Empirical Finance

Empirical Finance

Special Issue Editor

Shigeyuki Hamori

MDPI • Basel • Beijing • Wuhan • Barcelona • Belgrade

Special Issue Editor
Shigeyuki Hamori
Kobe University
Japan

Editorial Office
MDPI
St. Alban-Anlage 66
4052 Basel, Switzerland

This is a reprint of articles from the Special Issue published online in the open access journal *Journal of Risk and Financial Management* (ISSN 1911-8074) from 2018 to 2019 (available at: https://www.mdpi.com/journal/jrfm/special_issues/empirical)

For citation purposes, cite each article independently as indicated on the article page online and as indicated below:

LastName, A.A.; LastName, B.B.; LastName, C.C. Article Title. *Journal Name* **Year**, *Article Number*, Page Range.

ISBN 978-3-03897-706-3 (Pbk)
ISBN 978-3-03897-707-0 (PDF)

Contents

About the Special Issue Editor

Shigeyuki Hamori is a Professor of Economics, Graduate School of Economics, Kobe University, Japan. He holds a Ph.D. in Economics from Duke University, the United States. He is a Distinguished Fellow, International Engineering and Technology Institute (DFIETI), and Honorary Chair Professor, Asia University, Taiwan. His main research interests are applied time series analysis, empirical finance, data science, and international finance. He has published approximately 200 articles in international peer-reviewed journals, and he is presently a member of the editorial boards of *International Review of Financial Analysis*, *Singapore Economic Review*, *AGING AND HEALTH*, *Advances in Decision Sciences*, *Journal of Risk and Financial Management*, *Annals of Financial Economics*, *Journal of Management Information and Decision Sciences*, *International Economics and Finance Journal*, *Journal of Reviews on Global Economics*, and *Accounting and Finance Research*. He is also the Vice President of the International Research Institute for Economics and Management (IRIEM).

Article

Estimation of Cross-Lingual News Similarities Using Text-Mining Methods

Zhouhao Wang [1,*], Enda Liu [1], Hiroki Sakaji [1,*], Tomoki Ito [1], Kiyoshi Izumi [1,*], Kota Tsubouchi [2] and Tatsuo Yamashita [2]

[1] Izumi lab, Department of System Innovation, Graduate School of Engineering, The University of Tokyo, Hongo 7-3-1, Bunkyo-ku, Tokyo 113-0033, Japan; m2015eliu@socsim.org (E.L.); m2015titoh@socsim.org (T.I.)

[2] Yahoo! Japan Research, Kioicho 1-3, Chiyoda-ku, Tokyo 102-8282, Japan; ktsubouc@yahoo-corp.jp (K.T.); tayamash@yahoo-corp.jp (T.Y.)

[*] Correspondence: wangzhouhao94@gmail.com (Z.W.); sakaji@sys.t.u-tokyo.ac.jp (H.S.); izumi@sys.t.u-tokyo.ac.jp (K.I.); Tel.: +81-03-5841-6993 (K.I.)

Received: 31 December 2017; Accepted: 25 January 2018; Published: 31 January 2018

Abstract: In this research, two estimation algorithms for extracting cross-lingual news pairs based on machine learning from financial news articles have been proposed. Every second, innumerable text data, including all kinds news, reports, messages, reviews, comments, and tweets are generated on the Internet, and these are written not only in English but also in other languages such as Chinese, Japanese, French, etc. By taking advantage of multi-lingual text resources provided by Thomson Reuters News, we developed two estimation algorithms for extracting cross-lingual news pairs from multilingual text resources. In our first method, we propose a novel structure that uses the word information and the machine learning method effectively in this task. Simultaneously, we developed a bidirectional Long Short-Term Memory (LSTM) based method to calculate cross-lingual semantic text similarity for long text and short text, respectively. Thus, when an important news article is published, users can read similar news articles that are written in their native language using our method.

Keywords: text similarity; text mining; machine learning; SVM; neural network; LSTM

1. Introduction

Text similarity, as its name suggests, refers to how similar a given text query is to others. We normally tend to consider texts based mainly on their semantic characteristics, that is, how close (i.e., similar) their meanings are. Here, the text could be in the form of character level, word level, sentence level, paragraph level, or even longer, document level. In this paper, we mainly discuss text that is in the form of sentences (i.e., short text) and documents (i.e., long text).

The objective of this research could be summarized in three key points. The fundamental objective is to develop algorithms for estimation of semantic similarity for the given two pieces of text written in different languages, applicable for both long text and short text, by taking advantage the untapped vast suppository of text resources from Thomson Reuters economics news reports. Secondly, as a practical application and a verification of our model, we are aiming at developing a cross-lingual recommendation system and test benchmark, which could provide several of the most-related (for example, 10 results) pieces of Japanese or English text when given an English (or Japanese) article. Thirdly, we excavate cross-lingual resources from the enormous database of Thomson Reuters News and build an effective cross-lingual system by taking advantage of this un-developed treasure.

2. Related Work and Theories

Regardless of the length of the text, most of the state-of-the-art methods have recently been implemented based on word embedding methods and thus we discuss this in detail in a separate section. To solve semantic text similarity problems, one of the most typical and inspiring methods is Siamese LSTM structure, which is considered as both a basis and a competitive baseline of this research.

2.1. Embedding Techniques for Words and Documents

Word embedding technique, also known as distributed word representation, is one of the most basic concepts and applications prevalent nowadays. Word embedding could be further extended to be performed on documents. The embedding techniques capture both the semantic and syntactic information and convert them into meaningful feature vectors which help to train accurate models for natural language processing (NLP) tasks (Tang et al. 2014).

Word embedding can be implemented for both monolingual and multilingual tasks. There are several successful papers working on the monolingual word embedding such as the continuous bag of words models and skip-gram models (Mikolov et al. 2013), monolingual document embedding such as doc2vec (Le and Mikolov 2014), cross-lingual word embedding (Zou et al. 2013), as well as cross-lingual document embedding models such as Bilingual Bag-of-Words without Word Alignments (BilBOWA) (Gouws et al. 2015). Through embedding model, each word, phrase or document would be converted into a fixed length vector representation, where the similarity between two words, phrases, or documents could be derived by calculating the cosine distance of their vector representations. Methods are distinctly different for the text data with different length when solving the text similarity problem (Le and Mikolov 2014). With respect to the length of the text, a textual similarity task could be further categorized into two sub-tasks. Prevalent methods for cross-lingual document (i.e., long text) similarity could be categorized into four aspects (Rupnik et al. 2016), Dictionary-based approaches (Kudo et al. 2004), Probabilistic topic model based approaches (Taghva et al. 2005), Matrix factorization based approaches (Lo et al. 2014), and Monolingual approaches.

2.2. Text Similarities Using Siamese LSTM

Neural network-based Siamese recurrent architectures have recently proved to be one of the most effective ways for learning semantic text similarity on the sentence level. Mueller, in his work, implements a Siamese recurrent structure called Manhattan LSTM (MaLSTM) (Mueller and Thyagarajan 2016), which is practically used as the estimation of relativeness (i.e., similarity) when given any two sentences in English. This structure uses Long Short-Term Memory (LSTM) (Hochreiter and Schmidhuber 1997) and has a state-of-the-art performance on both semantic relatednesses scoring task and entailment classification using the SICK database, one of the NLP challenges provided by SemEval (Agirre et al. 2016). This model could identify how two sentences are similar to each other by trying to "understand" their true meaning on a deeper aspect, like the sentence pairs "He is smart" and "A truly wise man" as the figure demonstrates. They have no common words with different lengths, but they are indeed highly relevant to each other in terms of their implications, which a human cannot recognize without more consideration and logical analysis, suggesting the difficulty of this challenge.

In our work, we developed a new recurrent structure inspired by MaLSTM, by modifying the Siamese (i.e., symmetric) LSTM modules to "unbalanced" ones, and adding a full-connect neural network layer following the output of LSTM modules, which is more flexible and effective than a text similarity task.

3. Methods for Extracting Cross-Lingual News Pairs

In this section, we will introduce all fundamental and necessary methods applied in our research. There are mainly three aspects to be elaborated, including methods we applied regarding the foundation of natural language processing, such as word embedding and TF-IDF. We explained two applied methods, one of which is the classical methods learning SVM (Support Vector Machine). The other one is the neural network method, LSTM(Long-Short Term Memory).

3.1. Distribution Representation

The most traditional and naive way to consider words as features is to treat words as discrete symbols or numbers. This results in a discrete representation of each word and hinders the establishment of relations among these features. In contrast, vector space models consider (embedded) words in a continuous vector space, in which words with similar meanings are separated by small distances. There are two main categories for continuous word embedding: count-based (such as latent semantic analysis) models and predictive-based methods (such as neural probabilistic language models). The count-based models focus on the co-occurrence of the considered word and its neighboring words, whereas the predictive-based models predict a word based on its neighbors using embedding vectors Baroni et al. (2014). In this research, we implement a predictive-based model that is known as word2vec; it is based on the skip-gram or continuous bag-of-words model Mikolov et al. (2013).

We train each word from the training text sequence $w_1, w_2, w_3, ..., w_T$ to maximize the objective function

$$\frac{1}{T} \sum_{t=1}^{T} \sum_{-c \leq j \leq c, j \neq 0} \log p(w_{t+j} | w_t) \tag{1}$$

wherein c is the so-called "window size," which determines how much context information is to be considered for each of the training words. More specifically, we define $p(w_{t+j}|w_t)$ using a softmax function:

$$p(w_O | w_I) = \frac{\exp(v_{w_O}^T v_{w_I})}{\sum_{w=1}^{W} \exp(v_w^T v_{w_I})} \tag{2}$$

wherein W is the size of the vocabulary (i.e., the number of disparate words to be considered), and v is the vector representations for either the word w, the input word w_I, or the output word w_O.

However, the calculation of Equation (2) is impractical because the computational cost for calculating the gradient of $\log p(w_{t+j}|w_t)$ is proportional to W, which consists of as many as 10^5 to 10^7 terms. In practical terms, to train the model (i.e., optimize the cost function) in a more computationally efficient manner, we use Noise Contrastive Estimation for approximation during training, as described in Mikolov et al. (2013).

Finally, vector representations with fixed dimension (e.g., 200) can be extracted from the trained model. These word vectors have some outstanding attributes. Because we train our model for each word using its neighboring words, and words with similar meaning usually tend to have similar context, we can calculate the similarity among words using the cosine distance.

3.2. Term Frequency-Inversed Document Frequency (TF-IDF)

TF-IDF is one of the classical weighting models for words, which uses text representations. It is widely used in the natural language processing domain wherein it is commonly applied for weighting words or document features, such as in one-hot bag-of-words representation. The term frequency stands for the number of times a considered word occurs in a specific document, while the document frequency is the number of documents in the corpus that include the word. The inverse document frequency term for a specific word can be expressed as

$$idf = \log \frac{N}{1 + df} \tag{3}$$

wherein N is the total number of documents in the corpus. Combining these two concepts, the TF-IDF weight is the product of the TF and the IDF. This scheme loses semantic information for words; thus, it usually cannot achieve satisfactory performance. However, it measures the weights and importance of each word inside documents and among other documents according to a reasonable definition. In this study, we apply TF-IDF to weight words during document embedding.

3.3. TF-IDF Weighting for Word Vectors

Although there are several ways to form vector representations for documents (i.e., document embedding), we have experimentally discovered that the most effective strategy is to use the TF-IDF weighted sum of the word vectors that are present in each document as features. First, we calculate two TF-IDF weighting models, namely TF-IDF$_{jp}$ and TF-IDF$_{en}$, for each word from English training documents and Japanese training documents. Second, for each Japanese document, the weighted sum document representation can be derived as

$$\mathbf{J_i} = \sum_{m=0}^{N_i} t_{i,m} \cdot \mathbf{w_{i,m}} \tag{4}$$

wherein N_i refers to the number of words in this Japanese document (i.e., Japanese document i), and $t_{i,m}$ stands for the Japanese TF-IDF weight for the m-th word in document i with respect to the considered word. The final term $w_{i,m}$ is the word vector of the m-th word in document i, that is, the vector representation for this considered word.

We apply the same weighting scheme to the English documents. The vector representation for English document i can be expressed as

$$\mathbf{E_i} = \sum_{m=0}^{N_i} t_{i,m} \cdot \mathbf{w_{i,m}} \tag{5}$$

wherein all the definitions of the above variables are the same as those in the Japanese processing case, except the texts are in English.

3.4. Feature Engineering

The selection of features is possibly the most significant and tricky step, in particular, for classical machine learning algorithms such as SVM. This is called "feature engineering" because sometimes the choice of features can greatly affect the results. Fortunately, as one of the most exciting results in this research, we discover that satisfactory results can be generated using the joint cross-lingual document vector that is based on TF-IDF weighted word2vec as a training feature for the SVM model. Although both SVM and TF-IDF weighted word vectors are common in the text mining domain, to the best of our knowledge, this is the first time that the effectiveness of using joint cross-lingual text feature vectors as input for SVM on the cross-lingual text similarity problem has been proved.

More specifically, for the vector representation of a Japanese document $\mathbf{J_i}$ and an English document $\mathbf{E_j}$, the joint features are defined by

$$\mathbf{f_{i,j}} = (\mathbf{J_i}, \mathbf{E_j}) \tag{6}$$

Via feature engineering, we prepare our training datasets S, which contain a subset S_1 of instances for which the similarity scores are all equal to 1:

$$S_1 = \{(\mathbf{f_{1,1}}, 1), ..., (\mathbf{f_{N,N}}, 1)\} \tag{7}$$

and another subset S_0 of instances for which the similarity scores are all equal to 0:

$$S_0 = \{(\mathbf{f_{1,o}}, 0), ...(\mathbf{f_{Q,P}}, 0)\} \tag{8}$$

wherein N is the total number of cross-lingual training pairs with similarity of 1 (i.e., similar pairs) for training and o is an arbitrary number that belongs to $(1, N)$ and is not equal to 1, such that $\mathbf{f_{1,o}}$ is the set of dissimilar pairs with similarity of 0 (i.e., the pairs are totally unrelated). Moreover, note that $Q, P \in (1, N)$ and $Q \neq N$.

Hence, our final training data S is

$$S = S_1 \cup S_0 \qquad (9)$$

3.5. The SVM-Based Method

SVM is one of the most popular methods for solving both classification and regression tasks. It was originally purposed in 1990s and gradually proved to be effective in many fields including Natural language processing (NLP), pattern recognition and so on (Burges 1998; Malakasiotis and Androutsopoulos 2007; Béchara et al. 2015). TF-IDF and SVM are useful for tasks in the field of natural language processing. Therefore, we employ TF-IDF and SVM in our method as core technologies. Additionally, we propose a novel structure that uses TF-IDF and SVM effectively for this task. An overview of the structure is illustrated in Figure 1.

The system mainly contains three processing models. As our our training datasets, S only contains the data with label 0 or 1, the classification training objective of SVM is very similar to classification using Triplet Loss, which is proved to be quite effective in embedding and classification tasks (Schroff et al. 2015). The training procedures normally include the following steps:

1. Use the cross-lingual training data in the form of pre-trained word vectors as input, which is discussed in detail in Section 3.1.
2. Weight the word vectors for each of language models using TF-IDF, as introduced in Subsections 3.2 and 3.3.
3. Train the proposed model using SVM with Platt's probability estimation for the connected cross-lingual document features, each of which are the naive join of two weighted word sum vectors in English and Japanese. This is explained in Section 3.4.

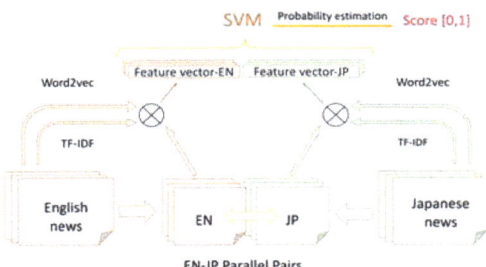

Figure 1. Illustration of our SVM-based method.

3.6. A Bidirectional LSTM Based Method

We implement the two independent modules of bi-directional LSTM recurrent neural networks on both English input and Japanese input respectively and the overview of this structure is shown in the Figure 2. We use the cross-lingual training data in the form of pre-trained word vectors as input. Feed the word vector sequentially to LSTM modules. This is discussed in detail in the Section 3.1. Furthermore, as a limitation of our LSTM modules, we have uniform length of data as input, denoted as "maxlen". The residue of the parts of sequence longer than maxlen will be abandoned, while those with input sequence shorter than "maxlen" will be padded with a predefined value (i.e., a word) such as "null" at the tail so that all the input data could have the same length. The two bi-LSTM modules are responsible for the English sequence and Japanese Sequence respectively. They generate four hidden layer outputs and we concatenate them into a joint feature. Details are elaborated in the Section 3.6.1. The joined feature is further fed into a densely-connected neural network of 1 depth, resulting in 1 dimension output $y \in [0, 1]$ as the final similarity score of the two inputs of cross-lingual data, by means of regression. In general, the LSTM-based model pays more attention to the order information of the input sequence, which might significantly determine the real meaning of a sentence written in natural languages.

3.6.1. The Bi-LSTM Layer

In this research, we take advantage of bi-LSTM (bi-directional long short-term memory), to enhance the ordinary RNN performance considering both forward and backward information and solve the problem of the long-term dependencies. The updates rules of LSTM for each sequential input $x_1, x_2, ..., x_t, ..., x_T$ could be express as:

$$i_t = \text{sigmoid}(W_i x_t + U_i h_{t-1} + b_i) \tag{10}$$

$$f_t = \text{sigmoid}(W_f x_t + U_f h_{t-1} + b_f) \tag{11}$$

$$\tilde{c}_t = \tanh(W_c x_t + U_c h_{t-1} + b_c) \tag{12}$$

$$c_t = i_t \odot \tilde{c}_t + f_t \odot c_{t-1} \tag{13}$$

$$o_t = \text{sigmoid}(W_o x_t + U_o h_{t-1} + b_o) \tag{14}$$

$$h_t = o_t \odot \tanh(c_t) \tag{15}$$

where h_{t-1} is the hidden layer value of the previous states and the sigmoid and tanh functions in the above equations are also used as activation functions:

$$\text{sigmoid}(x) = \frac{1}{1 + \exp(-x)} \tag{16}$$

$$\tanh(x) = \frac{2}{1 + \exp(-2x)} - 1 \tag{17}$$

The weights (i.e., parameters) we need to train include $W_i, W_f, W_c, W_o, U_i, U_f, U_c, U_o$ and bias vectors b_i, b_f, b_c, b_o. A more thorough exposition of the LSTM model and its variants is provided by (Graves 2012) and (Greff et al. 2017). In this layer, we use the cross-lingual training data in the form of pre-trained word vectors as input, which is discussed in detail in Section 3.1. There are four LSTM modules, constructing two bi-LSTM structures, where we only consider the final output (i.e., final value of the hidden layer) of each LSTM module: LSTM-a read Japanese text in a forward direction. The value of a hidden layer is denoted as $h_i^{(a)}$ where i is the i-th input of the sequence, while LSTM-b read backwards, denoted as $h_i^{(b)}$. Symmetrically, LSTM-c and LSTM-d are used to read English text, denoted as $h_i^{(c)}$ and $h_i^{(d)}$. As the results, we obtain four feature vectors derived from hidden layer values of the four LSTM modules, keeping all necessary information regarding to the cross-lingual inputs. We then merge these four features by concatenating them directly:

$$\mathbf{x}_{i,j} = (\mathbf{h}_L^{(a)}, \mathbf{h}_L^{(b)}, \mathbf{h}_L^{(c)}, \mathbf{h}_L^{(d)}) \tag{18}$$

where i and j refer to the document number of the input text for Japanese and English respectively, and vector $\mathbf{h}_L^{(a,b,c,d)}$ refers to the final status (i.e., the value) of the hidden layers of the LSTM module after feeding the last (or the first, if backwards) word.

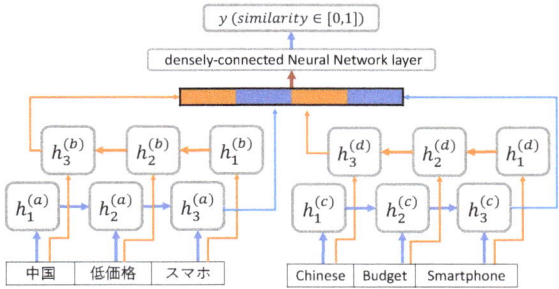

Figure 2. Illustration of the LSTM-based method.

3.6.2. Dense Layer

We use the most basic component of the basic full-dense Neural Network layer as the top layer. The function of this layer could be expressed as:

$$y_{i,j} = f(\mathbf{w}^T \mathbf{x_{i,j}} + b) \tag{19}$$

Here, the function f is also known as "activation" function, b is the one dimensional bias for the neural network and $\mathbf{w}$ is the weight (i.e., the parameters to be trained) of the neural network. In this project, we mainly apply the softplus Nair and Hinton (2010) function as the activation function in the dense layer:

$$f(x) = \ln[1 + \exp(x)] \tag{20}$$

As for the optimization, although we are handling a classification problem, based on the experimental results, we find that, instead of using ordinary cross-entropy cost, it performs better if we use Quadratic cost (i.e., mean square error) as the cost function, which could be described as:

$$C = \sum_{v=1}^{N} (y_{true,v} - y_{pred,v})^2 \tag{21}$$

where N is the total number of the training data, while $y_{true,v}$ and $y_{pred,v}$ refer to the true similarity and the predicted similarity, respectively. In practice, the stochastic gradient descent (SGD) is implemented by means of the back-propagation scheme. After computing the outputs and errors based on the cost function J, which is usually equal to the negative log of the maximum likelihood function, we update parameters by the gradient descent method, expressed as:

$$\mathbf{w} \leftarrow \mathbf{w} - \varepsilon \nabla_w J(\mathbf{w}) \tag{22}$$

where ε is known as "learning rate", defining the update speed of the hyper-parameters $\mathbf{w}$. However, the training process might fail due to either improper initialization regarding weights or the improper learning rate value set. Practically, based on the results of the experiments, the best performance is achieved by applying the Adam optimizer Kingma and Ba (2014) to perform the parameter updates.

4. Experiments and Results

4.1. Evaluation Methods

We mainly use two categories of the evaluations, TOP-N benchmark based on ranks, and traditional criteria for classification such as precision, recall as well as the F1-value. As the applications of this project aim to suggest several cross-lingual (For instance, English) alternative news stories to the users, when the user provides a Japanese article as a query, we make the system pick up 1, 5 and 10 of the most similar Japanese alternatives during the evaluation process. The Figure 3 illustrates the relationship and evaluation procedures for ranks, TOP-N index.For a given Japanese text (i.e., the query) J_x, calculate the similarity score between J_x and all English text of test data sets $(E_1, E_2, ..., E_x, ..., E_M)$ to derive a list of scores $L_x = (S_{x,1}, S_{x,2}, ..., S_{x,x}, ..., S_{x,M})$, where the corner mark M is the total number of English documents to be considered, and E_x is the true similar article with a similarity score of 1. Then sort this list in the order from large to small and find out the rank (i.e., position, index) of the score $S_{x,x}$ inside this sorted list noted as R_x, the rank for the query document J_x. Repeat this process recursively for N Japanese articles $(J_1, J_2, ..., J_N)$, result in a list of ranks $R = (R_1, R_2, ..., R_N)$ regarding the collections of J_x. Then we take the number of query documents with ranks smaller than N as TOP-N. In other words, TOP-1 refers to the number of query documents with rank equal to 1 and TOP-5 refers to the number of a query with rank equal to or smaller than 5.

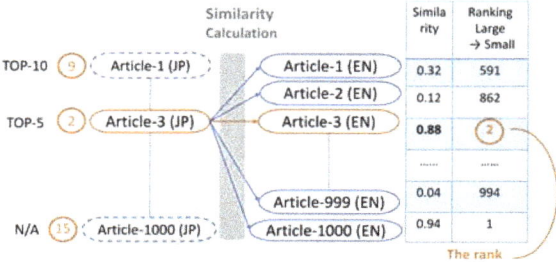

Figure 3. Illustration of an evaluation procedures using ranks and TOP-N index.

4.2. Baseline: Siamese LSTM with Google-Translation

Siamese LSTM is one of the deep learning-based models with the art-of-state performance on the semantic text similarity problems. In this research, we make this model a baseline by extending this model from a monolingual domain to a cross-lingual domain with the help of the Google Translation services. We first translate all Japanese text into the English version on both test and training data by using the google translate service[1] Then we implement the Siamese LSTM model as described in the original paper for Siamese LSTM Mueller and Thyagarajan (2016) with the help of the open source code on the Github[2] To illustrate this baseline method regarding a two cross-lingual input, we first translate the Japanese input into an English sentence using Google Translation service. Then, we can consider the cross-lingual task as monolingual one so that we can apply the Siamese LSTM model for training as a baseline.

4.3. Datasets and Pre-Processing

Thomson Reuters news[3] is a worldwide news agency providing worldwide news in multiple languages. Most of the reports are originally written in English and translated and edited into other languages including Chinese, Japanese, etc. These multi-lingual texts are expected to be highly potential resources for tasks related to the multi-lingual natural languages processing. In this research, we use 60,000 news articles in 2014 from Thomson Reuters News related to the economics. For the preprocessing of text, we convert raw data to normalized data, which could be further used to train word2vec models

---

[1] Google Translation Web API could be accessed from https://github.com/aditya1503/Siamese-LSTM.
[2] The open source code for Siamese LSTM can be accessed from https://github.com/aditya1503/Siamese-LSTM.
[3] Official websites of Thomson Reuters: http://www.reuters.com/.

for both English and Japanese text, respectively. We train the Japanese word2vec model and English word2vec model separately using news articles with the same contents in 2014. In our experiment, we use the model of a Continuous Bag of Words (CBOW), with 200 fixed dimensions of word embedding. Other parameters are set using the default value used in the Gensim package[4].

As discussed in Section 3.1, the word2vec could build relationships among words based on their original context. We could find several of the most similar words when given a query word by calculating their cosine similarity. The Tables 1 and 2 demonstrate examples to find the most similar words when given a word query in English and in Japanese respectively. All these results suggest the effectiveness of word2vec algorithms and success of the training processes.

Table 1. Example of similarity relationship for Japanese words (translated).

	Toyota		Sony	
TOP	**Word**	**Similarity**	**Word**	**Similarity**
1	Honda	0.612	PlayStation	0.612
2	Toyota corp	0.546	Entertainment	0.546
3	Hyundai corp	0.536	SonyBigChance	0.536
4	Chrysler	0.524	Game console	0.524
5	Nissan	0.519	Nexus	0.519
6	motor	0.511	X-BOX	0.511
7	LEXUS	0.506	spring	0.506
8	Acura	0.493	Windows	0.493
9	Mazda	0.492	Compatibility	0.492
10	Ford	0.486	application software	0.486

Table 2. Example of similarity relationship for English words.

	Lexus		Lenovo	
TOP	**Word**	**Similarity**	**Word**	**Similarity**
1	acura	0.636	huawei	0.636
2	corolla	0.588	zte	0.588
3	camry	0.571	xiaomi	0.571
4	2002–2005	0.570	dell	0.570
5	sentra	0.541	handset	0.541
6	prius	0.539	smartphone	0.539
7	2003–2005	0.537	hannstar	0.537
8	sedan	0.533	thinkpad	0.533
9	mazda	0.530	tcl	0.530
10	altima	0.524	medison	0.524

4.4. Experiments on Text Datasets

4.4.1. Training Data

Regarding Short Text, we firstly pick up 4000 pairs of parallel Japanese-English cross-lingual news titles from the database with the period from the January to February of 2014, all of which are labeled with a similarity score of 1. To provide balance training data, we also generated 4000 pairs of un-parallel Japanese-English cross-lingual news titles by a random combination. In order to simplify our model and experiments, we use the assumption that the similarity the random combination of Japanese text and English text is 0. Then, for Long Text, similar to the data preparation of experiments

---

4 To see more specific of the configuration of word2vec model, see the documentation of Word2Vec class from https://radimrehurek.com/gensim/models/word2vec.html

for short text introduced, we prepare 4000 parallel (i.e., similarity = 1) Japanese-English news articles and 4000 un-parallel (i.e., similarity = 0) ones for training data through random combination.

4.4.2. Test Data

For Short Text, in order to evaluate our model more comprehensively, we have prepared two sets of independent test data. TEST-1S contains 1000 pairs of parallel Japanese-English news titles, selected and split from the same period of training data, from January 2014 to the middle of February in 2014. Similarly, TEST-2S contains title pairs with time stamps of December 2014. For Long Text, similar to the case of short test evaluation, we have prepared two sets of independent test data. For training data, we prepared a similar dataset as for the short text experiments. TEST-1L and TEST-2L contain 1000 pairs of parallel Japanese-English long news articles respectively.

4.4.3. Ranks and TOP-N

Table 3 also summarizes and compares our two purposed models, LSTM-based model and SVM-based model respectively in terms of TOP-N benchmark regarding LONG text scenario and SHORT text scenario.

First, we could notice that both our purposed, LSTM-based model and SVM-based model, outperform the baseline in terms of all three TOP-N criteria. In terms of TOP-N, the LSTM-based model obtains around twice the performance of the baseline (511 vs. 243) on short test data, while LSTM-based model also has twice the performance of the baseline (685 vs. 302) on long test data, suggesting the effectiveness and efficiency of our purposed models. Furthermore, we may also easily notice that the SVM-based method outperforms the LSTM-based methods in terms of TOP-N criteria, in case of long text, around 50%. In contrast, the LSTM-based model has a TOP-10 score around 10% higher than that of the SVM-based model on both test datasets.

Table 3. Summary of in terms of TOP-N benchmark.

	TOP-10			
	SHORT		LONG	
	TEST-1S	TEST-2S	TEST-1L	TEST-1L
LSTM	**511**	**495**	456	432
SVM	453	422	**685**	**654**
baseline	243	-	302	-
	TOP-5			
	SHORT		LONG	
	TEST-1S	TEST-2S	TEST-1L	TEST-1L
LSTM	**339**	**338**	284	278
SVM	324	295	**520**	**491**
baseline	134	-	192	-
	TOP-1			
	SHORT		LONG	
	TEST-1S	TEST-2S	TEST-1L	TEST-1L
LSTM	90	**106**	61	58
SVM	**101**	96	**128**	**179**
baseline	39	-	50	-

The dominant performance of the SVM-based model on long test data is also maintained in terms of TOP-1 and TOP-5, twice the score compared to the LSTM-based model for TOP-5 and three times the score for the TOP-1 benchmark. On the other hand, although the LSTM-based model still performs better than SVM-based with respect to TOP-5, as for TOP-5 LSTM-based model failed to be in the lead anymore. We are going to discuss these results and propose possible hypotheses and provide explanations in Section 5. The performance of successful recommendation numbers from our bi-LSTM based model is twice that of the baseline.

5. Discussion

5.1. Comparison of the Baseline and the LSTM-Based Model

The performance of the LSTM-based model is twice that of the baseline, even though they are both based on LSTM structures. The differences, which are also the innovations for this purposed method, compared to the baseline, include the using of bi-LSTM, independent LSTM modules as well as using the fully connected neural network as the final layer.

First, the baseline method is able to calculate the similarity of two sentences, no matter whether there are different types of word arrangement for the two inputs, or if there are different words used referring to the same meaning, which proves the effectiveness of the encoding (i.e., embedding) ability for the input text. However, the baseline model has the "Siamese LSTM structure", which means, in other words, that the two LSTM instances always share the same parameters during the training. This might be effective for a monolingual case, but not good enough on the cross-lingual case. Thus, the LSTM instances used in our purposed model are all independently holding their own unique parameters. In addition, the bi-directional structure also helps to encode the feature of each input text more comprehensively. Finally, instead of using cosine similarity as the final layer in the baseline method, we used the fully connected neural network as output, making the output layer adjust (i.e., train) its parameters so as to learn precise patterns from the features generated by LSTMs. We believe these three modifications improve the final results for our LSTM-based model.

5.2. Comparison of the LSTM-Based Model and SVM-Based Model

The experiments above leave us with an interesting question about why the LSTM-based model and SVM-based model perform differently regarding the length of the target text we train and test. We explain this question in two aspects.

5.2.1. From the Point of View of the SVM-Based Model

Since the SVM-based methods use the TF-IDF weighting which is a classical and an effective method for NLP fields to extract the most important and representative features for each of document comprehensively, it could accurately identify the most significant feature, a few key words, from a very long and complex article containing hundreds of words, in both Japanese and English, and then finally feed them into the SVM classifier to get the similarity estimation universally. However, due to the attributes of TF-IDF algorithms, the shorter the length of each document is, the less information the TF-IDF could extract. This is because if there are fewer words in one document, every word could be either unique or common regarding other documents, resulting in the failure of TF-IDF. This might be the reason why SVM-based model performs well on long datasets but this performance becomes poor on shorter data sets.

5.2.2. From the Point of View of the LSTM-Based Model

On the other hand, the LSTM is good at understanding sentences by means of grasping the order information of each words, since for any natural languages, not only words themselves but also the order of words, to some extent, define the true meaning of a sentence. Especially for short text, a slight change of the order could alter the meaning of the sentences significantly and thus the LSTM-based model outperformed the LSTM model by around 10% on short datasets. However, LSTM is not good at extracting the key idea of longer documents since, although LSTM solves the problem of memorizing long text (i.e., solve of the problem of gradient vanishing and gradient explosion), it could tell the importance of each word as TF-IDF does. That might be the possible reason why it fails to perform effectively on a long text.

6. Conclusions

We developed a bi-LSTM-based model to calculate cross-lingual similarities given a pair of English and Japanese articles. Instead of using a translation module or a dictionary to translate from one to another language, our model has outstanding performance with short text. Furthermore, we modified and implemented a popular Siamese LSTM model as the baseline and we found both of our models outperform the baseline. For practical testing, we defined the concept of "TOP-N" and "ranks" to test the overall performance of the model, with visualized results. We also make a comparative study based on the results of the experiments that bi-LSTM based obtains better performance on short text data such as news titles and alert messages, which are on average shorter than 20 words, in contrast to normal news articles with more than 200 words on average. As the results show, both models obtained satisfactory performance with over half of the test documents of 1000 holding ranks lower than 10 (i.e., TOP-10). As a high-performance cross-lingual news calculating system, we expect that it could achieve optimal performance by taking advantage of both models to form a complete system.

Supplementary Materials: The following are available online at www.mdpi.com/1911-8074/11/1/8/s1.

Acknowledgments: Thanks three anonymous reviewers from JRFM for reviewing our paper, and providing valuable instructions to revise our paper.

Author Contributions: Zhouhao Wang, Enda Liu and Hiroki Sakaji conceived and designed the experiments. Enda Liu performed the experiments. Zhouhao Wang and Enda Liu analyzed the data. Tomoki Ito, Kiyoshi Izumi, Kota Tsubouchi and Tatsuo Yamashita contributed materials. Zhouhao Wang, Hiroki Sakaji and Kiyoshi Izumi wrote the paper.

Conflicts of Interest: The authors declare no conflict of interest.

References

Agirrea, Eneko, Carmen Baneab, Daniel Cerd, Mona Diabe, Aitor Gonzalez-Agirrea, Rada Mihalceab, German Rigaua, and Janyce Wiebe. 2016. Semeval-2016 task 1: Semantic textual similarity, monolingual and cross-lingual evaluation. Paper presented at the SemEval-2016, San Diego, CA, USA, June 16–17, pp. 497–511.

Baroni, Marco, Georgiana Dinu, and German Kruszewski. 2014. Don't count, predict! a systematic comparison of context-counting vs. context-predicting semantic vectors. Paper presented at the 52nd Annual Meeting of the Association for Computational Linguistics, Baltimore, MD, USA, June 23–25, pp. 238–47.

Béchara, Hanna, Hernani Costa, Shiva Taslimipoor, Rohit Gupta, Constantin Orasan, Gloria Corpas Pastor, and Ruslan Mitkov. 2015. Miniexperts: An svm approach for measuring semantic textual similarity. Paper presented at the 9th International Workshop on Semantic Evaluation (SemEval 2015), Denver, CO, USA, June 4–5, pp. 96–101.

Burges, Christopher J. C. 1998. A tutorial on support vector machines for pattern recognition. *Data Mining and Knowledge Discovery* 2: 121–67.

Gouws, Stephan, Yoshua Bengio, and Greg Corrado. 2015. Bilbowa: Fast bilingual distributed representations without word alignments. Paper presented at the 32nd International Conference on Machine Learning (ICML-15), Lille, France, July 7, pp. 748–56.

Graves, Alex. 2012. *Supervised Sequence Labelling with Recurrent Neural Networks*. Berlin and Heidelberg: Springer, vol. 385.

Greff, Klaus, Rupesh K. Srivastava, Jan Koutník, Bas R. Steunebrink, and Jürgen Schmidhuber. 2017. Lstm: A search space odyssey. *IEEE Transactions on Neural Networks and Learning Systems* 28: 2222–32.

Hochreiter, Sepp, and Jürgen Schmidhuber. 1997. Long short-term memory. *Neural Computation* 9: 1735–80.

Kingma, Diederik P., and Jimmy Ba. 2014. Adam: A Method for Stochastic Optimization. Available online: https://arxiv.org/abs/1412.6980 (accessed on 16 August 2017).

Kudo, Taku, Kaoru Yamamoto, and Yuji Matsumoto. 2004. Applying conditional random fields to japanese morphological analysis. Paper presented at the 2004 Conference on Empirical Methods in Natural Language Processing, Barcelona, Spain, July 25, vol. 4, pp. 230–37.

Le, Quoc, and Tomas Mikolov. 2014. Distributed representations of sentences and documents. Paper presented at the 31st International Conference on Machine Learning (ICML-14), Beijing, China, June 23, pp. 1188–96.

Lo, Chi-kiu, Meriem Beloucif, Markus Saers, and Dekai Wu. 2014. Xmeant: Better semantic mt evaluation without reference translations. Paper presented at the 52nd Annual Meeting of the Association for Computational Linguistics (Volume 2: Short Papers), Baltimore, MD, USA, June 23–25, vol. 2, pp. 765–71.

Malakasiotis, Prodromos, and Ion Androutsopoulos. 2007. Learning textual entailment using svms and string similarity measures. Paper presented at the ACL-PASCAL Workshop on Textual Entailment and Paraphrasing, Prague, Czech Republic, June 28–29. Stroudsburg: Association for Computational Linguistics, pp. 42–47.

Mikolov, Tomas, Ilya Sutskever, Kai Chen, Greg Corrado, and Jeffrey Dean. 2013. Distributed representations of words and phrases and their compositionality. Paper presented at the 26th International Conference on Neural Information Processing Systems, Lake Tahoe, NV, USA, December 5–10, pp. 3111–19.

Mueller, Jonas, and Aditya Thyagarajan. 2016. Siamese recurrent architectures for learning sentence similarity. Paper presented at the 30th AAAI Conference on Artificial Intelligence (AAAI 2016), Phoenix, AZ, USA, February 16, pp. 2786–92.

Nair, Vinod, and Geoffrey E. Hinton. 2010. Rectified linear units improve restricted boltzmann machines. Paper presented at the 27th International Conference on Machine Learning (ICML-10), Haifa, Israel, June 21–24, pp. 807–14.

Rupnik, Jan, Andrej Muhic, Gregor Leban, Blaz Fortuna, and Marko Grobelnik. 2016. News across languages-cross-lingual document similarity and event tracking. *Journal of Artificial Intelligence Research* 55: 283–316.

Schroff, Florian, Dmitry Kalenichenko, and James Philbin. 2015. Facenet: A unified embedding for face recognition and clustering. Paper presented at Proceedings of the IEEE Conference on Computer Vision and Pattern Recognition, Boston, MA, USA, June 7–12, pp. 815–23.

Taghva, Kazem, Rania Elkhoury, and Jeffrey Coombs. 2005. Arabic stemming without a root dictionary. Paper presented at International Conference on Information Technology: Coding and Computing, 2005 (ITCC 2005), Las Vegas, NV, USA, April 4–6, vol. 1, pp. 152–157.

Tang, Duyu, Furu Wei, Nan Yang, Ming Zhou, Ting Liu, and Bing Qin. 2014. Learning sentiment-specific word embedding for twitter sentiment classification. Paper presented at the 52nd Annual Meeting of the Association for Computational Linguistics, Baltimore, MD, USA, June 23–25, pp. 1555–65.

Zou, Will Y., Richard Socher, Daniel Cer, and Christopher D. Manning. 2013. Bilingual word embeddings for phrase-based machine translation. Paper presented at the 2013 Conference on Empirical Methods in Natural Language Processing, Seattle, WA, USA, October 19, pp. 1393–98.

Journal of
Risk and Financial
Management

Article

What Determines Utility of International Currencies?

Eiji Ogawa [1,2,*] and Makoto Muto [1]

[1]   Graduate School of Business Administration, Hitotsubashi University, Tokyo 186-8601, Japan;
cd162004@g.hit-u.ac.jp

[2]   Research Institute of Economy, Trade and Industry (RIETI), Tokyo 100-8901, Japan

*   Correspondence: eiji.ogawa@r.hit-u.ac.jp

Received: 7 December 2018; Accepted: 3 January 2019; Published: 8 January 2019

Abstract: In previous studies, we estimated a time series of coefficients on five international currencies (the US dollar, the euro, the Japanese yen, the British pound, and the Swiss franc) in a utility function. We call the coefficients utilities of international currencies. The time series show that the utility of the US dollar as an international currency has remained in the first position in the changing international monetary system despite of the fact that the euro was created as a single common currency for European countries. On one hand, the utility of the Japanese yen has been declining as an international currency. In this paper, we investigate what determines the utility of international currencies. We use a dynamic panel data model to analyze the issue with Generalized Method of Moments (GMM). Specifically, liquidity shortage in terms of an international currency means that it is inconvenient for economic agents to use the relevant currency for international economic transactions. In other words, liquidity shortages might reduce the utility of an international currency. In this analysis we focus on liquidity premium which represents a liquidity shortage in terms of an international currency. Our empirical results showed not only inertia in terms of change but also the impact of a liquidity shortage in an international currency on the utility of the relevant international currency.

Keywords: utility of international currency; inertia; liquidity risk premium; US dollar; Japanese yen

1. Introduction

The United States (US) dollar had been as a rule a key currency in the Bretton Woods international monetary system. The monetary authority of the United States fixed the US dollar to gold while the monetary authorities of other countries fixed their home currencies to the US dollar under the Bretton Woods system. It could keep stability of exchange rates among the currencies in the world economy. However, the Bretton Woods system was collapsed in 1971 because the monetary authority of the United States could not keep a value of the US dollar against gold to stop convertibility of the US dollar to gold. Afterwards, a position of the US dollar as a key currency has been still kept in the current international monetary system even though we have no longer the rule under which we have to use the US dollar as a key currency. The phenomenon is called as inertia of a key currency.

Given that a key currency is chosen for economic reasons which include costs and benefits of an international currency, comparison in costs and benefits of international currencies determines a key currency in the current international monetary policy. Also, inertia of a key currency should be related with inertia of costs and/or benefits of holding an international currency. The costs of holding an international currency are related with its depreciation that caused by inflation in the relevant country. On one hand, the benefits of holding an international currency are caused by utility of holding it.

In a Sidrauski (1967)-type of money-in-the-utility model (Calvo 1981, 1985; Obstfeld 1981; Blanchard and Fischer 1989), real balances of money as well as consumption are supposed as explanatory variables in a utility function. We can use the money-in-the-utility model to analyze costs and benefits of holding international currencies. Ogawa and Muto (2017a, 2017b) used expected inflation rates and Bank for International Settlements (BIS) data on total of domestic currency denominated debt and foreign currency denominated debt of the euro currency market to estimate time series of coefficients on five international currencies (the US dollar, the euro, the Japanese yen, the British pound, and the Swiss franc) in a utility function. We call the coefficients utility of an international currency. The time series show that utility of the US dollar as an international currency has kept at the first position even though the euro was introduced into some of the European Union (EU) states while it increased utility of the euro as an international currency. On one hand, utility of the Japanese yen has been declining as an international currency. Since 1973, although the US dollar is downward trend, it has kept the key currency in the changing international monetary system. This is probably because the US dollar has reduced the store of value function but maintained the medium of exchange function. Utility of the international currency means relative contribution of holding an international currency through such functions of international currency. Therefore, we can estimate relative position of international currency from a value of utility of the international currency.

In this paper, we have an objective to investigate what determines utility of the international currencies. We use a dynamic panel data model to analyze the issue with Generalized Method of Moments (GMM). Specifically, liquidity shortage in terms of an international currency means that it is inconvenient for economic agents to use the relevant currency for international economic transactions. In other words, the liquidity shortage might reduce utility of an international currency. In this analysis we focus on liquidity premium which represents liquidity shortage in terms of an international currency. We make empirical analysis of whether liquidity risk premium in an international currency affects utility of the relevant international currency. For example, if the currency authority aims to internationalize its home currency, results of this analysis will be useful for which variables should be focused.

We obtain the following results from the empirical study. Firstly, change in utility of the currency in the previous period has significantly a positive effect on the change of utility of the currency in the current period. This suggests that utility of the currency tends to fluctuate in the same direction as the change in the previous period. For example, if the utility of the currency declines, we assumed that the currency is less likely to be used than in the previous period, which will continue in the next period. Secondly, the change of liquidity risk premium has a significantly negative effect on the change of utility of the currency. This suggests that liquidity shortage reduce the utility of the international currency. Thirdly, the change of capital flow share has significantly a positive effect on the change of utility of the currency. This suggests that changes in economic scale, specifically capital flow, affect the utility of the international currency.

In the next section, we describe related literatures. In the third section, we explain our theoretical model in terms of utility of an international currency. In the fourth section, we explain empirical model for analyzing determinants of utility of an international currency. In the fifth section, we explain data used for the analysis and calculation method. In the sixth section, we discuss hypothesis of estimated coefficients and influence of each variable on utility of an international currency. In the seventh section, we show results of dynamic panel analysis. Finally, we conclude our empirical analysis.

2. Related Literature

Krugman (1984) adopted three functions of money as a medium of exchange, a unit of account, and a store of value to consider six roles of an international currency for both private and official sectors. According to his definition, it is used as a medium of exchange in private international economic transactions ("vehicle" currency or settlement currency), while it is transacted by monetary authorities in order to intervene in foreign exchange markets ("intervention" currency). Private sector makes trade contracts which are denominated in terms of a currency ("invoice" currency). Monetary authorities set par values for exchange rates which are stated in terms of a currency ("peg" currency). Private sector holds liquidity dollar denominated assets ("banking" role) as a store of value. Also, monetary authorities hold a currency as an international reserve ("reserve" currency) which is related with a store of value. Matsuyama et al. (1993) and Trejos and Wright (1996) used a search theory to investigate a role of international currency as a medium of exchange. Moreover, Kannan (2009) focused on the benefits arising from terms of trade as well as traditional seigniorage and presented models on the benefits of international currency. It was showed that the benefits arising from terms of trade are important.

Related studies focused on one of the functions of an international currency to investigate roles of a currency as an international currency and international monetary system with the US dollar as a key currency. For example, Chinn and Frankel (2007, 2008) focused on a role as international reserve currency. Eichengreen et al. (2016b) focused on a role of international reserve currency to investigate whether it has changed in the determinants of the currency composition of international reserves in before and after the collapse of the Bretton Woods regime. Goldberg and Tille (2008) analyzed the US dollar and other currencies as an invoice currency in international economic transactions. Ito et al. (2013) conducted a questionnaire survey on the choice of invoice currency with all Japanese manufacturing firms listed in the Tokyo Stock Exchange to show that the Japanese firms use the Japanese yen second to an importing country currency as invoice currency in exporting products to the US and Europe, while the Japanese yen is the first used in exporting them to Asia.

Catão and Terrones (2016) and Honohan (2008) focused on the dollarization of financial systems in emerging market economies. Especially, Catão and Terrones (2016) pointed out a broad global trend towards financial sector de-dollarization from the early 2000s to the eve of the global financial crisis. Kamps (2006) focused on the euro to investigate the decision on invoice currency in international trade. An analytical result is that economic agents in EU states played a role in determining the euro as an invoice currency. However, it was suggested that the US dollar is dominant as an invoice currency compared with the euro. ECB (European Central Bank 2015) reported increasing roles of the euro as an international currency in terms of each of the three functions in the international reserve, international trade, and financial markets.

Eichengreen et al. (2016a) conducted an empirical analysis on the international currency used in the settlement currency in the oil market using data from the 1930s to 1950s. Although the US dollar is said to be strongly dominant in the oil market, they showed that currencies other than dollars were used as the settlement currency to some extent in European countries and countries with stable currencies. These results showed that multiple international currencies were served as a means of settlement even in markets of such homogeneous goods as oil. They suggested that a transition from a dollar-based system to a multipolar system is not impossible.

3. Utility of International Currency

3.1. Estimation Equation of Utility of International Currency

Ogawa and Muto (2017a, 2017b) estimated a coefficient on each of international currencies in the utility function or utility of international currencies, given that economic agents make dynamic optimization of utility in a money-in-the-utility function while they faced depreciation of international currency holdings. They have optimal holdings of an international currency by comparing benefits or utility from holding it with costs or depreciation of holding it. We can derive invisible utility of an international currency as a function of visible economic variables which include holdings of an international currency and its depreciation. We can obtain an estimate of utility of an international currency i $\left(\gamma_t^i\right)$ according to the following estimation equation[1]:

---

[1] See Appendix A for derivation of Equation (1). We suppose that γ might change over time because we have an important objective to investigate what factors influence utility of the currency γ during the analytical period though it seems to be stable as an exogenous.

$$\gamma_t^i = \frac{1}{1 + \left(\frac{1}{\phi_t^i} - 1\right)\frac{\pi_t^O + \bar{r}}{\pi_t^i + \bar{r}}} \tag{1}$$

where ϕ_t^i: share of holdings of an international currency i, π_t^i: expected inflation (or depreciation) rate of country i, π_t^O: expected inflation (or depreciation) rate of the other countries, $\bar{r}$: real interest rate. Assumptions of both purchasing power parity and uncovered interest rate parity make real interest rates are equal to each other in the world.

In our previous study, we assumed real interest rates are 1.5%, 2.0%, 2.5%, and 3.0%.[2] In addition, there is also utility of an international currency calculated using the nominal interest rate as well as the expected inflation rate plus the real interest rate. However, the nominal interest rate has periods of zero-bound level. Moreover, it is considered that the nominal interest rate has a strong relationship with a liquidity risk premium. Therefore, in this analysis, utility of the international currency calculated using real interest rate was used.

3.2. Data for Estimating Utility of International Currencies

We should use data on shares of the international currencies according to the theoretical money-in-the-utility model in which they are regarded as real balances of international currencies. However, it is difficult to obtain data on the real balance of international currencies which include international currencies held by private sector in the world economy. Instead, we use BIS data on total of domestic currency denominated debt and foreign currency denominated debt of the euro currency market. The data are obtained from a BIS website.

The expected inflation rates are calculated rate of change between actual price level and expected price level estimated under the assumption that the price level of each period follows ARIMA (p, d, q) process[3]. We use monthly data on the price level for the last twenty-five years to estimate an ARIMA model. The Augmented Dickey–Fuller test is used to unit root test. The BIC is used for lag selection. The estimated ARIMA model is used to predict a price level of three periods ahead. Thus, we use the actual price level and the predicted price level of three periods ahead to calculate the expected inflation rate. Consumer price index (CPI) data are used as the price level. The data are obtained from the OECD website.

The expected inflation rate in the euro zone is a weighted average of the expected inflation rate in the original euro zone countries. The euro zone includes Austria, Belgium, Finland, France, Germany, Ireland, Italy, Luxembourg, Netherlands, Portugal, and Spain. A weight in calculating a weighted average of the expected inflation rate is based on their GDP share among the countries. The data were obtained from the *International Financial Statistics (IFS)* of International Monetary Fund (IMF) website.

3.3. Movements of Utility of International Currencies

We use Equation (1) to calculate utility of international currency in each period. Figure 1a–d show time series of utility of four international currencies. Throughout a whole period, changes in utility of the US dollar, the euro, the Japanese yen and the British pound are fluctuating around 0.5, 0.35, 0.03 and 0.08, respectively.

---

[2] An arithmetic average of real economic growth rates compared to the same quarter of previous year among the three countries and the region (the United States, the euro zone, Japan, and the United Kingdom) was about 1.1% from 2006Q3 to 2017Q4. However, if we exclude a period of 2008Q2 to 2010Q1 where the growth rate has greatly declined due to the global financial crisis, it was about 1.8%. Given the real economic growth rates, our setting the values as a real interest rate seem to be reasonable. The real economic growth rate data obtained from the OECD website.

[3] We used a method of Fama and Gibbons (1984) to estimate expected inflation rates. However, a sample period is much shorter than that by using the ARIMA model due to data constraints if we use the method. In addition, we could not use it because expected inflation rate of TIPS and survey data was only long-term expectation data, and Japan's TIPS data was a small sample. For those reasons, we choose to use the ARIMA model using CPI.

We can find that utility of the US dollar sharply decreased while the other currencies increased in 2008Q3. On the other hand, utility of other international currencies has increased. In particular, utility of the euro has greatly increased. Causes of this sharp change are considered as follows.

Inflation rate in the United States is relatively decreased compared with the other countries and region. At the Lehman Brothers bankruptcy in September 2008, housing price and rents in the United States sharp declined. Accordingly, CPI in the United States, which is greatly affected by housing price and rent, dropped in the period. Figure 2a–d show movements of CPI and expected price levels estimated from CPI. From the figures, from 2008Q3 to 2008Q4, the CPI of the United States is relatively lower than in other countries. Figure 3 shows movements of the four countries' expected inflation rate. From this figure, the expected inflation rate in the United States made larger decrease than the others in 2008Q3.

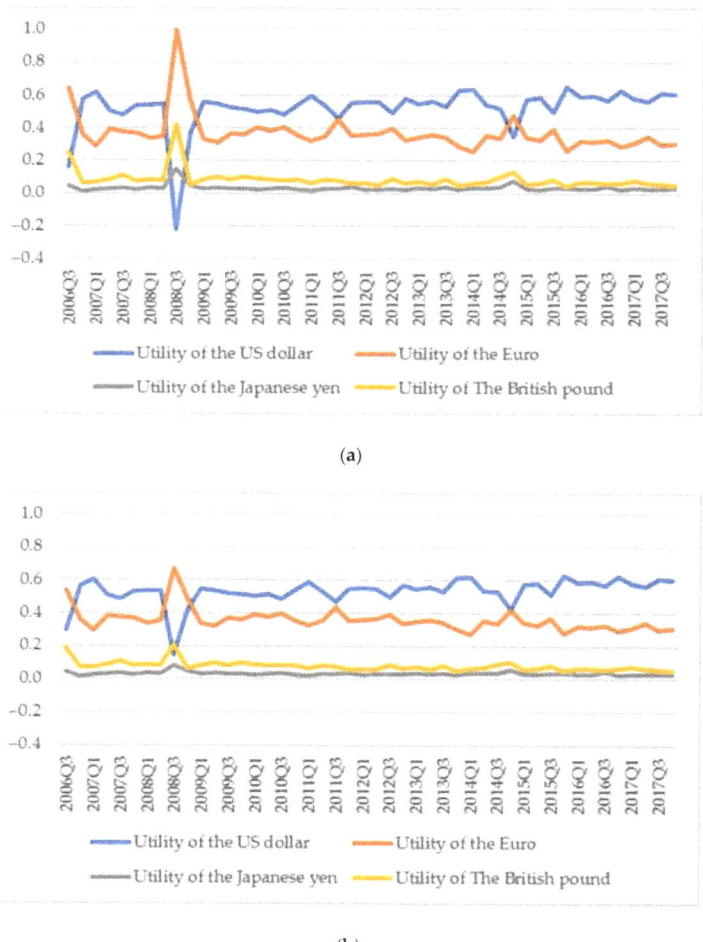

(a)

(b)

Figure 1. *Cont.*

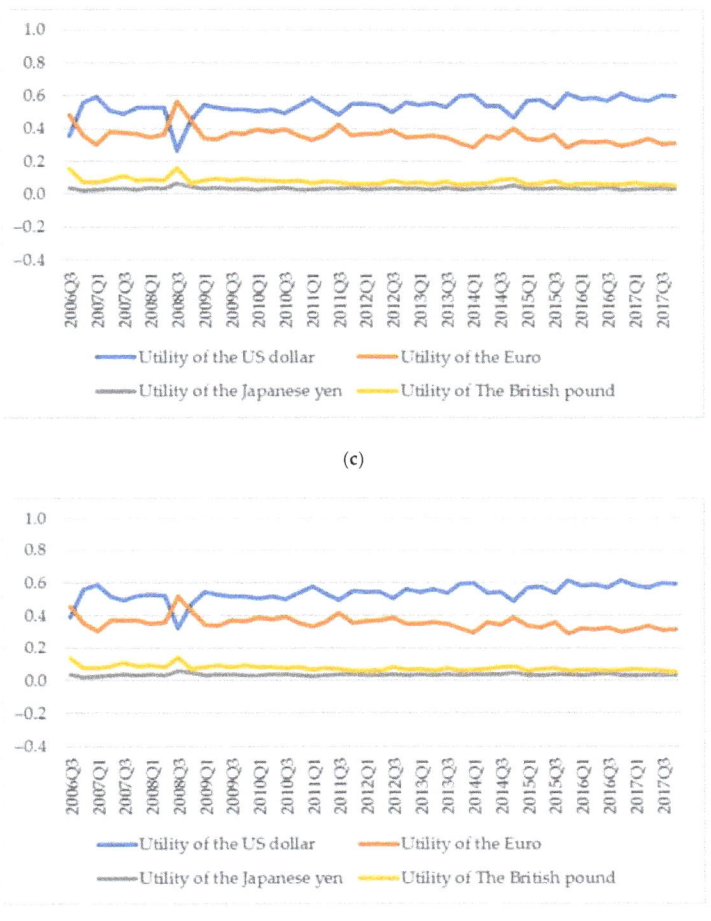

(c)

(d)

Figure 1. (**a**) Utility of international currencies (real interest rate = 1.5%). Notes: The four lines represent time series of estimated coefficients on four international currencies (the US dollar, the euro, the Japanese yen, and the British pound) in a money-in-the-utility function. The coefficients were estimated from share of holdings of an international currency and expected inflation rates with a real interest rate supposed to be 1.5%. We used BIS data on total of domestic currency denominated debt and foreign currency denominated debt of the euro currency market as the share of holdings of an international currency. The expected inflation rates are calculated rate of change of actual CPI level and expected CPI level estimated under the assumption that the price level of each period follows ARIMA (p, d, q) process. (**b**) Utility of international currencies (real interest rate = 2.0%). Notes: The four lines represent time series of estimated coefficients on four international currencies (the US dollar, the euro, the Japanese yen, and the British pound) in a money-in-the-utility function. The coefficients were estimated from share of holdings of an international currency and expected inflation rates with a real interest rate supposed to be 2.0%. We used BIS data on total of domestic currency denominated debt and foreign currency denominated debt of the euro currency market as the share of holdings of an international currency. The expected inflation rates are calculated rate of change of actual CPI level and expected CPI level estimated under the assumption that the price level of each period follows ARIMA (p, d, q) process. (**c**) Utility of international currencies (real interest rate = 2.5%). Notes: The four lines represent time series of estimated coefficients on four international currencies (the US dollar, the euro, the Japanese yen, and the British pound) in a money-in-the-utility function. The coefficients were estimated from share of holdings of an international currency and expected inflation rates with a real interest rate supposed to be 2.5%. We used BIS data on total of domestic currency denominated debt and foreign currency denominated debt of the euro currency market as the share of holdings of an international currency. The expected inflation rates are calculated rate of change of actual CPI level and expected CPI level estimated under the assumption that the price level of each period follows ARIMA (p, d, q) process. (**d**) Utility of international currencies (real interest rate = 3.0%). Notes: The four lines represent time series of estimated coefficients on four international currencies (the US dollar, the euro, the Japanese yen, and the British pound) in a money-in-the-utility function. The coefficients were estimated from share of holdings of an international currency and expected inflation rates with a real interest rate supposed to be 3.0%. We used BIS data on total of domestic currency denominated debt and foreign currency denominated debt of the euro currency market as the share of holdings of an international currency. The expected inflation rates are calculated rate of change of actual CPI level and expected CPI level estimated under the assumption that the price level of each period follows ARIMA (p, d, q) process.

Next, the share of holdings of US dollar did not decrease although the inflation rate relatively decreased. In general, when an inflation rate decreases, a share of holdings of a currency will increase if utility of the currency does not change. On the other hand, if the share of holdings of a currency does not change, utility of the relevant currency decreases when the inflation rate decreases. Figure 4 shows movements in shares of total of domestic currency denominated debt and foreign currency denominated debt of the euro currency market. Figure 5 shows rate of change in shares of total of domestic currency denominated debt and foreign currency denominated debt of the euro currency market. From these figures, change in US dollar share from 2008Q3 to 2008Q4 is the second smallest. Moreover, as mentioned above, inflation rate in the United States at this time has decreased relatively. Therefore, utility of the US dollar decreased, given that the share was not changed and that the inflation rate relatively decreased.

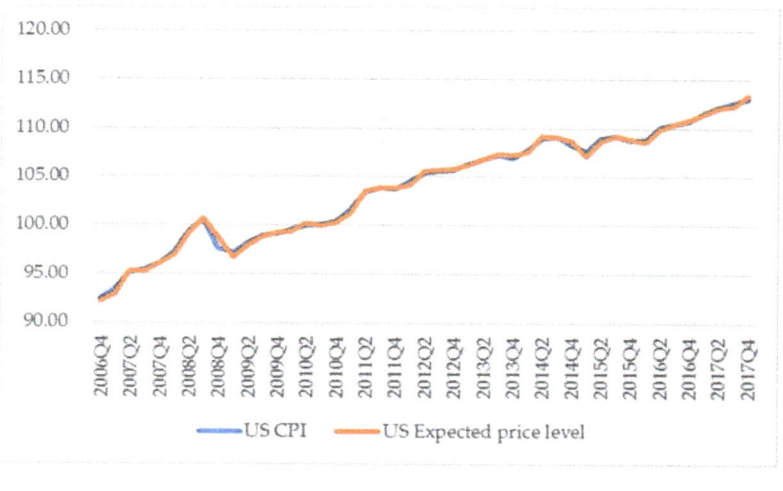

(**a**)

Figure 2. *Cont.*

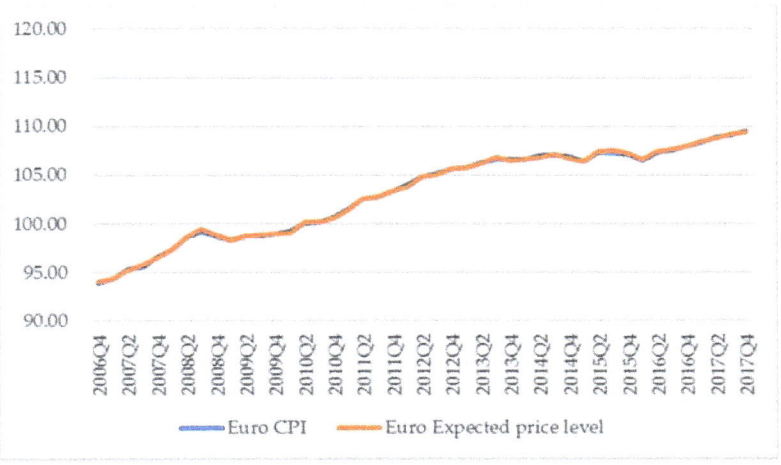

(**b**)

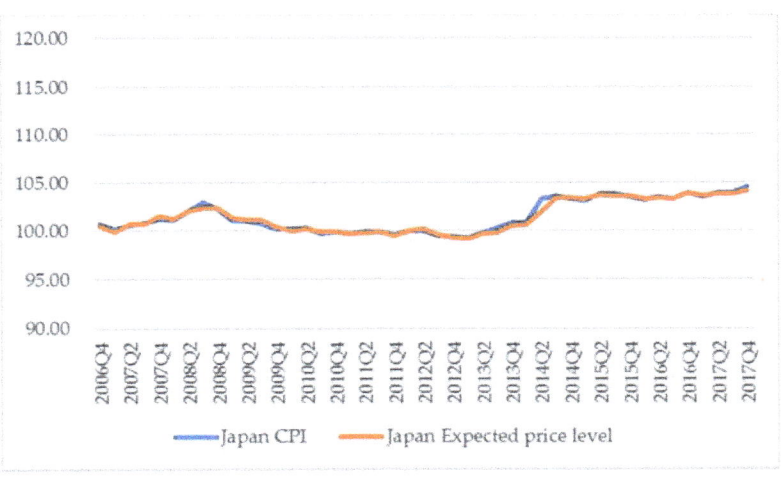

(**c**)

Figure 2. *Cont.*

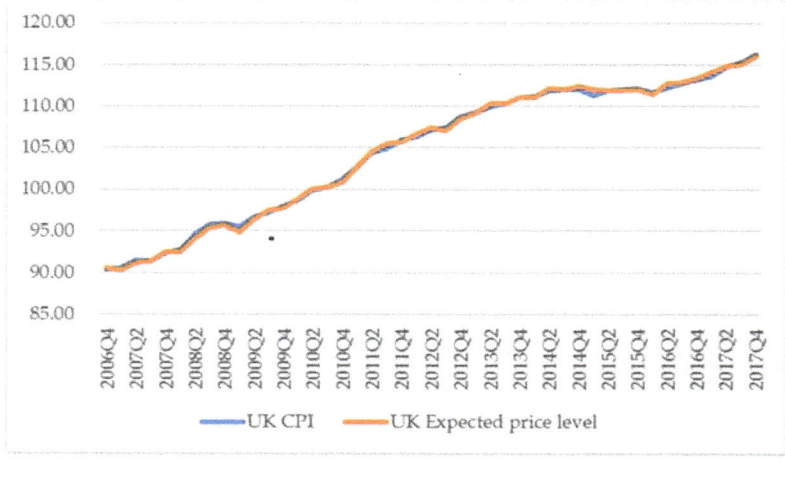

(**d**)

Figure 2. (**a**) CPI and expected price level in the United States. (**b**) CPI and expected price level in the euro zone. Notes: CPI is the weighted average of the original euro area. Weights are GDP share. (**c**) CPI and expected price level in Japan. (**d**) CPI and expected price level in the United Kingdom.

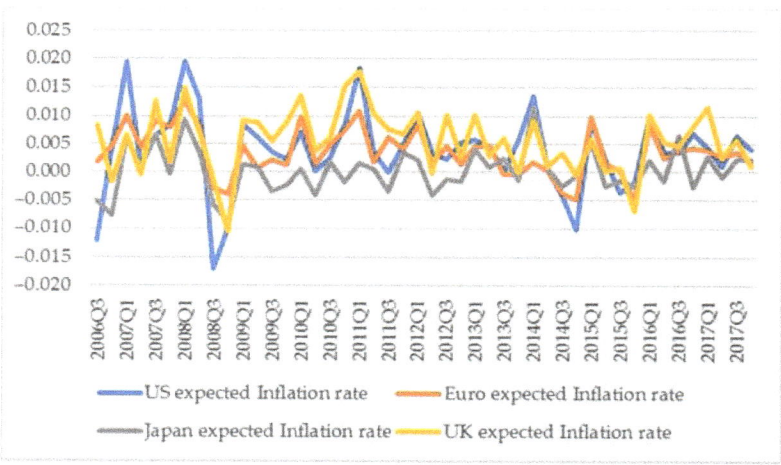

Figure 3. Expected inflation rate. Notes: The expected inflation rates are calculated rate of change between actual price level and expected price level estimated under the assumption that the price level of each period follows ARIMA (p, d, q) process. The price level data is CPI.

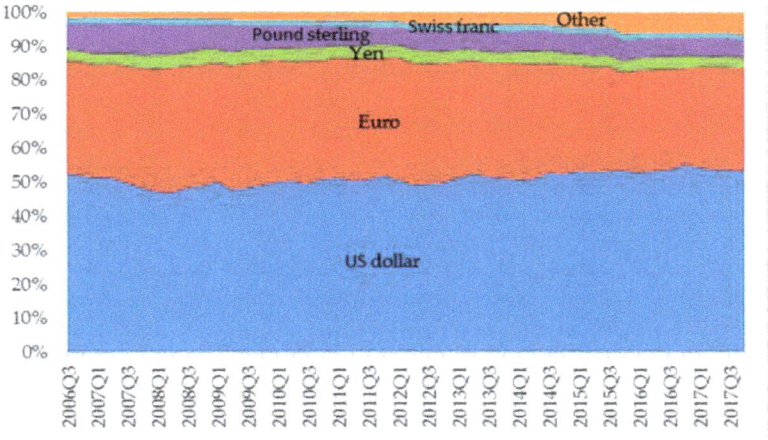

Figure 4. Total of domestic currency denominated debt and foreign currency denominated debt of the euro currency market. Data: BIS.

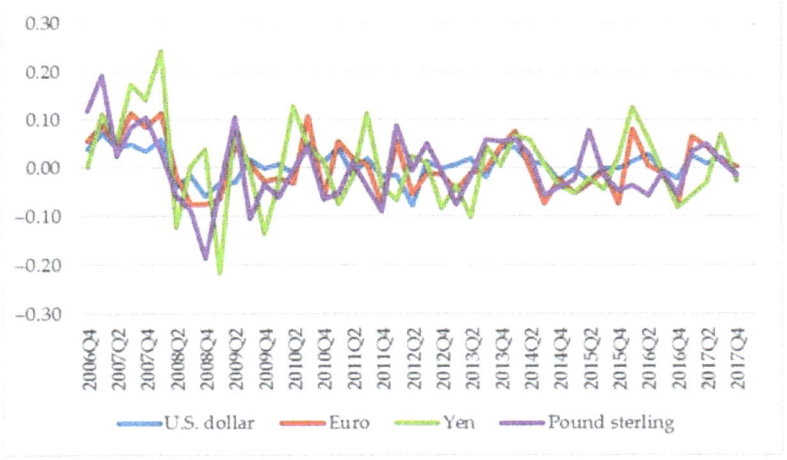

Figure 5. Rates of change of share of holdings of the international currencies. Data: BIS, rates of change of total of domestic currency denominated debt and foreign currency denominated debt of the euro currency market.

4. Empirical Model

4.1. Determinants of Utility of an International Currency

We explain economic variables that can affect utility of international currencies. Firstly, utility of an international currency in the previous period can affect that in the current period if an international currency has inertia in keeping its position. Utility of an international currency may be affected in the same direction as utility of an international currency in the previous period if they have inertia in terms of changes. For example, if utility of an international currency declines, we assumed that the currency is less likely to be used than in the previous period through decline of a medium of exchange function and economies of scale. In other words, utility of an international currency has inertia in terms of keeping changes in the same direction.

Secondly, supply of liquidity in terms of an international currency can affect its utility. A liquidity risk premium in terms of an international currency is an indicator of a liquidity condition in terms of the relevant international currency or its liquidity shortage. A liquidity shortage reduces utility of an international currency through deteriorating its function as a medium of exchange.

Thirdly, an international currency is more likely to be used in proportion to economic activity in the relevant country. A larger volume of international economic transactions with the relevant country make the international currency more useful in terms of its function as a medium of exchange because of its network externalities. The economic activity in the relevant country and the volume of international economic transactions with the relevant country can be represented by GDP, nominal economic growth rate, real economic growth rate, capitalization, total international trade, total exports, international capital flows, and money stock.

Fourthly, economic agents are likely to prefer a more stable value of currency in holding it as an international currency. Since standard deviation of nominal effective exchange rate is regarded as an indicator of the stability of relevant international currency, it can be a determinant of utility of the relevant international currency. In addition, economic agents are likely to prefer a higher value of currency in holding it as an international currency. An effective exchange rate of an international currency, that is an indicator of a currency value against the other currencies, could be a determinant of utility of the relevant international currency.

4.2. A Dynamic Panel Model

We analyze determinants of utility of international currencies by using panel data. In addition, the explanatory variables include a lag term of utility of an international currency as we explained above. For the reasons, we use a dynamic panel data model to analyze determinants of utility of international currencies. Given the above candidates for determinants of an international currency, a dynamic panel model is shown as follows:

$$
\begin{aligned}
Utility\ &of\ international\ currency_{it}\\
= \hat{b}_1 &Utility\ of\ international\ currency_{it-1} + \hat{b}_2 Liquidity\ risk\ premium_{it}\\
+ \hat{b}_3 &Money\ stock\ share_{it} + \hat{b}_4 Relative\ nominal\ economic\ growth_{it}\\
+ \hat{b}_5 &Relative\ real\ economic\ growth_{it} + \hat{b}_6 GDP\ share_{it}\\
+ \hat{b}_7 &Capitalization\ share_{it} + \hat{b}_8 Total\ trade\ share_{it} + \hat{b}_9 Total\ export\ share_{it}\\
+ \hat{b}_{10} &Capital\ flow\ share_{it} + \hat{b}_{11} SD\ of\ Nominal\ effective\ exchange\ rate_{it}\\
+ \hat{b}_{12} &LN\ nominal\ effective\ exchange\ rate_{it}\\
+ \hat{b}_{13} &LN\ real\ effective\ exchange\ rate_{it} + v_i + \varepsilon_{it}
\end{aligned}
\tag{2}
$$

where v_i: fixed effects, ε_{it}: disturbance term. We take a first difference of the above model (Equation (2)) and remove fixed effects. Thus, its first difference model is rewritten as follows:

$$
\begin{aligned}
\Delta Utility\ &of\ international\ currency_{it}\\
= \hat{b}_1 &\Delta Utility\ of\ international\ currency_{it-1} + \hat{b}_2 \Delta Liquidity\ risk\ premium_{it}\\
+ \hat{b}_3 &\Delta Money\ stock\ share_{it} + \hat{b}_4 \Delta Relative\ nominal\ economic\ growth_{it}\\
+ \hat{b}_5 &\Delta Relative\ real\ economic\ growth_{it} + \hat{b}_6 \Delta GDP\ share_{it}\\
+ \hat{b}_7 &\Delta Capitalization\ share_{it} + \hat{b}_8 \Delta Total\ trade\ share_{it} + \hat{b}_9 \Delta Total\ export\ share_{it}\\
+ \hat{b}_{10} &\Delta Capital\ flow\ share_{it} + \hat{b}_{11} \Delta SD\ of\ Nominal\ effective\ exchange\ rate_{it}\\
+ \hat{b}_{12} &\Delta LN\ nominal\ effective\ exchange\ rate_{it}\\
+ \hat{b}_{13} &\Delta LN\ real\ effective\ exchange\ rate_{it} + \Delta \varepsilon_{it}
\end{aligned}
\tag{3}
$$

where Δ: difference operator.

There is a correlation between $\Delta Utility\ of\ international\ currency_{it-1}$ and $\Delta \varepsilon_{it}$. Therefore, according to Arellano and Bond (1991), the first difference model is estimated by GMM.

5. Sample Period and Data

5.1. Sample Period

It is the US dollar, the euro, the Japanese yen, and the British pound that we analyze as international currencies in this paper. The Swiss franc has characteristics that is different from other international currencies and was excluded from the analysis in this paper.

A whole sample period covers a period from 2006Q3 to 2017Q4. The initial period of analysis (2006Q3) is due to constraint of data on the Japanese yen liquidity risk premium. Specifically, we investigate an effect of liquidity shortage on utility of international currencies. In this sample period, the world economy faced US dollar liquidity shortage. Moreover, the Federal Reserve Board (FRB) conducted quantitative easing monetary policy to solve the US dollar liquidity shortage from the end of 2008. The US dollar liquidity shortage could affect utility of the US dollar.

5.2. Data for Determinants of Utility of International Currencies

Figure 6a–d show movements in three spreads of London Interbank Offered Rate (LIBOR) (3 months) minus Treasury Bills (TB) rate (3 months), LIBOR (3 months) minus Overnight Indexed Swap (OIS) rate (3 months), and OIS rate (3 months) minus TB rate (3 months). The spread of LIBOR minus OIS rate is regarded as credit risk premium because LIBOR is the interest rate at which banks borrow unsecured funds from other banks. OIS rate is the interest rate at which banks borrow secured funds from other banks. Given that banks mainly face and liquidity risk as well as credit risk, the spread of OIS rate minus TB rate is regarded as liquidity risk premium. The data were obtained from *Datastream*.

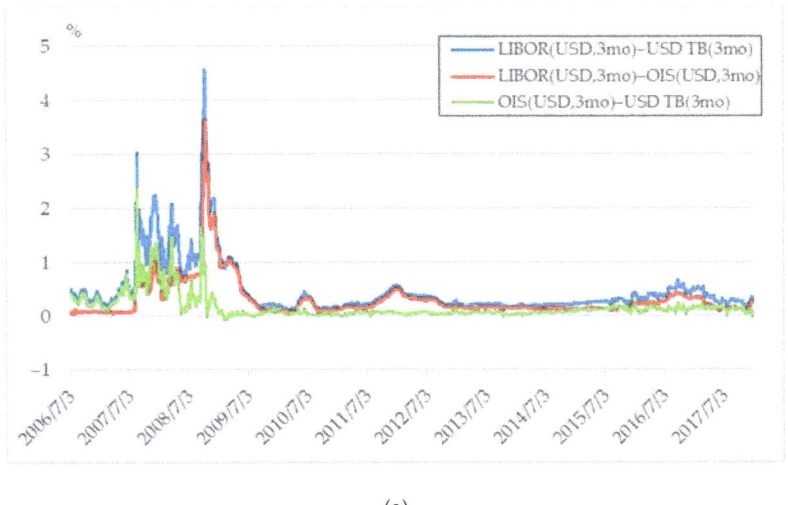

(a)

Figure 6. *Cont.*

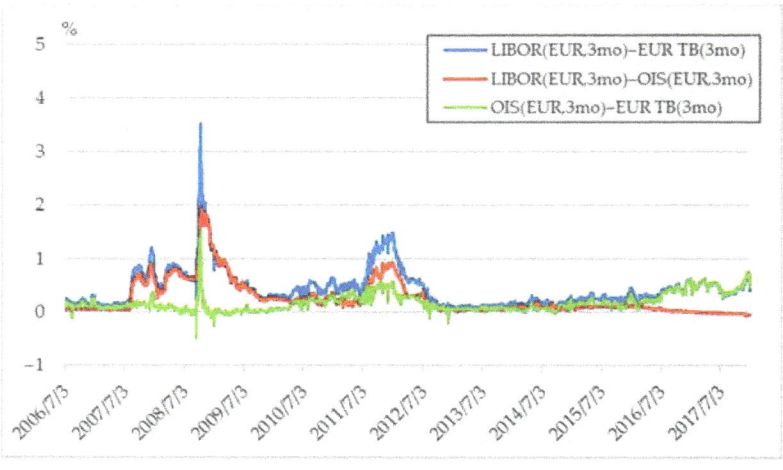

(**b**)

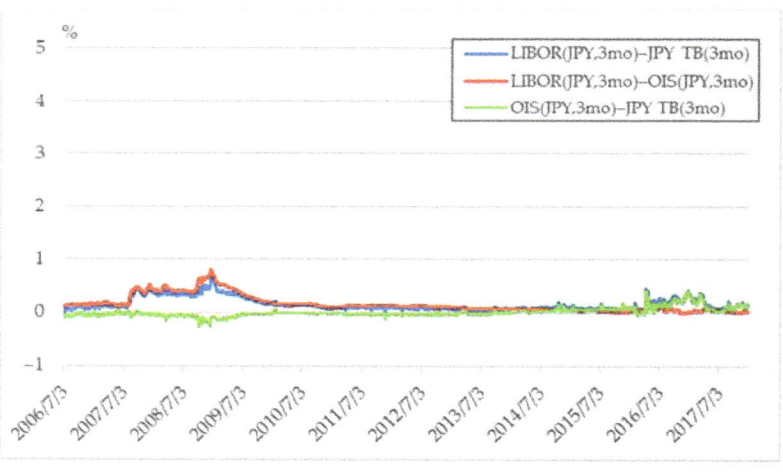

(**c**)

Figure 6. *Cont.*

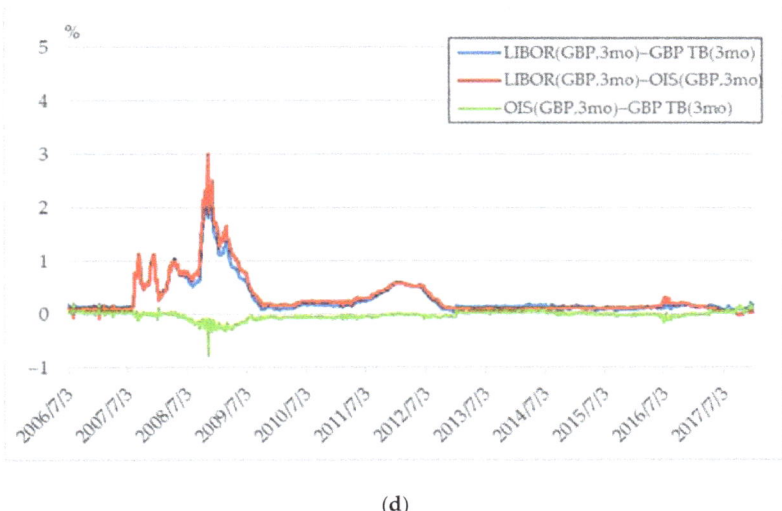

(**d**)

Figure 6. (**a**) Credit Risk Premium and Liquidity Risk Premium for the USD. Data: Datastream, Credit risk = London Interbank Offered Rate (LIBOR) (USD, 3 months) minus Overnight Indexed Swap (OIS) rate (USD, 3 months), liquidity risk = OIS minus US Treasury Bills (TB) rate (USD, 3 months). (**b**) Credit Risk Premium and Liquidity Risk Premium for the EUR. Data: Datastream, Credit risk = London Interbank Offered Rate (LIBOR) (EUR, 3 months) minus Overnight Indexed Swap (OIS) rate (EUR, 3 months), liquidity risk = OIS minus yields on German treasury discount paper (Bubills) (EUR TB rate) (euro, 3 months). (**c**) Credit Risk Premium and Liquidity Risk Premium for the JPY. Data: atastream, Credit risk = London Interbank Offered Rate (LIBOR) (JPY, 3 months) minus Overnight Indexed Swap (OIS) rate (JPY, 3 months), liquidity risk = OIS minus yields on Japanese Treasury Discount Bills (JPY TB rate) (JPY, 3 months). (**d**) Credit Risk Premium and Liquidity Risk Premium for the GBP. Data: Datastream, Credit risk = London Interbank Offered Rate (LIBOR) (GBP, 3 months) minus Overnight Indexed Swap (OIS) rate (GBP, 3 months), liquidity risk = OIS minus Yields on UK Government bonds (gilts) (GBP TB rate) (GBP, 3 months).

From Figure 6a, we can find that the US dollar liquidity shortage continues from 2006 to 2008. However, it has decreased to a level smaller than 0.1% since the FRB started quantitative easing monetary policy in late 2008 when it at the same time concluded and extended currency swap arrangements[4] with other major central banks to provide US dollar liquidity to other countries. From Figure 6b, we can find that the euro liquidity shortage from 2006 to 2008 has not occurred except for the Lehman Brothers bankruptcy in September 2008. However, the liquidity risk premium in terms of the euro increased from June 2010 to June 2012. Figure 6c,d do not show any significant increases in liquidity risk premium in terms of the Japanese yen and the British pound during the analysis period. The stable movements in the liquidity risk premium in terms of these currencies are different those in terms of the US dollar and the euro.

Money stock share is a share of money stock of each of the three countries and the region in terms of a total money stock of the three countries and the region. We used seasonally adjusted nominal money stock (M1). The data were obtained from the FRED website.

---

[4] The FRB concluded new currency swap arrangements with the ECB and the Swiss National Bank on 12 December 2007. Afterwards, it increased amount of currency swap arrangements and concluded them with other central banks.

GDP share is a share of GDP of each of the three countries and the region in terms of a total GDP of the three countries and the region (the United State, the euro Area, Japan, the United Kingdom). We used seasonally adjusted nominal GDP for the calculation. The data were obtained from the *IFS* of IMF website.

Relative nominal economic growth rate and relative real economic growth rate are ratio of GDP growth rate of each of the three countries and the region in terms of an arithmetic average of GDP growth rate of the three countries and the region. Nominal economic growth rate compared to previous quarter was calculated from seasonally adjusted nominal GDP. In addition, we used seasonally adjusted real economic growth rate compared to previous quarter to calculate a relative real economic growth rate. The data were obtained from the Organization for Economic Co-operation and Development (OECD) website.

Capitalization share is a share of capitalization of each of the three countries and the region in terms of a total capitalization of the three countries and the region. We could not obtain the data of United Kingdom in 2010 and quarterly data of the three countries and the region. For the reason, we estimated quarterly data using linear interpolation from annual data. We used data on market capitalization of listed domestic companies for the calculation. The data were obtained from website of the World Bank and the ECB.

Total trade share is a share of trade amount of each of the three countries and the region in terms of a total trade amount of the three countries and the region with the rest of the world. When we sum up the total trade amount for the three countries and the region, we exclude exports and imports among them. Also, total export share is a share of export value of each of the three countries and the region in terms of a total export value of the three countries and the region with the rest of the world. The data were obtained from the *Direction of Trade Statistics* of IMF website.

Capital flow share is a share of international capital flows of each of the three countries and the region in terms of a total international capital flows of the three countries and the region. We could not obtain quarterly data of Japan for 2006Q3 to 2010Q1. For the reason, we estimated quarterly data using linear interpolation from annual data. In this paper, the international capital flows are defined as sum of values of direct investments, portfolio investments, and other investments of net acquisition of financial assets and direct investments, portfolio investments, and other investments of net incurrence of liabilities. The data were obtained from the *Balance of Payments and International Investment Position* of IMF website.

Data on both nominal and real effective exchange rates of each of the currencies are taken logarithms. The data were obtained from BIS website and the *IFS* of IMF website. Table 1 shows mean and standard deviation of difference of each variable.

Table 1. Descriptive Statistics of difference of each variable.

	4 Countries		United States		Euro Area		Japan		United Kingdom	
	Mean	SD	Mean	SD	Mean	SD	Mean	SD	Mean	SD
ΔUtility of Currency (1.5%)$_t$	-0.0001	0.1153	0.0010	0.1666	-0.0015	0.1375	0.0004	0.0280	-0.0001	-0.0001
ΔUtility of Currency (2.0%)$_t$	0.0000	0.0614	0.0010	0.0921	-0.0013	0.0743	0.0003	0.0127	-0.0002	-0.0002
ΔUtility of Currency (2.5%)$_t$	0.0000	0.0441	0.0010	0.0665	-0.0012	0.0537	0.0003	0.0092	-0.0003	-0.0003
ΔUtility of Currency (3.0%)$_t$	0.0000	0.0352	0.0010	0.0530	-0.0011	0.0430	0.0002	0.0076	-0.0003	-0.0003
ΔUtility of Currency (1.5%)$_{t-1}$	-0.0005	0.1221	0.0093	0.1778	-0.0068	0.1437	-0.0004	0.0285	-0.0043	-0.0043
ΔUtility of Currency (2.0%)$_{t-1}$	-0.0003	0.0666	0.0063	0.1007	-0.0044	0.0787	-0.0002	0.0132	-0.0028	-0.0028
ΔUtility of Currency (2.5%)$_{t-1}$	-0.0002	0.0481	0.0049	0.0730	-0.0033	0.0569	-0.0002	0.0097	-0.0021	-0.0021
ΔUtility of Currency (3.0%)$_{t-1}$	-0.0001	0.0383	0.0041	0.0582	-0.0027	0.0454	-0.0001	0.0080	-0.0018	-0.0018
ΔLiquidity Risk Premium$_t$	0.0012	0.0754	-0.0036	0.1111	0.0054	0.0873	0.0028	0.0429	0.0004	0.0003
ΔMoney Stock Share$_t$	0.0000	0.0087	0.0012	0.0040	0.0003	0.0108	-0.0009	0.0122	-0.0009	-0.0007
ΔRelative Nominal Economic Growth$_t$	0.0000	3.9457	-0.0054	1.4781	0.0199	3.4264	-0.0083	5.0524	-0.0370	-0.0208
ΔRelative Real Economic Growth$_t$	0.0000	6.6128	0.0058	3.3296	-0.0024	5.4797	-0.0007	10.7073	0.0055	0.0049
ΔGDP Share$_t$	0.0000	0.0059	0.0012	0.0074	-0.0004	0.0049	-0.0007	0.0077	-0.0002	-0.0002
ΔCapitalization Share$_t$	0.0000	0.0042	0.0025	0.0044	-0.0017	0.0046	-0.0001	0.0039	-0.0007	-0.0007
ΔTotal Trade Share$_t$	0.0000	0.0068	0.0005	0.0072	-0.0002	0.0102	-0.0002	0.0050	-0.0001	-0.0001
ΔTotal Export Share$_t$	0.0000	0.0060	0.0007	0.0044	-0.0002	0.0088	-0.0004	0.0061	-0.0002	-0.0002
ΔCapital Flow Share$_t$	0.0000	0.0049	0.0010	0.0060	0.0006	0.0060	0.0004	0.0028	-0.0020	-0.0020
ΔSD of Nominal Effective Exchange Rate$_t$	0.0082	0.9941	0.0107	0.6415	0.0016	0.6647	0.0046	1.3446	0.0089	0.0159
ΔLN Nominal Effective Exchange Rate$_t$	-0.0005	0.0340	0.0023	0.0281	0.0007	0.0227	0.0020	0.0494	-0.0075	-0.0071
ΔLN Real Effective Exchange Rate$_t$	-0.0023	0.0339	0.0015	0.0272	-0.0017	0.0227	-0.0029	0.0491	-0.0065	-0.0060
number of observations	172		43		43		43		43	

6. Empirical Analysis on Determinants of Utility of International Currencies

6.1. Expected Effect of Determinant on Utility of International Currencies

We expect that each of determinants affects utility of international currencies in as a direction as follows.

If there is inertia of an international currency in terms of changes in utility, a change in utility of an international currency in the previous period has a positive effect on a change in utility of the international currency in the current period. For example, if utility of an international currency declines, demand for the relevant international currency as one with a function as medium of exchange should decrease. The decrease in the demand for the international currency, in turn, makes utility of an international currency decline further. We investigate a hypothesis that a change in utility of an international currency in the previous period has a positive effect on change in utility of the international currency in the current period.

An increase in the liquidity risk premium in terms of an international currency means liquidity shortage in terms of the relevant international currency. The liquidity shortage reduces convenience of the international currency for economic agents to use for medium of exchange. Thus, an occurrence of liquidity shortage decreases utility of the international currency. The liquidity risk premium, that is indicated by OIS rate minus TB rate, increases when the liquidity shortage worsens. Therefore, an increase in the liquidity risk premium reduces utility of the international currency. We investigate a hypothesis that liquidity risk premium has a negative effect on utility of the international currency. Figures 1a–d and 2a show that both we had both the increase in the US dollar liquidity risk premium in 2008 and the decrease in utility of the US dollar in 2008Q3 simultaneously.

Money stock share, relative nominal economic growth rate, relative real economic growth rate, GDP share, capitalization share, total trade share, total export share, and capital flow share are economic variables that represent relative economic size of the relevant country. Network externalities works in selecting an international currency as medium of exchange. For the reason, a change in an economic size of the relevant country has a positive effect on utility of the international currency. We investigate a hypothesis that coefficients of explanatory variables that represent relative economic size are positive.

As we have already explained, economic agents are likely to prefer a stabler and higher value of currency in holding it as an international currency. The standard deviation and value of effective exchange rate of an international currency, that is an indicator of a currency stable and value against the other currencies, could be a determinant of utility of the relevant international currency. We investigate a hypothesis that a stabler and higher value of an international currency increase. We analyze whether an increase in an effective exchange rate increases utility of the relevant international currency.

6.2. Empirical Results

Tables 2–5 show results of the dynamic panel analysis. A head line in Tables represents empirical analysis number. Table 2 shows determinants of utility of international currency supposing that a real interest rate is 1.5%. Coefficients on change in utility of international currencies in the previous period are significantly positive in 26 cases of total 36 cases. The coefficients are estimated from 0.15 to 0.26. Coefficients on change in liquidity risk premium are significantly negative in all of the cases at 1% of significance level. The coefficients are estimated from -0.25 to -0.20. In the analyses 1 to 4 and 12, the coefficients on change in money stock share are positive at 10% of significance level. The coefficients are estimated from 3.50 to 3.72. In the analyses 1 to 12 and 36, the coefficients on change in capital flow share are significantly positive. The coefficients are estimated from 1.21 to 2.93. However, economic scale variables excluding money stock share and capital flow share and effective exchange rate related variables do not satisfy a sign condition or significance levels.

Table 3 shows determinants of utility of international currency supposing that a real interest rate is 2.0%. Coefficients on change in utility of international currencies in the previous period are significantly positive in 20 cases of total 36 cases. The coefficients are estimated from 0.22 to 0.40. Coefficients on change in liquidity risk premium are significantly negative in all of the cases at 1% of significance level. The coefficients are estimated from −0.11 to −0.08. In the analysis 49, the coefficients on change in money stock share are positive at 5% of significance level. The coefficient is estimated 0.58. Coefficients on change in capital flow share are significantly positive in all of the cases at the significance level 1%. The coefficients are estimated from 0.86 to 1.71. In the analysis 62, Coefficients on change in nominal effective exchange rate are significantly positive at the significance level 10%. The coefficients are estimated 0.30. However, most of the coefficients on change in economic variables associated with relative economic scale excluding capital flow share and effective exchange rate do not satisfy a sign condition or significance levels.

Table 4 shows determinants of utility of international currency supposing that a real interest rate is 2.5%. Coefficients on change in utility of international currencies in the previous period are significantly positive in 22 cases of total 36 cases. The coefficients are estimated from 0.16 to 0.45. Coefficients on change in liquidity risk premium are significantly negative in all of the cases. The coefficients are estimated from −0.07 to −0.04. In the analysis 85, the coefficients on change in money stock share are positive at 5% of significance level. The coefficient is estimated 0.42. Coefficients on change in capital flow share are significantly positive in all of the cases except analysis 84. The coefficients are estimated from 0.65 to 1.07. In the analysis 98, the coefficients on change in nominal effective exchange rate are positive at 10% of significance level. The coefficient is estimated 0.24. However, most of the coefficients on change in economic variables associated with relative economic scale excluding capital flow share and effective exchange rate do not satisfy a sign condition or significance levels.

Table 5 shows determinants of utility of international currency supposing that a real interest rate is 3.0%. Coefficients on change in utility of international currencies in the previous period are significantly positive in 23 cases of total 36 cases. The coefficients are estimated to be from 0.06 to 0.43. Coefficients on change in utility of international currencies in the previous period are significantly negative in 14 cases out of 36 cases. The coefficients are estimated to be −0.04 and −0.03. In the analyses 136 and 144, coefficients on change in capital flow share are significantly positive. The coefficients are estimated to be 0.45 and 0.51. However, most of the coefficients on change in economic variables associated with relative economic scale and effective exchange rate do not satisfy the sign condition or the significance level.

We summarize the above empirical results. Firstly, the coefficients on utility of international currency in the previous period are significantly positive in the many cases. These results suggest that change in utility of an international currency in the previous period in the same direction has effect on change in utility of the international currency in the current period. There is inertia in terms of change in the international monetary system.

Secondly, the coefficients on liquidity risk premium are significantly negative in all of the cases except the real interest rate 3.0%. Even if the real interest rate is 3.0%, liquidity risk premium is significantly negative in about half of cases. The empirical result is consistent with the hypothesis that liquidity risk premium has a negative effect on utility of the international currency. We find that utility of an international currency is affected by liquidity condition or liquidity shortage. Specifically, the liquidity shortage reduces utility of the international currency through a reduction in convenience for economic agents to use the relevant international currency as a medium of exchange.

Thirdly, the coefficients on capital flow share are significant in many cases except in cases of real interest rate 3.0%. Capital flow share represent relative economic scale of the relevant country. Therefore, the above results suggest that utility of the international currency might be affected by changes in economic scale. However, since other economic scale variables did not become significant, the relative change in capital flows may be affecting utility of the international currency.

Table 2. Determinants utility of international currency (real interest rate 1.5%).

	1	2	3	4	5	6	7	8	9	10	11	12	13	14	15	16	17	18
ΔUtility of international currency$_{it-1}$	0.14 (0.30)	0.23 (0.10)	0.13 (0.28)	0.23* (0.09)	0.16 (0.25)	0.26* (0.07)	0.16 (0.22)	0.26* (0.05)	0.15 (0.28)	0.24* (0.08)	0.14 (0.27)	0.24* (0.07)	0.21** (0.01)	0.20** (0.05)	0.20** (0.04)	0.21** (0.02)	0.21** (0.02)	0.06 (0.43)
ΔLiquidity risk premium$_{it}$	-0.21*** (0.00)	-0.24*** (0.00)	-0.21*** (0.00)	-0.23*** (0.00)	-0.22*** (0.00)	-0.25*** (0.00)	-0.22*** (0.00)	-0.24*** (0.00)	-0.22*** (0.00)	-0.25*** (0.00)	-0.22*** (0.00)	-0.24*** (0.00)	-0.19*** (0.00)	-0.21*** (0.00)	-0.21*** (0.00)	-0.22*** (0.00)	-0.21*** (0.00)	-0.23*** (0.00)
ΔMoney stock share$_{it}$	3.50* (0.07)	3.55* (0.06)	3.57* (0.07)	3.64* (0.06)	3.36 (0.15)	3.49 (0.13)	3.44 (0.14)	3.58 (0.12)	3.50 (0.11)	3.62 (0.10)	3.60 (0.10)	3.72* (0.09)	0.85 (0.19)					
ΔRelative nominal economic growth$_{it}$	-0.0007 (0.63)	-0.0015 (0.35)			-0.0008 (0.59)	-0.0017 (0.33)			-0.0009 (0.58)	-0.0017 (0.33)				-0.0020 (0.32)				
ΔRelative real economic growth$_{it}$			-0.0005 (0.46)	-0.0006 (0.30)			-0.0005 (0.44)	-0.0006 (0.25)			-0.0006 (0.41)	-0.0006 (0.23)			-0.0003 (0.57)			
ΔGDP share$_{it}$	-2.97 (0.32)	-3.71 (0.17)	-2.97 (0.31)	-3.66 (0.15)	-3.69 (0.24)	-4.47 (0.11)	-3.62 (0.23)	-4.38* (0.10)	-3.46 (0.26)	-4.23 (0.12)	-3.39 (0.26)	-4.14 (0.11)						
ΔCapitalization share$_{it}$	-0.02 (0.98)	-0.29 (0.84)	-0.04 (0.96)	-0.28 (0.84)	0.13 (0.90)	-0.15 (0.93)	0.07 (0.94)	-0.18 (0.91)	-0.03 (0.98)	-0.30 (0.85)	-0.10 (0.90)	-0.35 (0.82)					-0.03 (0.88)	
ΔTotal trade share$_{it}$	-5.78*** (0.00)		-5.83*** (0.00)		-5.71*** (0.00)		-5.74*** (0.00)		-5.72*** (0.00)		-5.75*** (0.00)							-4.67*** (0.00)
ΔTotal export share$_{it}$		-3.45* (0.07)		-3.56* (0.08)		-3.41* (0.08)		-3.50* (0.08)		-3.48* (0.08)		-3.56* (0.08)						
ΔCapital flow share$_{it}$	2.36*** (0.00)	2.36** (0.02)	2.34*** (0.00)	2.30** (0.03)	2.85*** (0.00)	2.93*** (0.01)	2.78*** (0.00)	2.83** (0.02)	2.83*** (0.00)	2.91** (0.02)	2.76*** (0.00)	2.81** (0.04)						
ΔSD of Nominal effective exchange rate$_{it}$	-0.01 (0.16)	-0.01** (0.04)	-0.01 (0.16)	-0.01** (0.04)									-0.02 (0.25)	-0.02 (0.24)	-0.02 (0.25)	-0.02 (0.26)	-0.02 (0.23)	-0.01 (0.36)
ΔLN Nominal effective exchange rate$_{it}$					0.15 (0.65)	0.13 (0.72)	0.14 (0.65)	0.13 (0.71)										
ΔLN Real effective exchange rate$_{it}$									0.05 (0.87)	0.04 (0.92)	0.05 (0.89)	0.04 (0.91)						
Sargan test	0.95	0.97	0.95	0.97	0.99	0.99	0.99	0.99	0.98	0.99	0.98	0.99	0.97	0.98	0.98	0.97	0.98	0.87
AR(1) serial correlation test	0.08*	0.10*	0.08*	0.10*	0.08*	0.10	0.08*	0.10	0.08*	0.10*	0.08*	0.10*	0.09*	0.10*	0.10*	0.10*	0.10	0.08*
AR(2) serial correlation test	0.47	0.20	0.58	0.22	0.97	0.23	0.88	0.27	0.86	0.23	0.95	0.26	0.18	0.19	0.19	0.18	0.18	0.13

Table 2. Cont.

	19	20	21	22	23	24	25	26	27	28	29	30	31	32	33	34	35	36
ΔUtility of international currency$_{it-1}$	0.15 ** (0.05)	0.22 ** (0.01)	0.21 ** (0.04)	0.23 ** (0.02)	0.23 ** (0.02)	0.23 ** (0.02)	0.23 ** (0.04)	0.07 (0.50)	0.16 * (0.09)	0.25 *** (0.01)	0.20 ** (0.04)	0.22 ** (0.03)	0.22 ** (0.03)	0.23 ** (0.02)	0.23 ** (0.04)	0.07 (0.51)	0.16 * (0.10)	0.25 ** (0.01)
ΔLiquidity risk premium$_{it}$	−0.25 *** (0.00)	−0.21 *** (0.00)	−0.20 *** (0.00)	−0.21 *** (0.00)	−0.20 *** (0.00)	−0.21 *** (0.00)	−0.20 *** (0.00)	−0.22 *** (0.00)	−0.24 *** (0.00)	−0.21 *** (0.00)	−0.20 *** (0.00)	−0.21 *** (0.00)	−0.21 *** (0.00)	−0.21 *** (0.00)	−0.20 *** (0.00)	−0.22 *** (0.00)	−0.24 *** (0.00)	−0.22 *** (0.00)
ΔMoney stock share$_{it}$			0.61 (0.47)								0.90 (0.23)							
ΔRelative nominal economic growth$_{it}$				−0.0019 (0.35)								−0.0020 (0.34)						
ΔRelative real economic growth$_{it}$					−0.0002 (0.56)								−0.0002 (0.55)					
ΔGDP share$_{it}$							−0.31 (0.57)								−0.23 (0.71)			
ΔCapitalization share$_{it}$						−1.83 *** (0.00)								−1.68 ** (0.01)				
ΔTotal trade share$_{it}$								−5.57 *** (0.00)								−5.52 *** (0.00)		
ΔTotal export share$_{it}$	−2.70 (0.11)								−3.56 * (0.07)								−3.55 * (0.06)	
ΔCapital flow share$_{it}$		1.00 (0.26)								1.05 (0.15)								1.21 * (0.06)
ΔSD of Nominal effective exchange rate$_{it}$	−0.01 (0.26)	−0.02 (0.16)																
ΔLN Nominal effective exchange rate$_{it}$										0.11 (0.67)								
ΔLN Real effective exchange rate$_{it}$			0.01 (0.97)	0.14 (0.58)	0.17 (0.50)	0.45 (0.10)	0.17 (0.51)	0.43 (0.18)	0.33 (0.29)		−0.09 (0.78)	0.09 (0.72)	0.12 (0.62)	0.39 (0.15)	0.12 (0.64)	0.40 (0.19)	0.30 (0.32)	0.04 (0.86)
Sargan test	0.94	0.98	0.98	1.00	1.00	1.00	1.00	0.98	0.99	1.00	0.97	1.00	1.00	1.00	1.00	0.98	0.99	1.00
AR(1) serial correlation test	0.09 *	0.09 *	0.09 *	0.10 *	0.10 *	0.10	0.10 *	0.08 *	0.09 *	0.09 *	0.09 *	0.10 *	0.10 *	0.10	0.10	0.08 *	0.09 *	0.09 *
AR(2) serial correlation test	0.16	0.20	0.21	0.26	0.25	0.32	0.24	0.51	0.16	0.27	0.21	0.26	0.25	0.32	0.24	0.47	0.16	0.26

The parentheses are *p*-value. *, **, *** are significance level 10%, 5%, 1%. Instrument variables for period t are utility of the international currency of periods t-3. The null hypothesis of Sargan test is that over-identification is valid. The null hypothesis of AR(1) and AR(2) serial correlation test is that there is no serial correlation.

Table 3. Determinants utility of international currency (real interest rate 2.0%).

	37	38	39	40	41	42	43	44	45	46	47	48	49	50	51	52	53	54
ΔUtility of international currency$_{it-1}$	0.20 (0.38)	0.30 (0.22)	0.19 (0.35)	0.30 (0.20)	0.25 (0.32)	0.37 (0.18)	0.25 (0.28)	0.37 (0.14)	0.20 (0.35)	0.31 (0.18)	0.19 (0.31)	0.30 (0.14)	0.31*** (0.01)	0.29** (0.03)	0.28** (0.02)	0.31** (0.01)	0.32** (0.01)	0.12 (0.20)
ΔLiquidity risk premium$_{it}$	-0.08*** (0.00)	-0.10*** (0.00)	-0.08*** (0.00)	-0.10*** (0.00)	-0.10*** (0.00)	-0.11*** (0.00)	-0.10*** (0.00)	-0.11*** (0.00)	-0.10*** (0.00)	-0.11*** (0.00)	-0.09*** (0.00)	-0.11*** (0.00)	-0.07*** (0.00)	-0.08*** (0.00)	-0.08*** (0.00)	-0.08*** (0.00)	-0.08*** (0.00)	-0.09*** (0.00)
ΔMoney stock share$_{it}$	1.54 (0.17)	1.59 (0.16)	1.57 (0.16)	1.64 (0.13)	1.40 (0.36)	1.54 (0.32)	1.44 (0.34)	1.59 (0.29)	1.41 (0.30)	1.54 (0.27)	1.45 (0.28)	1.59 (0.23)	0.58** (0.05)					
ΔRelative nominal economic growth$_{it}$	-0.0007 (0.46)	-0.0012 (0.27)												-0.0014 (0.24)				
ΔRelative real economic growth$_{it}$			-0.0002 (0.56)	-0.0003 (0.40)	-0.0008 (0.48)	-0.0014 (0.28)	-0.0002 (0.54)	-0.0003 (0.34)	-0.0008 (0.47)	-0.0013 (0.27)	-0.0002 (0.51)	-0.0003 (0.30)			-0.0001 (0.71)			
ΔGDP share$_{it}$	-0.90 (0.60)	-1.36 (0.38)	-0.86 (0.59)	-1.29 (0.35)	-1.51 (0.42)	-2.00 (0.25)	-1.46 (0.40)	-1.94 (0.21)	-1.19 (0.46)	-1.66 (0.25)	-1.14 (0.44)	-1.59 (0.22)				0.20 (0.43)		
ΔCapitalization share$_{it}$	0.09 (0.85)	-0.08 (0.93)	0.10 (0.83)	-0.05 (0.95)	0.27 (0.67)	0.09 (0.93)	0.25 (0.68)	0.09 (0.93)	0.12 (0.80)	-0.05 (0.96)	0.09 (0.83)	-0.06 (0.94)					0.32 (0.19)	
ΔTotal trade share$_{it}$	-3.45*** (0.00)		-3.51*** (0.00)		-3.37*** (0.01)		-3.42*** (0.00)		-3.46*** (0.01)		-3.51*** (0.00)							-2.61*** (0.00)
ΔTotal export share$_{it}$		-2.12* (0.06)		-2.23* (0.05)		-1.97* (0.07)		-2.06* (0.05)		-2.13* (0.06)		-2.22* (0.05)						
ΔCapital flow share$_{it}$	1.32*** (0.00)	1.35*** (0.00)	1.28*** (0.00)	1.28*** (0.00)	1.63*** (0.00)	1.71*** (0.00)	1.57*** (0.00)	1.62*** (0.00)	1.51*** (0.00)	1.59*** (0.00)	1.46*** (0.00)	1.50*** (0.01)						
ΔSD of Nominal effective exchange rate$_{it}$	0.00 (0.18)	-0.01** (0.03)	-0.01 (0.18)	-0.01** (0.03)									-0.01 (0.24)	-0.01 (0.26)	-0.01 (0.26)	-0.01 (0.25)	-0.01 (0.21)	-0.01 (0.40)
ΔLN Nominal effective exchange rate$_{it}$					0.14 (0.49)	0.12 (0.60)	0.15 (0.47)	0.13 (0.57)										
ΔLN Real effective exchange rate$_{it}$									0.08 (0.71)	0.05 (0.82)	0.08 (0.69)	0.06 (0.79)						
Sargan test	0.80	0.88	0.80	0.89	0.94	0.97	0.95	0.98	0.84	0.92	0.84	0.92	0.91	0.89	0.89	0.91	0.92	0.51
AR(1) serial correlation test	0.09*	0.13	0.09*	0.13	0.11	0.15	0.11	0.15	0.10*	0.13	0.09*	0.13	0.10	0.12	0.12	0.11	0.12	0.11
AR(2) serial correlation test	0.55	0.26	0.62	0.27	0.99	0.23	0.91	0.23	0.70	0.22	0.77	0.22	0.22	0.21	0.20	0.21	0.21	0.16

Table 3. *Cont.*

	55	56	57	58	59	60	61	62	63	64	65	66	67	68	69	70	71	72
ΔUtility of international currency$_{t+1}$	0.22** (0.03)	0.34** (0.01)	0.31** (0.01)	0.36*** (0.00)	0.36*** (0.00)	0.37*** (0.00)	0.38** (0.01)	0.16 (0.24)	0.27* (0.05)	0.40*** (0.01)	0.29** (0.01)	0.35*** (0.00)	0.35*** (0.00)	0.36*** (0.00)	0.37** (0.02)	0.16 (0.25)	0.26* (0.06)	0.40** (0.01)
ΔLiquidity risk premium$_{it}$	−0.09*** (0.00)	−0.09*** (0.00)	−0.08*** (0.00)	−0.09*** (0.00)	−0.09*** (0.00)	−0.08*** (0.00)	−0.09*** (0.00)	−0.09*** (0.00)	−0.10*** (0.00)	−0.10*** (0.00)	−0.08*** (0.00)	−0.09*** (0.00)	−0.09*** (0.00)	−0.09*** (0.00)	−0.09*** (0.00)	−0.09*** (0.00)	−0.10*** (0.00)	−0.10*** (0.00)
ΔMoney stock share$_{it}$			0.29 (0.61)								0.44 (0.43)							
ΔRelative nominal economic growth$_{it}$				−0.0014 (0.28)								−0.0014 (0.27)						
ΔRelative real economic growth$_{it}$					−0.0001 (0.75)								−0.0001 (0.76)					
ΔGDP share$_{it}$						−0.62*** (0.00)								−0.49** (0.02)				
ΔCapitalization share$_{it}$							0.15 (0.81)								0.21 (0.75)			
ΔTotal trade share$_{it}$								−3.29*** (0.00)								−3.25*** (0.00)		
ΔTotal export share$_{it}$	−1.45* (0.07)								−2.01* (0.05)								−2.02** (0.05)	
ΔCapital flow share$_{it}$		0.89*** (0.00)								0.86*** (0.00)								0.97*** (0.00)
ΔSD of Nominal effective exchange rate$_{it}$	−0.01 (0.29)	−0.01* (0.09)																
ΔLN Nominal effective exchange rate$_{it}$			0.07 (0.76)	0.12 (0.36)	0.14 (0.28)	0.25 (0.17)	0.14 (0.36)	0.30* (0.10)	0.24 (0.16)	0.09 (0.52)								
ΔLN Real effective exchange rate$_{it}$											0.00 (0.99)	0.09 (0.47)	0.11 (0.36)	0.20 (0.25)	0.10 (0.48)	0.29 (0.11)	0.22 (0.17)	0.05 (0.72)
Sargan test	0.79	0.94	0.95	0.99	0.99	0.99	0.99	0.93	0.98	0.99	0.91	0.98	0.99	0.99	0.99	0.92	0.97	0.99
AR(1) serial correlation test	0.12	0.11	0.11	0.11	0.11	0.12	0.11	0.10*	0.11	0.10	0.11	0.11	0.12	0.12	0.12	0.10	0.12	0.11
AR(2) serial correlation test	0.18	0.22	0.21	0.25	0.24	0.26	0.24	0.72	0.17	0.25	0.21	0.25	0.23	0.25	0.24	0.66	0.17	0.25

The parentheses are *p*-value. *, **, *** are significance level 10%, 5%, 1%. Instrument variables for period t are utility of the international currency of periods t-3. The null hypothesis of Sargan test is that over-identification is valid. The null hypothesis of AR(1) and AR(2) serial correlation test is that there is no serial correlation.

Table 4. Determinants utility of international currency (real interest rate 2.5%).

	73	74	75	76	77	78	79	80	81	82	83	84	85	86	87	88	89	90
ΔUtility of international currency$_{it-1}$	0.12 (0.55)	0.23 (0.37)	0.12 (0.52)	0.22 (0.33)	0.20 (0.48)	0.32 (0.34)	0.21 (0.42)	0.33 (0.29)	0.11 (0.50)	0.22 (0.29)	0.11 (0.43)	0.22 (0.23)	0.32*** (0.00)	0.31** (0.03)	0.30** (0.03)	0.33** (0.01)	0.34*** (0.01)	0.16** (0.05)
ΔLiquidity risk premium$_{it}$	−0.04* (0.08)	−0.05* (0.09)	−0.04* (0.10)	−0.05* (0.09)	−0.05** (0.03)	−0.07** (0.04)	−0.05** (0.03)	−0.06** (0.04)	−0.05* (0.06)	−0.06* (0.06)	−0.05* (0.07)	−0.06* (0.06)	−0.03* (0.06)	−0.04** (0.01)	−0.04** (0.02)	−0.04** (0.02)	−0.04** (0.01)	−0.04*** (0.00)
ΔMoney stock share$_{it}$	0.79 (0.29)	0.82 (0.26)	0.82 (0.26)	0.86 (0.22)	0.69 (0.53)	0.80 (0.47)	0.73 (0.50)	0.85 (0.43)	0.64 (0.46)	0.75 (0.40)	0.67 (0.42)	0.79 (0.35)	0.42** (0.04)					
ΔRelative nominal economic growth$_{it}$	−0.0005 (0.45)	−0.0009 (0.25)			−0.0006 (0.50)	−0.0010 (0.30)			−0.0005 (0.46)	−0.0009 (0.24)				−0.0011 (0.22)				
ΔRelative real economic growth$_{it}$			−0.0001 (0.76)	−0.0001 (0.62)			−0.0001 (0.69)	−0.0001 (0.45)			−0.0001 (0.71)	−0.0001 (0.49)			−0.0001 (0.76)			
ΔGDP share$_{it}$	−0.09 (0.94)	−0.39 (0.68)	−0.07 (0.94)	−0.36 (0.66)	−0.60 (0.65)	−0.93 (0.44)	−0.60 (0.62)	−0.92 (0.40)	−0.27 (0.76)	−0.59 (0.46)	−0.25 (0.76)	−0.56 (0.42)				0.25 (0.14)		
ΔCapitalization share$_{it}$	0.00 (0.99)	−0.14 (0.75)	0.01 (0.94)	−0.12 (0.79)	0.16 (0.62)	0.01 (0.99)	0.17 (0.62)	0.02 (0.97)	0.04 (0.82)	−0.11 (0.81)	0.03 (0.85)	−0.11 (0.80)					0.27** (0.02)	
ΔTotal trade share$_{it}$	−2.72*** (0.00)		−2.76*** (0.00)		−2.63** (0.01)		−2.65*** (0.01)		−2.77*** (0.00)		−2.79*** (0.00)							−1.82*** (0.00)
ΔTotal export share$_{it}$		−1.83* (0.05)		−1.89** (0.05)		−1.64* (0.07)		−1.69* (0.06)		−1.84** (0.05)		−1.89** (0.04)						
ΔCapital flow share$_{it}$	0.80*** (0.00)	0.81** (0.02)	0.78*** (0.01)	0.76* (0.06)	1.02*** (0.00)	1.07*** (0.00)	0.99*** (0.00)	1.02*** (0.00)	0.89** (0.02)	0.94** (0.04)	0.87** (0.05)	0.89 (0.10)						
ΔSD of Nominal effective exchange rate$_{it}$	0.00 (0.35)	0.00 (0.16)	0.00 (0.34)	0.00 (0.15)									−0.01 (0.24)	−0.01 (0.26)	−0.01 (0.26)	−0.01 (0.23)	−0.01 (0.20)	0.00 (0.38)
ΔLN Nominal effective exchange rate$_{it}$					0.12 (0.39)	0.09 (0.52)	0.12 (0.36)	0.10 (0.48)										
ΔLN Real effective exchange rate$_{it}$									0.07 (0.57)	0.04 (0.74)	0.07 (0.54)	0.05 (0.70)						
Sargan test	0.54	0.71	0.57	0.74	0.81	0.90	0.84	0.93	0.54	0.74	0.56	0.77	0.89	0.85	0.86	0.90	0.90	0.42
AR(1) serial correlation test	0.09*	0.15	0.09*	0.14	0.14	0.20	0.13	0.19	0.10*	0.14	0.10*	0.13	0.10*	0.12	0.13	0.11	0.12	0.13
AR(2) serial correlation test	0.35	0.25	0.38	0.26	0.63	0.23	0.73	0.23	0.32	0.20	0.34	0.19	0.24	0.22	0.22	0.23	0.23	0.18

Table 4. Cont.

	91	92	93	94	95	96	97	98	99	100	101	102	103	104	105	106	107	108
ΔUtility of international currency$_{t+1}$	0.24 ** (0.02)	0.36 ** (0.02)	0.34 ** (0.01)	0.42 *** (0.00)	0.42 *** (0.00)	0.43 *** (0.00)	0.44 *** (0.02)	0.21 (0.18)	0.31 * (0.08)	0.45 ** (0.03)	0.31 *** (0.01)	0.41 *** (0.01)	0.41 *** (0.00)	0.42 *** (0.00)	0.44 ** (0.02)	0.21 (0.20)	0.31 * (0.09)	0.45 ** (0.04)
ΔLiquidity risk premium$_{it}$	−0.05 *** (0.00)	−0.04 ** (0.05)	−0.04 ** (0.03)	−0.05 *** (0.00)	−0.05 *** (0.00)	−0.05 *** (0.01)	−0.05 *** (0.00)	−0.05 *** (0.00)	−0.06 *** (0.01)	−0.06 *** (0.00)	−0.04 ** (0.04)	−0.05 *** (0.00)	−0.05 *** (0.00)	−0.05 *** (0.00)	−0.05 *** (0.00)	−0.05 *** (0.00)	−0.06 *** (0.01)	−0.06 *** (0.00)
ΔMoney stock share$_{it}$			0.17 (0.69)								0.27 (0.52)							
ΔRelative nominal economic growth$_{it}$				−0.0011 (0.27)								−0.0011 (0.26)						
ΔRelative real economic growth$_{it}$					−0.0001 (0.81)								0.0000 (0.82)					
ΔGDP share$_{it}$						−0.31 * (0.09)								−0.20 (0.40)				
ΔCapitalization share$_{it}$							0.17 (0.74)								0.22 (0.70)			
ΔTotal trade share$_{it}$	−1.03 * (0.08)							−2.39 *** (0.00)								−2.37 *** (0.00)		
ΔTotal export share$_{it}$									−1.44 * (0.06)								−1.46 ** (0.05)	
ΔCapital flow share$_{it}$		0.66 *** (0.00)								0.65 ** (0.01)								0.73 *** (0.01)
ΔSD of Nominal effective exchange rate$_{it}$		0.00 * (0.07)								0.07 (0.48)								
ΔLN Nominal effective exchange rate$_{it}$			0.07 (0.69)	0.10 (0.30)	0.12 (0.22)	0.17 (0.21)	0.11 (0.33)	0.24 * (0.08)	0.18 (0.12)									
ΔLN Real effective exchange rate$_{it}$											0.02 (0.90)	0.08 (0.40)	0.10 (0.30)	0.13 (0.34)	0.08 (0.45)	0.23 * (0.09)	0.17 (0.14)	0.04 (0.70)
Sargan test	0.75	0.90	0.95	0.99	0.99	0.99	0.99	0.93	0.98	0.99	0.89	0.98	0.99	0.99	0.99	0.92	0.98	0.98
AR(1) serial correlation test	0.13	0.11	0.11	0.11	0.11	0.12	0.11	0.11	0.13	0.11	0.10	0.11	0.12	0.12	0.12	0.11	0.13	0.12
AR(2) serial correlation test	0.19	0.23	0.22	0.25	0.24	0.24	0.25	0.75	0.19	0.25	0.21	0.25	0.24	0.24	0.24	0.68	0.19	0.25

The parentheses are *p*-value. *, **, *** are significance level 10%, 5%, 1%. Instrument variables for period t are utility of the international currency of periods t-3. The null hypothesis of Sargan test is that over-identification is valid. The null hypothesis of AR(1) and AR(2) serial correlation test is that there is no serial correlation.

Table 5. Determinants utility of international currency (real interest rate 3.0%).

	109	110	111	112	113	114	115	116	117	118	119	120	121	122	123	124	125	126
ΔUtility of international currency$_{it-1}$	−0.03 (0.69)	0.06 * (0.06)	−0.02 (0.79)	0.06 ** (0.04)	0.03 (0.55)	0.14 (0.24)	0.05 (0.42)	0.16 (0.20)	−0.06 (0.57)	0.05 (0.26)	−0.05 (0.63)	0.06 (0.17)	0.29 *** (0.00)	0.27 ** (0.01)	0.27 ** (0.01)	0.30 *** (0.01)	0.30 *** (0.00)	0.17 *** (0.00)
ΔLiquidity risk premium$_{it}$	−0.02 (0.42)	−0.03 (0.33)	−0.02 (0.42)	−0.03 (0.33)	−0.03 (0.29)	−0.04 (0.25)	−0.03 (0.28)	−0.04 (0.24)	−0.03 (0.38)	−0.04 (0.29)	−0.03 (0.37)	−0.04 (0.28)	−0.02 (0.41)	−0.02 (0.28)	−0.02 (0.33)	−0.02 (0.32)	−0.02 (0.31)	−0.03 (0.14)
ΔMoney stock share$_{it}$	0.36 (0.28)	0.37 (0.28)	0.38 (0.25)	0.40 (0.23)	0.24 (0.67)	0.33 (0.57)	0.28 (0.63)	0.38 (0.51)	0.20 (0.58)	0.28 (0.49)	0.22 (0.53)	0.32 (0.43)	0.31 (0.16)					
ΔRelative nominal economic growth$_{it}$	−0.0003 (0.32)	−0.0006 (0.14)			−0.0003 (0.44)	−0.0007 (0.21)			−0.0002 (0.31)	−0.0006 (0.12)				−0.0009 (0.20)				
ΔRelative real economic growth$_{it}$			0.0000 (0.99)	0.0000 (0.90)			0.0000 (1.00)	−0.0001 (0.80)			0.0000 (0.94)	0.0000 (0.88)			−0.0001 (0.79)			
ΔGDP share$_{it}$	0.39 (0.28)	0.18 (0.33)	0.39 (0.25)	0.18 (0.25)	0.03 (0.94)	−0.19 (0.64)	0.00 (0.99)	−0.22 (0.59)	0.27 (0.24)	0.05 (0.88)	0.27 (0.24)	0.04 (0.90)				0.23 (0.20)		
ΔCapitalization share$_{it}$	−0.06 (0.83)	−0.20 (0.18)	−0.05 (0.86)	−0.17 (0.25)	0.06 (0.77)	−0.09 (0.72)	0.07 (0.72)	−0.07 (0.79)	−0.02 (0.94)	−0.17 (0.26)	−0.02 (0.93)	−0.16 (0.30)					0.17 (0.10)	
ΔTotal trade share$_{it}$	−2.45 *** (0.00)		−2.46 *** (0.00)		−2.40 *** (0.00)		−2.39 *** (0.00)		−2.52 *** (0.00)		−2.52 *** (0.00)							−1.41 *** (0.00)
ΔTotal export share$_{it}$		−1.78 ** (0.02)		−1.81 ** (0.02)		−1.65 ** (0.01)		−1.65 ** (0.02)		−1.80 ** (0.01)		−1.82 ** (0.02)						
ΔCapital flow share$_{it}$	0.53 (0.28)	0.52 (0.38)	0.52 (0.30)	0.49 (0.42)	0.65 (0.19)	0.67 (0.23)	0.64 (0.20)	0.65 (0.26)	0.57 (0.39)	0.60 (0.41)	0.56 (0.41)	0.57 (0.45)						
ΔSD of Nominal effective exchange rate$_{it}$	0.00 (0.53)	0.00 (0.42)	0.00 (0.52)	0.00 (0.40)									0.00 (0.30)	0.00 (0.30)	0.00 (0.30)	0.00 (0.29)	0.00 (0.27)	0.00 (0.37)
ΔLN Nominal effective exchange rate$_{it}$					0.10 (0.23)	0.07 (0.38)	0.11 (0.22)	0.08 (0.35)										
ΔLN Real effective exchange rate$_{it}$									0.07 (0.32)	0.04 (0.55)	0.07 (0.31)	0.05 (0.50)						
Sargan test	0.29	0.51	0.32	0.56	0.48	0.68	0.55	0.76	0.25	0.49	0.29	0.55	0.86	0.81	0.83	0.88	0.87	0.41
AR(1) serial correlation test	0.14	0.13	0.13	0.13	0.15	0.18	0.15	0.18	0.23	0.17	0.22	0.17	0.09 *	0.12	0.12	0.10 *	0.11	0.14
AR(2) serial correlation test	0.08 *	0.15	0.08 *	0.15	0.19	0.13	0.21	0.13	0.18	0.12	0.19	0.11	0.23	0.22	0.22	0.23	0.22	0.17

Table 5. *Cont.*

	127	128	129	130	131	132	133	134	135	136	137	138	139	140	141	142	143	144
ΔUtility of international currency$_{it-1}$	0.22 *** (0.00)	0.30 *** (0.00)	0.31 *** (0.00)	0.42 *** (0.01)	0.42 *** (0.01)	0.43 *** (0.00)	0.43 ** (0.02)	0.23 (0.11)	0.31 * (0.10)	0.42 ** (0.03)	0.27 *** (0.00)	0.41 *** (0.01)	0.42 *** (0.01)	0.42 *** (0.00)	0.43 ** (0.03)	0.23 (0.13)	0.30 (0.10)	0.41 ** (0.04)
ΔLiquidity risk premium$_{it}$	−0.03 (0.13)	−0.02 (0.36)	−0.03 (0.24)	−0.03 * (0.06)	−0.03 * (0.07)	−0.03 * (0.08)	−0.03 ** (0.04)	−0.04 ** (0.05)	−0.04 * (0.08)	−0.04 * (0.07)	−0.02 (0.32)	−0.03 * (0.05)	−0.03 * (0.06)	−0.03 * (0.06)	−0.03 ** (0.04)	−0.04 * (0.05)	−0.04 * (0.09)	−0.03 * (0.06)
ΔMoney stock share$_{it}$			0.09 (0.75)								0.15 (0.55)							
ΔRelative nominal economic growth$_{it}$				−0.0009 (0.27)								−0.0009 (0.26)						
ΔRelative real economic growth$_{it}$					0.0000 (0.83)								0.0000 (0.84)					
ΔGDP share$_{it}$						−0.18 (0.20)								−0.08 (0.64)				
ΔCapitalization share$_{it}$							0.11 (0.76)								0.14 (0.72)			
ΔTotal trade share$_{it}$								−1.91 *** (0.00)								−1.90 *** (0.00)		
ΔTotal export share$_{it}$	−0.84 (0.13)								−1.17 * (0.06)								−1.20 ** (0.05)	
ΔCapital flow share$_{it}$		0.47 (0.20)								0.45 *** (0.00)								0.51 *** (0.00)
ΔSD of Nominal effective exchange rate$_{it}$	0.00 (0.32)	0.00 (0.16)																
ΔLN Nominal effective exchange rate$_{it}$			0.06 (0.63)	0.08 (0.31)	0.10 (0.22)	0.13 (0.24)	0.09 (0.32)	0.20 * (0.08)	0.15 (0.11)	0.06 (0.45)								
ΔLN Real effective exchange rate$_{it}$											0.03 (0.81)	0.07 (0.41)	0.08 (0.30)	0.09 (0.40)	0.07 (0.44)	0.19 * (0.10)	0.14 (0.13)	0.03 (0.67)
Sargan test	0.73	0.82	0.93	0.99	0.99	0.99	0.99	0.94	0.98	0.97	0.86	0.98	0.99	0.99	0.99	0.93	0.97	0.96
AR(1) serial correlation test	0.13	0.10	0.11	0.11	0.11	0.12	0.11	0.11	0.14	0.10	0.10	0.11	0.11	0.11	0.11	0.12	0.15	0.11
AR(2) serial correlation test	0.19	0.22	0.21	0.25	0.25	0.24	0.25	0.68	0.20	0.25	0.21	0.25	0.24	0.24	0.25	0.60	0.19	0.24

The parentheses are *p*-value. *, **, *** are significance level 10%, 5%, 1%. Instrument variables for period t are utility of the international currency of periods t-3. The null hypothesis of Sargan test is that over-identification is valid. The null hypothesis of AR(1) and AR(2) serial correlation test is that there is no serial correlation.

7. Conclusions

In this paper, we investigated what determines utility of the international currencies among the current major currencies which include the US dollar, the euro, the Japanese yen, and the British pound. We used a dynamic panel data model to analyze the issue with GMM. We focused on effects of liquidity shortage in terms of an international currency on utility of the international currencies as well as inertia of the US dollar as the key currency. We made empirical analysis of whether liquidity risk premium in an international currency as well as other possible determinant factors affect utility of the relevant international currency.

We obtained the following results from the empirical analysis. Firstly, change in utility of the international currency in the previous period has significantly a positive effect on the change of utility of the international currency in the current period. This suggests that utility of the international currency tends to fluctuate in the same direction as the change in the previous term. For example, if the utility of the international currency decreases, we assumed that the currency is less likely to be used than in the previous period, which will continue in the next period. Secondly, the change of liquidity risk premium has significantly a negative effect on the change of utility of the currency. This suggests that liquidity shortage reduce the utility of the international currency. Thirdly, the change of capital flow share has significantly a positive effect on the change of utility of the international currency. This suggests that increase in economic scale may increase utility of the international currency.

We mention policy implications from the empirical results. As mentioned above, liquidity risk premium and capital flow had influence on utility of the international currency. If the monetary authorities try to internationalize their home currencies, it is necessary to focus on these variables. It is considered that utility of the international currency will increase by conducting policies that increase liquidity of the currency or increase international capital flows. It might be possible to push internationalization of the home currencies through this increase of utility of the international currencies.

Moreover, in this analysis, we found a strong relationship between utility of the international currency and liquidity of the international currency. We should also deeply analyze relationship between the two variables. In this analysis, as we supposed that utility of the international currency is dependent variable, changes in liquidity of the international currency have influenced changes in the utility of the international currency. However, it is necessary for us to suppose causality between the liquidity of the international currency and its utility in the opposite direction. If utility of an international currency declines, it may reduce liquidity of the international currency through reduction in convenience of the currency.

We used liquidity risk premium as a variable for liquidity of the international currency in this paper. There are such other variables as bid-ask spreads that represent liquidity of the international currency. Moreover, it is capital adequacy of financial institution that could affect liquidity of the international currency. It is necessary to conduct robustness tests for the analysis result by conducting any analysis using the variables in the future. Furthermore, we used ARIMA model using CPI for the expected inflation rate. Other expected inflation rate data include TIPS data and survey data, which may reflect the reality. Robustness check using these data as future work is also necessary.

In addition, we have further study regarding what factors are important to help an emerging new international currency which includes the Chinese yuan. In recent years, the Chinese government has been promoting the Chinese yuan to be internationalized while the IMF has added it into major international currencies that is component currencies of the Special Drawing Rights (SDR). It is important for us to investigate how a local currency can emerge as an international currency and, in turn, make it into a key currency in the current international monetary system where we do not as a rule set any currencies as a key currency.

Author Contributions: Conceptualization, E.O.; methodology, E.O.; formal analysis, M.M.; investigation, M.M.; writing—original draft preparation, E.O. and M.M.; writing—review and editing, E.O. and M.M.; visualization, E.O. and M.M.; supervision, E.O.; project administration, E.O.

Funding: This research received no external funding.

Acknowledgments: This study is conducted as a part of the project "Exchange Rate and International Currency" undertaken at the Research Institute of Economy, Trade and Industry (RIETI). The authors are grateful to the three anonymous referees, Keiichiro Kobayashi, Etsuro Shioji, Shinichi Fukuda, Jorg Mayer, Stephan Gerlach and other participants in the RIETI research seminar, a research meeting of the Ministry of Finance, and conferences of the Asia-Pacific Economic Association and Japan Economic Network for their useful comments and suggestions.

Conflicts of Interest: The authors declare no conflict of interest.

Appendix A. Derivation of Equation (1)

We base on a Sidrauski (1967)-type of money-in-the-utility model in which real balances of money as well as consumption are supposed as explanatory variables in a utility function. According to Ogawa and Sasaki (1998), we extend the money-in-the-utility model to a dynamic one with parallel international currencies[5]. We suppose that the international currencies are held by private economic agents in a third country. For simplicity, we suppose that two monetary authorities supply international currencies.

For convenience, we suppose that it is both the monetary authorities in the Country i and other countries O that supply their international currencies. The monetary authorities in Country i supply currency i while the monetary authorities in other countries O supply their own currencies O. The private sector in the third country A is able to use both the currencies i and O as international currencies in international economic transactions. The monetary authorities in country A adopt a flexible exchange rate system.

We suppose a situation that bonds in currencies i and O are available to the private sector in country A and that no bonds denominated in currency A are issued in country A. We assume perfect capital mobility and perfect substitution for the bonds of different currencies. Moreover, we assume that the private sector has perfect foresight. Thus, uncovered interest parity holds in the model. On one hand, we assume perfect flexible prices and a law of one price. Thus, the purchasing power parity always holds in the model. For simplicity, we assume that its rate of time preference is constant over time and is equal to a real interest rate. Given the assumptions, the real interest rate is constant over time. Real interest rates in all countries are equal to each other by both the uncovered interest parity and purchasing power parity.

The private sector in country A holds home currency A, international currencies i and O, and bonds in currencies i and O. Instantaneous budget constraints for the private sector are represented in real terms:

$$\dot{w}_t^p = \bar{r}w_t^p + y_t - c_t - \tau_t - i_t^A m_t^A - i_t^i m_t^i - i_t^O m_t^O \tag{A1a}$$

$$w_t^p = b_t^i + b_t^O + m_t^A + m_t^i + m_t^O \tag{A1b}$$

where y: real gross domestic products, τ: real taxes, c: real consumption, i^j: nominal interest rate in currency j ($j = A, i, O$), w^p: real balance of financial assets held by the private sector, m^j: real balance of home currency j ($j = A, i, O$) held by the private sector, b^j: real balance of bond in currency j ($j = i, O$) held by the private sector, $\bar{r}$: real interest rate. A dot over variables implies a change in the relevant variables. We assume no-Ponzi game conditions for the real balance of financial assets held by the private sector (w^p).

$$\lim_{t \to \infty} w_t^p e^{-\bar{r}t} \geq 0 \tag{A2}$$

We assume that the private sector maximizes its utility over an infinite horizon subject to budget constraints (A1a) and (A1b). We specify a Cobb-Douglas type of instantaneous utility function:

$$\int_0^\infty U(c_t, m_t^A, m_t^i, m_t^O)e^{-\delta t}dt \tag{A3a}$$

---

[5] See Ogawa and Muto (2017a) for the detailed derivation.

$$U(c_t, m_t^A, m_t^i, m_t^O) \equiv \frac{\left[c_t^\alpha \left\{ m_t^{A\beta} \left(m_t^{i\gamma} m_t^{O1-\gamma} \right)^{1-\beta} \right\}^{1-\alpha} \right]^{1-R}}{1-R}$$

(A3b)

$$0 < \alpha < 1, \ 0 < \beta < 1, \ 0 < \gamma < 1, \ 0 < R < 1$$

where δ: rate of time preference, R: reciprocal of instantaneous elasticity of substitution between intertemporal consumption σ: $\sigma \equiv -\frac{U_c}{U_{cc} c_t}$.

We assume that the public sector in country A holds only bonds in currencies i and O. Instantaneous budget constraints for the public sector are represented in real terms:

$$\dot{f}_t = \bar{r} f_t + \tau_t + \mu_t^A m_t^A - g_t$$

(A4a)

$$f_t \equiv f_t^i + f_t^O$$

(A4b)

where g: real government expenditures, f: foreign assets held by the public sector, μ^A: growth rate of currency A. We assume no-Ponzi game conditions for foreign assets held by the public sector.

$$\lim_{t \to \infty} f_t e^{-\bar{r} t} \geq 0$$

(A5)

A stock of foreign exchange reserves held by the monetary authorities should be unchanged under a flexible exchange rate system because the monetary authorities will not intervene in foreign exchange markets $(f_t = \bar{f})$. Also, they are able to control nominal money supply. Here, we assume that they increase the nominal money supply at a constant growth rate μ^A.

Thus we obtain an instantaneous budget constraint equation for the public sector under a flexible exchange rate system:

$$g_t - \tau_t = \bar{r} \bar{f} + \bar{\mu}^A m_t^A$$

(A6)

From the instantaneous budget constraint equations for the private sector and the public sector Equations (A1a) and (A6), we derive an instantaneous budget constraint equation for the whole economy of country A under a flexible exchange rate system:

$$\dot{b}_t^i + \dot{b}_t^O + \dot{m}_t^i + \dot{m}_t^O = \bar{r}(b_t^i + b_t^O + m_t^i + m_t^i + \bar{f}) + y_t - c_t - g_t - i_t^i m_t^i - i_t^O m_t^O$$

(A7)

The private sector maximizes its utility Functions (A3a) and (A3b) subject to budget constraint Equation (A7). We assume that the private sector has perfect foresight that economic variables do not diverge to infinity but converge to equilibrium values along a saddle path to rule out a possibility of multiplicity of equilibria in the model.

From the first-order conditions for maximization, we derive optimal real balances of international currencies:

$$m_t^i = \frac{(1-\alpha)(1-\beta)\gamma}{\alpha} \frac{\bar{c}}{i_t^i} = \frac{(1-\alpha)(1-\beta)\gamma}{\alpha} \frac{\bar{c}}{i_t^i + \bar{r}}$$

(A8a)

$$m_t^O = \frac{(1-\alpha)(1-\beta)(1-\gamma)}{\alpha} \frac{\bar{c}}{i_t^O} = \frac{(1-\alpha)(1-\beta)(1-\gamma)}{\alpha} \frac{\bar{c}}{i_t^O + \bar{r}}$$

(A8b)

where π_t^j: inflation rate of currency $j(j = i, O)$,

$$\bar{c} = \bar{r} \left\{ a_0 + \int\limits_0^\infty y_t e^{-\bar{r} t} dt - \int\limits_0^\infty g_t e^{-\bar{r} t} dt - \int\limits_0^\infty (i_t^i m_t^i - i_t^O m_t^O) e^{-\bar{r} t} dt \right\}$$

From Equations (A8a) and (A8b), an optimal share ϕ of i is derived:

$$\phi_t \equiv \frac{m_t^i}{m_t^i + m_t^O} = \frac{1}{1 + \frac{1-\gamma}{\gamma} \frac{i_t^i}{i_t^O}} = \frac{1}{1 + \frac{1-\gamma}{\gamma} \frac{\pi_t^i + \bar{r}}{\pi_t^O + \bar{r}}} \qquad (A9)$$

Equation (A9) implies that the optimal share of i depends on both the inflation or depreciation rates of the international currencies (π^i and π^O) and a parameter γ in the utility function Equation (A3b). From Equation (A9), the parameter γ_t^i is derived:

$$\gamma_t^i = \frac{1}{1 + \left(\frac{1}{\phi_t^i} - 1 \right) \frac{\pi_t^O + \bar{r}}{\pi_t^i + \bar{r}}} \qquad (A10)$$

References

Arellano, Manuel, and Stephen Bond. 1991. Some Tests of Specification for Panel Data: Monte Carlo Evidence and an Application to Employment Equations. *The Review of Economic Studies* 58: 277–97. [CrossRef]

Blanchard, Olivier J., and Stanley Fischer. 1989. *Lectures on Macroeconomics*. Cambridge: MIT Press.

Calvo, Guillermo A. 1981. Devaluation: Levels versus Rates. *Journal of International Economics* 11: 165–72. [CrossRef]

Calvo, Guillermo A. 1985. Currency Substitution and the Real Exchange Rate: The Utility Maximization Approach. *Journal of International Money and Finance* 4: 175–88. [CrossRef]

Catão, Luis, and Marco Terrones. 2016. *Financial De-Dollarization—A Global Perspective and the Peruvian Experience*. IMF Working Paper WP/16/97. Washington, DC: International Monetary Fund. [CrossRef]

Chinn, Menzie, and Jeffrey A. Frankel. 2007. Will the Euro Eventually Surpass the Dollar as Leading International Reserve Currency? In *G7 Current Account Imbalances: Sustainability and Adjustment*. Edited by Richard H. Clarida. Chicago: University of Chicago Press, pp. 283–338.

Chinn, Menzie, and Jeffrey A. Frankel. 2008. Why the Euro Will Rival the Dollar. *International Finance* 11: 49–73. [CrossRef]

Eichengreen, Barry, Livia Chiţu, and Arnaud Mehl. 2016a. Network Effects, Homogeneous Goods and International Currency Choice: New Evidence on Oil Markets from an Older Era. *Canadian Journal of Economics/Revue Canadienne d'économique* 49: 173–206. [CrossRef]

Eichengreen, Barry, Livia Chiţu, and Arnaud Mehl. 2016b. Stability or Upheaval? The Currency Composition of International Reserves in the Long Run. *IMF Economic Review* 64: 354–80. [CrossRef]

European Central Bank. 2015. *The International Role of the Euro*. Frankfurt: European Central Bank.

Fama, Eugene F., and Michael R. Gibbons. 1984. A Comparison of Inflation Forecasts. *Journal of Monetary Economics* 13: 327–48. [CrossRef]

Goldberg, Linda S., and Cédric Tille. 2008. Vehicle Currency Use in International Trade. *Journal of International Economics* 76: 177–92. [CrossRef]

Honohan, Patrick. 2008. The Retreat of Deposit Dollarization. *International Finance* 11: 247–68. [CrossRef]

Ito, Takatoshi, Satoshi Koibuchi, Kiyotaka Sato, and Junko Shimizu. 2013. Choice of Invoicing Currency: New Evidence from a Questionnaire Survey of Japanese Export Firms. Discussion Paper. Research Institute of Economy, Trade and Industry (RIETI) Discussion Paper Series, No. 13-E-034. Available online: https://econpapers.repec.org/paper/etidpaper/13034.htm (accessed on 7 January 2019).

Kamps, Annette. 2006. The Euro as Invoicing Currency in International Trade (August 2006). ECB Working Paper No. 665. Available online: https://papers.ssrn.com/abstract=926402 (accessed on 7 January 2019).

Kannan, Prakash. 2009. On the Welfare Benefits of an International Currency. *European Economic Review* 53: 588–606. [CrossRef]

Krugman, Paul R. 1984. The International Role of the Dollar: Theory and Prospect. In *Exchange Rate Theory and Practice*. Chicago: University of Chicago Press, pp. 261–78.

Matsuyama, Kiminori, Nobuhiro Kiyotaki, and Akihiko Matsui. 1993. Toward a Theory of International Currency. *The Review of Economic Studies* 60: 283–307. [CrossRef]

Obstfeld, Maurice. 1981. Macroeconomic Policy, Exchange-Rate Dynamics, and Optimal Asset Accumulation. *Journal of Political Economy* 89: 1142–61. [CrossRef]

Ogawa, Eiji, and Makoto Muto. 2017a. Inertia of the US Dollar as a Key Currency Through the Two Crises. *Emerging Markets Finance and Trade* 53: 2706–24. [CrossRef]

Ogawa, Eiji, and Makoto Muto. 2017b. Declining Japanese Yen in the Changing International Monetary System. *East Asian Economic Review* 21: 317–42. [CrossRef]

Ogawa, Eiji, and Yuri Nagataki Sasaki. 1998. Inertia in the Key Currency. *Japan and The World Economy* 10: 421–39. [CrossRef]

Sidrauski, Miguel. 1967. Rational Choice and Patterns of Growth in a Monetary Economy. *The American Economic Review* 57: 534–44.

Trejos, Alberto, and Randall Wright. 1996. Search—Theoretic Models of International Currency. *Review* 78. [CrossRef]

Article

Can We Forecast Daily Oil Futures Prices? Experimental Evidence from Convolutional Neural Networks

Zhaojie Luo [1], Xiaojing Cai [2], Katsuyuki Tanaka [2], Tetsuya Takiguchi [1,*], Takuji Kinkyo [2] and Shigeyuki Hamori [2]

[1] Graduate School of System Informatics, Kobe University, 2-1 Rokkodai, Nada-Ku, Kobe 657-8501, Japan; luozhaojie@hotmail.com

[2] Graduate School of Economics, Kobe University, 2-1 Rokkodai, Nada-Ku, Kobe 657-8501, Japan; xiaojing_cai@yahoo.com (X.C.); katsutanaka@econ.kobe-u.ac.jp (K.T.); kinkyo@econ.kobe-u.ac.jp (T.K.); hamori@econ.kobe-u.ac.jp (S.H.)

[*] Correspondence: takigu@kobe-u.ac.jp

Received: 21 November 2018; Accepted: 2 January 2019; Published: 8 January 2019

Abstract: This paper proposes a novel approach, based on convolutional neural network (CNN) models, that forecasts the short-term crude oil futures prices with good performance. In our study, we confirm that artificial intelligence (AI)-based deep-learning approaches can provide more accurate forecasts of short-term oil prices than those of the benchmark Naive Forecast (NF) model. We also provide strong evidence that CNN models with matrix inputs are better at short-term prediction than neural network (NN) models with single-vector input, which indicates that strengthening the dependence of inputs and providing more useful information can improve short-term forecasting performance.

Keywords: crude oil futures prices forecasting; convolutional neural networks; short-term forecasting

---

1. Introduction

Crude oil is a vital fuel, accounting for 32.9% of global energy consumption in 2016 according to BP's Statistical Energy Outlook, which indicates that crude oil will continue to play an important role until 2035. It is fair to argue that the movement in the crude oil price should have a significant effect on macroeconomic aggregates, such as the GDP and inflation of oil-exporting and -importing countries. On the other hand, as one of the most actively traded commodities in the world (Alvarez-Ramirez et al. (2012)), crude oil futures have become an important financial asset and an additional investment tool. Owing to the increasing correlation between traditional financial markets, such as stocks, bonds, and foreign exchange, international investors are searching for new investment tools, such as crude oil futures, to enhance returns, diversify portfolios, and hedge against inflation. Therefore, forecasting oil futures prices accurately is crucial and helps international investors to diversify risk.

Many researchers have proposed and developed economic models to forecast crude oil spot prices (De Souza e Silva et al. (2010); Ye et al. (2006); Merino and Ortiz (2005); Wang et al. (2016); Wen et al. (2016); Baumeister et al. (2015); Naser (2016)). However, studies forecasting futures prices are scarce. According to Sklibosios Nikitopoulos et al. (2017), futures prices depend on the value of deferred use. For example, decreasing futures prices show that the value of immediate use (consumption) or the yield to holders of physical inventory is reducing. Therefore, futures prices are vulnerable to many complex natural, economic, and political factors, such as the economic development conditions of oil giants, oil wars, international petroleum organizations and so on. A large number of these factors are random, resulting in sharp fluctuations in the crude oil futures markets and showing very complex nonlinear characteristics. Thus, it is difficult to predict the futures prices accurately.

Recently, as new technologies are developed, artificial intelligence (AI) techniques (e.g., neural networks (NNs)) have been applied to the prediction of time series. AI-based models emulate the human brain to provide feedback on large quantities of data, and to learn to recognize information patterns. Thus, NN models can create a breakthrough opportunity in the analysis of the non-linear behavior of the time series of the crude oil markets (Refenes (1994); Ongkrutaraksa (1995); Moshiri and Foroutan (2006); Jammazi and Aloui (2012); Mingming and Jinliang (2012); Wang et al. (2005)). For example, Moshiri and Foroutan (2006) compared linear (Autoregressive moving average models and Generalized autoregressive conditional heteroscedasticity models) and nonlinear NN models, and found that NNs are superior and produce a more statistically significant forecast. Jammazi and Aloui (2012) combined the wavelet transform and NNs to forecast the crude oil monthly price. Mingming and Jinliang (2012) constructed a multiple-wavelet recurrent NN model to analyze crude oil monthly prices. Wang et al. (2005) present an NN-based model to forecast crude oil monthly prices, and claimed superior performance by their model. These results prove that an AI-based forecasting model can provide greater efficiency and higher accuracy than other models.

Here, we propose a novel, deep-learning forecasting approach based on a convolutional neural networks (CNNs) model for short-term[1] forecasting using daily data of crude oil futures prices. Unlike NNs with a single-vector neuron, the layers of the CNN model have neurons arranged in two dimensions (width and height). The CNNs take advantage of the fact that the inputs consist of matrices, which can strengthen the dependence and connections between neurons and constrain the architecture in a more sensible way. Moreover, instead of all the neurons in NNs being fully connected, the neurons of the CNN in a layer are only connected to a small region of the previous layer, which enables CNN models to share connections among neurons more flexibly. These characteristics may improve the short-term forecasting of crude oil prices. CNNs have recently been applied to large-scale image and video recognition (Krizhevsky et al. (2012); Zeiler and Fergus (2014); Simonyan and Zisserman (2014)) and traffic-speed prediction (Ma et al. (2017)). To the best of our knowledge, our study is the first CNN approach applied in the economic and financial field, and particularly to crude oil futures prices forecasting. CNN models are used in modeling problems related to spatial inputs like images. They are not suitable for processing and predicting events at relatively long intervals and delays in the time series. However, in our forecasting task, we used the daily oil prices to predict a short-term future price. Thus, CNN is suitable for this task due to its ability to capture the relevant features from the nearby daily prices in an image (one-week daily prices matrix). In addition, we normalized our data to overcome non-stationary time series and focus on the short-term oil futures prices trends using the daily data. We employ CNN models to forecast crude oil daily prices, which has become possible owing to the large daily data set.

Our study offers two contributions to the literature. First, we confirm that the non-linear deep-learning approaches perform better for short-term forecasting by comparing AI-based deep-learning methods with the naive forecast (NF) and Autoregressive-Generalized autoregressive conditional heteroscedasticity (AR-GARCH) model as two benchmarks, in terms of the accuracy of the short-term crude oil price forecasting. Second, we find that strengthening the dependence of inputs and providing more useful information connections between neurons can improve the short-term forecasting performance. Here we show that the CNN models are more powerful than the benchmark models.

The remainder of this paper is organized as follows. In Section 2, we introduce our related work in technology. In Section 3, we describe the model specifications. We show our data and empirical results in Sections 4 and 5. Finally, our concluding remarks are presented in Section 6.

---

[1]   In this paper, the short-term forecast means the next day forecast that is the forecast is 1-step-ahead.

2. Neural Networks and Convolutional Neural Networks

Neural networks (NNs) are trained on a frame error (FE) minimization criterion, and the corresponding weights are adjusted to minimize the error squares over the whole source-target, stereo training data set. As shown in Equation (1), the mapping error is given by:

$$\epsilon = \sum_t ||y_t - G(x_t)||^2,$$
(1)

where $G(x_t)$ denotes the NNs mapping of x_t and is defined as:

$$G(x_t) = (G^1 \circ G^2 \circ \cdots \circ G^L) = \bigodot_{l=1}^{L} G^{(l)}(x_t)$$
(2)

$$G^{(l)}(x_t) = \sigma(W^{(l)}x_t).$$
(3)

Here, $\bigodot_{l=1}^{L}$ denotes a composition of L functions. For instance, $\bigodot_{l=1}^{2} G^{(l)}(x_t) = \sigma(W^{(2)}\sigma(W^{(1)}(x_t)))$. $W^{(l)}$ represents the weight matrix of layer l in the NNs. σ denotes an activation function sigmoid, which has the mathematical form $\sigma(x) = 1/(1 + e^{-x})$.

CNNs typically have a standard structure in which the basic design is prevalent in the image (matrix) classification. In recent years, CNNs have been applied in many fields owing to their advanced detection and classification performance (LeCun et al. (1989)). CNNs consist of a sequence of layers. The typical layers in CNNs are: the convolutional layer, pooling layer, and fully-connected layer.

Convolutional layer: As with NNs, CNNs also are made up of neurons with learnable weights Please confirm meaning is retained. and biases, where each neuron receives inputs and performs a dot product, after which the output is computed through non-linearity functions, and called the activation function. However, neurons in the convolutional layer are arranged in 3 dimensions, and they are only connected to small local regions of the previous layer, instead of all outputs. The output of regions is patched out by multiple filters, called convolutional filters. When one convolutional filter W_l^r is applied to the input, the output can be formulated as:

$$y_{conv} = \sum_{e=1}^{m} \sum_{f=1}^{n} \left((W_l^r)_{ef} d_{ef} \right),$$
(4)

where m and n are two dimensions of the filter, d_{ef} is the data value of the input matrix at positions e and f, $(W_l^r)_{ef}$ is the coefficient of the convolutional filter at positions e and f, and y_{conv} is the output. In the convolutional layers, each filter comprises a local path from lower-level into higher-level features.

Pooling layer: Down sampling is performed in the pooling layer to compress the size of representation. This helps in the computation of the network.

Fully-connected layer: Similar to ordinary NNs, all outputs neurons of previous layers are collected to each neuron in the layer, computing the class scores by linear classifiers, such as SVM and Softmax.

Even though the overall network remains as a single, differentiable score function, as with NNs, CNNs are proven to be more effective with two-dimensional input, such as a matrix, since CNN architectures enable the encoding of certain properties into the architecture by taking advantage of the input structure.

3. Model Design

3.1. Method 1: Neural Networks

The methodology formulation of NNs is described in Section 2. In this section, we introduce the NN architecture used to predict the oil price and the steps of the training process.

(1) Transform a sequence of oil prices into segment-level features. We segment a sequence of oil prices by window size w and shift the window by day.

$$X_N = [x_1, ..., x_m, ..., x_N]^\mathrm{T}. \tag{5}$$

Equation (5) represents N examples of w-dimensional source features, which are composed of daily oil prices input. The daily oil prices of the output are one day after the input daily oil prices. In the proposed model, we set $w = 5$, which represents five days of oil price inputs. To guarantee the coordination between the initial input and output features, we adopt the same approach for the target features composed of the daily oil price output, that is, a day after input.

(2) After transforming one-dimensional features to five-dimensional features, we train them using different NNs with different parameters as shown in Figure 1. As shown in the left part of the figure, there are two kinds of input and output data sets: five days' oil prices and a combination of five days' oil prices and their delta values. The target output is the input's next days' oil prices. The right part of the figure shows four different architecture NNs. The top left model NNs_A uses the two-layer NNs model to train the oil prices. The number of nodes from the input layer x to the output layer are [5, 10, 5]. The top right model NNs_B uses the three layers with the nodes [5, 10, 10, 5]. The bottom model NNs_A and NNs_B use oil prices and their delta values as the input and output, NNs_A uses the two layers with the nodes [10, 20, 10], and NNs_B uses the three layers with the nodes [10, 20, 20, 10]. Every model is trained with sigmoid and tanh activation functions, respectively. As shown in the training model, W1, W2, and W3 represent the weight matrix of the first, second, and third layers of NNs, respectively. In this paper, we train the oil prices from start to $N - 100$ (N denotes sample size) and we test the last 100 days of oil prices. The results are introduced in the experiment section.

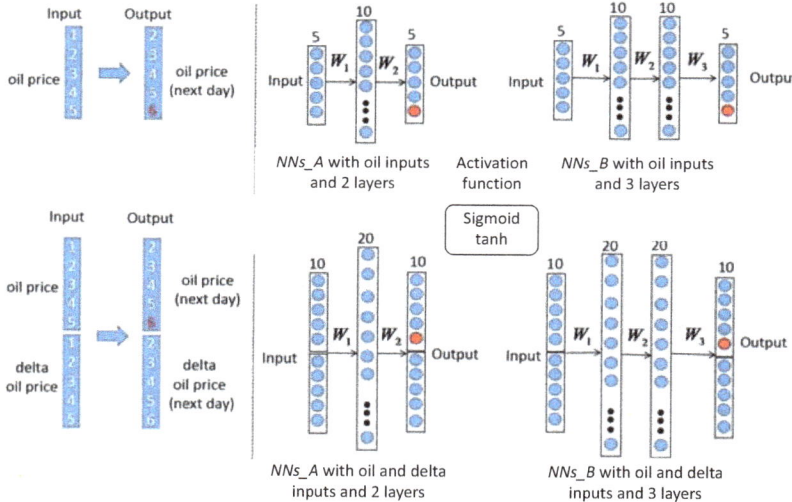

Figure 1. Neural network (NN) models with different layers and parameters.

3.2. Method 2: Convolutional Neural Networks

The basic model of a convolutional neural network is described in Section 2. In this section, we describe how to translate the data to the matrix. Then, the architectures used for predicting the oil price are introduced. Since the image is small, we do not apply a pooling layer in this paper.

(1) Transform the sequence of oil prices into a matrix suitable for CNN training. As shown in Figure 2, a, b, c, d, and e represent normalized oil values in Monday, Tuesday, Wednesday, Thursday,

and Friday, respectively. For example, a_1-e_1 represent the prices from Monday to Friday of the first week, and a_n-e_n represent the prices from Monday to Friday of the n-th week. We copy each week's oil prices five times and transform them to 5×5-size images, where the colors represent different oil prices.

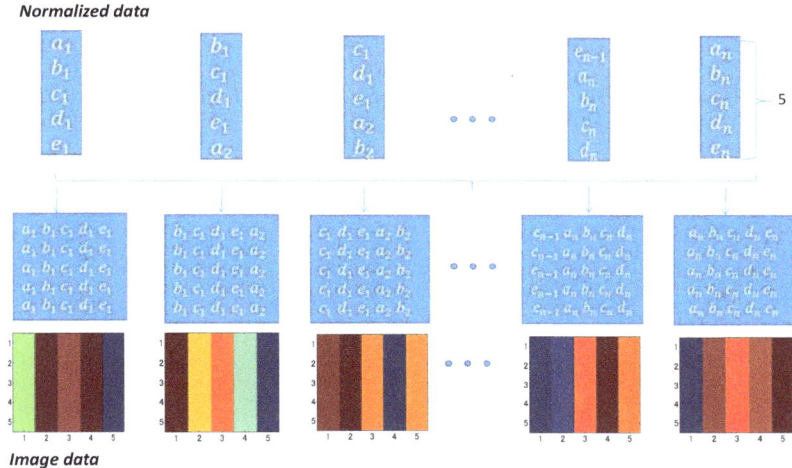

Figure 2. Transform data to matrix inputs (*a-e* denote the normalized oil prices from Monday to Friday, for example a_1-e_1 represent the prices from Monday to Friday of the first week and a_n-e_n represent the prices from Monday to Friday of the n-th week).

(2) An overview of our CNN architectures is depicted in Figure 3. We train the two CNN architectures with different parameters using the data. As shown in the figure, *CNN_A* net contains two layers with weight; the first is convolutional and the second is fully-connected layers. *CNN_B* net contains three layers with weights; the first two are convolutional and the last is a fully-connected layer. The outputs of the last fully-connected layer are all fed to a five-way[2] Softmax, which produces the predicted oil values over the true values. The kernels of all convolutional layers are connected to the previous layer, and neurons in the fully-connected layers are connected to all neurons. The two models are trained with sigmoid and tanh activation functions, respectively. For the two models, the first convolutional layer filters the 5×5 image with the three kernels of size $n \times n$ with a stride of one pixel. The stride is the distance between the receptive field centers of neighboring neurons in a kernel map, and we set the stride of the filters to one pixel for all the other layers. For comparison, n will be set to 2 and 3 in the experiment section. In *CNN_A*, the output of the first convolutional layer is the input of the *CNN_A*'s last fully-connected layer. In *CNN_B*, the output of the first convolutional layer is the input of *CNN_B*'s second convolutional layer, and the second convolutional layer filters the input with six kernels of size $2 \times 2 \times 3$. The output of the second convolutional layer is the input of the *CNN_B*'s last fully-connected layer. The image size of each layer is calculated as follows:

$$W1 = (W - n + 2P)/S,$$
$$W2 = (W - 2 + 2P)/S \tag{6}$$

---

[2]   In fact, we also used the 2 and 3 output layers and we find there are not obvious differences among 5 output nodes in forecast performance, which implies the robustness of our CNN models.

W is the input image size. S is the stride with which we slide the filter. When the stride is 1, we move the filters one pixel at a time. When the stride is 2, then the filters jump two pixels at a time as we slide them around. P represents the zero-padding, which pads the input volume with zeros around the border. As described above, n is the kernel size. In this case, the input image is 5×5, so W is 5, the stride S is set to 1, and no zero-padding is $P = 0$. $W1$ and $W2$ represent the image size after the convolutional processing. When training the CNN models, we used the Adam optimizer Kingma and Ba (2014) with a mini-batch size of 20. The learning rate was set to 0.01, and the momentum term was set to 0.1.

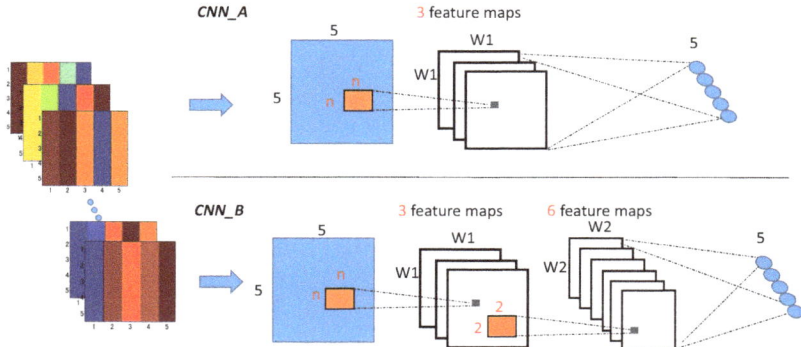

Figure 3. Train the 5×5-size economic data images by two different architectures. Convolutional neural network (CNN). *CNN_A* (**top**): two-layers model with one convolutional layer and one fully-connected layer. *CNN_B* (**bottom**): three-layers model with two convolutional layers and one fully-connected layer.

4. Data

In this study, we use the daily Brent crude oil generic series of the first month's futures prices, traded on the Intercontinental Exchange (ICE). The data cover the period from 24 June 1988, to 3 November 2018, consisting of 7942 observations. The data were obtained from Bloomberg.

For training neural networks, data normalization is an effective way to obtain better performance and quick convergence. Usually, we subtract the mean value to make the input mean zero to prevent weights changing in the same directions, which is called the zero-mean normalization method.

The values of attribute X are normalized using the mean and standard deviation of X. A new value X_n is obtained using the following expression:

$$X_n = \frac{(X - U_x)}{S_x},$$ (7)

where U_x and S_x are the mean and standard deviation of attribute X, respectively. If U_x and S_x are not known, they can be estimated from the samples. After zero-mean normalizing, each feature will have a mean value of 0. In addition, the unit of each value will be the number of (estimated) standard deviations away from the (estimated) mean. When zero-mean normalization is applied, all data in each profile are slid vertically so that their average is zero. In most neural networks, they normalize the data by the mean of all data. As shown in Figure 4, the middle curve is obtained from the top one by a vertical translation so that the average of the profile is zero. Our method draws its strength from making normalization a part of the model architecture and performing the normalization for different training segmentation using the following formula:

$$n = Numl(X)/k$$ (8)

$$X_{si} = \frac{(X_i - U_i)}{S_i}, \ i = 1, 2, 3, ..., n. \tag{9}$$

Here, $Numl(X)$ represents the sample size of the attribute X. k is the scale of segmentation days, and denotes how many days are concluded in one batch for normalization. For instance, if we set k to 100, it means using the mean value and standard deviations calculated in each 100-day period for normalization. n is the batch number in normalization, and U_i and S_i are the mean and standard deviation, respectively, of each segmentation attribute X_i. X_{si} is the new normalized value obtained from each batch. As shown in Figure 4, the bottom curve represents the normalized value for $k = 20$. Different batch sizes used in normalization lead to different results in the training part. We describe the results in the experiment section.

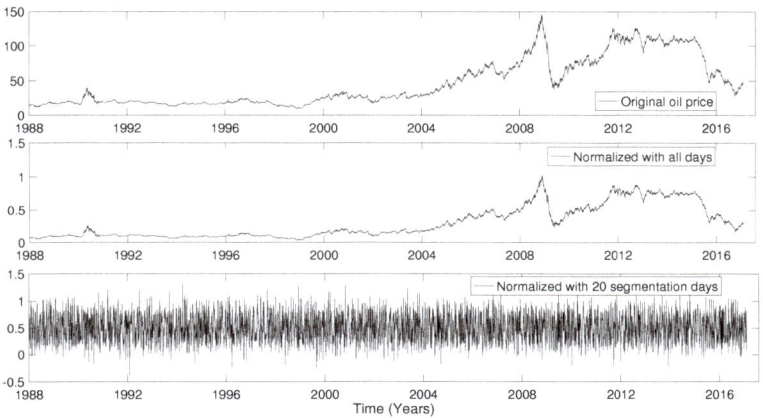

Figure 4. The original oil price (**top**), the normalized oil price by zero-mean normalization with all data (**middle**), and 20 segmentation days (**bottom**), respectively.

5. Empirical Results

5.1. Evaluation Criteria

To evaluate the forecasting performance, we calculate the directional accuracy (DA), the root mean absolute error (RMAE), and Theil's U between the actual values and predicted values, which are often used in the literature (Jammazi and Aloui (2012); Drachal (2016); Yu et al. (2017); Zhao et al. (2017)).

The DA can represent the directional accuracy of each day between the actual data and predicted data, which can be expressed as follows:

$$DA = \frac{1}{N} \sum_{t=1}^{N} Z_t, t = 1, 2, ..., N \tag{10}$$

$$Z_t = \begin{cases} 1 & (V_t^a - V_{t-1}^a)(V_t^p - V_{t-1}^p) \geq 0 \\ 0 & otherwise \end{cases} \tag{11}$$

where V_t^a and V_t^p denote the actual value and predicted value, respectively. N represents the number of days in the testing data. A lower RMAE means a smaller difference between the actual value and predicted value, while a lager DA represents a higher directional accuracy of the predicted value.

The RMAE can reflect the disparity between the actual values and predicted values, which is as follows:

$$RMAE = \sqrt{\frac{1}{N}\sum_{t=1}^{N}\left|V_t^a - V_t^p\right|} \qquad (12)$$

Thus, a higher value of DA and a lower RMAE represent the better forecasting performance of the model.

We also calculate the Theil's U to compare the forecast performance of different models with benchmark models.

$$U = \sqrt{\frac{\sum_{t=1}^{N}(\frac{V_{t+1}^p - V_{t+1}^a}{V_t^a})^2}{\sum_{t=1}^{N}(\frac{V_{t+1}^a - V_t^a}{V_t^a})^2}} \qquad (13)$$

If $U = 1$, that means the proposed model forecast with an accuracy equal to that of the benchmark-NF model. If $U > 1$, that implies the NF model offers a better forecast performance than the proposed model. And if $U < 1$, that means the proposed model provides evidence of a better forecasting performance.

Moreover, we use the Diebold-Mariano (DM) test to investigate whether two competing forecasts have equal predictive accuracy. According to Diebold and Mariano (1995), we first define the forecast errors as:

$$e_{it} = \hat{y}_{it} - y_{it}, i = 1,2 \quad t = 1,2,...,N \qquad (14)$$

The loss associated with forecast i is assumed to be a function of the forecast error e_{it}, and is denoted by $g(e_{it}) = e_{it}^2$ in this paper. We then define the loss differential between the two forecasts by:

$$d_t = g(e_{1t}) - g(e_{2t}) \qquad (15)$$

The null hypothesis is $H_0 : E(d_t) = 0$, meaning that the forecasts of two different models have the same accuracy while the alternative hypothesis $H_1 : E(d_t) \neq 0$ is that they have different levels of forecast accuracy. Finally, we define the Diebold-Mariano statistics as

$$DM = \frac{\bar{d}}{\sqrt{\frac{1}{N} \times s}} \qquad (16)$$

where $\bar{d} = \frac{1}{N} \times \sum_{t=1}^{N}(d_t)$, s denotes the variance of d_t. If DM is positive, that means the forecast errors of the second model are smaller than the first model. Under the null hypothesis, the test statistics DM is asymptotically $N(0,1)$ distributed.

5.2. Normalization Influence

In this section, we test the last 100-day oil price forecasting using the NN model and the two types of normalization methods described in Sections 3.1 and 4. We report the results in Figure 5. As shown in the top portion of Figure 5, the red curve represents the actual oil prices in the testing part. The black curve represents the predicted oil prices that are calculated by the normalization method using all sample data. The blue one represents the predicted price calculated by the segmentation normalization method of every 20-day period as a batch. The bottom portion of Figure 5 shows the predicted error of the two segmentation normalization methods. We can intuitively see that the latter normalization method can achieve a lower predicted error, which means a better forecasting performance. Thus, we use the 20-day period as a batch to normalize the input data in the training model for short-term oil price forecasting.

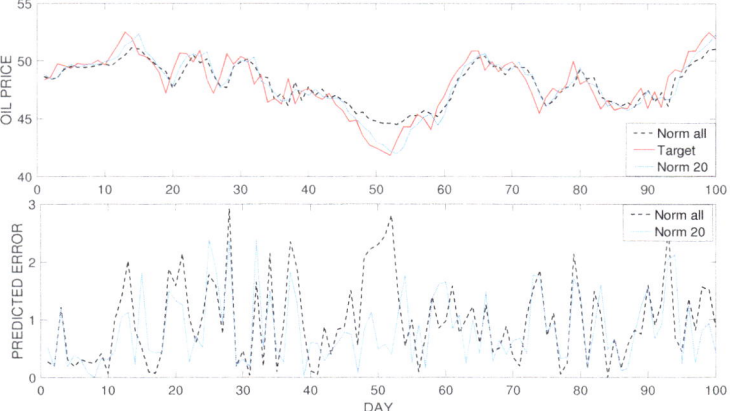

Figure 5. (**Top**) Target oil price (red) and the predicted price by the normal normalization method (black) and the segmentation normalization method (blue); (**Bottom**) The predicted error calculated from different normalization methods.

5.3. Results

In this subsection, the empirical results of NNs and CNNs are given. For each model, different kinds of activation functions, inputs, and layers will be set for comparison. Table 1 shows the forecasting performance of the NF, AR-GARCH, and NN models. In the NF model, the oil price tomorrow is set equal to today's price and the probability of an increase (decrease) in the price next day is 50%. From Table 1, we can see that all NN models achieve larger DA and smaller RMAE values than the NF and AR-GARCH models, confirming that the AI-based forecasting model can provide greater efficiency and higher accuracy. As shown in Table 1, NNs_A denotes the two-layer NN model without and with the delta values of oil prices, while NNs_B represents the three-layer NN model without and with the delta values. We find that most NNs_B with two and three layers of different activation functions show a better forecasting performance than those of NNs_A, implying that the model with deep layers provides higher accuracy of forecasting than the shallow architecture model. The result is in line with Bengio (2009). The three-layer NN model NNs_B can obtain the largest DA values by using the sigmoid activation function and achieves the smallest RMAE values by using the tanh activation function. Moreover, we also find that the Theil's U value of AR-GARCH is very close to 1, implying that the forecast accuracy of AR-GARCH is equal with the benchmark of the NF model, while all Theil's U values of NN models are less than 1, which means NN models offer better forecasting performances than NF and AR-GARCH models.

Table 2 shows the results of the NF, AR-GARCH, and our proposed CNN models with different parameters, where CNN_A and CNN_B represent two-layer and three-layer CNN models, respectively. For each model, we set two kernel sizes-2×2 and 3×3. As shown in Table 2, we find that all CNN models have larger DA and smaller RMAE and Theil's U values than the NF and AR-GARCH models, which suggests that the deep-learning model can provide higher accuracy for short-term forecasting. This result is consistent with Table 1. In addition, by comparing the CNN with NN models with the same activation functions and layers, we can see that most of the DA (RMAE) values of the CNN models are larger (smaller) than those of NN models, providing strong evidence that CNN models with matrix inputs have better short-term prediction performance than the NN models with single-vector input. We also find that CNN_A/CNN_B with 3×3 kernel size achieves the higher DA and lower RMAE values than CNN_A/CNN_B with 2×2 kernel size, suggesting that the large kernel size works on the short-term forecasting performance. In addition, we find that the CNN models with the sigmoid function obtain the lower RMAE values while the higher DA values occur in the CNN models with the tanh function.

We also forecast the crude oil prices during two different sub-periods, including the pre-crisis period (24 June 1988–15 September 2008) and the post-crisis period (14 September 2009–3 December 2018) to test the robustness of our CNN models. The empirical results are shown in Tables 3 and 4. Similarly, the proposed CNN models have higher DA and smaller RMAE and Theil's U values than the NF and AR-GARCH models during both two sub-periods. Specifically, CNN_B with 3×3 kernel size offers the best forecast performance.

Table 5 shows the results of the DM test in terms of the statistics and p-values. According to the statistic values, we find most values are positive, meaning that the second model gives smaller forecast errors than the first one. According to the results of the DM test, it can be found that in most cases the difference in forecasting performance seems significant, with a confidence level of 99%. The results provide evidence that the compared two forecasts have different levels of accuracy.

Table 1. Directional accuracy (DA), root mean absolute error (RMAE) and Theil's U results of NN models.

Models	Functions	Inputs	Layers	DA	RMAE	Theil's U
NF	-	-	-	0.495	0.909	1
AR-GARCH	-	-	-	0.450	0.910	1.000
NNs_A	Sigmoid	Oil	2	0.536	0.816	0.865
NNs_B	Sigmoid	Oil	3	0.567	0.785	0.814
NNs_A	Sigmoid	Oil-delta	2	0.541	0.801	0.832
NNs_B	Sigmoid	Oil-delta	3	**0.575**	0.808	0.802
NNs_A	Tanh	Oil	2	0.514	0.835	0.838
NNs_B	Tanh	Oil	3	0.557	0.793	0.813
NNs_A	Tanh	Oil-delta	2	0.545	0.811	0.821
NNs_B	Tanh	Oil-delta	3	0.556	**0.776**	**0.782**

Notes: NF denotes naive forecast. In the NF, the oil price tomorrow is equal to today's price, and the probability of an increase (decrease) in the price tomorrow is 50%; AR-GARCH denotes the AR(1)-GARCH(1, 1) model; NNs_A and NNs_B represent 2-layer NNs models with [5, 10, 5] and 3-layer with the nodes [5, 10, 10, 5], respectively. The numbers in bold represent the best forecast performance.

Table 2. DA, RMAE and Theil's U results of CNN models (Full sample: 24 June 1988 to 3 December 2018).

Models	Functions	Inputs	Kernel Size	Layers	DA	RMAE	Theil's U
NF	-	-	-	-	0.495	0.909	1
AR-GARCH	-	-	-	-	0.450	0.910	1.000
CNN_A	Sigmoid	Oil	2×2	2	0.523	0.732	0.781
CNN_B	Sigmoid	Oil	2×2	3	0.542	0.745	0.763
CNN_A	Sigmoid	Oil	3×3	2	0.535	**0.728**	**0.743**
CNN_B	Sigmoid	Oil	3×3	3	0.550	0.741	0.762
CNN_A	Tanh	Oil	2×2	2	0.561	0.753	0.776
CNN_B	Tanh	Oil	2×2	3	0.574	0.772	0.791
CNN_A	Tanh	Oil	3×3	2	**0.595**	0.739	0.752
CNN_B	Tanh	Oil	3×3	3	0.558	0.785	0.755

Notes: NF denotes naive forecast. In the NF, the oil price tomorrow is equal to the today's price and the probability of an increase (decrease) in the price tomorrow is 50%; AR-GARCH denotes the AR(1)-GARCH(1, 1) model; CNN_A and CNN_B represent 3-layer and 4-layer CNN models, respectively. The numbers in bold represent the best forecast performance.

Table 3. DA, RMAE and Theil's U results of CNN models (Subperiod 1: 24 June 1988 to 15 September 2008).

Models	Functions	Inputs	Kernel Size	Layers	DA	RMAE	Theil's U
NF	-	-	-	-	0.415	1.363	1
AR-GARCH	-	-	-	-	0.400	1.374	1.001
CNN_A	Sigmoid	Oil	2 × 2	2	0.436	1.259	0.821
CNN_B	Sigmoid	Oil	2 × 2	3	0.441	1.245	0.814
CNN_A	Sigmoid	Oil	3 × 3	2	0.455	1.129	**0.796**
CNN_B	Sigmoid	Oil	3 × 3	3	0.475	1.191	0.842
CNN_A	Tanh	Oil	2 × 2	2	0.483	1.162	0.806
CNN_B	Tanh	Oil	2 × 2	3	0.478	1.213	0.829
CNN_A	Tanh	Oil	3 × 3	2	**0.492**	**1.125**	0.811
CNN_B	Tanh	Oil	3 × 3	3	0.459	1.257	0.801

Notes: NF denotes naive forecast. In the NF, the oil price tomorrow is equal to the today's price and the probability of an increase (decrease) in the price tomorrow is 50%; AR-GARCH denotes the AR(1)-GARCH(1, 1) model; *CNN_A* and *CNN_B* represent 3-layer and 4-layer CNN models, respectively. The numbers in bold represent the best forecast performance.

Table 4. DA, RMAE and Theil's U results of CNN models (Subperiod 2: 14 September 2009 to 3 December 2018).

Models	Function	Inputs	Kernel Size	Layers	DA	RMAE	Theil's U
NF	-	-	-	-	0.495	0.909	1
AR-GARCH	-	-	-	-	0.490	0.910	1.000
CNN_A	Sigmoid	Oil	2 × 2	2	0.505	0.891	0.983
CNN_B	Sigmoid	Oil	2 × 2	3	0.517	0.863	0.956
CNN_A	Sigmoid	Oil	3 × 3	2	0.495	0.851	0.942
CNN_B	Sigmoid	Oil	3 × 3	3	0.523	0.865	**0.923**
CNN_A	Tanh	Oil	2 × 2	2	0.491	0.874	0.996
CNN_B	Tanh	Oil	2 × 2	3	0.501	0.881	0.962
CNN_A	Tanh	Oil	3 × 3	2	**0.525**	0.884	0.950
CNN_B	Tanh	Oil	3 × 3	3	0.519	**0.785**	0.956

Notes: NF denotes naive forecast. In the NF, the oil price tomorrow is equal to the today's price and the probability of an increase (decrease) in the price tomorrow is 50%; AR-GARCH denotes the AR(1)-GARCH(1, 1) model; *CNN_A* and *CNN_B* represent 3-layer and 4-layer CNN models, respectively. The numbers in bold represent the best forecast performance.

Table 5. Diebold-Mariano (DM) test results.

	NF vs. AR-GARCH	NF vs. NN	NF vs. CNN
Statistics	−0.313	4.039	3.640
P-values	0.755	0.000	0.000
	AR-GARCH vs. NN	AR-GARCH vs. CNN	NN vs. CNN
Statistics	4.035	3.635	2.308
P-values	0.000	0.000	0.023

Notes: NF denotes naive forecast. In the NF, the oil price tomorrow is equal to the today's price and the probability of an increase (decrease) in the price tomorrow is 50%; AR-GARCH denotes the AR(1)-GARCH(1, 1) model; *NN* represents the best forecast performance model in NN models; *CNN* represents the best forecast performance model in our CNN models.

6. Conclusions

As one of the major drivers of the global economy, the crude oil price fluctuation affects the real economy worldwide. Specifically, the importance of the oil futures markets as a common investment alternative to traditional markets has increased. Thus, forecasting oil futures prices accurately can provide useful information that helps international investors to diversify risk. However, the prices of crude oil are influenced by many complex natural, economic, and political factors, which cause the crude oil futures prices show very complex nonlinear characteristics. Thus, it is very hard to predict the prices of crude oil accurately by using the traditional economic models. The evolution of a good forecasting model for oil prices is of great importance.

In this study, we develop a new forecasting methodology based on CNNs to forecast the short-term crude oil futures prices. We first compare the AI-based deep-learning model with the benchmark models. We then employ the CNN model with matrix inputs for short-term prediction. In our paper, we confirm that the non-linear AI-based deep-learning approach can provide higher accuracy than the benchmark models. We also find that the CNNs are more powerful than the benchmark models. These results imply that increasing the dependence of inputs and providing more useful information are effective ways of improving the forecasting performance.

Author Contributions: Conceptualization: S.H. and T.T.; Formal Analysis: Z.L. and X.C.; Writing—Original draft preparation: Z.L. and X.C.; Writing—Reviewing and editing: K.T., T.T., T.K. and S.H.; Funding Acquisition: T.T. and S.H.

Funding: This work was supported by JSPS KAKENHI Grant Number 17K18564 and (A) 17H00983.

Acknowledgments: We would like to acknowledge the valuable comments from the Reviewers of Journal of Risk and Financial Management.

Conflicts of Interest: The authors declare no conflicts of interest.

References

Alvarez-Ramirez, Jose, Eduardo Rodriguez, Esteban Martina, and Carlos Ibarra-Valdez. 2012. Cyclical behavior of crude oil markets and economic recessions in the period 1986–2010. *Technological Forecasting and Social Change* 79: 47–58. [CrossRef]

Baumeister, Christiane, Pierre Guérin, and Lutz Kilian. 2015. Do high-frequency financial data help forecast oil prices? The MIDAS touch at work. *International Journal of Forecasting* 31: 238–52. [CrossRef]

Bengio, Yoshua. 2009. Learning deep architectures for AI. *Foundations and Trends® in Machine Learning* 2: 1–127. [CrossRef]

De Souza e Silva, Edmundo G., Luiz F.L. Legey, and Edmundo A. de Souza e Silva. 2010. Forecasting oil price trends using wavelets and hidden Markov models. *Energy Economics* 32: 1507–19. [CrossRef]

Diebold, Francis X., and Roberto S. Mariano. 1995. Comparing predictive accuracy. *Journal of Business and Economic Statistics* 13: 253–63.

Drachal, Krzysztof. 2016. Forecasting spot oil price in a dynamic model averaging framework—Have the determinants changed over time? *Energy Economics* 60: 35–46. [CrossRef]

Jammazi, Rania, and Chaker Aloui. 2012. Crude oil price forecasting: Experimental evidence from wavelet decomposition and neural network modeling. *Energy Economics* 34: 828–41. [CrossRef]

Kingma, Diederik P., and Jimmy Ba. 2014. Adam: A method for stochastic optimization. *arXiv*, arXiv:1412.6980.

Krizhevsky, Alex, Ilya Sutskever, and Geoffrey E. Hinton. 2012. Imagenet classification with deep convolutional neural networks. Paper presented at the 25th International Conference on Neural Information Processing Systems, Lake Tahoe, NV, USA, December 3–6, pp. 1097–105.

LeCun, Yann, Bernhard E. Boser, John Denker, Don Henderson, Richard E. Howard, Wayne Hubbard, and Larry Jackel. 1989. Backpropagation applied to handwritten zip code recognition. *Neural Computation* 1: 541–51. [CrossRef]

Ma, Xiaolei, Zhuang Dai, Zhengbing He, Jihui Na, Yong Wang, and Yunpeng Wang. 2017. Learning traffic as images: A deep convolutional neural network for large-scale transportation network speed prediction. *Sensors* 17: 818. [CrossRef] [PubMed]

Merino, Antonio, and Álvaro Ortiz. 2005. Explaining the so-called "price premium" in oil markets. *OPEC Energy Review* 29: 133–52. [CrossRef]

Moshiri, Source, and Faezeh Foroutan. 2006. Forecasting nonlinear crude oil futures prices. *The Energy Journal* 27: 81–95. [CrossRef]

Naser, Hanan. 2016. Estimating and forecasting the real prices of crude oil: A data rich model using a dynamic model averaging (DMA) approach. *Energy Economics* 56: 75–87. [CrossRef]

Ongkrutaraksa, Worapot. 1995. *Fractal Theory and Neural Networks in Capital Markets*. Working Paper at Kent State University. Kent: Kent State University.

Refenes, Apostolos Paul. 1994. *Neural Networks in the Capital Markets*. New York: John Wiley & Sons, Inc.

Simonyan, Karen, and Andrew Zisserman. 2014. Two-stream convolutional networks for action recognition in videos. In *Advances in Neural Information Processing Systems*. Cambridge: MIT Press, pp. 568–76.

Sklibosios Nikitopoulos, Christina, Matthew Squires, Susan Thorp, and Danny Yeung. 2017. Determinants of the crude oil futures curve: Inventory, consumption and volatility. *Journal of Banking and Finance* 84: 53–67. [CrossRef]

Tang, Mingming, and Jinliang Zhang. 2012. A multiple adaptive wavelet recurrent neural network model to analyze crude oil prices. *Journal of Economics and Business* 64: 275–86.

Wang, Shouyang, Lean Yu, and Kin Keung Lai. 2005. Crude oil price forecasting with TEI@ I methodology. *Journal of Systems Science and Complexity* 18: 145–66.

Wang, Yudong, Chongfeng Wu, and Li Yang. 2016. Forecasting crude oil market volatility: A Markov switching multifractal volatility approach. *International Journal of Forecasting* 32: 1–9. [CrossRef]

Wen, Fenghua, Xu Gong, and Shenghua Cai. 2016. Forecasting the volatility of crude oil futures using HAR-type models with structural breaks. *Energy Economics* 59: 400–13. [CrossRef]

Yu, Lean, Yang Zhao, and Ling Tang. 2017. Ensemble forecasting for complex time series using sparse representation and neural networks. *Journal of Forecasting* 36: 122–38. [CrossRef]

Ye, Michael, John Zyren, and Joanne Shore. 2006. Forecasting short-run crude oil price using high-and low-inventory variables. *Energy Policy* 34: 2736–43. [CrossRef]

Zeiler, Matthew D., and Rob Fergus. 2014. Visualizing and understanding convolutional networks. Paper presented at the European Conference on Computer Vision, Zurich, Switzerland, September 6–12, pp. 818–33.

Zhao, Yang, Jianping Li, and Lean Yu. 2017. A deep learning ensemble approach for crude oil price forecasting. *Energy Economics* 66: 9–16. [CrossRef]

Journal of
Risk and Financial Management

Article

Take Profit and Stop Loss Trading Strategies Comparison in Combination with an MACD Trading System

Dimitrios Vezeris [1,*], **Themistoklis Kyrgos** [2] and **Christos Schinas** [1]

[1] Department of Electrical and Computer Engineering, Democritus University of Thrace,
    67100 Xanthi, Greece; cschinas@ee.duth.gr
[2] COSMOS4U, 67100 Xanthi, Greece; thkyrgos@kyrgos.gr
*   Correspondence: d.vezeris@ioniki.net; Tel.: +30-254-108-4084

Received: 22 August 2018; Accepted: 17 September 2018; Published: 19 September 2018

Abstract: A lot of strategies for Take Profit and Stop Loss functionalities have been propounded and scrutinized over the years. In this paper, we examine various strategies added to a simple MACD automated trading system and used on selected assets from Forex, Metals, Energy, and Cryptocurrencies categories and afterwards, we compare and contrast their results. We conclude that Take Profit strategies based on faster take profit signals on MACD are not better than a simple MACD strategy and of the different Stop Loss strategies based on ATR, the sliding and variable ATR window has the best results for a period of 12 and a multiplier of 6. For the first time, to the best of our knowledge, we implement a combination of an adaptive MACD Expert Advisor that uses back-tested optimized parameters per asset with price levels defined by the ATR indicator, used to set limits for Stop Loss.

Keywords: algorithmic trading; take profit; stop loss; MACD; ATR

1. Introduction

When trading on an asset, investors are exposed to a potentially high risk if the price moves towards a direction which is the opposite from the one they had anticipated. This could result in considerable losses in the investment capital, unless immediate action is taken to exit the non-profitable position as soon as possible. On the other hand, if the price moves towards a direction that makes the current position profitable, an investor might want to close the position and cash in the profits gained so far, as there is always the possibility that winning trades could turn into losing positions and lead to catastrophic losses.

Different strategies of securing profits (Take Profit) and averting losses (Stop Loss) have been proposed and examined, usually involving the prices at which a position was opened, and are frequently used by traders, as well as automated trading systems. In this research, we tested and compared six different Take Profit and Stop Loss strategies used in combination with an algorithmic trading system, based on the MACD indicator on eleven different assets over a six-month period. With the results of these comparisons, we aim to provide some practical insights into every day traders about which Take Profit and Stop Loss technics to incorporate with an existing MACD strategy and which to avoid. There have been numerous studies about MACD, which is a 30-year-old tool, such as those by Chong and Ng (2008) and Yazdi and Lashkari (2013), focused on MACD's performance in various markets and timeframes, or such as that by Ni and Yin (2009), who examined, among others, Take Profit and Stop Loss technics in MACD using neural networks. But there has not yet been a study of MACD combined with the Take Profit/Stop Loss strategies we examined based on ATR and in a faster timeframe.

2. Materials and Methods

2.1. Trading Systems

2.1.1. Automated Trading

Nowadays, trading is almost exclusively conducted electronically through a computer (Jain 2005). In addition to that, investors have replaced the broker with a platform of automated trading (algorithmic trading), as was postulated by Hendershott and Moulton (2007).

The decrease in the cost of this technology has led to its fast-paced adoption by the financial industry. The resulting technological change has brought about a revolution in the financial markets and the way the assets are traded. Many institutions today trade through algorithms and algorithmic trades improve liquidity. It has been proven that the increased algorithmic trades limit wrong price choices and decrease the proportion of offer risk over different price levels of an asset associated with the trades. These results show that algorithmic trading lowers the cost of trades and enhances the informativeness of quotes, as demonstrated by Hendershott et al. (2011).

On the other hand, it seems that Forex manual trading outweighs automated trading systems. Humans are more informed than systems (Chaboud et al. 2014). However, on closer inspection, we realize that there are some indications pointing to the fact that algorithmic trading contributes to an efficient price discovering process (Brogaard et al. 2014) through the elimination of opportunities for triangular arbitrage and faster "integration" of macroeconomic news into the price (Foucault et al. 2011). Also, in the same paper, it was established that algorithmic trades tend to correlate, demonstrating that automated strategies are not that different from those used by a human. Despite that correlation, there are no indications that algorithmic trading causes excess variability. In addition, the volume of algorithmic trading in the market has a small, but positive, impact on the liquidity of the market.

In this research, only algorithmic trades are executed without human intervention, with an automated high frequency trading system. Consequently, commissions and the cost of position swap are kept to a minimum, in contrast with using human intermediaries, and are subsequently presented. But the main element is the fact that they are automatically included in the results by the trading terminal we used. Consequently, the profit rate presented in this paper is pure, after the deduction of commissions.

2.1.2. Private Investors

As more brokers adopt electronic trading platforms, more private investors opt for automated algorithmic trading. It is estimated that private investors lose 2% in the USA market and 3.8% in Taiwan annually (Barber et al. 2008). It has also been calculated that institutional profits are enhanced by 1.5% annually as a result of the small transactions' cost and corresponding profits of the same actions.

The feeling of the individual investors in relation to weekly and monthly profits and the variability of NYSE stocks was studied by Kaniel et al. (2004). Private investors who are more aware of the risk may force them to provide liquidity to other market participants who seek an instant service. The buying orders from bigger, stock-accumulating investors can cause a coercion of sales by increasing the prices. In the same way, individual buyers are attracted to lower prices caused when these larger investors choose to sell their stocks. Liquidity is actually provided by both professional traders (e.g., specialists) and individuals. If we assume that market liquidity is only provided by individual investors and they are more active in relation to the demand for immediacy, then there would be an excess supply of liquidity. In this case, individual investors that have contracts and are silent liquidity providers will amount losses, while more terms-informed investors will perform trades in adverse conditions. If, on the other hand, there are fewer investors than the market immediacy demands, the silent liquidity providers will amount profits. Understanding the predictability of the short-term profits calls for an understanding of the silent liquidity provision to individuals, as well as the explicit liquidity provision to professional investors. Specifically, the provision of liquidity can be regarded as the interaction between different types of investors that trade on the same market.

A lot of individuals, in parallel with these systems, adopt long-term positions, instead of strategic buying and holding, strategies whose trends are reflected on Google Trends, an analysis by Preis et al. (2013) quantifying the behavior of the market. In this research, there is no liquidity problem, especially for the $10,000 of initial capital, as the automated systems tested in this research can be implemented by institutes, as well as by private investors. On the other hand, it has been proven through back-testing that whether or not data from the profits of an asset or data from Google Trends are used for the same asset, the results are the same. The results have been tested on a non-linear machine learning system by Challet and Ayed (2014). In the current work, the problem of back-testing period selection is evident.

2.2. Take Profit & Stop Loss

Returns can be either absolute or relative. As a rule, we avoid absolute numbers because they will have to be calculated for each asset individually. Leung and Li (2015) proved that the stop loss function has to be calculated at every moment because it is related to the price of an asset at every tick since that price is within the price range $x \in (L, b \times L)$, or the investor, if x is the entering price, can simply set a constant I (proportional to the fluctuation we add), where $x-I$ is the stop loss price. In addition, returns change over seasons and periods, according to the influences an asset undergoes as a result of outside or inside factors. It is obvious that orders with stop loss and take profit, when activated, oppose the market trend (take profit) or intensify the movement (stop loss), with great influence even over the liquidity during a flash crash (Easley et al. 2011). In all these adoptive trading systems, special consideration should be given to the use of these functions, as shown by Austin et al. (2004). In addition, the use of cut-loss orders and take profit orders and the range of these orders reflect the risk-taking desire of the investor (Au et al. 2003).

With regard to absolute numbers, we see a 3% take profit and a 2% stop loss in the work by Bolgün et al. (2010) on stocks of the Istanbul Stock Exchange. Constant take profit was used by Krishnan and Menon (2009), defined at 20 pips, in an interesting work that examined the influence that rate, closing price times, and indicators participating in trading systems (RSI, BB, Stoch, SAR, MACD, ADX, CCI, Williams %R, Mom, A/D) have on profit. Take profit was also set at 20 pips by Barbosa and Belo (2010). Even in systems that are based on the flow of buy and sell orders and not on the price itself, as postulated by Bates et al. (2003), stop loss and take profit were used as a function of returns 0–0.5%, 0.5–1%, etc. Similarly, Azzini and Tettamanzi (2008b) set staggering take profit signals on returns of 0.33%, 0.67%, etc., while in another work, Azzini and Tettamanzi (2008a) took three returns as take profit, logarithmically setting the constant at rTP = 0.006, 0.008, or 0.0046. Martinez et al. (2009) conducted experiments that converted the percentage of loss break from 0.1% to 2.0%. A small loss break percentage could impede profitable transactions, while a high one could cause bigger losses. The system executes more profitable transactions with the stop loss rules and the 0.5% percent yielded the best results.

As for the fluctuation range, we consider that take profit and stop loss functions display flexibility of profitability adjusted on each asset. In this way, with the range (R), stop loss = 0,5R and take profit = 1R were set by Cervelló-Royo et al. (2015). It is obvious that profit>stop loss is the only fair deal. Consequently, we make sure that 1R > 0.5R. Klement (2013) set the stop loss (c) in combination with a reentry condition (d), where (c) as the stop loss level is expressed in units of annual standard deviation of the return of an asset. The same applies for (d). Similarly, Chevallier et al. (2012) set a dynamic stop loss and reduced the losses on S&P500, for which the rule is as follows: if the proposed rate of return against the variability reaches a lower limit (n), that is, the number of fluctuation days of the market that will activate the stop loss rule, then this is a signal for the selling of the investment.

We prove here that the addition of take profit and stop loss could considerably improve the results, to the point that they become profitable, in contrast to the claim laid by Clare et al. (2013).

More specifically, this became more evident after the proof put forward by Han et al. (2016), who, with a stop loss at 10% of the monthly returns of a strategy based on the momentum, achieved a reduction of losses from −49.79% to −11.36%. Likewise, for monthly data from 1950 to 2004 setting stop loss on American long-term bonds investment, Kaminski and Lo (2014), improved the return over the buying and holding strategy by 50–100 basis points.

Lei and Li (2009) applied a constant price stop loss, as well as trailing stop loss, for stocks of NYSE and AMEX from 1970 to 2005. They concluded that the stop loss function shields investors from holding a non-profitable position for a long period of time, which could result in big losses of capital. On the other hand, they found a distinction between the profits' enhancement and the risk reduction. The analysis of exchange rates of high frequency by Osler (2005) yields facts that provide support for the idea that orders of stop loss have an influence on the fall of prices. First of all, the change in exchange rates is faster when the prices reach levels at which stop loss orders are usually placed. Secondly, the effect of stop loss orders is greater than the effect of the take profit orders, which also helps the fast changes in prices by creating an opposite trend. Thirdly, the effect of stop loss orders has a broader time duration than that of take profit orders.

All of the above stop loss and take profit rules and conditions can be evaluated and sorted with regard to the profitability of the investment through a number of ways, where the aggregate profit would be the ultimate result, but with an evaluation framework proposed by Chan and Ma (2015).

The take profit and stop loss functions we use and analyze below are dynamic, follow the average fluctuation and the current price for every tick, and are activated instantaneously.

2.3. Automated Trading Strategy Development and Combinations

For this research, we used an automated trading system (Expert Advisor) based on the MACD indicator. We started with a simple system and progressively added more complex features, implementing Take Profit and Stop Loss functionalities.

2.3.1. The MACD Indicator and Expert Advisor

The MACD (Moving Average Convergence/Divergence) is a well-known indicator created in 1979 by Appel (2005). It calculates the difference of two exponential moving averages of different periods over a time-series. The moving average with the smaller period is called the fast moving average and the moving average with the bigger period is called the slow moving average.

$$\text{MACD line} = \text{EMA}_{p_{fast}}(\text{Timeseries}) - \text{EMA}_{p_{slow}}(\text{Timeseries}), \quad p_{fast} < p_{slow} \tag{1}$$

Another exponential moving average is calculated on the MACD line, called the Signal line:

$$\text{Signal line} = \text{EMA}_{p_{signal}}(\text{MACD line}) \tag{2}$$

When the MACD line is above the Signal line, this is an indication of an upward trend momentum in the time-series and when the MACD line is below the Signal line, this is an indication of a downward trend momentum in the time-series.

The default values of the three periods used in the calculations of the MACD indicator are usually $p_{fast} = 12$, $p_{slow} = 26$, and $p_{signal} = 9$ in the daily timeframe. An example of the MACD indicator can be seen in Figure 1.

Figure 1. EURUSD chart with an MACD line (blue) and a Signal line (red) below.

An automated trading system (Expert Advisor) can be formulated on the basis of the MACD indicator following the rules below:

When the MACD line crosses above the Signal line, this constitutes a buy signal and any short positions are closed and a long position is opened.

When the MACD line crosses below the Signal line, this constitutes a sell signal and any long positions are closed and a short position is opened.

The abovementioned trading strategy in the form of a pseudocode can be found in Appendix A.

2.3.2. The MACD Expert Advisor with a quicker Take Profit Signal

Sometimes, the rate of change of a time-series can be more rapid than the rate at which the MACD indicator can provide us with a signal. If a position was open during that time, even if it was a successful one up until that moment, potential profits could be diminished and never materialize or even turn into losses.

A potential solution to that problem is the use of a different Signal line to judge when to exit a position, with a faster (smaller) period than that of the normal Signal line:

$$\text{Take Profit Signal line} = \text{EMA}_{p_{take\ profit\ signal}}(\text{MACD line}) \tag{3}$$

where

$$p_{take\ profit\ signal} = \frac{p_{signal}}{N}, \quad N = 2,\ 3,\ \dots \tag{4}$$

An example of the MACD indicator with a Take Profit Signal Line can be seen in Figure 2.

Now, the Expert Advisor, in addition to the two previous rules, closes any long positions when the MACD line crosses below the Take Profit Signal line and any short positions when the MACD line crosses above the Take Profit Signal line. After that and until the next time, the MACD line crosses the Signal line, and no position is open, in contrast with the previous strategy, where there was always a long or a short position open. The abovementioned trading strategy in the form of a pseudocode can be found in Appendix A.

Figure 2. EURUSD chart with an MACD line (blue), a Signal line (red), and a Take Profit Signal line (green) below.

2.3.3. The MACD Expert Advisor with Signal Lines' Hierarchy

There can be time periods when the time-series of an asset does not follow a clear upward or downward trend, but instead oscillates around a value. During these periods, the previous strategies produce a lot of signals and change positions frequently, which can potentially lead to losses, because there is not enough time for the price to move to profitable levels and every transaction and position change comes at a cost. A more effective option might involve staying out of the market during these periods and only opening a new position when clear upward or downward trends occur.

The clarity of a trend can be judged by means of the MACD, Signal, and Take Profit Signal lines. When the prevailing trend is bullish, then we have the MACD line above the Take Profit Signal line and the Take Profit Signal line above the Signal line. Likewise, when the trend is bearish, we have the MACD line below the Take Profit Signal line and the Take Profit Signal line below the Signal line.

The Expert Advisor still closes positions using the Take Profit Signal line in the same way as in the previous case, but only opens new positions if the hierarchy of the MACD, Take Profit Signal, and Signal lines matches the one outlined in the above paragraph. The abovementioned trading strategy in the form of a pseudocode can also be found in Appendix A.

2.3.4. The Average True Range Indicator

The Average True Range or ATR indicator is a measure of volatility introduced in 1978 by Wilder (1978). The True Range for a specific interval is defined as

$$TR = \max\left[(\text{high} - \text{low}),\, \text{abs}(\text{high} - \text{close}_{\text{prev}}),\, \text{abs}(\text{low} - \text{close}_{\text{prev}})\right] \qquad (5)$$

The ATR of period N is calculated as

$$ATR = \frac{1}{N}\sum_{i=1}^{N} TR_i \qquad (6)$$

for the first instance and after that as

$$ATR_t = \frac{ATR_{t-1} \times (N-1) + TR_t}{N} \qquad (7)$$

2.3.5. The MACD Expert Advisor combined with the ATR Indicator for Stop Loss Strategies

The ATR indicator can be used to set a Stop Loss barrier when a new position is opened following an MACD Expert Advisor signal. When the MACD Expert Advisor opens a new long position, a Stop Loss barrier can be set at

$$\text{Stop Loss Barrier} = \text{Opening Price} - x \times \text{ATR(N)} \tag{8}$$

where Opening Price is the price the long position was opened at, ATR(N) is the value of the ATR indicator of period N at that moment, and x is a constant multiplier used to adjust the barrier's width. When the asset's price moves below that barrier, the long position is closed.

Likewise, when a short position is opened, a Stop Loss barrier can be set at

$$\text{Stop Loss Barrier} = \text{Opening Price} + x \times \text{ATR(N)} \tag{9}$$

When the asset's price moves above this barrier, then the short position is closed.

After a Stop Loss is triggered and a position closed, it is possible that the MACD indicator keeps signaling for the same type of position to be opened. To avoid the immediate reopening of the same type of position after a Stop Loss, a new barrier can be created in the same way. Until the price moves above

$$\text{New Position Barrier} = \text{Closing Price} + y \times \text{ATR(N)} \tag{10}$$

a long signal will not result in a new long position after a Stop Loss, and until the price moves below

$$\text{New Position Barrier} = \text{Closing Price} - y \times \text{ATR(N)} \tag{11}$$

a short signal will not result in a new short position after a Stop Loss. The y parameter is a constant multiplier used to adjust the barrier's width, as is the case with x. Examples of Stop Loss Barriers and New Position Barriers can be seen in Figure 3. The abovementioned trading strategy in the form of a pseudocode can also be found in Appendix A.

Figure 3. A segment from an MACD Expert Advisor's trading on EURUSD. The green dots on the price chart indicate the $\pm 2 \times \text{ATR(24)}$ Stop Loss barrier after opening a new position and the red dots indicate the $\pm 2 \times \text{ATR(24)}$ barrier for new positions prevention after Stop Loss.

2.3.6. The MACD Expert Advisor with sliding ATR barrier zone

The ATR Stop Loss barriers described in the above section are drawn around the price at which a new position is opened and stay fixed, even if the price follows an upward, profitable trend, until there is a new MACD signal or the price moves back to the barrier.

In the second case, when the price moves back to the Stop Loss barrier, the potential gains from the previous profitable movements are never materialized. To prevent this, the $\pm x \times$ ATR(N) zone can be redrawn each time the price moves out of it and follows a profitable direction. This slides the Stop Loss barrier to values that secure some of the profits gained so far.

On the other hand, the position prevention barrier should stay at the same level and not slide, as it could prevent the Expert Advisor from opening a new position for a long time. An example of this strategy can be seen in Figure 4.

Figure 4. A segment from an MACD Expert Advisor's trading on EURUSD. The green dots show how the $\pm 2 \times$ ATR(24) zone slides upwards as the price moves to more profitable values. Eventually, a stop loss is triggered and the position is closed at a higher price than the one we would have in the event of waiting for the next MACD signal.

2.3.7. The MACD Expert Advisor with sliding and variable ATR barrier zone

An asset's price can show large or small variability as it changes over time, which reflects the value of ATR. In the previous cases, ATR barriers were of a constant range, calculated with the ATR value at the moment when a position opened. Using the latest ATR value to form an ATR window with a variable range through time, could prevent the expert advisor from exiting a position prematurely in periods when variability spikes and help him follow the price trends, as seen in Figure 5.

Figure 5. A segment from an MACD Expert Advisor's trading on EURUSD. The green dots show how the ATR window changes in width as the ATR value changes over time.

2.4. Data and Implementation

We conducted our experiments on the different Take Profit – Stop Loss strategies for nine assets from the Forex, Metals, Commodities, Energy, and Cryptocurrencies categories: AUDUSD, EURGBP, EURUSD, GBPUSD, USDCHF, USDJPY, XAUUSD, OIL, and BTCUSD. This choice mainly came from the need for assets that are traded on global markets on a 24 h base (or close to 24 h), as we wanted to examine the automated trading systems in a High Frequency Trading mode (hourly timeframe). The MACD Indicator has mainly been used for stock trading, but we opted to not trade stocks as the relatively big time intervals that exist between their trade sessions, in combination with the multinational activities of most of these corporations, can cause a lot of gaps and noise in their prices. The period we examined was from 3 September 2017 to 24 February 2018 with historical data from FXTM, GEBINVEST, and OctaFX. Because our systems were used in High Frequency Trading mode, we determined that a six-month period would be enough to draw conclusions about their performance.

For the testing, we used the Metatrader 5 trading terminal from Metaquotes, and Microsoft SQL Server for the initial data processing.

We set the initial test amount at $10,000 at a 1:100 leverage ratio for all assets except for BTCUSD, whose high price and spread required an equally high margin on the broker we used, so we set the initial amount at $10,000,000 and adjusted the results in such a way as to be comparable to the other assets. For each new position the automated trading system opens, it risks 20% of its current balance and no capital is deposited or withdrawn for the six-month period apart from the initial capital. The spreads for every asset (in pips) as reported by the brokers used were AUDUSD:0.7, EURGBP:0.6, EURUSD:0.4, GBPUSD:0.7, USDCHF:0.9, USDJPY:0.5, XAUUSD:21.0, OIL:5.0, and BTCUSD:11.5. The Metatrader 5 trading terminal also automatically adds the cost of each transaction to the Gross Losses so the Net Profits represent the actual pure number a trader has won or lost at the end.

2.4.1. Back testing Limitations

The Metatrader 5 terminal offers the ability to test an automated trading system over a past time period with various methods for simulating the price changes, such as every tick, every open-high-low-close value, every open value for a specific timeframe, etc. It also offers the ability to test a rage of the parameters used by the Expert Advisor in order to identify the best combination of parameters for a back testing period. In order to speed up back-tests, Metatrader 5 also offers the ability to use distributed testing agents utilizing the resources of a local network of computers. We used this ability to form a local cluster of computers, mainly with i5, i7, and Xeon Intel CPUs for a total capacity of 130 distributed agents, in order to run our backtesting experiments. We also used a Microsoft SQL Server in order to save and process the results of our experiments during the stage of parameter selection.

It should be noted that the wider the parameters' ranges, the greater the number of combinations of parameters. Also, back testing with an every tick simulation is far more time- and resource-consuming than back testing with open-high-low-close value, which is in turn more time-consuming than an open value only simulation.

The values of the MACD and ATR indicators are calculated over one-hour timeframes, but during an hourly timeframe, the price of an asset can reach levels that would trigger a Take Profit/Stop Loss in some strategies or an automatic Stop Loss from the broker, so we chose to run our experiments with every tick simulations.

2.4.2. Parameter Selection

For our tests, we had to choose a set of parameters for each asset that would allow for the demonstration of an improvement or worsening in the MACD Expert Advisor's behavior with the introduction of each Take Profit/Stop Loss strategy.

Since the different periods in the MACD averages can generate widely different results and in order to render the role of these parameters less significant for our tests, we decided to choose sets of parameters that are centered on neighborhoods (± 2) of similar results, with the results indicating there is room for both improvement and worsening.

The simple MACD Expert Advisor has three parameters, the periods of its moving averages, which means that even for small parameter ranges, the number of combinations is significant. Performing a back test for every asset with full parameter sweeping on an every tick simulation would be prohibitive because of the time and electrical energy it would require. We circumvented this firstly by running the simulations on open-high-low-close prices ticks, which produces results close enough to the real tick simulation, and secondly by incrementing each parameter by a step of 2 instead of 1, which reduces the combinations to $1/8$, allowing us to check a wider range. Potentially suitable neighborhoods can still be identified as a step of 2 still hits a ± 2 neighborhood in eight or 27 of its 125 members.

Next, we defined some requirements for a suitable neighborhood, such as a minimum amount of trades and profit range, and chose the best 100 neighborhoods that fulfilled them, sorted by the smallest relative range defined as

$$\text{Relative Range} = \frac{\max(\text{Profits}) - \min(\text{Profits})}{\text{average}(\text{Profits})} \qquad (12)$$

The specific requirements for each asset can be seen in Table 1.

Table 1. Requirements set for neighborhood selection for each asset.

	Profits $\in$	Trades$\geq$	Central Value
AUDUSD	[0, 22500]	59	
EURGBP	[−2800, 10800]	75	
EURUSD	[1500, 6500]	75	MinProfit < 4000 < MaxProfit
GBPUSD	[0, 8500]	75	MinProfit < 4000 < MaxProfit
USDCHF	[400, 7600]	75	MinProfit < 4000 < MaxProfit
USDJPY	[200, 7800]	75	MinProfit < 4000 < MaxProfit
XAUUSD	[0, 1300]	75	MinProfit < 400 < MaxProfit
OIL	[0, 30000]	70	
BTCUSD	[0, 220]	75	

To be more certain, we ran back tests with every tick value for these 100 neighborhoods of each asset, with range ±2 around their center with step 1. The missing combinations changed the min, max and average profits of the neighborhoods, which resulted in changes in their order of classification. Finally, we conducted a supervisory review of the best options and chose a neighborhood for each asset that seemed the most fitting one and served our purposes. The final parameters are presented in Table 2.

Table 2. Final parameters chosen for each asset and characteristics of their neighborhoods.

	Fast	Slow	Signal	MinProfit	MaxProfit	AvgProfit	Relative Range	MinTrades
AUDUSD	57	284	34	3693.40	8969.10	5918.32	0.8914	59
EURGBP	27	118	6	−672.23	4324.72	1274.10	3.9220	135
EURUSD	27	280	28	2403.46	6166.85	4210.10	0.8939	79
GBPUSD	15	82	14	1063.08	8268.69	4648.14	1.5502	129
USDCHF	29	132	22	736.39	6780.59	4161.61	1.4524	80
USDJPY	33	64	32	1702.63	5914.10	3545.61	1.1878	86
XAUUSD	17	160	16	240.32	1230.11	792.88	1.2484	108
OIL	51	60	34	5537.31	21058.19	12217.25	1.2704	76
BTCUSD	53	210	14	48.46	219.93	143.53	1.1946	77

3. Results and Discussion

3.1. Default/Selected Parameters and Weekends

Firstly, we compared the results for a) the simple MACD Expert Advisor with the default parameters $p_{fast} = 12$, $p_{slow} = 26$, and $p_{signal} = 9$ and without holding positions over weekends; b) the simple MACD Expert Advisor with our selected parameters and without holding positions over weekends; and c) the simple MACD Expert Advisor with our selected parameters with holding open positions over the weekends. Although the default MACD parameters refer to the daily timeframe, attempting to express two weeks, one month, and 1.5 weeks, respectively, we opted to keep them the same in the hourly timeframe instead of using the equivalent $p_{fast} = 288$, $p_{slow} = 624$, and $p_{signal} = 216$ of days expressed in hours since that would move the scale outside the HFT. By porting the default parameters to the hourly timeframe, they then expressed $\frac{1}{2}$ of a day, one day, and one work-day, which is closer to the timeframe of a daily trader doing HFT. The results of these three experiments can be seen in Tables A1 and A2 and Figures 6 and 7.

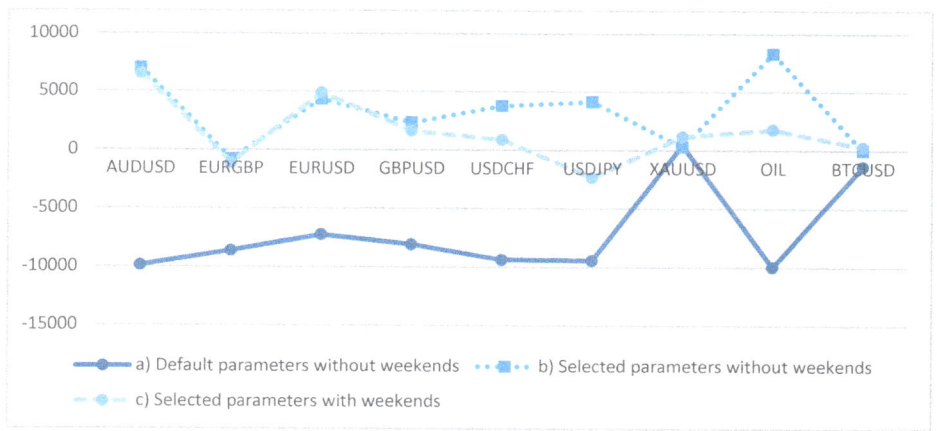

Figure 6. Net Profits of experiments (a), (b), and (c).

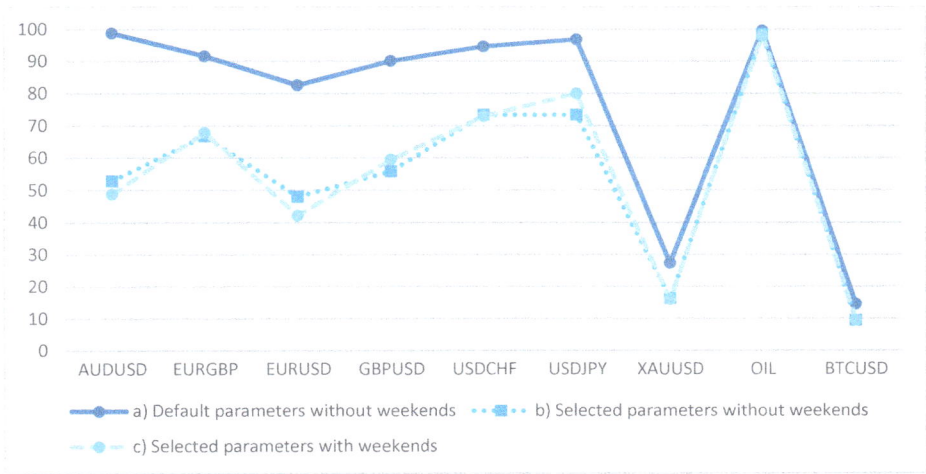

Figure 7. Drawdown, as percentage of equity, of experiments (a), (b), and (c).

It can be concluded that holding open positions over the weekends helps cut one's losses, but it also takes away a proportion of the profits for all the examined assets. Figure 6 makes clear that the net profits in most cases are diminished and Figure 7 shows the usually higher drawdown when holding positions open over the weekend. Also, using the default parameters almost always results in losses. Because of differences in contract sizes, trading hours, variability, etc., the XAUUSD, OIL, and BTCUSD show different numbers compared with the FOREX pairs (a behavior that also presents itself to the rest of the experiments) but, in the relativity of the experiments' comparisons, their numbers still support the conclusions. The Net Profits in Table A1 and, by extension, for all later experiments, are a result of the parameter selection described in Section 2.4.2., which is a posteriori process. The actual amount of returns and the profitability of the MACD Expert Advisor are not something we actually concern ourselves with in this research, but rather how these returns change by adding each Take Profit and Stop Loss strategy.

From now on, in our experiments, we will be using our selected parameters for each asset and open positions will be closed for the weekends.

3.2. Fast Take Profit Signal and Signals' Hierarchy

Next, we compared the (b) simple MACD Expert Advisor with the (d) MACD Expert Advisor, with the addition of a faster take profit signal, as described in Section 2.3.2. The determined value of the divisor N of the Fast Signal period was set as follows: N = {2,3,4}. With N = 1, the (d) Expert Advisor effectively becomes the same as (b), as the Fast Signal line becomes identical to the Signal line. Their results can be seen in Tables A3 and A4 and Figures 8 and 9.

The simple MACD yields better results in most cases, both in terms of net profits and drawdown, especially on Forex pairs. Even when assets which are traded using the MACD do not yield the most profitable results, it is postulated that the MACD ranks second after a neck-and-neck round, with a fast Take Profit signal of N = 2.

Next, we compared the (b) simple MACD Expert Advisor with the (e) MACD Expert Advisor that only opens new positions when the hierarchy of the MACD and Signal lines is right, as described in Section 2.3.3. The divisor N of the Fast Signal period assumed values of N = {2,3,4}. With N = 1, the e) Expert Advisor becomes the same as (b). Their results can be seen in Tables A5 and A6 and Figures 10 and 11.

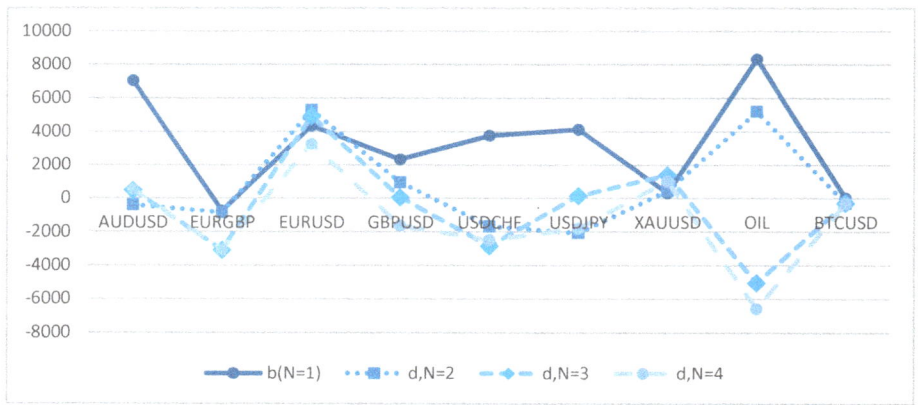

Figure 8. Net Profits of experiment (d) for various values of N.

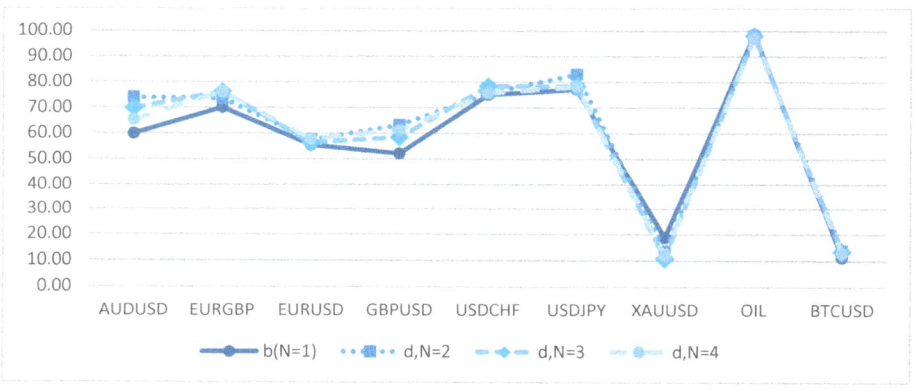

Figure 9. Drawdown, as percentage of equity, of experiment (d) for various values of N.

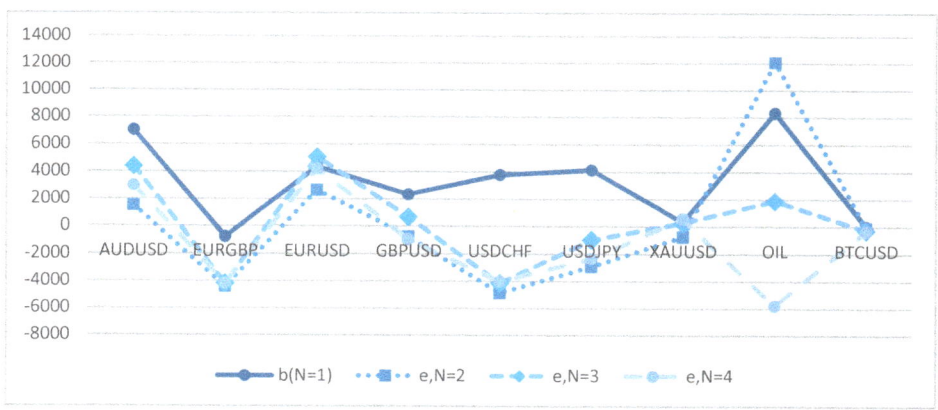

Figure 10. Net Profits of experiment (e) for various values of N.

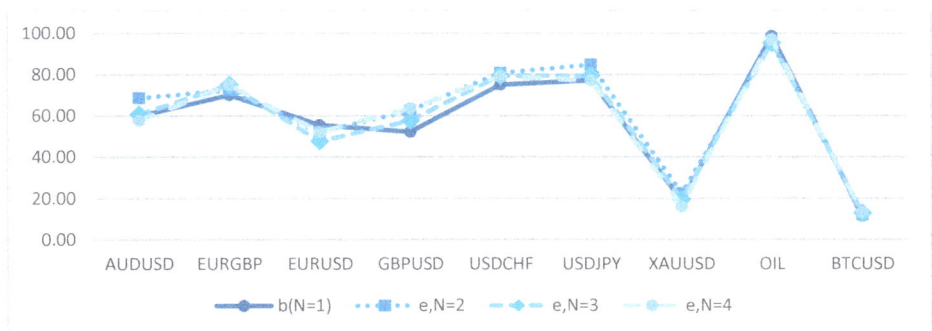

Figure 11. Drawdown, as percentage of equity, of experiment (e) for various values of N.

Again, it is evident that the simple MACD Expert Advisor generally produces better results than the MACD, which opens positions with the hierarchy of lines.

3.3. Constant ATR Zone, Sliding ATR Zone, Sliding and Variable ATR Zone

The first Stop Loss strategy we examined was f) a MACD Expert Advisor that creates a Stop Loss zone at $\pm x \times$ ATR(N) when it opens a new position and a new position prevention zone at $\pm y \times$ ATR(N), after a position has to be closed due to a Stop Loss that has been triggered. We tested every combination of parameters for N:{12,24,36,48}, x:{1,2,3,4,5,6,7}, and y:{1,2,3,4}. The Net Profits for each asset for every combination of N, x, y have been outlined in Figure 12 and Drawdown in Figure 13.

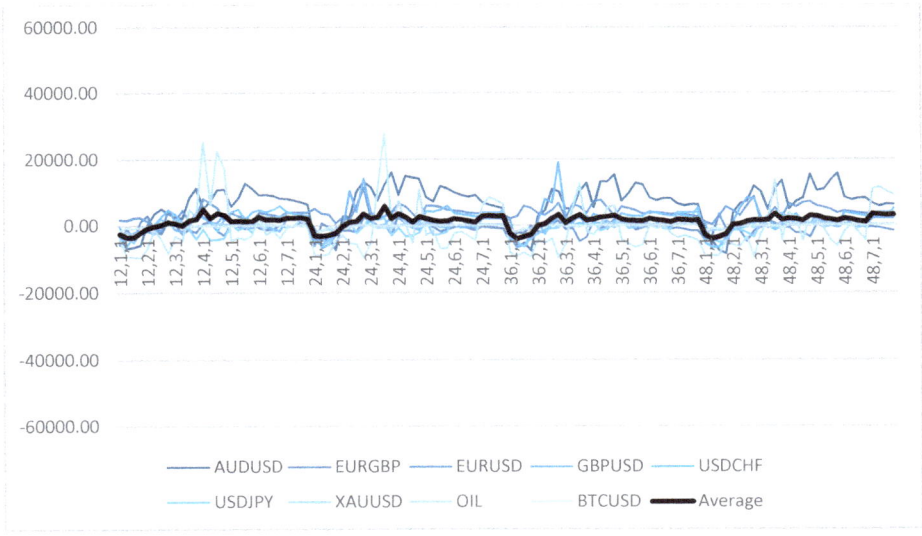

Figure 12. Net Profits of experiment (f) for various combinations of N, x, y.

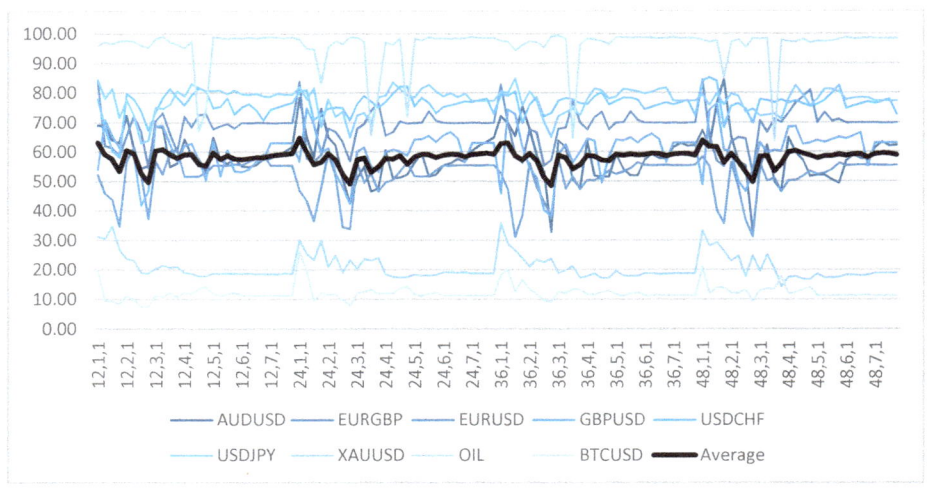

Figure 13. Drawdown, as percentage of equity, of experiment (f) for various combinations of N, x, y.

The periodicity that can be seen in Figure 12 indicates that the x multiplier plays a significant role in this strategy. For small values of x (=1), net profits are diminished for all assets, while with larger values of x (5,6,7), profits are more constant and approach those of the simple MACD, as the big ATR zone does not trigger a Stop Loss very often. Values of x (2,3,4) yield the best results compared to the others. In the drawdown diagram, there also seems to be periodicity for y, with bigger values (y = 3,4) having lower drawdown.

Next, we examined g) an MACD Expert Advisor with a sliding Stop Loss zone $\pm x \times$ ATR(N) as described in Section 2.3.6 and a constant new position prevention zone at $\pm y \times$ ATR(N). We tested every combination of parameters for N:{12,24,36,48}, x:{1,2,3,4,5,6,7}, and y:{1,2,3,4}. The Net Profits for each asset for every combination of N, x, y are displayed in Figure 14 and Drawdown in Figure 15.

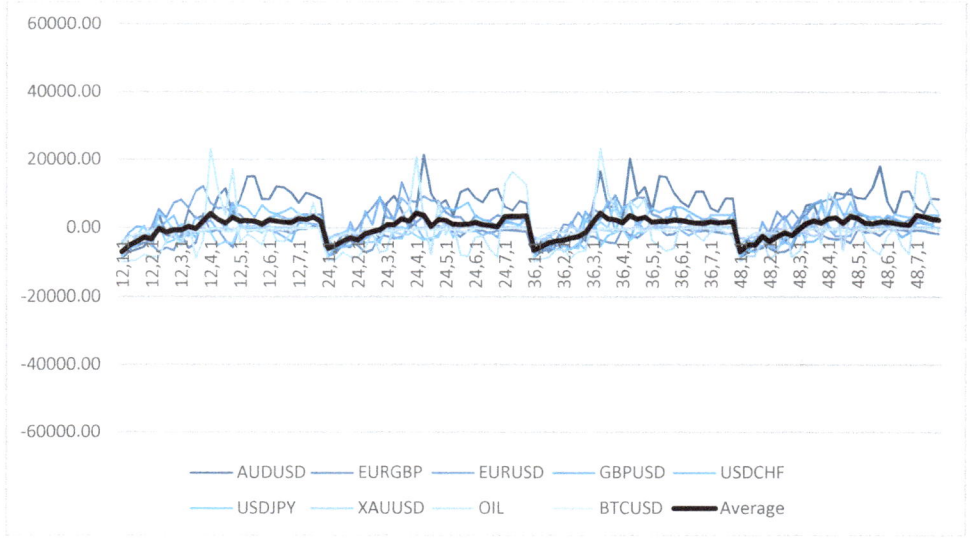

Figure 14. Net Profits of experiment (g) for various combinations of N, x, y.

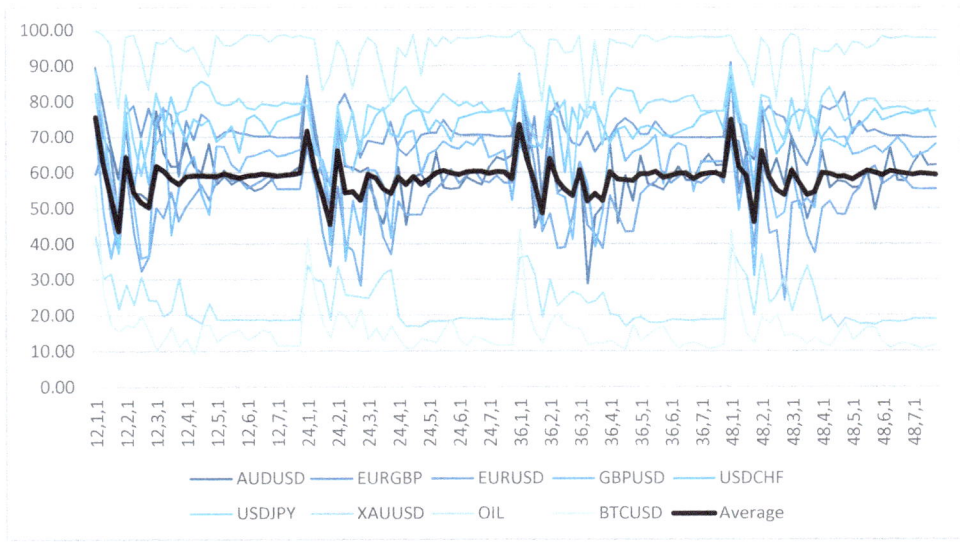

Figure 15. Drawdown, as percentage of equity, of experiment (g) for various combinations of N, x, y.

The general picture is the same as the case of (f). For small values of x, the profits are diminished, while for larger values of x, they tend to stay constant and approach the Simple MACD's results. Additionally, large values of y tend to have lower drawdown.

Finally, we examined (h) an MACD Expert Advisor with a sliding and variable Stop Loss zone $\pm x \times \text{ATR}(N)$, with a new value of ATR used at hourly intervals as described in Section 2.3.7 and a constant new position prevention zone at $\pm y \times \text{ATR}(N)$. We tested every combination of parameters for N:{12,24,36,48}, x:{1,2,3,4,5,6,7}, and y:{1,2,3,4}. The Net Profits for each asset for every combination of N, x, y have been outlined in Figure 16 and Drawdown in Figure 17.

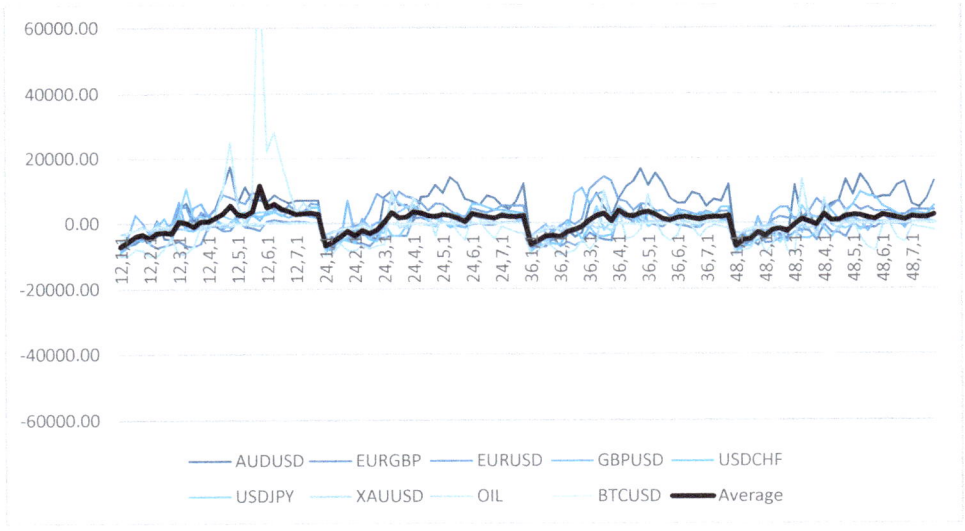

Figure 16. Net Profits of experiment (h) for various combinations of N, x, y.

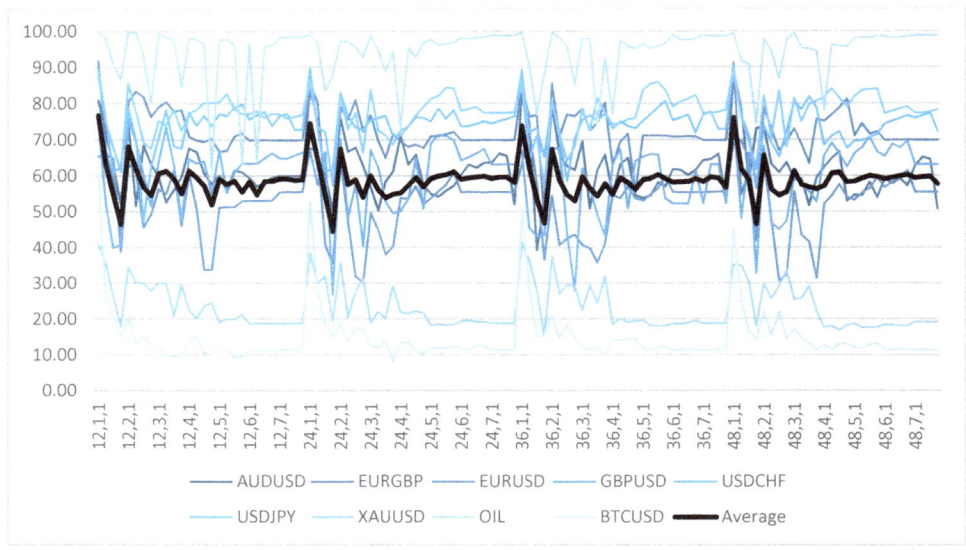

Figure 17. Drawdown, as percentage of equity, of experiment (h) for various combinations of N, *x*, *y*.

In this case, apart from the same conclusions that can be reached in the two previous tests, we can observe a clear peak in the profits in the neighborhood of (12,6,2), even when accounting for the big spikes from the OIL profits (the drawdown is also below total average in this area). This becomes more evident when we draw the diagram, Figure 18, of average profits for the (b) Simple MACD, (f) MACD with a constant ATR zone, (g) MACD with a sliding ATR zone, and (h) MACD with a sliding and variable ATR zone.

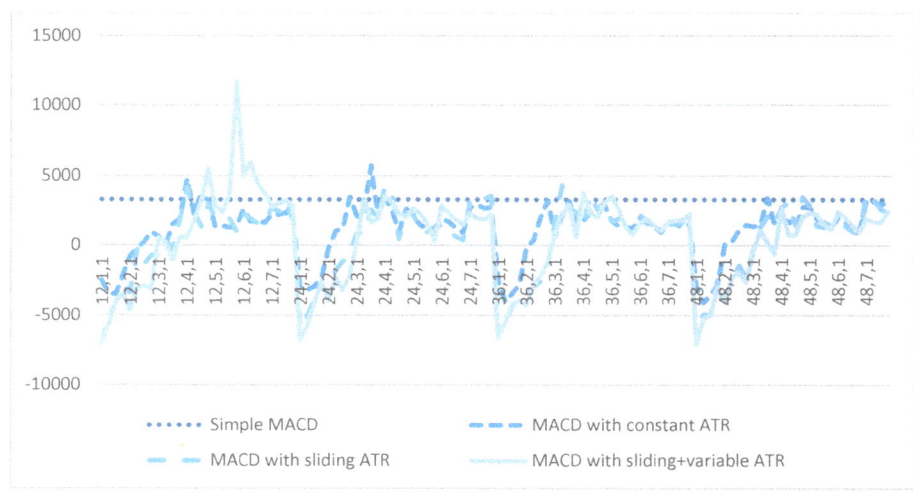

Figure 18. The averages of profits for experiments (f), (g), and (h) and the simple MACD system.

A neighborhood around 12,6,2 of MACD with sliding and variable ATR windows clearly stands out, consistently having the edge over the simple MACD, as well as the other Stop Loss strategies. Apart from some solitary peaks, the other strategies do not outperform the simple MACD system.

4. Conclusions

In the present research, we examined various Take Profit and Stop Loss strategies added to a simple MACD automated trading system used in trading 10 assets from the Forex, Metals, Energy, and Cryptocurrencies categories. In order to make the MACD parameters less important in our research, we chose parameters based on the characteristics of their neighborhoods of ± 2 and used them for all our experiments.

In our research, we first of all concluded that it is generally less profitable to keep positions open during weekends. Another conclusion we reached is that Take Profit strategies based on faster take profit signals on MACD are not far better than a simple MACD strategy. We also showed that among the different Stop Loss strategies based on ATR windows, the best and safest results come from a sliding and variable $\pm x \times \text{ATR}(N)$ window with period $N = 12$ and multiplier $x = 6$ after opening a position and a constant $\pm y \times \text{ATR}(N)$ with period $N = 12$ and multiplier $y = 2$ after stop loss closing.

Since the MACD Indicator is used quite prevalently by a lot of traders and our results are general enough, a trader could incorporate them in their technical analysis/trading strategy for Stop Loss and Take Profit without interfering with the rest of their strategy (portfolio management, capital allocation, MACD parameter selection, etc.)

Author Contributions: Conceptualization, D.V.; Investigation, D.V.; Methodology, D.V.; Software, T.K.; Supervision, C.S.; Visualization, T.K.

Funding: This research has been co-financed by the European Union and Greek national funds through the Operational Program Competitiveness, Entrepreneurship and Innovation, under the call RESEARCH—CREATE—INNOVATE (project code:T1EDK-02342).

Acknowledgments: We would like to thank COSMOS4U for providing the infrastructure used to conduct this research. We would also like to thank the anonymous referees who reviewed our paper and provided us with valuable insights and suggestions.

Conflicts of Interest: The authors declare no conflict of interest. The funders had no role in the design of the study; in the collection, analyses, or interpretation of data; in the writing of the manuscript, and in the decision to publish the results.

Appendix A

Pseudocode of the basic MACD trading strategy as described in Section 2.3.1.

```
OnTick()
{
    if(MACD line > Signal line)
    {
        if(ShortPositionsExist) CloseShortPositions();

        if(!LongPositionsExist) OpenLongPosition();
    }
    else if(MACD line < Signal line)
    {
        if(LongPositionsExist) CloseLongPositions();

        if(!ShortPositionsExist) OpenShortPosition();
    }
}
```

Pseudocode of the MACD trading strategy with a faster Take Profit Signal, as described in Section 2.3.2.

```
OnTick()
{
    if(MACD line > Take Profit Signal line)
        CloseShortPositions();
    else if(MACD line <  Take Profit Signal line)
        CloseLongPositions();

    if( (MACD line > Signal line) && (MACD line > Take Profit Signal line) )
    {
        if(ShortPositionsExist) CloseShortPositions();

        if(!LongPositionsExist) OpenLongPosition();
    }
    else if( (MACD line <  Signal line) && (MACD line <  Take Profit Signal line) )
    {
        if(LongPositionsExist) CloseLongPositions();

        if(!ShortPositionsExist) OpenShortPosition();
    }
}
```

Pseudocode of the MACD trading strategy using the Signal Lines' Hierarchy, as described in Section 2.3.3.

```
OnTick()
{
    if(MACD line > Take Profit Signal line)
        CloseShortPositions();

    else if(MACD line <  Take Profit Signal line)
        CloseLongPositions();

    if( MACD line > Take Profit Signal line > Signal line )
    {
        if(ShortPositionsExist) CloseShortPositions();

        if(!LongPositionsExist) OpenLongPosition();
    }
    else if( MACD line < Take Profit Signal line < Signal line )
    {
        if(LongPositionsExist) CloseLongPositions();

        if(!ShortPositionsExist) OpenShortPosition();
    }
}
```

Pseudocode of the MACD trading strategy with a constant ATR Stop Loss barrier zone, as described in Section 2.3.5.

```
OnTick()
{
    if(LongPositionExists)
    {
        if(Current Price < PositionOpeningPrice - x*ATR(N) )
        {
            CloseLongPosition();
        }
    }
    if(ShortPositionExists)
    {
        if(Current Price > PositionOpeningPrice + x*ATR(N) )
        {
            CloseShortPosition();
        }
    }

    if(NoPositionsExist)
    {
        if(MACD line > Signal line)
        {
            if(AfterStopLoss && Current Price < PositionClosingPrice + y*ATR(N) )
                return;
            else
            {
                CloseShortPositions();
                OpenLongPosition();
            }
        }
        else if(MACD line <  Signal line)
        {
            if(AfterStopLoss && Current Price > PositionClosingPrice - y*ATR(N) )
                return;
            else
            {
                CloseLongPositions();
                OpenShortPosition();
            }
        }
    }
}
```

Appendix B

Table A1. Results of experiments (a), (b), and (c).

	Gross Profits			Gross Losses			Net Profits		
	a	b	c	a	b	c	a	b	c
AUDUSD	13,966.24	37,297.78	31,166.56	−23,816.08	−30,282.34	−24,627.67	−9849.84	7015.44	6538.89
EURGBP	22,526.94	54,321.39	49,798.47	−31,113.62	−55,099.62	−50,929.09	−8586.68	−778.23	−1130.62
EURUSD	45,671.48	36,106.59	32,522.98	−52,901.34	−31,757.62	−27,630.16	−7229.86	4348.97	4892.82
GBPUSD	56,474.11	48,025.86	44,737.63	−64,529.80	−45,705.37	−43,091.59	−8055.69	2320.49	1646.04
USDCHF	18,662.64	27,822.32	19,855.93	−28,019.51	−24,060.67	−18,962.81	−9356.87	3761.65	893.12
USDJPY	20,697.02	27,060.23	14,940.23	−30,106.48	−22,931.07	−17,282.76	−9409.46	4129.16	−2342.53
XAUUSD	17,208.71	9107.39	9749.19	−16,773.68	−8800.84	−8564.85	435.03	306.55	1184.34
OIL	9098.18	81,584.58	57,452.95	−19,058.36	−73,261.17	−55,665.34	−9960.18	8323.41	1787.61
BTCUSD	3297.66	2410.97	2462.69	−4681.72	−2404.57	−2175.06	−1384.05	6.40	287.62

Table A2. Additional results of experiments (a), (b), and (c).

	Drawdown			Trades		
	a	b	c	a	b	c
AUDUSD	98.79	52.90	48.82	266	59	40
EURGBP	91.62	66.82	67.88	242	162	141
EURUSD	82.51	47.95	42.18	243	81	60
GBPUSD	90.03	55.78	59.42	248	152	133
USDCHF	94.56	73.40	72.92	254	83	64
USDJPY	96.80	73.36	79.95	240	86	69
XAUUSD	27.32	16.40	16.04	228	119	99
OIL	99.60	98.43	98.07	188	80	59
BTCUSD	14.45	9.44	9.50	221	84	64

Table A3. Results of experiment (d) for various values of N.

	Gross Profits				Gross Losses				Net Profits			
	b (N = 1)	d, N = 2	d, N = 3	d, N = 4	b (N = 1)	d, N = 2	d, N = 3	d, N = 4	b (N = 1)	d, N = 2	d, N = 3	d, N = 4
AUDUSD	37,294	25,474	24,725	544	−30,278	−25,896	−24,269	−29	7015	−422	456	515
EURGBP	54,415	59,520	55,503	55,503	−55,194	−60,383	−58,596	−58,596	−778	−863	−3094	−3094
EURUSD	36,116	37,642	38,389	40,268	−31,767	−32,361	−37,011	−37,011	4349	5281	4929	3257
GBPUSD	47,999	48,220	54,566	47,588	−45,679	−47,279	−54,533	−49,227	2320	941	33	−1639
USDCHF	27,829	20,634	18,821	20,256	−24,067	−22,316	−21,671	−22,752	3762	−1683	−2850	−2496
USDJPY	27,056	21,233	26,475	26,142	−22,927	−23,304	−26,338	−27,942	4129	−2072	137	−1799
XAUUSD	9115	9048	9864	9928	−8809	−8618	−8476	−8912	307	430	1388	1016
OIL	81,593	71,421	51,236	51,994	−73,269	−66,204	−56,279	−58,578	8323	5217	−5043	−6584
BTCUSD	2377	2247	2284	2265	−2371	−2554	−2586	−2576	6	−307	−302	−311

Table A4. Additional results of experiment (d) for various values of N.

	Drawdown				Trades			
	b (N = 1)	d, N = 2	d, N = 3	d, N = 4	b (N = 1)	d, N = 2	d, N = 3	d, N = 4
AUDUSD	59.84	73.92	69.72	65.13	59	67	68	74
EURGBP	70.03	73.49	76.14	76.14	162	186	210	210
EURUSD	55.44	57.48	56.33	57.82	81	88	96	104
GBPUSD	52.13	63.16	58.47	61.14	152	171	192	216
USDCHF	74.98	75.60	78.35	75.70	83	101	112	118
USDJPY	77.06	83.04	78.24	78.21	86	101	104	112
XAUUSD	18.73	13.47	10.78	11.96	119	136	152	161
OIL	98.80	97.80	98.14	97.35	80	87	93	99
BTCUSD	11.30	13.81	13.42	12.84	84	89	96	105

Table A5. Results of experiment (e) for various values of N.

	Gross Profits				Gross Losses				Net Profits			
	b (N = 1)	e, N = 2	e, N = 3	e, N = 4	b (N = 1)	e, N = 2	e, N = 3	e, N = 4	b (N = 1)	e, N = 2	e, N = 3	e, N = 4
AUDUSD	37,294	24,838	26,666	29,074	−30,278	−23,346	−22,296	−26,120	7015	1492	4370	2954
EURGBP	54,415	36,836	44,974	44,974	−55,194	−41,263	−49,168	−49,168	−778	−4428	−4194	−4194
EURUSD	36,116	28,172	35,252	37,813	−31,767	−25,534	−30,184	−33,621	4349	2638	5068	4192
GBPUSD	47,999	39,274	49,657	51,052	−45,679	−40,010	−48,985	−51,998	2320	−736	671	−946
USDCHF	27,829	15,949	16,941	17,136	−24,067	−20,830	−21,086	−21,171	3762	−4880	−4146	−4035
USDJPY	27,056	17,328	23,076	25,002	−22,927	−20,258	−24,040	−27,339	4129	−2929	−964	−2338
XAUUSD	9115	7220	7882	8678	−8809	−7950	−7623	−8112	307	−730	259	566
OIL	81,593	84,182	74,125	59,685	−73,269	−72,111	−72,253	−65,487	8323	12,071	1871	−5802
BTCUSD	2377	2085	2208	2179	−2371	−2171	−2476	−2512	6	−86	−267	−333

Table A6. Additional results of experiment (e) for various values of N.

	Drawdown				Trades			
	b (N = 1)	e, N = 2	e, N = 3	e, N = 4	b (N = 1)	e, N = 2	e, N = 3	e, N = 4
AUDUSD	59.84	68.68	60.71	57.72	59	63	65	71
EURGBP	70.03	72.45	75.01	75.01	162	175	205	205
EURUSD	55.44	51.98	47.68	52.07	81	77	91	100
GBPUSD	52.13	62.45	57.63	63.58	152	153	178	206
USDCHF	74.98	80.71	79.28	78.96	83	97	109	115
USDJPY	77.06	84.73	79.44	77.03	86	92	97	105
XAUUSD	18.73	22.35	19.39	15.90	119	124	143	153
OIL	98.80	95.67	95.32	97.05	80	76	85	91
BTCUSD	11.30	12.00	12.85	13.20	84	80	91	102

References

Appel, Gerald. 2005. *Technical Analysis: Power Tools for Active Investors*. Upper Saddle River: FT Press.

Au, Kevin, Forrest Chan, Denis Wang, and Ilan Vertinsky. 2003. Mood in foreign exchange trading: Cognitive processes and performance. *Organizational Behavior and Human Decision Processes* 91: 322–38. [CrossRef]

Austin, Mark P., Graham Bates, Michael AH Dempster, Vasco Leemans, and Stacy N. Williams. 2004. Adaptive systems for foreign exchange trading. *Quantitative Finance* 4: 37–45. [CrossRef]

Azzini, Antonia, and Andrea GB Tettamanzi. 2008a. Evolving neural networks for static single-position automated trading. *Journal of Artificial Evolution and Applications*, 17. [CrossRef]

Azzini, Antonia, and Andrea GB Tettamanzi. 2008b. Evolutionary single-position automated trading. In *Workshops on Applications of Evolutionary Computation*. Berlin/Heidelberg: Springer.

Barbosa, Rui Pedro, and Orlando Belo. 2010. Multi-Agent Forex Trading System. In *Agent and Multi-agent Technology for Internet and Enterprise Systems*. Berlin: Springer, vol. 289, pp. 91–118.

Bates, R. Graham, Michael AH Dempster, and Yazann S. Romahi. 2003. Evolutionary reinforcement learning in FX order book and order flow analysis. Paper presented at IEEE International Conference on Computational Intelligence for Financial Engineering, Hong Kong, China, March 20–23.

Bolgün, Kaan Evren, Engin Kurun, and Serhat Güven. 2010. Dynamic Pairs Trading Strategy for the Companies Listed in the Istanbul Stock. *International Review of Applied Financial Issues and Economics* 2: 37. [CrossRef]

Barber, Brad M., Yi-Tsung Lee, Yu-Jane Liu, and Terrance Odean. 2008. Just how much do individual investors lose by trading? *The Review of Financial Studies* 22: 609–32. [CrossRef]

Brogaard, Jonathan, Terrence Hendershott, and Ryan Riordan. 2014. High-frequency trading and price discovery. *The Review of Financial Studies* 27: 2267–306. [CrossRef]

Osler, Carol L. 2005. Stop-loss orders and price cascades in currency markets. *Journal of International Money and Finance* 24: 219–41. [CrossRef]

Cervelló-Royo, Roberto, Francisco Guijarro, and Karolina Michniuk. 2015. Stock market trading rule based on pattern recognition and technical analysis: Forecasting the DJIA index with intraday data. *Expert Systems with Applications* 42: 5963–75. [CrossRef]

Chaboud, Alain P., Benjamin Chiquoine, Erik Hjalmarsson, and Clara Vega. 2014. Rise of the machines: Algorithmic trading in the foreign exchange market. *The Journal of Finance* 69: 2045–84. [CrossRef]

Challet, Damien, and Ahmed Bel Hadj Ayed. 2014. Do Google Trend data contain more predictability than price returns? Available online: https://arxiv.org/abs/1403.1715 (accessed on 24 July 2018).

Chan, Oliver, and Alfred Ka Chun Ma. 2015. A Framework for Stop-Loss Analysis on Trading Strategies. *The Journal of Trading* 10: 87–95. [CrossRef]

Chevallier, Julien, Wei Ding, and Florian Ielpo. 2012. Implementing a Simple Rule for Dynamic Stop-Loss Strategies. *The Journal of Investing* 21: 111–14. [CrossRef]

Chong, Terence Tai-Leung, and Wing-Kam Ng. 2008. Technical analysis and the London stock exchange: testing the MACD and RSI rules using the FT30. *Applied Economics Letters* 15: 1111–14. [CrossRef]

Clare, Andrew, James Seaton, Peter N. Smith, and Stephen Thomas. 2013. Breaking into the blackbox: Trend following, stop losses and the frequency of trading–The case of the S&P500. *Journal of Asset Management* 14: 182–94.

Easley, David, MM Lopez De Prado, and Maureen O'Hara. 2011. The microstructure of the flash crash: Flow toxicity, liquidity crashes and the probability of informed trading. *Journal of Portfolio Management* 37: 118–28. [CrossRef]

Foucault, Thierry, Bruno Biais, and Sophie Moinas. 2011. Equilibrium High Frequency Trading. Paper presented at International Conference of the French Finance Association, Montpellier, France, May 11.

Han, Yufeng, Guofu Zhou, and Yingzi Zhu. 2016. Taming Momentum Crashes: A Simple Stop-Loss Strategy. Available online: https://ssrn.com/abstract=2407199 or http://dx.doi.org/10.2139/ssrn.2407199 (accessed on 26 July 2018).

Hendershott, Terrence, Charles M. Jones, and Albert J. Menkveld. 2011. Does algorithmic trading improve liquidity? *The Journal of Finance* 66: 1–33. [CrossRef]

Hendershott, Terrence, and Pam Moulton. 2007. *The Shrinking New York Stock Exchange Floor and the Hybrid Market*. Technical Report. Berkeley: University of California, Available online: https://docplayer.net/13539804-The-shrinking-new-york-stock-exchange-floor-and-the-hybrid-market.html (accessed on 25 July 2018).

Jain, Pankaj K. 2005. Financial market design and the equity premium: Electronic versus floor trading. *The Journal of Finance* 60: 2955–85. [CrossRef]

Kaminski, Kathryn, and Andrew W. Lo. 2014. When do stop-loss rules stop losses? *Journal of Financial Markets* 18: 234–54. [CrossRef]

Kaniel, Ron, Saar Gideon, and Titman Sheridan. 2004. Individual Investor Sentiment and Stock Returns. Available online: https://ssrn.com/abstract=1294447 (accessed on 24 July 2018).

Klement, Joachim. 2013. Assessing Stop-Loss and Re-Entry Strategies. Available online: https://ssrn.com/abstract=2277722 or http://dx.doi.org/10.2139/ssrn.2277722 (accessed on 26 July 2018).

Lei, Adam YC, and Huihua Li. 2009. The Value of Stop Loss Strategies. *Financial Services Review* 18: 23–51. [CrossRef]

Leung, Tim, and Xin Li. 2015. Optimal mean reversion trading with transaction costs and stop-loss exit. *International Journal of Theoretical and Applied Finance* 18: 1550020. [CrossRef]

Martinez, Leonardo C., Diego N. da Hora, Joao R. de M. Palotti, Wagner Meira, and Gisele L. Pappa. 2009. From an artificial neural network to a stock market day-trading system: A case study on the BM&F BOVESPA. Paper presented at International Joint Conference on Neural Networks, Atlanta, GA, USA, June 14–19.

Ni, He, and Hujun Yin. 2009. Exchange rate prediction using hybrid neural networks and trading indicators. *Neurocomputing* 72: 2815–23. [CrossRef]

Preis, Tobias, Helen Susannah Moat, and H. Eugene Stanley. 2013. Quantifying trading behavior in financial markets using Google Trends. *Scientific Reports* 3: 1684. [CrossRef] [PubMed]

Krishnan, Rajeswari, and S. Sandhya Menon. 2009. Impact of Currency Pairs, Time Frames and Technical Indicators on Trading Profit in Forex Spot Market. *International Journal of Business Insights & Transformation* 2: 34–51.

Wilder, J. Welles. 1978. *New Concepts in Technical Trading Systems*. Chicago: Investor Publishing, Inc.

Yazdi, Seyed Hadi Mir, and Ziba Habibi Lashkari. 2013. Technical Analysis of Forex by MACD Indicator. *International Journal of Humanities and Management Sciences* 1: 159–65.

Article

Predicting Currency Crises: A Novel Approach Combining Random Forests and Wavelet Transform

Lei Xu, Takuji Kinkyo and Shigeyuki Hamori *

Graduate School of Economics, Kobe University, 2-1, Rokkodai, Nada-Ku, Kobe 657-8501, Japan;
joker0813@hotmail.com (L.X.); kinkyo@econ.kobe-u.ac.jp (T.K.)
* Correspondence: hamori@econ.kobe-u.ac.jp

Received: 1 November 2018; Accepted: 1 December 2018; Published: 4 December 2018

Abstract: We propose a novel approach that combines random forests and the wavelet transform to model the prediction of currency crises. Our classification model of random forests, built using both standard predictors and wavelet predictors, and obtained from the wavelet transform, achieves a demonstrably high level of predictive accuracy. We also use variable importance measures to find that wavelet predictors are key predictors of crises. In particular, we find that real exchange rate appreciation and overvaluation, which are measured over a horizon of 16–32 months, are the most important.

Keywords: currency crisis; random forests; wavelet transform; predictive accuracy

JEL Classification: F31; F37; F47

1. Introduction

Severe economic collapse in developing countries often involves currency crises triggered by speculative attacks on the currency and sudden stops to capital inflows. An unexpectedly sharp exchange rate depreciation tends to have a contractionary effect on economic activities, owing to an extensive dollarization of liabilities in both bank and corporate balance sheets. Thus, preventing serious currency crises is considered a priority task of macroeconomic management in developing countries.

Having observed the severe economic consequences of emerging market currency crises during the 1990s, economists have searched for a reliable currency crisis prediction model. The seminal works include Frankel and Rose (1996) and Kaminsky et al. (1998). Frankel and Rose (1996) define a currency crash as the nominal depreciation of a currency's value by at least 25%, which is also at least a 10% increase in the rate of depreciation. They estimate multivariate logistic regressions and find that a currency crash tends to occur when output growth is low, the growth of domestic credit is high, and the foreign interest level is high. Kaminsky et al. (1998) propose a signaling approach, which seeks to identify the threshold values for individual predictors. They find that exports, real exchange rate overvaluation, GDP growth, foreign exchange reserves, and equity prices are the most reliable predictors of crises. Berg and Pattillo (1999) use panel probit models and show that their forecasting ability outperforms the signaling approach. Bussiere and Fratzscher (2006) use multinomial logistic regressions, which distinguish between tranquil periods, crisis periods, and post-crisis periods. They use the exchange market pressure (EMP) index originally proposed by Eichengreen et al. (1995) to define a currency crisis and show that the multinomial logistic model predicts crises better than the binomial logistic model. In a similar vein, Abiad (2003) and Peria (2002) use a Markov-switching model, which identifies and characterizes crisis periods endogenously. Shimpalee and Breuer (2006) focus on the role of institutional factors and use the probit model to show that corruption, de facto fixed exchange rates, weak government stability, and weak law and order increase the probability of crises.

The global financial crisis of 2008 has rekindled interest in this topic. Rose and Spiegel (2011, 2012) regressed the measure of crisis intensity on a set of potential predictors; however, they found few clear and reliable predictors for the cross-country incidence of severe recessions during the global financial crisis. Frankel and Frankel and Saravelos (2012) investigated whether traditional indicators can help explain why some countries were badly impacted by the global financial crisis and found that foreign exchange reserves and real exchange rate overvaluation are the most useful predictors. Gourinchas and Obstfeld (2012) employed the methods of event studies and logit regressions and found that domestic credit expansion, real exchange rate appreciation, and foreign exchange reserves are useful predictors of crises in emerging market economies. Sevim et al. (2014) used decision trees and artificial neural networks to predict currency crises in Turkey and showed that results from these two methods are superior to those obtained by logistic regressions.

In this study, we propose a novel approach that combines a machine learning technique of random forests and a signal processing method of the wavelet transform to model the prediction of currency crises. We demonstrate that our model can achieve a high level of accuracy in predicting currency crises. Our contribution to the literature is two-fold. First, we use the wavelet transform to extract key features of exchange rate behavior that may signal the risk of currency crises. The existing studies tend to focus on a particular aspect of exchange rate behavior, such as overvaluation or volatility over a particular period of time. By applying the wavelet transform, we can systemically extract various features of exchange rate behavior across different time horizons. Recent literature in economics and finance makes extensive use of wavelet analysis, indicating its usefulness as a tool for feature extraction (Reboredo and Rivera-Castro 2013; Cai et al. 2017; Faria and Verona 2018). Second, we construct a prediction model by applying the random forests method, which is a variant of decision trees. The existing literature is generally more concerned with identifying the key predictors of crises than improving the predictive accuracy (Frankel and Saravelos 2012). We choose the random forests method to construct a prediction model because it can significantly improve predictive accuracy by building a large number of trees using random input selection (Breiman 2001). In addition, the random forests method provides variable importance measures that rank predictors according to their contribution to the prediction. Thus, the random forests method also addresses the traditional question of which predictors are most reliable. Owing to its superior performance, the random forests method has been increasingly employed in the area of economic and financial forecasting (Tanaka et al. 2018).

The rest of the paper is organized as follows. In Section 2, we explain the methodology and the data. In Section 3, we evaluate the predictive accuracy of the models and present the variable importance measures. Section 4 provides our conclusions.

2. Methodology and Data

2.1. Discrete Wavelet Transformation

We applied the discrete wavelet transform (DWT) to a time series of monthly exchange rates and systemically extracted key features of exchange rate behavior over different time horizons. Specifically, we used a modified version of DWT known as the maximal overlap DWT (MODWT) because its sample size need not be restricted to a power of two. Existing studies typically measure the deviation from the trend and the volatility of exchange rates over an arbitrarily selected period of time. Our approach has an advantage over the existing methods because it evaluates various aspects of exchange rate behavior over different time horizons. The MODWT was computed using the pyramid algorithm proposed by Percival and Walden (2000)[1].

---

[1]   The computation of the MODWT is conducted using the "Wavelets" package in the R software package.

The sample variance of the exchange rate series can be decomposed into parts corresponding to the variance of the series on different scales. For a partial DWT of level J_0, the decomposition is given by:

$$\hat{\sigma}_X^2 = \frac{1}{N} \sum_{j=1}^{J_0} \left\| \widetilde{\mathbf{W}}_j \right\|^2 + \frac{1}{N} \|\widetilde{\mathbf{V}}_{J_0}\|^2 - \overline{X}^2, \tag{1}$$

where $\hat{\sigma}_X^2$ denotes the sample variance of the exchange rate series; $\widetilde{\mathbf{W}}_j$ denotes an N dimensional vector, whose element $\widetilde{W}_{j,t}$ is the jth level wavelet coefficient corresponding to a scale of $\tau_j = 2^{j-1}$; $\widetilde{\mathbf{V}}_{J_0}$ denotes an N dimensional column vector, whose element $\widetilde{V}_{J_0,t}$ is the J_0th level scaling coefficient corresponding to a scale of $\lambda_j = 2^j$; and $\overline{X}$ denotes the sample average of the exchange rate series[2]. The jth level wavelet coefficients of $\widetilde{\mathbf{W}}_j$ and the scaling coefficients of $\widetilde{\mathbf{V}}_{J_0}$ are given by:

$$\widetilde{\mathbf{W}}_j = \widetilde{B}_j \widetilde{\mathbf{V}}_{j-1} = \widetilde{B}_j \widetilde{A}_{j-1} \cdots \widetilde{A}_1 \mathbf{X}, \tag{2}$$

$$\widetilde{\mathbf{V}}_{J_0} = \widetilde{A}_{J_0} \widetilde{\mathbf{V}}_{J_0-1} = \widetilde{A}_{J_0} \widetilde{A}_{J_0-1} \cdots \widetilde{A}_1 \mathbf{X}, \tag{3}$$

where $\widetilde{B}_j$ and $\widetilde{A}_j$ are $N \times N$ matrices whose rows contain circularly shifted and up-sampled versions of the wavelet filter, $\{\widetilde{h}_l\}$, and scaling filter, $\{\widetilde{g}_l\}$, periodized to length N; N denotes the sample size; and $\mathbf{X}$ denotes an N dimensional vector, whose element $\{X_t\}$ is the exchange rate series[3].

The multi-resolution analysis (MRA) decomposes a time series of exchange rates into parts corresponding to the variation of the series on different scales. For a partial DWT of level J_0, the MRA is given by:

$$\mathbf{X} = \sum_{j=1}^{J_0} \widetilde{D}_j + \widetilde{S}_{J_0}, \tag{4}$$

where $\widetilde{D}_j$ denotes an N dimensional vector whose element $\widetilde{D}_{j,t}$ is the jth level wavelet detail corresponding to a scale, $\tau_j = 2^{j-1}$, and $\widetilde{S}_{J_0}$ denotes an N dimensional vector, whose element $\widetilde{S}_{J_0,t}$ is the J_0th level smooth function corresponding to a scale, $\lambda_j = 2^j$. The jth level details of $\widetilde{D}_j$ and the smooth function of $\widetilde{S}_{J_0}$ are given by:

$$\widetilde{D}_j = \widetilde{A}_1^T \cdots \widetilde{A}_{j-1}^T \widetilde{B}_j^T \widetilde{\mathbf{W}}_j \tag{5}$$

and

$$\widetilde{S}_{J_0} = \widetilde{A}_1^T \cdots \widetilde{A}_{J_0-1}^T \widetilde{A}_{J_0}^T \widetilde{\mathbf{V}}_{J_0}, \tag{6}$$

respectively, where $\widetilde{B}_j^T$ and $\widetilde{A}_j^T$ denote the transposers of $\widetilde{B}_j$ and $\widetilde{A}_j$, respectively[4].

A cascade of wavelet filters relating $\widetilde{W}_{j,t}$ to X_t is an approximation to a band-pass filter with the pass-band given by $[1/2^{j+1}, 1/2^j]$, while a cascade of scaling filters relating $\widetilde{V}_{j,t}$ to X_t is an approximation to a low-pass filter with the pass-band given by $[0, 1/2^{j+1}]$. Correspondingly, $\widetilde{D}_{j,t}$ represents the variation of monthly exchange rates over $2^j - 2^{j+1}$ months, while $\widetilde{S}_{j,t}$ represents the trend obtained after the sum of $\widetilde{D}_{j,t}$, up to the jth level, is removed from the series.

---

[2] Equation (1) is derived from the energy preserving condition: $\|\mathbf{X}\|^2 = \sum_{j=1}^{J_0} \left\| \widetilde{\mathbf{W}}_j \right\|^2 + \|\widetilde{\mathbf{V}}_{J_0}\|^2$.

[3] While Fourier transform coefficients are associated with frequencies, wavelet coefficients are associated with a particular scale and set of times.

[4] Using the orthonormality of DWT, the MRA is obtained by pre-multiplying both sides of Equations (2) and (3) by the transposer of $\widetilde{B}_j \widetilde{A}_{j-1} \cdots \widetilde{A}_1$ and $\widetilde{A}_{J_0} \widetilde{A}_{J_0-1} \cdots \widetilde{A}_1$, respectively.

We set $J_0 = 5$ and computed each level of $\widetilde{W}_{j,t}$, $\widetilde{V}_{j,t}$, $\widetilde{D}_{j,t}$, and $\widetilde{S}_{j,t}$ up to the fifth level. Our choice of MODWT wavelet and scaling filters are Harr filters[5], which are given by:

$$\widetilde{h}_0 = 1/2, \widetilde{h}_1 = -1/2, \widetilde{g}_0 = 1/2, \widetilde{g}_1 = -1/2. \tag{7}$$

We used a time series of $\widetilde{W}_{j,t}$, $\widetilde{V}_{j,t}$, $\widetilde{D}_{j,t}$, and $\widetilde{S}_{j,t}$ as predictors for building a classification model of random forests. Specifically, we used the square of $\widetilde{W}_{j,t}$ and $\widetilde{V}_{j,t}$ to capture the scale-by-scale contribution to the volatility of nominal exchange rates, while we used $\widetilde{D}_{j,t}$ to capture the variation of real exchange rates over various time horizons. In addition, we measured the overvaluation of real exchange rates by computing the difference between the actual value of the real exchange rates and the corresponding $\widetilde{S}_{j,t}$ on each scale. The nominal exchange rate was the end-of-period monthly bilateral dollar exchange rate, while the real exchange rate is computed by deflating the nominal exchange rate with the consumer price index (CPI). Both nominal and real exchange rates were transformed into logarithmic terms.

2.2. The EMP Index

A currency crisis can be characterized as a situation in which a country's currency is under a severe attack that leads to a sharp depreciation of exchange rates and/or a substantial loss in foreign exchange reserves. To measure the extent of downward pressures on exchange rates, many studies employ the EMP index originally proposed by Eichengreen et al. (1995). In this study, we used the modified version of the EMP index employed by Bussiere and Fratzscher (2006). The modified index is the weighted average of the annual changes of real exchange rates and foreign exchange reserves given by:[6]

$$EMP_{i,t} = \omega_{exr}\left(\frac{rexr_{i,t} - rexr_{i,t-1}}{rexr_{i,t-1}}\right) - \omega_{resr}\left(\frac{res_{i,t} - res_{i,t-1}}{res_{i,t-1}}\right), \tag{8}$$

where $rexr_{i,t}$ denotes the real exchange rate as defined above; $res_{i,t}$ denotes the foreign exchange reserves; ω_{exr} and ω_{resr} denote the inverse of the variance of change rates in exchange rates and foreign exchange reserves, respectively; and the subscripts i and t denote a specific country and time, respectively. Using this EMP index, a binary variable of currency crises is defined as follows:

$$Crisis_{i,t} = \begin{cases} 1 & \text{if } EMP_{i,t} > \mu_{EMP_{i,t}} + 2\sigma_{EMP_{i,t}} \\ 0 & \text{otherwise} \end{cases}, \tag{9}$$

where $\mu_{EMP_{i,t}}$ and $\sigma_{EMP_{i,t}}$ denote the sample mean and the standard deviation of the EMP index, respectively, for each country.

Table 1 shows the number of currency crises obtained during the sample period by using Equation (9).

---

[5] In addition to the Harr filter, we also used LA8 and D4 to derive wavelet predictors and evaluate the predictive accuracy. The reason we have chosen to use the Harr filter is because it is the only filter that produces consistent results. When we used LA8 and D4, the random forests method performed better than the logistic regression based on the balanced accuracy and the F-measure, while the latter performed better than the former based on AUC. By contrast, the random forests method consistently outperformed the logistic regression when the Harr filter was used.

[6] Although the original index also includes interest rate differentials, Kaminsky et al. (1998) removed it from their index because developing countries often adopt interest rate control. Since our sample includes many developing countries, we exclude interest rate differentials from the index. Note also that real exchange rates are used instead of nominal exchange rates to take into account differences in inflation rates across countries.

Table 1. Number of currency crises.

Year	No. of Crises
1992	1
1993	2
1994	3
1997	2
1998	1
1999	5
2002	1
2003	3
2007	1
2015	4
Total	23

2.3. Classification Model of Random Forests

In this paper, we built a classification model of random forests for predicting currency crises. An alternative method is to estimate a probit or a logistic regression, in which the probability of a crisis is regressed on a set of predictors, such as exchange rates, foreign exchange reserves, and domestic credit supply. In this study, we employed the method of random forests because it tends to perform better in terms of predictive accuracy. The random forests classification model is a variant of classification trees, which split the data at each node into smaller, more homogeneous groups. To achieve homogeneity, the classification trees search the predictor to split the data and the value at which they are split (Kuhn and Johnson 2013). The homogeneity is measured by the Gini index, which is defined for the two-class problem as:

$$Gini = p_1(1 - p_1) + p_2(1 - p_2), \tag{10}$$

where p_1 and p_2 are the probabilities for the classes. A smaller value of the Gini index implies a greater degree of homogeneity in the group.

Compared with a basic classification tree, the random forests method performs better in terms of classification accuracy for two main reasons. First, it seeks to reduce the prediction variance and, thus, to improve predictive performance over a single tree by so-called bagging, which is the building of many trees using different bootstrapped training data sets and averaging the resulting predictions. Second, it seeks to lessen correlation among trees by adding randomness to the selection of predictors at each split (Breiman 2001).

We followed Kuhn and Johnson (2013) method for building a random forests classification model and evaluated its performance[7]. Our selection of predictors was guided by Frankel and Saravelos (2012), who conducted an extensive literature survey and concluded that the most reliable indicators for predicting crises include foreign exchange reserves, the real exchange rate, the growth rate of credit, GDP, and the current account. Hence, we used the annual series of the following indicators to predict whether a crisis occurs in the following year: (i) the ratio of total reserves to GDP (res_gdp); (ii) the growth rate of total reserves; (gr_res); (iii) the growth rate of real GDP (gr_gdp); (iv) the current account balance as a percentage of GDP (ca); (v) the growth rate of broad money (gr_bm); (vi) the ratio of broad money to GDP (bm_gdp); (vii) the ratio of broad money to total reserves (bm_res); (viii) $\widetilde{D}_{j,t}\{j = 1 \sim 5\}$ for real exchange rates (dj_rer); (ix) real exchange rate overvaluation, measured by the difference between the actual value and $\widetilde{S}_{j,t}\{j = 1 \sim 5\}$ (ovj_rer); (x) the square of $\widetilde{W}_{j,t}\{j = 1 \sim 5\}$ for nominal exchange rates (wj_ner); and (xi) the square of $\widetilde{V}_{j,t}\{j = 5\}$ for nominal exchange rates (v5_ner). Note that the annual data for the wavelet predictors corresponding to

---

[7] The computation is conducted using "caret", "randomForest", and "pROC" packages in the R software package.

indicators (viii)–(xi) were constructed by averaging the monthly series obtained from the DWT for each year.

The sample for predictors covers 40 developing countries over the period 1991–2015. Thus, the corresponding sample of the EMP index covers the same countries over the period 1992–2016. The list of the sample countries is provided in the Appendix A. We selected countries for which the proportion of missing data of monthly exchange rates or CPI in the total sample was not more than 10%. The k-nearest-neighbor imputation was used to deal with the missing data. The data sources were the International Financial Statistics of the International Monetary Fund (IMF) and the World Development Indicators of the World Bank. Table 2 shows the summary statistics of the variables.

Table 2. Summary statistics. EMP: exchange market pressure.

	EMP_index	res_gdp	gr_res	gr_gdp	ca	gr_bm
Obs.	1000	1000	1000	1000	1000	1000
Mean	−0.4671	−0.0025	0.0165	−0.0009	0.0037	0.0013
Sd. dev.	1.5397	0.9801	0.9856	0.9795	0.9752	0.9773
Min	−7.6276	−2.4292	−2.8799	−4.3650	−4.2418	−2.1852
Max	4.9584	2.8716	4.6392	4.3375	2.8742	4.5146

	bm_gdp	bm_res	d1_rer	d2_rer	d3_rer	d4_rer
Obs.	1000	1000	1000	1000	1000	1000
Mean	0.0044	0.0035	−0.0001	−0.0001	−0.0001	−0.0007
Sd. dev.	0.9813	0.9799	0.0088	0.0148	0.0351	0.0837
Min	−3.7706	−2.1113	−0.0772	−0.1122	−0.2180	−0.5096
Max	3.0995	4.7506	0.0861	0.1279	0.2288	0.5434

	d5_rer	ov1_rer	ov2_rer	ov3_rer	ov4_rer	ov5_rer
Obs.	1000	1000	1000	1000	1000	1000
Mean	−0.0037	−0.0001	−0.0001	−0.0002	−0.0009	−0.0046
Sd. dev.	0.1417	0.0088	0.0229	0.0554	0.1342	0.2586
Min	−0.9524	−0.0772	−0.1684	−0.3621	−0.7815	−1.7339
Max	0.9170	0.0861	0.1924	0.4113	0.8296	1.4932

	w1_ner	w2_ner	w3_ner	w4_ner	w5_ner	v5_ner
Obs.	1000	1000	1000	1000	1000	1000
Mean	0.0025	0.0047	0.0098	0.0208	0.0445	0.8894
Sd. dev.	0.0120	0.0165	0.0300	0.0604	0.1142	1.2783
Min	0.0000	0.0000	0.0000	0.0000	0.0000	0.0000
Max	0.1614	0.2000	0.3433	0.7592	1.0942	10.6675

3. Results

3.1. Wavelet Predictors

Table 3 compares the mean and standard deviations of wavelet predictors between the crisis and non-crisis samples. The former includes the observations of wavelet predictors in the year immediately before a crisis, while the latter includes those in the year immediately before a year with no crisis.

There are three points worth noting here. First, the means for all levels of dj_rer in the crisis sample were negative, while those in the non-crisis sample were positive. The *t*-test rejects the null hypothesis that the mean is the same across the two samples for all levels of dj_rer. These results indicate that the appreciation of the real exchange rate over various time horizons was associated with a crisis in the following year. In other words, the appreciation of the real exchange rate signals the risk of a crisis. Second, the means for all levels of ovj_rer in the crisis sample were negative, while those in the non-crisis sample were positive. The corresponding *t*-test rejects the null hypothesis of the same mean for all levels of ov_rer. The results indicate that the overvaluation of the real exchange rate over various time horizons signals the risk of a crisis. Third, the means of wj_ner (*j* = 1~5) and v5_ner in the crisis sample were larger than those in the non-crisis sample. However, the *t*-test rejects the null hypothesis of the same mean only for W5_ner at the 5% significance level. The results indicate that a greater volatility of the nominal exchange rate measured by the square of W5_ner signals the risk of a crisis.

Table 3. Wavelet predictors (crisis vs. non-crisis).

	d1_rer		d2_rer		d3_rer		d4_rer		d5_rer	
	Mean	Std. dev.	Mean	Std. dev.	Mean	Std. dev.	Mean	Std. dev.	Mean	Std. dev.
Crisis	−0.0083	0.0155	−0.0164	0.0215	−0.0438	0.0405	−0.1163	0.0800	−0.1775	0.1416
Non-crisis	0.0001	0.0085	0.0003	0.0144	0.0010	0.0343	0.0020	0.0818	0.0004	0.1392
t-test (*p*-value)	0.0084		0.0006		0.0000		0.0000		0.0000	

	ov1_rer		ov2_rer		ov3_rer		ov4_rer		ov5_rer	
	Mean	Std. dev.	Mean	Std. dev.	Mean	Std. dev.	Mean	Std. dev.	Mean	Std. dev.
Crisis	−0.0083	0.0155	−0.0246	0.0366	−0.0684	0.0759	−0.1847	0.1511	−0.3622	0.2516
Non-crisis	0.0001	0.0085	0.0005	0.0222	0.0014	0.0538	0.0034	0.1308	0.0038	0.2528
t-test (*p*-value)	0.0084		0.0017		0.0001		0.0000		0.0000	

	w1_ner		w2_ner		w3_ner		w4_ner		w5_ner	
	Mean	Std. dev.	Mean	Std. dev.	Mean	Std. dev.	Mean	Std. dev.	Mean	Std. dev.
Crisis	0.0117	0.0349	0.0180	0.0467	0.0355	0.0860	0.0741	0.1726	0.1613	0.2912
Non-crisis	0.0023	0.0108	0.0044	0.0150	0.0092	0.0272	0.0195	0.0547	0.0417	0.1053
t-test (*p*-value)	0.1056		0.0888		0.0784		0.0720		0.0309	

	v5_ner	
	Mean	Std. dev.
Crisis	1.1793	1.5044
Non-crisis	0.8826	1.2719
t-test (*p*-value)	0.1790	

Note: *t*-test is Welch's test for one-sided hypothesis.

Based on these analyses, we speculate that wavelet predictors will play an important role in constructing prediction models for currency crises.

3.2. Predictive Accuracy of the Random Forests Classification Model

We constructed a random forests classification model using both standard predictors and wavelet predictors, as discussed in Section 2.3. For the purpose of comparison, we also estimated a conventional logistic regression. We kept the subset of the predictor sample covering the period 2011–2015 as the test set for evaluating model performance. Thus, the training set used for building the model was the subset of the sample covering the period 1991–2010. To reduce model bias arising from the imbalance in sizes between the crisis and non-crisis samples, we truncated the non-crisis sample by selecting only those observations for crisis-hit countries corresponding to the two years prior to the crisis. Hence, if a country was hit by a crisis in 1997, the observation of the predictors for 1996 was included in the crisis sample and the observations of the predictors for 1994–1995 were included in the non-crisis sample. This represents an addition of three observations to the training set[8].

Table 4 shows the evaluation of the predictive accuracy of the two models[9]. The results are shown for probability thresholds of 50% and 70%. In the former, we predicted a crisis if the probability of a crisis predicted by a model exceeds 50%, while in the latter we predicted a crisis only if the probability exceeds 70%.

---

[8] As a result of the truncation, the number of observations in the training set is 53, of which the number of crisis and non-crisis is 19 and 34, respectively. The test set includes all 200 observations, of which the number of crises and non-crisis is 4 and 196, respectively.

[9] We use the set.seed ( ) function in R to reproduce the results. Our results for predictive accuracy and variable importance measures are obtained when the function takes the value of 10. Regarding the choice of key parameters, notably, the number of tress to grow, the minimum size of terminal nodes, and the maximum number of terminal nodes, we use the default values given by "randomForests" package, which are 500, 1, and NULL (which implies that trees are grown to the maximum possible, subject to limits by the minimum size of terminal nodes), respectively.

Table 4. Predictive accuracy of the models. AUC: area under the receiver operating characteristic curve.

	50%	Threshold	70%	Threshold
	Random Forests	**Logistic Regression**	**Random Forests**	**Logistic Regression**
Sensitivity	0.9565	0.8696	0.8696	0.8696
Specificity	0.8608	0.8270	0.9222	0.8301
Balanced accuracy	0.9087	0.8483	0.8959	0.8499
F-measure	0.9061	0.8478	0.8951	0.8494
	Random Forests	**Logistic Regression**		
AUC	0.9496	0.857		

The sensitivity is defined as the ratio that a crisis is predicted accurately for all samples having a crisis event, and is given by:

$$\text{sensitivity} = \frac{\text{samples with a crisis event and predicted to have a crisis}}{\text{samples with a crisis event}}.$$

The sensitivity is synonymous with the true-positive rate. By contrast, the specificity is defined as the ratio that a non-crisis is predicted accurately for all samples without a crisis event, which is given by:

$$\text{specificity} = \frac{\text{samples without a crisis event and predicted to have no crisis}}{\text{samples without a crisis event}}.$$

The false-positive rate is defined as one minus the specificity. Since there tends to be a trade-off between the sensitivity and the specificity, the balanced accuracy and the F-measure are often used to evaluate the overall accuracy. The former is the arithmetic mean of the sensitivity and the specificity, while the latter is the harmonic mean. As can be seen from the table, the levels of sensitivity, specificity, balanced accuracy, and the F-measure are fairly high for both the random forests method and the logistic regression. Overall, the random forests method performs better than the logistic regression in terms of classification accuracy. Note that both the balanced accuracy and the F-measure for the random forests method exceed 0.9 based on the 50% threshold.

We also used a receiver operating characteristic (ROC) curve to evaluate the predictive accuracy of the models. A ROC curve was constructed by plotting the true-positive rate and the false-positive rate against each other for each candidate threshold. The measure of the overall performance of the model was given by the area under the ROC curve (AUC). A larger value of AUC implies a better predictive performance of the model. The level of AUC was fairly high for both the random forests and the logistic regression, and the former performed better than the latter in terms of overall accuracy.

3.3. Variable Importance Measures

A valuable property of the random forests method is that it provides variable importance measures that rank predictors according to their contribution to the prediction. The variable importance measure was calculated by adding up the total reduction in the Gini index by splits over a given predictor, averaged over all bagged trees.

Figure 1 shows the variable importance measure for each predictor. Among the range of wavelet predictors, ov4_rer and d4_rer are the most important crisis predictors. The result is in line with the existing literature that emphasizes the importance of the real exchange rate overvaluation in signaling the risk of currency crises (see, for example, Kaminsky et al. 1998; Frankel and Saravelos 2012; Gourinchas and Obstfeld 2012). The remaining top five predictors include ov3_rer, d3_rer, and w5_ner. It is worth noting that the volatility of nominal exchange rates is also an important crisis predictor. In contrast to common perception, the level of foreign exchange reserves or the growth rate of domestic credit are less important crisis predictors in our model.

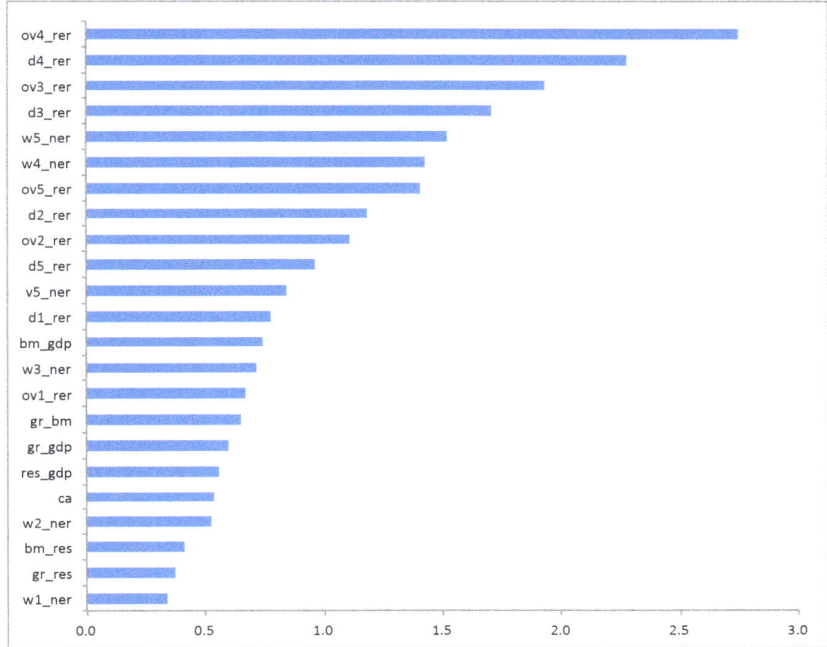

Figure 1. Variable importance measures.

To summarize, we found that wavelet predictors, which capture the features of exchange rate behavior over various time horizons, are the key currency crisis predictors. In particular, we found that real exchange rate appreciation and overvaluation, which are measured over a horizon of 16–32 months, are the most important predictors. We also found that nominal exchange rate volatility, which was measured over a horizon of 32–64 months, is an important predictor.

4. Conclusions

In this study, we proposed a novel approach that combines a machine learning technique of random forests and a signal processing method of the wavelet transform to model the prediction of currency crises. In the first step, we used the wavelet transform to systemically extract key features of exchange rate behavior that may signal the risk of currency crises. Next, we built a random forests classification model using both standard predictors identified in the literature and wavelet predictors obtained from the wavelet transform. We demonstrated that the prediction model constructed by the random forests method can achieve a high level of predictive accuracy, presumably because the wavelet transform can better extract key features of exchange rate behavior while the random forests can improve accuracy by combining a large number of trees using random input selection. We also used the variable importance measures to find that wavelet predictors, which capture the features of exchange rate behavior over various time horizons, are key currency crisis predictors. In particular, we find that real exchange rate appreciation and overvaluation, which are measured over a horizon of 16–32 months, are the most important crisis predictors.

We believe that our novel approach to modeling the prediction of currency crises will prove useful in detecting the risk of crises and, thus, in taking preemptive action. One constraint on the practical use of our model is the limited availability of monthly data on exchange rates and price indices in developing countries. Future research may focus more on establishing an effective method of imputation that renders our approach more robust to missing data.

Author Contributions: S.H. and T.K. conceived and designed the experiments; L.X. performed the experiments, analyzed the data, and contributed reagents/materials/analysis tools; L.X., S.H., and T.K. wrote the paper.

Funding: This research was supported by JSPS KAKENHI Grant Number 17K18564, (A) 17H00983, and 18K01610.

Acknowledgments: We are grateful to two anonymous referees for their helpful comments and suggestions.

Conflicts of Interest: The authors declare no conflict of interest. The founding sponsors had no role in the design of the study, in the collection, analyses, or interpretation of data, in the writing of the manuscript, or in the decision to publish the results.

Appendix A. List of Sample Countries

Algeria, Bulgaria, Burundi, Cabo Verde, Central African Republic, Chad, Chile, China, Colombia, Dominican Republic, Egypt, Equatorial Guinea, Gabon, Gambia, Guatemala, Honduras, Hungary, Kenya, Madagascar, Malawi, Malaysia, Mauritius, Mexico, Namibia, Nigeria, Peru, Philippines, Poland, Romania, Seychelles, South Africa, Sri Lanka, Sudan, Thailand, Tunisia, Turkey, Uganda, Uruguay, Venezuela, Zambia.

References

Abiad, Abdul. 2003. Early Warning Systems: A Survey and a Regime Switching Approach. IMF Working paper No. 03/23, International Monetary Fund, Washington, DC, USA.

Berg, Andrew, and Catherine Pattillo. 1999. Predicting currency crises: The indicator approach and an alternative. *Journal of International Money and Finance* 18: 561–86. [CrossRef]

Breiman, Leo. 2001. Random forests. *Machine Learning* 45: 5–32. [CrossRef]

Bussiere, Matthieu, and Marcel Fratzscher. 2006. Towards a new early warning system of financial crises. *Journal of International Money and Finance* 25: 953–73. [CrossRef]

Cai, Xiao Jing, Shuairu Tian, Nannan Yuan, and Shigeyuki Hamori. 2017. Interdependence between Oil and East Asian Stock Markets: Evidence from Wavelet Coherence Analysis. *Journal of International Financial Markets, Institutions and Money* 48: 206–23. [CrossRef]

Eichengreen, Barry, Andrew K. Rose, and Charles Wyplosz. 1995. Exchange market mayhem: The antecedents and aftermath of speculative arracks. *Economic Policy* 21: 249–312. [CrossRef]

Faria, Gonçalo, and Fabio Verona. 2018. Forecasting stock market returns by summing the frequency decomposed parts. *Journal of Empirical Finance* 45: 228–42. [CrossRef]

Frankel, Jeffrey A., and Andrew K. Rose. 1996. Currency crashes in emerging markets: An empirical treatment. *Journal of International Economics* 41: 351–66. [CrossRef]

Frankel, Jeffrey, and George Saravelos. 2012. Can leading indicators assess country vulnerability? Evidence from the 2008–2009 global financial crisis. *Journal of International Economics* 87: 216–31. [CrossRef]

Gourinchas, Pierre-Olivier, and Maurice Obstfeld. 2012. Stories of the twentieth century for the twenty-first. *American Economic Journal: Macroeconomics* 4: 226–65. [CrossRef]

Kaminsky, Graciela, Saul Lizondo, and Carmen M. Reinhart. 1998. The leading indicators of currency crises. *IMF Staff Paper* 45: 1–48. [CrossRef]

Kuhn, Max, and Kjell Johnson. 2013. *Applied Predictive Modeling*. New York: Springer.

Percival, Donald B., and Andrew T. Walden. 2000. *Wavelet Methods for Time Series Analysis*. Cambridge: Cambridge University Press.

Peria, Maria Soledad Martinez. 2002. A regime-switching approach to the study of speculative attacks: A focus on EMS crises. *Empirical Economics* 27: 299–334. [CrossRef]

Reboredo, Juan C., and Miguel A. Rivera-Castro. 2013. A Wavelet decomposition approach to crude oil price and exchange rate dependence. *Economic Modelling* 32: 42–57. [CrossRef]

Rose, Andrew K., and Mark M. Spiegel. 2011. Cross-country causes and consequences of the crisis: An update. *European Economic Review* 55: 309–24. [CrossRef]

Rose, Andrew K., and Mark M. Spiegel. 2012. Cross-country causes and consequences of the 2008 crisis: Early warning. *Japan and the World Economy* 24: 1–16. [CrossRef]

Sevim, Cuneyt, Asil Oztekin, Ozkan Bali, Serkan Gumus, and Erkam Guresen. 2014. Developing an early warning system to predict currency crises. *European Journal of Operational Research* 237: 1095–104. [CrossRef]

Shimpalee, Pattama L., and Janice Boucher Breuer. 2006. Currency crises and institutions. *Journal of International Money and Finance* 25: 125–45. [CrossRef]

Tanaka, Katsuyuki, Takuji Kinkyo, and Shigeyuki Hamori. 2018. Financial hazard map: Financial vulnerability predicted by a random forests classification model. *Sustainability* 10: 1530. [CrossRef]

Article

Predicting Micro-Enterprise Failures Using Data Mining Techniques

Aneta Ptak-Chmielewska

Institute of Statistics and Demography, Warsaw School of Economics, Warsaw 02-554, Poland;
aptak@sgh.waw.pl; Tel.: +48-22-564-92-70

Received: 30 December 2018; Accepted: 3 February 2019; Published: 10 February 2019

Abstract: Research analysis of small enterprises are still rare, due to lack of individual level data. Small enterprise failures are connected not only with their financial situation abut also with non-financial factors. In recent research we tend to apply more and more complex models. However, it is not so obvious that increasing complexity increases the effectiveness. In this paper the sample of 806 small enterprises were analyzed. Qualitative factors were used in modeling. Some simple and more complex models were estimated, such as logistic regression, decision trees, neural networks, gradient boosting, and support vector machines. Two hypothesis were verified: (i) not only financial ratios but also non-financial factors matter for small enterprise survival, and (ii) advanced statistical models and data mining techniques only insignificantly increase the prediction accuracy of small enterprise failures. Results show that simple models are as good as more complex model. Data mining models tend to be overfitted. Most important financial ratios in predicting small enterprise failures were: operating profitability of assets, current assets turnover, capital ratio, coverage of short-term liabilities by equity, coverage of fixed assets by equity, and the share of net financial surplus in total liabilities. Among non-financial factors only two of them were important: the sector of activity and employment.

Keywords: data mining; bankruptcy prediction; financial and non-financial variables

1. Introduction

Since the announcement of the Altman's Z-Score model (Altman 1968), a large number of statistical bankruptcy prediction studies were written using the traditional methods, like discriminant analysis (Back et al. 1996), logistic regression (Aziz and Dar 2006; Back et al. 1996), and probit analysis (Zmijewski 1984). Recent studies in this area focus on more advanced and sophisticated methods, like case-based reasoning (Sartori et al. 2016), genetic algorithms (Back et al. 1996), and neural networks (Blanco-Oliver et al. 2013) or support vector machines (Kim and Sohn 2010).

Sartori et al. (2016) applied the case-based reasoning (CBR) paradigm to forecast the bankruptcy and compared the results received with the Z-Score model. The CBR method turned out to be good in predicting bankruptcy. The authors found that this approach could be useful to cluster enterprises according to opportune similarity metrics.

Genetic algorithms (GAs) were another method used in SMEs' default prediction analysis. Gordini (2014) compared the potential of genetic algorithms with two other methods: logistic regression (LR) and support vector machine (SVM). The results obtained suggest that GAs are a very effective and promising method in assessing the probability of SMEs bankruptcy compared with LR and SVM, especially in reducing type II misclassification rates. The author also investigated whether the size of firms and the geographical area of their operation can influence the accuracy of the models and, again, the results obtained from separate models built to custom for separate geographical areas show that GAs prediction accuracy in each area is superior to that of the other models.

Lahmiri (2016a) in this paper compared several predictive models that combine features selection techniques with data mining classifiers in the context of credit risk assessment in terms of accuracy, sensitivity, and specificity. He used the support vector machine (SVM), back-propagation neural network, radial basis function neural network, linear discriminant analysis, and naive Bayes classifier. Results from three datasets using a 10-fold cross-validation technique showed that the SVM provides the best accuracy. The SVM seems to be an attractive classifier to be used in real applications for bankruptcy prediction. In his later works Lahmiri (2017) proposed a two-step system to improve prediction of telemarketing outcomes and to help the marketing management team effectively manage customer relationships in the banking industry. Several neural networks were trained with different categories of information to make initial predictions. Next, all initial predictions were combined by a single neural network to make a final prediction. Empirical results indicated that the two-step system presented performs better than all its individual components. According to author the proposed two-step system seems to be robust to noisy and nonlinear data, easy to interpret, suitable for large and heterogeneous marketing databases, fast and easy to implement.

Sohn et al. (2016) proposed an approach based on fuzzy logistic regression that can be used in the default prediction models. Moreover, the authors showed that the proposed approach outperforms the logistic regression model in terms of discriminatory power. Similarly, Chaudhuri and De (2011) used the fuzzy support vector machine which outperformed traditional bankruptcy prediction methods.

Traditional analysis of company financial condition is based on financial factors. However, it is worth considering whether other indicators can be significant. This problem was addressed by few researchers. Jiménez and Saurina (2004) discussed the role of a limited set of variables, namely: collateral, type of lender and bank-borrower relationship. According to their results, collateralized loans have higher probability of default and loans granted by savings banks are riskier. Additionally, authors found that a close relationship between the bank and the customer increases the willingness to take more risk.

Psillaki et al. (2010) showed that non-financial performance indicators are useful ex ante determinants of business failure. Using the companies' datasets from three different French manufacturing industries they proved that managerial inefficiencies are an important ex ante indicator of a firm's financial risk. The results suggest that more efficient firms, as well as firms with more liquid assets are less likely to fail. A similar approach was taken by Fabling and Grimes (2005), who used regional as well as national data. They analyzed the role of property prices, which influenced the collateral values. According to the authors' findings the interactions between economic activity, leverage and property price (collateral) shocks indicate that region-specific shocks can compound into significant localized economic cycles.

A variation of the approach was suggested by Kalak and Hudson (2016). Using a US dataset of companies that became insolvent in between 1980 and 2013, the authors built four discrete-time duration-dependent hazard models for SMEs, micro-, small-, and medium-sized companies. Authors indicated that there are significant differences between micro and small firms and these categories should be considered separately when building the credit risk models. Analogous to Kalak and Hudson (2016), Gupta et al. (2015) investigated how the SMEs size can affect credit risk. Their research results suggest that separate models for micro firms are desired. In case of small and medium companies, there is no such a need as the determinants present similar level of hazard.

Ong et al. (2005) analyzed usage of the genetic programming in building credit scoring models. According to their results, model built with genetic programming (GP) outperformed models built with other methods, namely the artificial neural networks ANN, decision trees, rough sets, and logistic regression. Huang et al. (2006), proposed building a two-stage genetic programming (2SGP) model as it achieves better results than other models. Berg (2007) used different accounting-based models for bankruptcy prediction. Obtained results suggest that generalized additive models outperform models like linear discriminant analysis, generalized linear models and neural networks. In order to identify defaulted SMEs, Calabrese et al. (2015) investigated a binary regression accounting-based model. Results obtained suggest that their approach outperformed the classical logistic regression model for different default horizons considered.

Lahmiri (2016b) also compared the forecasting ability of different data mining techniques like the backpropagation neural network (BPNN) and the nonlinear autoregressive moving average with exogenous inputs (NARX) network trained with different optimization algorithms. The simulation results showed that in general the NARX which is a dynamic system outperforms the popular BPNN. In addition, conjugate gradient algorithms provide better prediction accuracy than the Levenberg-Marquardt algorithm widely used in the literature in modeling exponential signals. However, the LM performed the best when used for forecasting the Moroccan and South African stock price indices under both the BPNN and NARX systems.

In his later paper Lahmiri (2016c) compared the accuracy of three hybrid intelligent systems in forecasting ten international stock market indices; namely the CAC40, DAX, FTSE, Hang Seng, KOSPI, NASDAQ, NIKKEI, S and P 500, Taiwan stock market price index, and the Canadian TSE. Based on out-of-sample simulation results, he found that contrary to the literature GA-TDNN significantly outperforms GA-ATDNN. In addition, ANFIS was found to be more effective in forecasting CAC40, FTSE, Hang Seng, NIKKEI, Taiwan, and the TSE price level. In contrary, GA-TDNN and GA-ATDNN were found to be superior to ANFIS in predicting DAX, KOSPI, and NASDAQ future prices.

In Poland the first corporate bankruptcies took place in 1990 after start of economic transformation. Predicting corporate bankruptcies in Poland have been of interest to the researchers since 1990s, but since then the studies dealing with this subject have been numerous. For this reason, only an overview of the selected literature on this topic is mentioned below. The very first research was aimed at applying foreign models, like the Altman model, to predict bankruptcies of Polish enterprises (Mączyńska 1994). At the same time the Polish researchers started using financial ratios analysis (Wędzki 2000; Stępień and Strąk 2003; Prusak 2005), and build first national models (Pogodzińska and Sojak 1995; Gajdka and Stos 1996; Hadasik 1998; Wierzba 2000). Due to the limited access to the data, these models were based on small samples and mainly on multivariate linear discriminant analysis. Later on other models were applied and the sizes of the data samples were larger (Hołda 2001; Sojak and Stawicki 2000; Mączyńska 2004; Appenzeller and Szarzec 2004; Korol 2004; Hamrol et al. 2004; Prusak 2005; Jagiełło 2013). Next the newer statistical techniques also were used, such as the logit models (Gruszczyński 2003; Michaluk 2003; Wędzki 2004; Stępień and Strąk 2004; Prusak and Więckowska 2007; Jagiełło 2013; Pociecha et al. 2014; Karbownik 2017), neural networks, other genetic algorithms, classification trees or survival analysis using the Cox model (Michaluk 2003; Korol 2004; Pociecha et al. 2014; Gąska 2016; Ptak-Chmielewska 2016), the k-nearest neighbors method, kernel classifiers, random forests, Bayesian networks, support vectors, and fuzzy logic and methods for ensemble models (Korol 2010b; Gąska 2016, Zięba et al. 2016). In addition to universal models, many sectoral models were created (Brożyna et al. 2016; Balina and Bąk 2016; Jagiełło 2013; Karbownik 2017). The criterion of enterprise size were utilized (Jagiełło 2013). Not only financial ratios, but also non-financial factors and macroeconomic variables were used as explanatory variables to construct the models of enterprise bankruptcy risk assessment (Korol 2010a; Ptak-Chmielewska and Matuszyk 2017). In addition, the risk of bankruptcy depends on the economic cycle and therefore suggested that enterprise bankruptcy forecasting models should consider measures showing changes in economic conditions (Pociecha and Pawełek 2011).

Błażej (2018) Prusak's article *Review of Research into Enterprise Bankruptcy Prediction in Selected Central and Eastern European Countries* (International Journal of Financial Studies, published: 22 June 2018) used a literature review as a research method. The author presented the results of the research on corporate bankruptcy prediction related to highly-developed countries, which reached many years back and covered the main research and a comparative basis for the Central and Eastern European countries. Collected material included countries which founded the CMEA (Council for Mutual Economic Assistance) or which later emerged as a result of its collapse (Poland, Lithuania, Latvia, Estonia, Ukraine, Hungary, Russia, Slovakia, Czech Republic, Romania, Bulgaria, Belarus). Information on the publications covered the period of Q4 2016–Q3 2017 from Google Scholar and ResearchGate databases. Based on such wide literature review author proposed the ratings described below (Prusak 2018, p. 17):

- Rating 0—There are no studies in enterprise bankruptcy risk prediction in the given country.
- Rating 1—Analyses are conducted to assess the risk of bankruptcy of enterprises using only foreign models in the country concerned.
- Rating 2—Both national and foreign models are used to assess the risk of business insolvency in the country concerned, with national models being constructed using less sophisticated statistical methods, i.e., linear multidimensional discriminant analysis, logit and probit methods, etc.
- Rating 3—Both national and foreign models are used to assess the risk of business insolvency in the country concerned, with national models being constructed using also more advanced methods: artificial neural networks, genetic algorithms, the support vector method, fuzzy logic, etc. Moreover, national sectoral models are also estimated.
- Rating 4—The most advanced methods are used in enterprise bankruptcy risk forecasting in the country concerned and the researchers propose new solutions that affect the development of this discipline.

According to author's assessment Poland grade was the highest 4.0 with following comment (Prusak 2018, p. 17): "Numerous studies have been performed in this area. Many national and sectoral models have been evaluated using the latest statistical methods. Both financial and non-financial information have been used as explanatory variables. Additionally, attention was paid to the impact of the economic climate on the efficiency of models for the forecasting of enterprise insolvency."

Other rated countries got grades from the lowest: Belarus (1.5), Bulgaria (1.5), Latvia (2.0), Romania (2.0), Lithuania (2.5), Ukraine (2.5), medium grade like: Estonia (3.0), Hungary (3.0), Russia (3.0), Slovakia (3.5) to the highest: Czech Republic (4.0).

In my research I focused on two research hypothesis to be verified:

Hypothesis 1 (H1): *Not only financial ratios but also non-financial factors matter for small enterprises survival.*

Hypothesis 2 (H2): *Advanced statistical models and data mining techniques only insignificantly increase the prediction accuracy of small enterprise failures modeling.*

2. Materials and Methods

In this research the sample of 806 small enterprises was used including 311 bankruptcies and 495 non-bankrupted enterprises for bankruptcy prediction. Sample covered the equal proportion of enterprises from sectors: industry, trade and services. The financial statements covered the period of 2008–2010. The bankruptcy events took place between 2009 and 2012, a 12-month observation period was considered. The data were kindly provided by a consultancy firm operating on the Polish market. From a long list of financial ratios only 16 were selected based on univariate analysis:

		Mean	SD
w1	Current liquidity	1.877	1.584
w2	Quick ratio	1.351	1.236
w3	Liquidity cash	0.406	0.655
w4	Capital share in assets	0.149	0.326
w5	Gross margin	0.058	0.134
w6	Operating profitability of sales	0.022	0.101
w7	Operating profitability of assets	0.040	0.189

w8	Net profitability of equity	0.180	0.583
w9	Assets turnover	2.419	1.484
w10	Current assets turnover	3.860	2.308
w11	Receivables turnover	10.521	10.458
w12	Inventory turnover	4.740	3.689
w13	Capital ratio	0.336	0.328
w14	Coverage of short-term liabilities by equity	1.592	2.294
w15	Coverage of fixed assets by equity	2.948	5.294
w16	Share of net financial surplus in total liabilities	0.226	0.473

There are 16 administrative regions in Poland, so called voivodeships. Those 16 regions were grouped according to hierarchical clustering into 4 groups (low risk, lower-medium, higher-medium, and high risk of bankruptcy) to create the variable: region. All together five non-financial factors were used: sector of the company's activity (industry, trade, services); company's legal form (self-employed, joint stock company, limited liability company, limited partnership company, other); region (grouped as mentioned above); age of the company (in years); employment (number of employed workers at the date of financial statement).

The sample was partitioned into a training sample (70%) and a test sample (30%) with the same proportion of bankruptcy events in each sample.

Models used for estimation and comparison consisted of six different models: logistic regression with interval variables, logistic regression with discretized variables, decision tree, gradient boosting, neural network, and support vector machines.

2.1. Logistic Regression

The logistic regression function is S-shaped and described by the following formula:

$$P(Y = 1) = \frac{1}{1 + \exp^{-(\beta_0 + \beta_1 x_1 + \ldots + \beta_k x_k)}},$$

where:

β_0—intercept,
β_i—coefficients ($i = 1, 2, \ldots, k$),
x_i—explanatory variables ($i = 1, 2, \ldots, k$).

The $P(Y = 1)$ takes the values from interval [0; 1]. The cut-off point is an important element in the logistic regression model. Estimation based on a balanced sample usually takes the 0.5 as the cut-off value. The structure of the sample (the percentage of bankrupted enterprises) determines the cut-off value. Interpretation of results is usually based on odds ratios (the ratio of odds in two groups or in change of one unit in explanatory variable). Logistic regression requires a number of different assumptions to be fulfilled. The most important assumptions are: randomness of the sample, a large sample, no collinearities in explanatory variables, and independence of observations.

2.2. Decision Tree

A decision tree is a tool mainly used in hierarchical segmentation (division) of the dataset. The main element is the so-called root that includes the entire dataset. Subsequent splits of the data (observations) are carried out in the so-called nodes, or segments, according to the rules created on the basis of the values of explanatory variables. A segment that is subdivided into subsegments is being referred to as the parent node (or intermediate node) and the subsegments as children nodes. The tree branch creates a node with further subsegments. A leaf (group) is the final segment that is no longer divided. Each observation from the output node is assigned to only one final leaf. The decision tree contains intermediate and final nodes, while the decision tree model contains only the final leaves that are used to predict or classify data (see Figure 1).

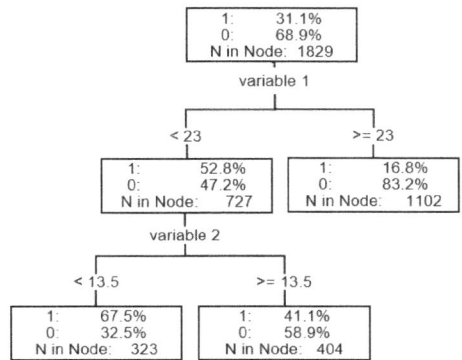

Figure 1. Decision tree—graphical representation.

In order for decision trees to be used, a large collection of observations is required, as well as sufficiently numerous cases for the dependent variable. Any (very) unusual observations may distort the results, though this is not a major risk. A big risk in building the tree is overfitting, which can cause instability of the model. The decision tree, unlikely the binary logistic regression, does not contain any equations or coefficients, it is based only on the rules of dividing the dataset into separate groups. As estimation of probabilities posteriori probabilities for each leaf are used. The rules generated by the model from the learning set can be used for prediction (resulting in binary decisions).

The basic ways to measure the quality of the division for binary dependent variables or discrete dependent variables with several categories include:

1. The degree of separation achieved by the division (measured by the Pearson chi-squared test),
2. The degree of pollution reduction achieved by the division (measured by the reduction of entropy or by the Gini coefficient).

The stopping criteria may be the following: the minimal number of observations in any final leaf, the critical size of any node, the number of splits in any path. After building a tree, it should be pruned into an optimal size. The advantages of a decision tree are twofold: the results are easily interpretable and the model is flexible. Additionally, decision trees are not sensitive to missing data and do not require the normality of distributions or the equality of covariance matrices (as discriminant analysis does). The explanatory variables may differ in character, being either qualitative or quantitative. Decision trees automatically select important variables and may explain non-linear dependencies. The disadvantage of the decision trees is the fact that they can prove unstable and sensitive to the size of the training sample, validation or test sample results. The large size of the training sample is critical. Probabilities are approximated on the final leaf level. Overtraining is quite common in decision trees and the results for the training sample are usually much better than for the testing sample. All those disadvantages must be considered while building a model.

2.3. Gradient Boosting

Nowadays, a more popular method is the random forest, initially proposed by Breiman. It is a method that takes together many classification trees. Firstly, we draw K bootstrap samples, then we create a classification tree for each of them in such a way that in each node we draw m (fewer than the number of all features) features which will participate in the selection of the best division. Trees are built without pruning. Finally, the observations are classified by the voting method. The only parameter of the method is the m coefficient, which should be much smaller than the dimension of data. The ease and speed with which random forests can be created makes them a feasible option even for very large data. Random forests are currently one of the most efficient classification methods, apart from the SVM and boosting. The boosting method makes it possible to cope with an opposite situation: it allows to aggregate many stable but less efficient classifiers (weak learners). The classification abilities of weak learners are small—the probability of correct classification slightly exceeds 1/2. The main idea is that in the iteration process the observations should be assigned weights which suggest to weak learners on which examples they should concentrate in their next approach to the classification task. The final decision regarding the classification of observations is made in majority voting. The main feature of boosting is the ability to decrease the training error: a group of weak learners acts together as a single good learner. What is more important, the error decreases exponentially, which is very important in practical usage. An additional advantage is that the boosting algorithms are not subject to overfitting.

2.4. Neural Network

The neural network, i.e., the fourth analyzed method, is formed by the neurons (information processing elements) along with the connections among them (weights modified during the learning process). This network is a simplified model of the human brain. A neuron contains many inputs x_i, where $i = 1, 2, ..., n$ and one output. Neural inputs are selected by the explanatory variables. When neural networks are used to forecast the risk of bankruptcy, these are typically financial ratios. Each input variable is assigned a specific weight w_i. Once the weights are determined, the total neuron activation (e) is calculated as the sum of the product of the explanatory variables and their weights assigned. Then y is calculated, which is the difference between the value of e and the threshold value Θ. The output signal depends on the neuron activation and the activation function $\varphi(y)$. The form of this function determines the neuron type (see Figure 2).

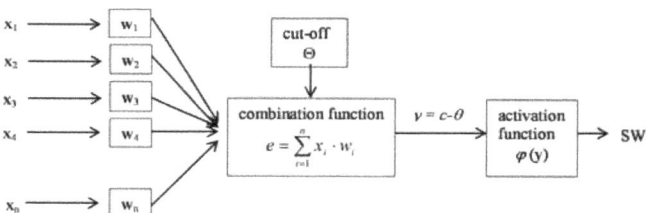

Figure 2. Neural network model.

In practice, artificial neural networks are usually made of a large number of interconnected neurons. We can distinguish the following neural networks:

- double layer neural networks—consisting of the input and output layers;
- multi-layered neural networks—consisting of input and output layers and hidden layers between them.

In predicting the bankruptcy of enterprises multi-layer perceptron (MLP) neural networks are frequently used. Neural networks are flexible and they quickly adapt to changes. They are resistant to any chaotic information and do not require assumptions like normality etc. The explanatory variables can be both qualitative and quantitative in type. Neural networks enable the modeling of any type of non-linear dependencies in the data.

Unfortunately, neural network models also have significant limitations. The long-term learning process for networks with extensive structures prevents the model from achieving an optimal level of error reduction. The weights selection process is difficult and complex. Neural networks do not select explanatory variables for the model. The analyst conducts a selection of explanatory variables by himself. Similarly as in the case of decision trees, there is a risk of overtraining. Selecting network architecture is a subjective choice. The worst disadvantage of the neural networks approach is the fact that they operate on the "black box" basis—without the ability to provide the rules that resulted in the obtained outcome. In neural network model all variables were used. Results are not as easily interpretable as in the decision tree model.

2.5. Support Vector Machines

Support vector machines are based on the concept of decision planes that define decision boundaries. A decision plane is one that separates between a set of objects having different class memberships. The classic example of a separation is a linear classifier that separates a set of objects into their respective groups with a line. Most classification tasks, however, are not that simple, and often more complex structures are needed in order to make an optimal separation, i.e., to correctly classify new objects (test cases) on the basis of the examples that are available (train cases). This situation is depicted in the illustration below (Figure 3a). A full separation of the "green" and "red" objects would require a curve (which is more complex than a line). Classification tasks based on drawing separating lines to distinguish between objects of different class memberships are known as hyperplane classifiers. Support vector machines handle such tasks. The illustration below (Figure 3b) shows the basic idea behind support vector machines. The original objects (left side of the schematic) mapped, i.e., rearranged, using a set of mathematical functions, known as kernels. The process of rearranging the objects is known as mapping (transformation).

(a)   (b)

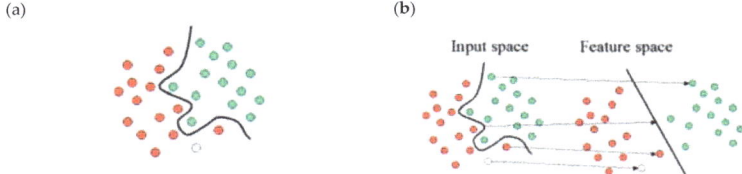

Figure 3. SVM mechanism. (**a**) Optimal classification; (**b**) mapping.

The support vector machine (SVM) is primarily a classier method that performs classification tasks by constructing hyperplanes in a multidimensional space that separates cases of different class labels. SVM supports both regression and classification tasks and can handle multiple continuous and categorical variables. For categorical variables a dummy variable is created with case values as either 0 or 1. To construct an optimal hyperplane, SVM employs an iterative training algorithm, which is used to minimize an error function. According to the form of the error function, SVM models can be classified into four distinct groups: C-SVM classification, nu-SVM classification, epsilon-SVM regression, and nu-SVM regression.

3. Results

3.1. Logistic Regression with Interval Variables

The stepwise selection method was used (significance level at entry and at exit equal 0.05) for variables selection. All types of variables were included: interval financial ratios and non-financial variables.

Legal form of the company as variable was significant but the differences between categories were not significant. The differences between sectors were significant. The risk of bankruptcy in the trade sector was 63.6% higher comparing to services (at a 0.1 significance level), and the risk of bankruptcy was almost 2.3 times higher in production comparing to services. Ratios: current liquidity (w1) and (w10) current assets turnover had positive sign, higher values of ratios were connected with higher risk of bankruptcy. Ratios: capital ratio (w13) and operating profitability of assets (w7) had negative sign, negative effect, meaning higher values of those ratios were connected with lower risk of bankruptcy (see Table 1).

Table 1. Results of estimation of logistic regression with interval variables.

Variable	DF	Parameter	Std Err	Wald Chi-sqr	*p*-Value	Exp(x)
Intercept	1	−1.0053	0.3845	6.83	0.0089	0.366
legal_form 2	1	0.4244	0.3065	1.92	0.1661	1.529
legal_form 3	1	−0.7052	0.4612	2.34	0.1262	0.494
legal_form 4	0	0	.	.	.	.
Sector 1	1	0.4922	0.2631	3.50	0.0613	1.636
Sector 2	1	0.8228	0.2609	9.95	0.0016	2.277
Sector 3	0	0	.	.	.	.
w1	1	0.0893	0.0323	7.64	0.0057	1.093
w10	1	0.1426	0.0335	18.09	<0.0001	1.153
w13	1	−2.8207	0.4264	43.75	<0.0001	0.060
w7	1	−2.1131	0.5771	13.41	0.0003	0.121

3.2. Logistic Regression with Discretized Variables

The stepwise selection method was used (significance level at entry and at exit equal 0.05) for variables selection. All types of variables were included: discretized financial ratios and non-financial variables. Interval variables were divided into five equally frequent classes and dichotomized. The last class was set up as reference category. Different variables were significant comparing to logistic regression with interval variables. Among non-financial variables only employment was significant with positive nonlinear effect. Smaller enterprises with lower number of employee are more risky compared to the largest. The receivables turnover ratio (w11) had negative sign in all groups comparing to the highest group. The effect of capital ratio (w13) is positive but nonlinear. The share of net financial surplus in total liabilities (w16) is non-linear. There is a large difference between the lowest and the highest groups (see Table 2).

Table 2. Results of estimation of logistic regression with discretized variables.

Variable	DF	Parameter	Std Err	Wald Chi-sqr	*p*-Value	Exp(x)
Intercept	1	−0.9796	0.4283	5.23	0.0222	0.375
GRP_employment 1	1	0.8388	0.3806	4.86	0.0275	2.314
GRP_employment 2	1	0.0969	0.3413	0.08	0.7765	1.102
GRP_employment 3	1	0.1829	0.3726	0.24	0.6235	1.201
GRP_employment 4	1	0.8616	0.3454	6.22	0.0126	2.367
GRP_employment 5	0	0	.	.	.	.
GRP_w11 1	1	−1.2379	0.3450	12.87	0.0003	0.290
GRP_w11 2	1	−1.4883	0.3486	18.23	<0.0001	0.226
GRP_w11 3	1	−1.6453	0.3540	21.60	<0.0001	0.193
GRP_w11 4	1	−1.7106	0.3587	22.74	<0.0001	0.181
GRP_w11 5	0	0	.	.	.	.
GRP_w13 1	1	1.3206	0.4528	8.51	0.0035	3.746
GRP_w13 2	1	1.2484	0.4367	8.17	0.0043	3.485
GRP_w13 3	1	0.2725	0.4296	0.40	0.5258	1.313
GRP_w13 4	1	−0.5903	0.4334	1.85	0.1732	0.554
GRP_w13 5	0	0	.	.	.	.
GRP_w16 1	1	2.4878	0.4438	31.42	<0.0001	12.034
GRP_w16 2	1	1.1336	0.4505	6.33	0.0119	3.107
GRP_w16 3	1	0.2847	0.4624	0.38	0.5381	1.329
GRP_w16 4	1	−0.3871	0.4548	0.72	0.3947	0.679
GRP_w16 5	0	0	.	.	.	.

3.3. Decision Tree CART (Classification And Regression Tree)

For decision tree the CART tree was used. For interval variables the splitting was based on F test and for nominal variables the chi-square test with a 0.2 *p*-value. A maximum of two subgroups in one split was allowed and maximum 6 splits in depth as the stopping criteria. Eight different financial ratios were used in splitting and two of them were used twice. Only one non-financial factor was used in splitting: sector (see Table 3). Results in graphical form are presented in Figure 4.

Table 3. Importance of variables in the decision tree.

Variable	Number of Rules	Importance
w16	1	1.0000
w4	2	0.4884
w11	1	0.4349
w15	2	0.3930
w14	1	0.3236
w8	1	0.3079
w13	1	0.3047
sector	1	0.2673
w10	1	0.2128

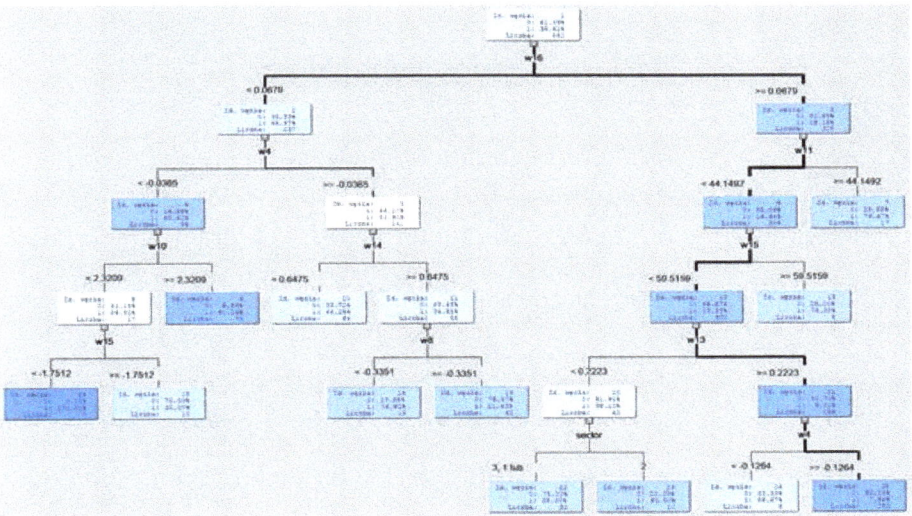

Figure 4. Results of the estimation of the decision tree.

The first split was done according to ratio w16 into a group with almost a twice higher level of bankruptcy, w16 < 0.0679, and a group with almost twice lower level of bankruptcy, w16 ≥ 0.0679. Among those with w16 < 0.0679 there was a group with w4 < −0.0365 resulting in bankruptcy level 85.4% and further split according w10 < 2.32 giving the bankruptcy rate above 91% (more than 2.4 times higher comparing to total sample). The lowest risk of bankruptcy was characteristic for enterprises with w16 ≥ 0.0679, and w11 < 44.15 and w15 < 59.5 and w13 ≥ 0.22 and w4 ≥ −0.12. In this group the bankruptcy rate was about 7.9% (more than 4.75 times lower comparing to total sample).

3.4. Gradient Boosting

The fourth applied model was gradient boosting based on trees with split into two subgroups and a maximum depth of 2. Subtree was selected based on lowest misclassification rate. In gradient boosting similar financial ratios were important. Among non-financial factors employment was more important compared to other factors (see Table 4).

Table 4. Importance of variables in the decision tree.

Variable	Number of Rules	Importance
w16	16	1.00000
w13	6	0.60837
w11	14	0.60156
w15	5	0.40503
employment	11	0.38090
w14	7	0.33149
w7	4	0.32444
w5	6	0.31146
w6	6	0.30114
w1	4	0.28198
w3	6	0.27084
age	4	0.24969
w12	5	0.23794
w2	5	0.23771
w10	5	0.20920
sector	3	0.19020
legal_form	3	0.18527
w4	2	0.16845
w8	3	0.15562
w9	2	0.12812
region_cluster	2	0.12418

3.5. Neural Network

The most popular architecture of neural network was used the multi-layer perceptron (MLP) with one hidden layer. Number of neurons in the layer equals number of explanatory variables. pseudo-Newton optimization technique was used with maximum 200 iterations. A total of 106 parameters were estimated in total. The iteration history is shown in Figure 5.

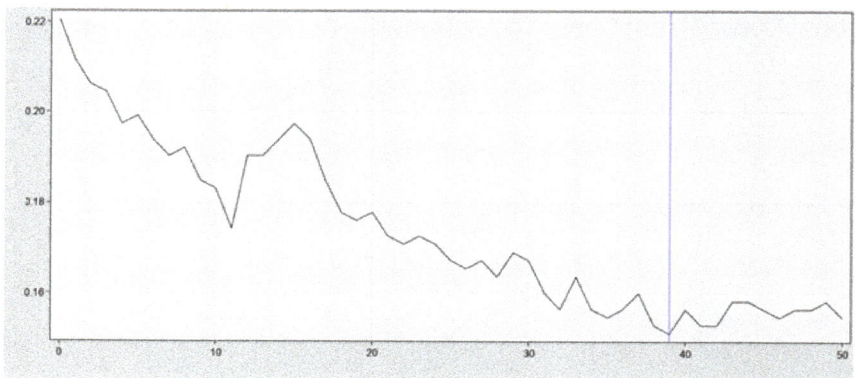

Figure 5. Neural network—iterations history (misclassification rate—training sample).

3.6. Support Vectors Machine

As a final model, the SVM was estimated. As an optimization method the interior point was set with scaling and polynomial function (two degrees).

The penalization method was C with a penalization parameter equal 1. Maximum iterations was set to 25 with a tolerance 1×10^{-6}. The results are presented in Table 5.

Table 5. Results of SVM training.

Internal product of weights	46.3039131
Burden	−21.744579
Total stock (violation of restrictions)	305.767624
Norm of the longest vector	11.6448785
Number of support vectors	387
Number of support vectors on margin	334
Maximal F	2.84554647
Minimal F	−21.760742
Number of effects	21
Columns of data matrix	36
Columns of kernel matrix	703

3.7. Model Comparison

Model evaluation was based on the Gini (accuracy ratio—AR) coefficient on the test sample, which is a measure based on ROC, i.e., the curve used to measure the discriminative power of the model. It is applied in the case when the dependent variable is binary (it has two unique values). The Figure 6 presents the relation of the specificity to the sensitivity of the model. Both of those measures provide information on how effective the classification is in the context of both levels of the dependent variable. The ROC curve is a sensitivity function (on the vertical axis) and 1-specificity (on the horizontal axis). Each point of the curve corresponds to a given point of split (section). Points in the right upper corner correspond to a low q level. Points in the left bottom corner relate to a high q level. ROC does not depend on the assumed point of split. The rates are drawn for all points of split. While selecting a given point of split we can establish the specificity and sensitivity of the model for that point. Selecting a given point of split we can establish the number of successes and failures predicted by the model, and then calculate the sensitivity and the specificity of the model. The correspondent sensitivity and specificity levels are easy to read from the graph of the ROC curve. A good model has the ROC curve close to the upper-left boundary of the graph. Then we can find points on the curve representing high values both in terms of sensitivity and specificity (e.g., so that c > 0.8 and s > 0.8). The random model has the ROC curve lying on the diagonal. Then the sensitivity + specificity = 1 for all the threshold values of q. In such a case while establishing the value c > 0.8 we cannot ensure that the specificity is greater than 0.2. The ROC curve is helpful when selecting the optimal point of division. For example, we choose the threshold that gives equal probability of misclassification in each class. We also have to take into account the different cost of both types of misclassification and decide whether to provide high sensitivity or high specificity. The area under the ROC curve is a measure of the quality of the model. This way we can compare the quality of different models. The AUC (area under the ROC curve) for an ideal model equals 1 and for a random model 0.5.

The similar measure to ROC is the CAP curve, where the cumulative frequencies for good customers are substituted by frequencies for all customers. The area under the CAP curve is called the accuracy ratio. The CAP curve represents the $y\%$ of bankrupted enterprises that can be found in the $x\%$ of the worst assessed enterprises within the model. The curve should be concave. The accuracy ratio (Gini coefficient) based on the CAP curve is defined as:

$$AR = \frac{\int\limits_0^1 f(x)dx - \frac{1}{2}}{\frac{1}{2} - \frac{1}{2}BR},$$ (1)

where:

BR—bankruptcy rate;

$\int\limits_0^1 f(x)dx - \frac{1}{2}$—area under the CAP curve.

The value of *AR* is normalized in the range of [0; 1].

Comparing models Gini coefficient for test sample was used. The highest Gini coefficient for the test sample was reached by SVM and amounted at 0.69 (see Table 6). This model was not overfitted because Gini for the training sample was similar (0.67). Regression with interval ratios was also stable with similar results for train and test sample but slightly worse comparing to SVM. Neural network and decision tree models were overfitted because Gini was much higher for the training sample comparing to test sample. Gradient boosting had a high Gini for the test sample, but the difference for training and testing samples was too high. The shape of the ROC curve was correct for all models with the highest AUC for SVM (see Figure 3).

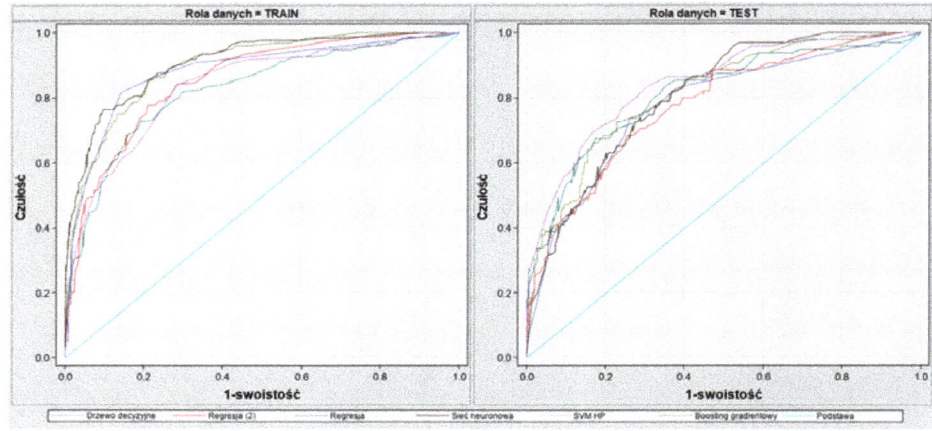

Figure 6. ROC curve for all models, train and test sample.

Table 6. Comparison of models based on test and train sample.

Model	Test Gini	Train MSE	Train MSC	Train ROC	Train Gini
SVM	0.690	0.19078	0.23665	0.835	0.671
Boost	0.632	0.12880	0.18327	0.895	0.791
Reg1	0.622	0.16336	0.23665	0.823	0.647
Neural	0.612	0.11745	0.15125	0.907	0.814
Reg2	0.554	0.14974	0.23310	0.854	0.708
Tree	0.552	0.12275	0.15836	0.881	0.762

It is also important to compare the error rate for bankruptcy classifications and for non-bankruptcy classifications (see Table 7). Classification table was compared for the train sample (see Table 8). SVM with the highest Gini on the test sample had the highest rate of misclassification of bankruptcies (50%). Regression with interval ratios had lower rates of misclassifications of bankruptcies (44%). The decision tree with the lowest Gini coefficient for the test sample had the lowest misclassifications of bankruptcies (18%) for the training sample. The choice of the final model must be in equilibrium between accuracy and stability of the model (overfitting).

Table 7. Classification table.

	Model = 0	Model = 1	
Level = 0	TP	FP	OP
Level = 1	FN	TN	ON
	PP	PN	Total

TP—true positive, FP—false positive, FN—false negative, TN—true negative, PP—predicted positive, PN—predicted negative, OP—original positive, ON—original negative.

Table 8. Classification table—training sample.

Model	FN	TP	FP	TN	% (FN/ON)
SVM	108	320	25	109	50%
Boost	65	307	38	152	30%
Reg1	96	308	37	121	44%
Neural	51	311	34	166	24%
Reg2	78	292	53	139	36%
Tree	40	296	49	177	18%

Taking into account different financial ratios and non-financial factors only six financial ratios and two non-financial factors were significant in at least two different models (see Table 9).

Table 9. Financial ratios and non-financial factors—significance in different models.

Model	x1	x2	x3	x4	x5	x6	x7	x8	x9	x10	x11	x12	x13	x14	x15	x16
SVM																
Boost				x	x	x							x	x	x	x
Reg1	x					x				x			x			
Neural																
Reg2											x		x			x
Tree				x				x		x	x		x	x	x	x

Model	Legal Form	Sector	Age	Region	Employment
SVM					
Boost					x
Reg1	x	x			
Neural					
Reg2					x
Tree		x			

4. Discussion and Conclusions

Summing up above estimation we can conclude that simple models like logistic regression were as good as more complex models like neural networks (NN), decision trees (DT), or support vector machines (SVM). However, in other research, like Zięba et al. (2016), who applied the extreme gradient boosting model, results gained by the selected classifier were significantly better than the results gained by all other simpler methods that were applied by authors to the problem of predicting financial condition of the companies. In different classification analysis not only concerning financial ratios quite often SVM is stated as promising method (see Lahmiri et al. 2017; Lahmiri and Shmuel 2018).

Data mining models are less stable and tend to be overfitted (see Gradient Boosting, Neural Network, and Decision Tree sections). The difference of accuracy between train and test sample was too high.

Financial ratios that were most important in predicting small enterprise failures were: operating profitability of assets, current assets turnover, capital ratio, coverage of short-term liabilities by equity, coverage of fixed assets by equity, and share of net financial surplus in total liabilities. Results may be compared to results recently obtained for Polish bankruptcy data by Zięba et al. (2016). The authors examined data for Polish bankrupted companies from period 2007–2013. They analyzed a five-year period and only three indicators: adjusted share of equity in financing of assets, current ratio, liabilities turnover ratio appeared in each analyzed year. According to authors those ratios can be considered as useful in predicting bankruptcy of enterprises.

Among non-financial factors two of them were important: sector of activity and employment. The usage of non-financial ratios improves the results of all models which confirmed our expectations and other research. The legal form of the company seems to be the most important variable among all the considered non-financial factors. Employment and sector also plays a role, which confirms the results obtained by Chava and Jarrow (2004). Gordini (2014) confirmed that building models tailored to specific geographical areas increases the accuracy. However, in our models two variables, region and age of the company, seem to play a much less important role.

The hypotheses were positively verified:

Hypothesis 3 (H3): *Non-financial factors are important in case of predicting small enterprises success and failures.*

Hypothesis 4 (H4): *More advanced and complicated models are not necessary to predict small enterprise failures. Simple models are as effective as more complex ones.*

As always the greatest problem is the access to good quality data. Depending on the data availability future research would cover the interaction with the macroeconomic situation. Financial situations expanded by non-financial factors do not give the full view of the bankruptcy causes. Deeper analysis of causality mechanisms is needed.

Funding: This research received no external funding.

Conflicts of Interest: The authors declare no conflict of interest.

References

Altman, Edward I. 1968. Financial ratios, Discriminant analysis and the prediction of corporate bankruptcy. *Journal of Finance* 23: 589–609. [CrossRef]

Appenzeller, Dorota, and Katarzyna Szarzec. 2004. Forecasting the bankruptcy risk of Polish public companies. *Rynek Terminowy* 1: 120–28.

Aziz, M. Adnan, and Humayon A. Dar. 2006. Predicting Corporate Bankruptcy: Where do We Stand? *Corporate Governance International Journal of Business in Society* 6: 18–33. [CrossRef]

Back, Barbro, Teija Laitinen, Kaisa Sere, and Michiel van Wezel. 1996. *Choosing Bankruptcy Predictors Using Discriminant Analysis, Logit Analysis, and Genetic Algorithms*. Technical Report. Turku: Turku Centre for Computer Science.

Balina, Rafał, and Maksymilian Jan Bąk. 2016. *Discriminant Analysis as a Prediction Method for Corporate Bankruptcy with the Industrial Aspects*. Waleńczów: Wydawnictwo Naukowe Intellect.

Blanco-Oliver, Antonio, Rafael Pino-Mejías, Juan Lara-Rubio, and Salvador Rayo. 2013. Credit scoring models for the microfinance industry using neural networks: Evidence from Peru. *Expert Systems with Applications* 40: 356–64. [CrossRef]

Brożyna, Jacek, Grzegorz Mentel, and Tomasz Pisula. 2016. Statistical methods of the bankruptcy prediction in the logistics sector in Poland and Slovakia. *Transformations in Business & Economics* 15: 80–96.

Calabrese, Raffaella, Giampiero Marra, and Silvia Angela Osmetti. 2015. Bankruptcy prediction of small and medium enterprises using a flexible binary generalized extreme value model. *Journal of the Operational Research Society* 67: 604–15. [CrossRef]

Chaudhuri, Arindam, and Kajal De. 2011. Fuzzy support vector machine for bankruptcy prediction. *Applied Soft Computing* 11: 2472–86. [CrossRef]

Chava, Sudheer, and Robert A. Jarrow. 2004. Bankruptcy prediction with industry effects. *Review of Finance* 8: 537–569. [CrossRef]

Gajdka, Jerzy, and Daniel Stos. 1996. The use of discriminant analysis in assessing the financial condition of enterprises. In *Restructuring in the Process of Transformation and Development of Enterprises*. Edited by Ryszard Borowiecki. Kraków: Wydawnictwo Akademii Ekonomicznej w Krakowie.

Gąska, Damian. 2016. Predicting Bankruptcy of Enterprises with the use of Learning Methods. Ph.D. dissertation, Wrocław University of Economics, Wrocław, Poland.

Gordini, Niccolo. 2014. A genetic algorithm approach for SMEs bankruptcy prediction: Empirical evidence from Italy. *Expert Systems with Applications* 41: 6067–536. [CrossRef]

Gruszczyński, Marek. 2003. *Models of Microeconometrics in the Analysis and Forecasting of the Financial Risk of Enterprises*. Warszawa: Zeszyty Polskiej Akademii Nauk nr 23.

Gupta, Jairaj, Andros Gregoriou, and Jerome Healy. 2015. Forecasting bankruptcy for SMEs using hazard function: A review of quantitative finance and accounting. *Review of Quantitative Finance and Accounting* 45: 845–69. [CrossRef]

Hadasik, Dorota. 1998. *The Bankruptcy of Enterprises in Poland and Methods of its Forecasting*. Poznań: Wydawnictwo Akademii Ekonomicznej w Poznaniu, vol. 153.

Hamrol, Mirosław, Bartłomiej Czajka, and Maciej Piechocki. 2004. Enterprise bankruptcy—discriminant analysis model. *Przegląd Organizacji* 6: 35–39.

Hołda, Artur. 2001. Forecasting the bankruptcy of an enterprise in the conditions of the Polish economy using the discriminatory function ZH. *Rachunkowość* 5: 306–10.

Jagiełło, Robert. 2013. *Discriminant and Logistic Analysis in the Process of Assessing the Creditworthiness of Enterprises*. Materiały i Studia, Zeszyt 286. Warszawa: NBP.

Jiménez, Gabriel, and Jesus Saurina. 2004. Collateral, type of lender and relationship banking as determinants of credit risk. *Journal of Banking & Finance* 28: 2191–212.

Kalak, El Izidin, and Robert Hudson. 2016. The effect of size on the failure probabilities of SMEs: An empirical study on the US market using discrete hazard model. *International Review of Financial Analysis* 43: 135–45. [CrossRef]

Karbownik, Lidia. 2017. *Methods for Assessing the Financial Risk of Enterprises in the TSI Sector in Poland*. Łódź: Wydawnictwo Uniwersytetu Łódzkiego.

Kim, Hong Sik, and So Young Sohn. 2010. Support Vector Machines for Default Prediction of SMEs Based on Technology Credit. *European Journal of Operational Research* 201: 838–46. [CrossRef]

Korol, Tomasz. 2004. Assessment of the Accuracy of the Application of Discriminatory Methods and Artificial Neural Networks for the Identification of Enterprises Threatened with Bankruptcy. Doctoral dissertation, University of Gdańsk, Gdańsk, Poland.

Korol, Tomasz. 2010a. *Early Warning Systems of Enterprises to the Risk of Bankruptcy*. Warszawa: Wolters Kluwer.

Korol, Tomasz. 2010b. Forecasting bankruptcies of companies using soft computing techniques. *Finansowy Kwartalnik Internetowy "e-Finanse"* 6: 1–14.

Lahmiri, Salim. 2016a. Features selection, data mining and financial risk classification: A comparative study. Intelligent Systems in Accounting. *Finance and Management* 23: 265–75.

Lahmiri, Salim. 2016b. On simulation performance of feedforward and NARX networks under different numerical training algorithms. In *Handbook of Research on Computational Simulation and Modeling in Engineering*. Hershey: IGI.

Lahmiri, Salim. 2016c. Prediction of International Stock Markets Based on Hybrid Intelligent Systems. In *Handbook of Research on Innovations in Information Retrieval, Analysis, and Management*. Hershey: IGI.

Lahmiri, Salim. 2017. A two-step system for direct bank telemarketing outcome classification. Intelligent Systems in Accounting. *Finance and Management* 24: 49–55.

Lahmiri, Salim, Debra Ann Dawson, and Amir Smuel. 2017. Performance of machine learning methods in diagnosing Parkinson's disease based on dysphonia measures. *Biomedical Engineering Letters* 8: 1–11. [CrossRef] [PubMed]

Lahmiri, Salim, and Amir Shmuel. 2018. Performance of machine learning methods applied to structural MRI and ADAS cognitive scores in diagnosing Alzheimer's disease. *Biomedical Signal Processing and Control*. [CrossRef]

Mączyńska, Elżbieta. 1994. Assessment of the condition of the enterprise. Simplified methods. *Życie Gospodarcze* 38: 42–45.

Mączyńska, Elżbieta. 2004. Early warning systems. *Nowe Życie Gospodarcze* 12: 4–9.

Michaluk, Krzysztof. 2003. Effectiveness of corporate bankruptcy models in Polish economic conditions. In *Corporate Finance in the Face of Globalization Processes*. Edited by Leszek Pawłowicz and Ryszard Wierzba. Warszawa: Wydawnictwo Gdańskiej Akademii Bankowej.

Ong, Chorng-Shyong, Jih-Jeng Huang, and Gwo-Hshiung Tzeng. 2005. Building credit scoring models using genetic programming. *Expert Systems with Applications* 29: 41–47. [CrossRef]

Pociecha, Józef, and Barbara Pawełek. 2011. Bankruptcy Prediction and Business Cycle, Contemporary Problems of Transformation Process in the Central and East European Countries. Paper presented at 17th Ukrainian-Polish-Slovak Scientific Seminar, Lviv, Ukraine, September 22–24; Lviv: The Lviv Academy of Commerce, pp. 9–24.

Pociecha, Józef, Barbara Pawełek, Mateusz Baryła, and Sabina Augustyn. 2014. *Statistical Methods of Forecasting Bankruptcy in the Changing Economic Situation*. Kraków: Fundacja Uniwersytetu Ekonomicznego w Krakowie.

Pogodzińska, Marzanna, and Sławomir Sojak. 1995. *The Use of Discriminant Analysis in Predicting Bankruptcy of Enterprises*. Ekonomia XXV, Zeszyt 299. Toruń: AUNC.

Prusak, Błażej. 2018. Review of Research into Enterprise Bankruptcy Prediction in Selected Central and Eastern European Countries. *International Journal of Financial Studies* 6: 60. [CrossRef]

Prusak, Błażej, and Agnieszka Więckowska. 2007. Multidimensional models of discriminant analysis in the study of the bankruptcy risk of Polish companies listed on the WSE. In *Economic and Legal Aspects of Corporate Bankruptcy*. Edited by Błażej Prusak. Warszawa: Difin.

Prusak, Błażej. 2005. *Modern Methods of Forecasting Financial Risk of Enterprises*. Warszawa: Difin.

Psillaki, Maria, Ioannis E. Tsolas, and Dimitris Margaritis. 2010. Evaluation of credit risk based on firm performance. *European Journal of Operational Research* 201: 873–81. [CrossRef]

Ptak-Chmielewska, Aneta, and Anna Matuszyk. 2017. The importance of financial and non-financial ratios in SMEs bankruptcy prediction. *Bank i Kredyt* 49: 45–62.

Ptak-Chmielewska, Aneta. 2016. Statistical Models for Corporate Credit Risk Assessment—Rating Models. *Acta Universitatis Lodziensis Folia Oeconomica* 3: 98–111. [CrossRef]

Sartori, Fabio, Alice Mazzucchelli, and Angelo Di Gregorio. 2016. Bankruptcy forecasting using case-based reasoning: The CRePERIE approach. *Expert Systems with Applications* 64: 400–11. [CrossRef]

Sohn, So Young, Dong Ha Kim, and Jin Hee Yoon. 2016. Technology credit scoring model with fuzzy logistic regression. *Applied Soft Computing* 43: 150–58. [CrossRef]

Sojak, Sławomir, and Józef Stawicki. 2000. The use of taxonomic methods to assess the economic condition of enterprises. *Zeszyty Teoretyczne Rachunkowości* 3: 55–66.

Stępień, Paweł, and Tomasz Strąk. 2003. Signs of the threat of bankruptcy of Polish enterprises—Empirical study. In *Time for Money, t. II*. Edited by Dariusz Zarzecki. Szczecin: Wydawnictwo Uniwersytetu Szczecińskiego.

Stępień, Paweł, and Tomasz Strąk. 2004. Multidimensional logit models for assessing the risk of bankruptcy of Polish enterprises. In *Time for Money, t. I*. Edited by Dariusz Zarzecki. Szczecin: Wydawnictwo Uniwersytetu Szczecińskiego.

Wędzki, Dariusz. 2000. The problem of using the ratio analysis to predict the bankruptcy of Polish enterprises—Case study. *Bank i Kredyt* 5: 54–61.

Wędzki, Dariusz. 2004. Logit model of bankruptcy for the Polish economy—Conclusions from the study. In *Time for Money. Corporate Finance. Financing Enterprises in the EU*. Edited by Dariusz Zarzecki. Szczecin: Wydawnictwo Uniwersytetu Szczecińskiego.

Wierzba, Dariusz. 2000. *Early Detection of Enterprises Threatened with Bankruptcy Based on the Analysis of Financial Ratios—Theory and Empirical Research*. Zeszyty Naukowe nr 9. Warszawa: Wydawnictwo Wyższej Szkoły Ekonomiczno-Informatycznej w Warszawie.

Zięba, Maciej, Sebastian K. Tomczak, and Jakub M. Tomczak. 2016. Ensemble boosted trees with synthetic features generation in application to bankruptcy prediction. *Expert Systems with Applications* 58: 93–101. [CrossRef]

Zmijewski, Me. 1984. Methodological issues related to the estimation of financial distress prediction models. *Journal of Accounting Research* 22: 59–82. [CrossRef]

Article

Ensemble Learning or Deep Learning? Application to Default Risk Analysis

Shigeyuki Hamori [1,*] , **Minami Kawai** [2], **Takahiro Kume** [2], **Yuji Murakami** [2]
and Chikara Watanabe [2]

[1]   Graduate School of Economics, Kobe University, Kobe 657-8501, Japan
[2]   Department of Economics, Kobe University, Kobe 657-8501, Japan; minami.hehe@gmail.com (M.K.);
    takahiro-2479@outlook.jp (T.K.); yuji.murakami0410@gmail.com (Y.M.); 4751.power.wc@gmail.com (C.W.)
*   Correspondence; hamori@econ.kobe-u.ac.jp; Tel.: +81-78-803-6832

Received: 19 January 2018; Accepted: 28 February 2018; Published: 5 March 2018

Abstract: Proper credit-risk management is essential for lending institutions, as substantial losses can be incurred when borrowers default. Consequently, statistical methods that can measure and analyze credit risk objectively are becoming increasingly important. This study analyzes default payment data and compares the prediction accuracy and classification ability of three ensemble-learning methods—specifically, bagging, random forest, and boosting—with those of various neural-network methods, each of which has a different activation function. The results obtained indicate that the classification ability of boosting is superior to other machine-learning methods including neural networks. It is also found that the performance of neural-network models depends on the choice of activation function, the number of middle layers, and the inclusion of dropout.

Keywords: credit risk; ensemble learning; deep learning; bagging; random forest; boosting; deep neural network

---

1. Introduction

Credit-risk management is essential for financial institutions whose core business is lending. Thus, accurate consumer or corporation credit assessment is of utmost importance because significant losses can be incurred by financial institutions when borrowers default. To control their losses from uncollectable accounts, financial institutions therefore need to properly assess borrowers' credit risks. Consequently, they endeavor to collate borrower data, and various statistical methods have been developed to measure and analyze credit risk objectively.

Because of its academic and practical importance, much research has been conducted on this issue. For example, Boguslauskas and Mileris (2009) analyzed credit risk using Lithuanian data for 50 cases of successful enterprises and 50 cases of bankrupted enterprises. Their results indicated that artificial neural networks are an efficient method to estimate the credit risk.

Angelini, Tollo, and Roli (Angelini et al. 2008) presented the application of an artificial neural network for credit-risk assessment using the data of 76 small businesses from a bank in Italy. They used two neural architectures to classify borrowers into two distinct classes: in bonis and default. One is a feedforward neural network and is composed of an input layer, two hidden layers and an output layer. The other is a four-layer feedforward neural network with ad hoc connections and input neurons grouped in sets of three. Their results indicate that neural networks successfully identify the in bonis/default tendency of a borrower.

Khshman (2009) developed a system of credit-risk evaluation using a neural network and applied the system to Australian credit data (690 cases; 307 creditworthy instances and 383 non-creditworthy instances). He compared the performance of the single-hidden layer neural network (SHNN) model and double-hidden layer network (DHNN). His experimental results indicated that the system with

SHNN outperformed the system with DHNN for credit-risk evaluation, and thus the SHNN neural system was recommended for the automatic processing of credit applications.

Yeh and Lien (2009) compared the predictive accuracy of probability of default among six data-mining methods (specifically, K-nearest neighbor classifier, logistic regression, discriminant analysis, naive Bayesian classifier, artificial neural networks, and classification trees) using customers' default payments data in Taiwan. Their experimental results indicated that only artificial neural networks can accurately estimate default probability.

Khashman (2010) employed neural-network models for credit-risk evaluation with German credit data comprising 1000 cases: 700 instances of creditworthy applicants and 300 instances where applicants were not creditworthy.[1] The results obtained indicated that the accuracy rates for the training data and test data were 99.25% and 73.17%, respectively. In this data, however, if one always predicts that a case is creditworthy, then the accuracy rate naturally converges to 70%. Thus, the results imply that there is only a 3.17% gain for the prediction accuracy of test data using neural network models.

Gante et al. (2015) also used German credit data and compared 12 neural-network models to assess credit risk. Their results indicated that a neural network with 20 input neurons, 10 hidden neurons, and one output neuron is a suitable neural network model for use in a credit risk evaluation system.

Khemakhem and Boujelbene (2015) compared the prediction of a neural network with that of discriminant analysis using 86 Tunisian client companies of a Tunisian commercial bank over three years. Their results indicated that a neural network outperforms discriminant analysis in predicting credit risk.

As is pointed out by Oreski et al. (2012), the majority of studies have shown that neural networks are more accurate, flexible and robust than conventional statistical methods for the assessment of credit risk.

In this study, we use 11 machine-learning methods to predict the default risk based on clients' attributes, and compare their prediction accuracy. Specifically, we employ three ensemble learning methods—bagging, random forest, and boosting—and eight neural network methods with different activation functions. The performance of each method is compared in terms of their ability to predict the default risk using multiple indicators (accuracy, rate of prediction, results, receiver operating characteristic (ROC) curve, area under the curve (AUC), and F-score).[2]

The results obtained indicate that the classification ability of boosting is superior to other machine-learning methods including neural networks. It is also found that the performance of neural-network models depends on the choice of activation function and the number of middle layers.

The remainder of this paper is organized as follows. Section 2 explains the data employed and the experimental design. Section 3 discusses the empirical results obtained. Section 4 presents concluding remarks.

2. Data and Experimental Design

2.1. Machine-Learning Techniques

Three ensemble-learning algorithms are employed in this study: bagging, random forest, and boosting. Bagging, developed by Breiman (1996), is a machine-learning method that uses bootstrapping to create multiple training datasets from given datasets. The classification results generated using the data are arranged and combined to improve the prediction accuracy. Because the bootstrap samples are mutually independent, learning can be carried out in parallel.

---

[1] The German credit dataset is publicly available at UCI Machine Learning data repository, https://archive.ics.uci.edu/ml/datasets/statlog+(german+credit+data).

[2] Lantz (2015) provides good explanation for machine learning methods.

Random forest, also proposed by Breiman (2001), is similar to bagging. It is a machine-learning method in which the classification results generated from multiple training datasets are arranged and combined to improve the prediction accuracy. However, whereas bagging uses all input variables to create each decision tree, random forest uses subsets that are random samplings of variables to create each decision tree. This means that random forest is better suited than bagging for the analysis of high-dimensional data.

Boosting is also a machine-learning method. Whereas bagging and random forest employ independent learning, boosting employs sequential learning (Schapire 1999; Shapire and Freund 2012). In boosting, on the basis of supervised learning, weights are successively adjusted, and multiple learning results are sought. These results are then combined and integrated to improve overall accuracy. The most widely used boosting algorithm is AdaBoost, proposed by Freund and Schapire (1996).

A neural network (NN) is a network structure comprising multiple connected units. It consists of an input layer, middle layer(s), and an output layer. The neural network configuration is determined by the manner in which the units are connected; different configurations enable a network to have different functions and characteristics. The feed-forward neural network is the most frequently used neural-network model and is configured by the hierarchical connection of multiple units. When the number of middle layers is greater than or equal to two, the network is called a deep neural network (DNN).

The activation function in a neural network is very important, as it expresses the functional relationship between the input and output in each unit. In this study, we employed two types of activation functions: Tanh and rectified linear unit (ReLU). These functions are defined as follows:

$$Tanh : f(x) = \frac{e^x - e^{-x}}{e^x + e^{-x}}$$

$$ReLU : f(x) = \max(0, x)$$

The Tanh function compresses a real-valued number into the range $[-1, 1]$. Its activations saturate, and its output is zero-centered. The ReLU function is an alternative activation function in neural networks.[3] One of its major benefits is the reduced likelihood of the gradient vanishing.

Although DNNs are powerful machine-learning tools, they are susceptible to overfitting. This is addressed using a technique called dropout, in which units are randomly dropped (along with their incoming and outgoing connections) in the network. This prevents units from overly co-adapting (Srivastava et al. 2014).

Thus, we use the following 11 methods to compare performance:

1. Bagging.
2. Random forest.
3. Boosting.
4. Neural network (activation function is Tanh).
5. Neural network (activation function is ReLU).
6. Neural network (activation function is Tanh with Dropout).
7. Neural network (activation function is ReLU with Dropout).
8. Deep neural network (activation function is Tanh).
9. Deep neural network (activation function is ReLU).
10. Deep neural network (activation function is Tanh with Dropout).
11. Deep neural network (activation function is ReLU with Dropout).

---

[3]   See LeCun et al. (2015).

2.2. Data

The payment data in Taiwan used by Yeh and Lien (2009) are employed in this study. The data are available as a default credit card client's dataset in the UCI Machine Learning Repository. In the dataset used by Yeh and Lien (2009), the number of observations is 25,000, in which 5529 observations are default payments. However, the current dataset in the UCI Machine Learning Repository has a total number of 30,000 observations, in which 6636 observations are default payments. Following Yeh and Lien (2009), we used default payment (No = 0, Yes = 1) as the explained variable and the following 23 variables as explanatory variables:

X1: Amount of given credit (NT dollar).

X2: Gender (1 = male; 2 = female).

X3: Education (1 = graduate school; 2 = university; 3 = high school; 4 = others).

X4: Marital status (1 = married; 2 = single; 3 = others).

X5: Age (year).

X6–X11: History of past payment tracked via past monthly payment records (−1 = payment on time; 1 = payment delay for one month; 2 = payment delay for two months; . . . ; 8 = payment delay for eight months; 9 = payment delay for nine months and above).

X6: Repayment status in September 2005.

X7: Repayment status in August 2005.

X8: Repayment status in July 2005.

X9: Repayment status in June 2005.

X10: Repayment status in May 2005.

X11: Repayment status in April 2005.

X12: Amount on bill statement in September 2005 (NT dollar).

X13: Amount on bill statement in August 2005 (NT dollar).

X14: Amount on bill statement in July 2005 (NT dollar).

X15: Amount on bill statement in June 2005 (NT dollar).

X16: Amount on bill statement in May 2005 (NT dollar).

X17: Amount on bill statement in April 2005 (NT dollar).

X18: Amount of previous payment in September 2005 (NT dollar).

X19: Amount of previous payment in August 2005 (NT dollar).

X20: Amount of previous payment in July 2005 (NT dollar).

X21: Amount of previous payment in June 2005 (NT dollar).

X22: Amount of previous payment in May 2005 (NT dollar).

X23: Amount of previous payment in April 2005 (NT dollar).

Because of the high proportions of no-default observations (77.88%), the accuracy rate inevitably remains at virtually 78% when all observations are used for analysis. It is difficult to understand the merit of using machine learning if we use all data. Thus, in this study we extracted 6636 observations randomly from all no-default observations to ensure that no-default and default observations are equal, thereby preventing distortion. As regards the ratio of training to test datasets, this study uses two cases, i.e., 90% to 10% and 75% to 25%.[4]

It is well known that data normalization can improve performance. Classifiers are required to calculate the objective function, which is the mean squared error between the predicted value

---

[4] There are two typical ways to implement machine learning. One is to use training data, validation data, and test data, and the other is to use training data and test data. In the first approach, the result of the test is randomly determined and we cannot obtain robust results. Also, it is not advisable to divide the small sample into three pieces. Thus, we use the second approach in this study. We repeat the test results over 100 times to obtain robust results.

and the observation. If some of the features have a broad range of values, the mean squared error may be governed by these particular features and objective functions may not work properly. Thus, it is desirable to normalize the range of all features so that each feature equally contributes to the cost function (Aksoy and Haralick 2001). Sola and Sevilla (1997) point out that data normalization prior to neural network training enables researchers to speed up the calculations and to obtain good results. Jayalakshmi and Santhakumaran (2011) point out that statistical normalization techniques enhance the reliability of feed-forward backpropagation neural networks and the performance of the data-classification model.

Following Khashman (2010), we normalize the data based on the following formula:

$$z_i = \frac{x_i - x_{min}}{x_{max} - x_{min}}$$

where z_i is normalized data, x_i is each dataset, x_{min} is the minimum value of x_i, and x_{max} is the maximum value of x_i. This method rescales the range of features to between 0 and 1. We analyze both normalized and original data in order to evaluate the robustness of our experimental results.

2.3. Performance Evaluation

We use accuracy to evaluate the performance of each machine-learning method. In our two-class problem, the confusion matrix (Table 1) gives us a summary of prediction results on a classification problem as follows:

Table 1. Confusion matrix.

		Actual Class	
		Event	No-Event
Predicted Class	Event	TP (True Positive)	FP (False Positive)
	No-Event	FN (False Negative)	TN (True Negative)

Note that "true positive" indicates the case for correctly predicted event values; "false positive" indicates the case for incorrectly predicted event values; "true negative" indicates the case for correctly predicted no-event values: and "false negative" indicates the case for incorrectly predicted no-event values. Then, prediction accuracy rate is defined by,

$$\text{prediction accuracy rate} = \frac{TP + TN}{TP + FP + FN + TN}$$

Furthermore, we repeat the experiments 100 times and calculate the average and standard deviation of the accuracy rate for each dataset.[5]

Next, we analyzed the classification ability of each method by examining the ROC curve and the AUC value. When considering whether a model is appropriate, it is not sufficient to rely solely on accuracy rate. The ratio of correctly identified instances in the given class is called the true positive rate. The ratio of incorrectly identified instances in the given class is called the false positive rate. When the false positive rate is plotted on the horizontal axis and the true positive rate on the vertical axis, the combination of these produces an ROC curve. A good model is one that shows a high true positive rate value and low false positive value. The AUC refers to the area under the ROC curve. A perfectly random prediction yields an AUC of 0.5. In other words, the ROC curve is a straight line connecting the origin (0, 0) and the point (1, 1).

---

[5] We used set. seed(50) to remove the difference caused by random numbers in drawing the ROC curve and calculating the AUC.

We also report the F-score of each case, which is defined as follows:

$$F - score = \frac{2 \times recall \times precision}{recall + precision}$$

where *recall* is equal to TP/(TP + FN) and *precision* is equal to TP/(TP +FP). Thus, the F-score is the harmonic average of recall and precision.

3. Results

We implement the experiments using R—specifically, the "ipred" package for bagging, "randomForest" for random forest, "ada" package for boosting (adaboost algorithm), and "h2o" package for NN and DNN. Furthermore, we analyze the prediction accuracy rate of each method for two cases i.e., original and normalized data. Then, we examine the classification ability of each method based on the ROC curve, AUC value, and F-score.

Table 2a,b report the results obtained using the original data. The tables show that boosting has the best performance and yields higher than 70% prediction accuracy rate on average, with a small standard deviation for both training and test data. None of the neural network models exceed a 70% average accuracy rate for test data. Furthermore, they have relatively large standard deviation for test data. Thus, it is clear that boosting achieves a higher accuracy prediction than neural networks. The prediction accuracy rate for test data is less than 60% for bagging and random forest. In addition, the difference of ratios between training and test data (90%:10% or 75%:25%) does not have an obvious influence on the results of our analysis.[6]

Table 3a,b summarize the results obtained using normalized data. The tables show that boosting has the highest accuracy rate on test data, which is similar to the results obtained for the original data case. The average accuracy rate for boosting is more than 70% and it has the smallest standard deviation for both training and test data. None of the neural network models has an average prediction accuracy rate exceeding 70% for test data. Furthermore, they have relatively large standard deviation for test data. The prediction accuracy rate of bagging and random forest does not reach 60% on average for test date, which is similar to the case for the original data. In addition, the difference of ratios between training and test data (90%:10% or 75%:25%) does not have a major influence on the result, which is similar to the case with the original data. Our comparison of the results of the original data with the results of the normalized data reveals no significant difference in prediction accuracy rate.

Figures 1–11 display ROC curves with AUC and F-score for the case using normalized data and the ratio between the training and test data of 75% to 25%. In each figure, sensitivity (vertical axis) corresponds to the true positive ratio, whereas 1—specificity (horizontal axis) corresponds to the false positive ratio. The graphs indicate that the ROC curve for boosting and neural network models have desirable properties except for the case for the Tanh activation function with dropout.

The AUC values and F-score are also shown for each figure. It is found that the highest AUC value is obtained for boosting (0.769). The highest F-score is also obtained for boosting (0.744). Thus, the classification ability of boosting is superior to other machine-learning methods. This may be because boosting employs sequential learning of weights.

It is also found that the AUC value and F-score of NN are better than those of DNN when Tanh is used as an activation function. However, this result is not apparent when ReLU is used as an activation function. It is interesting to see the results of neural-network models with respect to the influence of dropout in terms of AUC value and F-score. When Tanh is used as an activation function, NN (DNN) outperforms NN (DNN) with dropout. On the other hand, when ReLU is used as an activation function, NN (DNN) with dropout outperform NN (DNN). Thus the performance of neural networks

---

[6]   The number of units in the middle layers of NN and DNN is determined based on the Bayesian optimization method. (See Appendix A for details.)

may be sensitive to the model setting i.e., the number of middle layers, the type of activation function, and inclusion of dropout.

Table 2. Prediction accuracy of each method for original data.

(a) Original data: the ratio of training and test data is 75% to 25%						
Method			**Accuracy Ratio of Training Data**		**Accuracy Ratio of Test Data**	
			Average (%)	Standard Deviation	Average (%)	Standard Deviation
Bagging			80.13	0.003	55.98	0.008
Boosting			71.66	0.003	71.06	0.008
Random Forest			69.59	0.544	58.50	0.844
Method			**Accuracy Ratio of Training Data**		**Accuracy Ratio of Test Data**	
Model	**Activation Function**	**Middle Layer**	Average (%)	Standard Deviation	Average (%)	Standard Deviation
DNN	Tanh	2	70.66	0.721	68.93	0.972
NN	Tanh	1	71.01	0.569	69.59	0.778
DNN	Tanh with Dropout	2	58.47	3.566	58.46	3.404
NN	Tanh with Dropout	1	67.27	1.237	67.14	1.341
DNN	ReLU	2	69.57	0.707	68.61	0.863
NN	ReLU	1	68.81	0.708	68.30	1.008
DNN	ReLU with Dropout	2	69.97	0.903	69.01	0.956
NN	ReLU with Dropout	1	70.12	0.637	69.48	0.881
(b) Original Data: the Ratio of Training and Test Data is 90% to 10%						
Method			**Accuracy Ratio of Training Data**		**Accuracy Ratio of Test Data**	
			Average (%)	Standard Deviation	Average (%)	Standard Deviation
Bagging			79.58	0.003	56.23	0.015
Boosting			71.57	0.003	70.88	0.011
Random Forest			68.55	0.453	58.77	1.331
Method			**Accuracy Ratio of Training Data**		**Accuracy Ratio of Test Data**	
Model	**Activation Function**	**Middle Layer**	Average (%)	Standard Deviation	Average (%)	Standard Deviation
DNN	Tanh	2	69.64	0.683	69.31	1.325
NN	Tanh	1	70.49	0.550	69.61	1.312
DNN	Tanh with Dropout	2	57.29	3.681	57.27	4.117
NN	Tanh with Dropout	1	66.37	1.619	66.25	1.951
DNN	ReLU	2	69.49	0.695	68.76	1.408
NN	ReLU	1	69.16	0.728	68.54	1.261
DNN	ReLU with Dropout	2	69.74	0.796	68.84	1.438
NN	ReLU with Dropout	1	70.26	0.573	69.55	1.210

Table 3. Prediction accuracy of each method for normalized data.

(a) Normalized data: the ratio of training and test data is 75% to 25%					
Method			Accuracy Ratio of Training Data		Accuracy Ratio of Test Data	
			Average (%)	Standard Deviation	Average (%)	Standard Deviation
Bagging			80.12	0.003	56.15	0.008
Boosting			71.66	0.004	70.95	0.007
Random Forest			69.67	0.565	58.39	0.880
Method			Accuracy Ratio of Training Data		Accuracy Ratio of Test Data	
Model	Activation Function	Middle Layer	Average (%)	Standard Deviation	Average (%)	Standard Deviation
DNN	Tanh	2	71.14	0.732	68.75	0.912
NN	Tanh	1	70.64	0.652	69.42	0.763
DNN	Tanh with Dropout	2	57.00	4.324	56.69	4.485
NN	Tanh with Dropout	1	68.09	0.641	68.01	0.904
DNN	ReLU	2	70.37	0.627	69.35	0.856
NN	ReLU	1	70.92	0.615	69.37	0.943
DNN	ReLU with Dropout	2	70.00	0.811	68.96	0.946
NN	ReLU with Dropout	1	70.25	0.692	69.56	0.813

(b) Normalized data: the ratio of training and test data is 90% to 10%					
Method			Accuracy Ratio of Training Data		Accuracy Ratio of Test Data	
			Average (%)	Standard Deviation	Average (%)	Standard Deviation
Bagging			79.54	0.003	56.28	0.013
Boosting			71.50	0.003	70.80	0.012
Random Forest			68.66	0.475	58.83	1.368
Method			Accuracy Ratio of Training Data		Accuracy Ratio of Test Data	
Model	Activation Function	Middle Layer	Average (%)	Standard Deviation	Average (%)	Standard Deviation
DNN	Tanh	2	70.18	0.698	69.35	1.382
NN	Tanh	1	70.52	0.594	69.51	1.309
DNN	Tanh with Dropout	2	58.04	5.134	58.14	5.016
NN	Tanh with Dropout	1	67.33	1.285	67.13	1.787
DNN	ReLU	2	71.41	0.710	69.17	1.334
NN	ReLU	1	69.55	0.772	68.97	1.426
DNN	ReLU with Dropout	2	69.76	0.785	69.13	1.426
NN	ReLU with Dropout	1	69.88	0.701	69.25	1.279

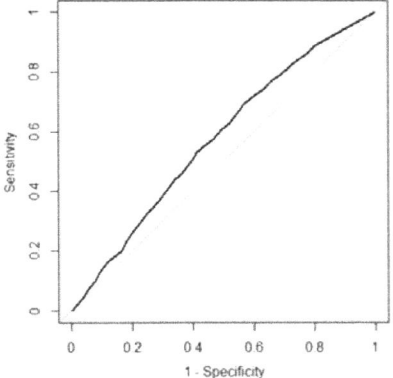

Figure 1. Receiver operating characteristic (ROC) curve for bagging. (Area under the curve (AUC) = 0.575, F-score = 0.520).

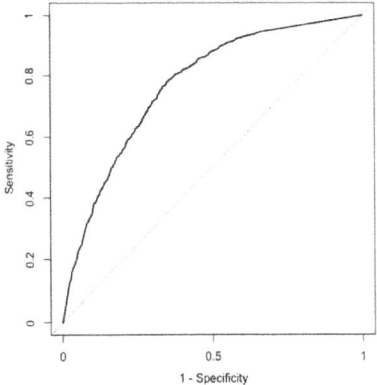

Figure 2. ROC curve for boosting. (AUC = 0.769, F-score = 0.744).

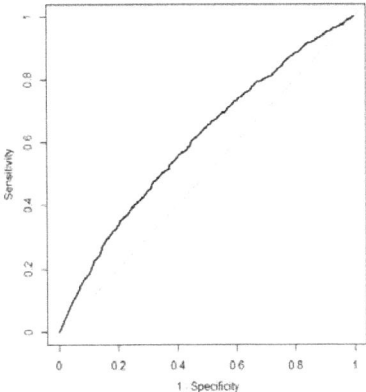

Figure 3. ROC curve for random forest. (AUC = 0.605, F-score = 0.714).

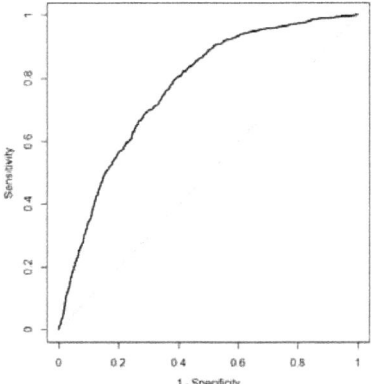

Figure 4. ROC curve for deep neural network (DNN) (Tanh). (AUC = 0.753, F-score = 0.721).

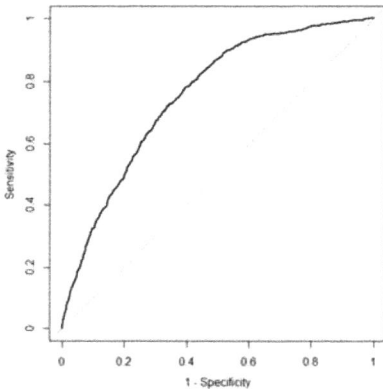

Figure 5. ROC curve for neural network (NN) (Tanh). (AUC = 0.768, F-score = 0.741).

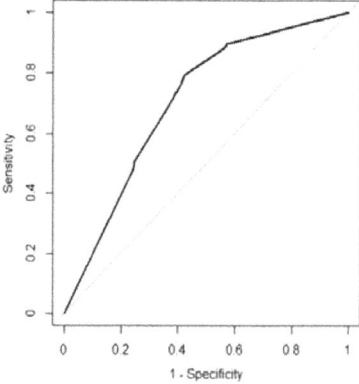

Figure 6. ROC curve for DNN (Tanh w/Dropout). (AUC = 0.600, F-score = 0.620).

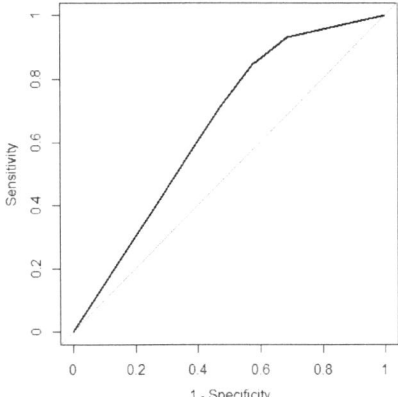

Figure 7. ROC curve for NN (Tanh w/Dropout). (AUC = 0.704, F-score = 0.717).

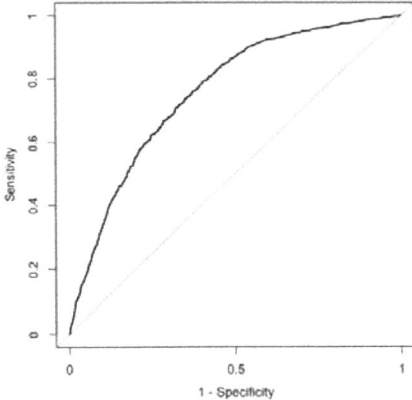

Figure 8. ROC curve for DNN (ReLU). (AUC = 0.751, F-score = 0.734).

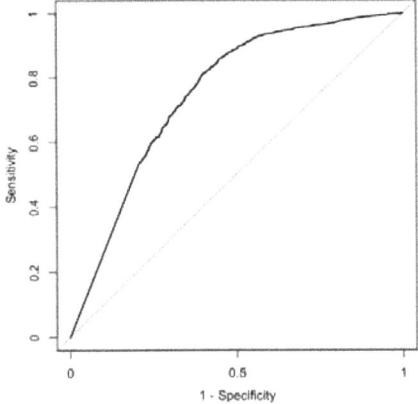

Figure 9. ROC curve for NN (ReLU). (AUC = 0.757, F-score = 0.727).

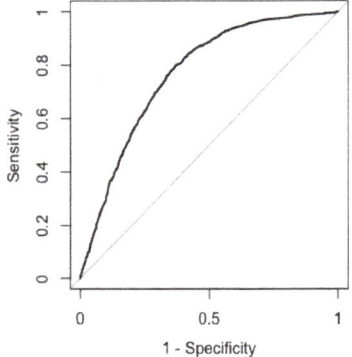

Figure 10. ROC curve for DNN (ReLU w/Dropout). (AUC = 0.765, F-score = 0.735).

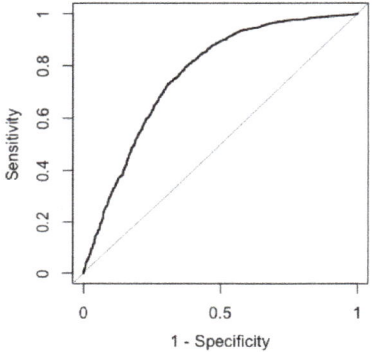

Figure 11. ROC curve for NN (ReLU w/Dropout). (AUC = 0.767, F-score = 0.730).

4. Conclusions

In this study, we analyzed default payment data in Taiwan and compared the prediction accuracy and classification ability of three ensemble-learning methods: bagging, random forest, and boosting, with those of various neural-network methods using two different activation functions. Our main results can be summarized as follows:

(1)   The classification ability of boosting is superior to other machine-learning methods.
(2)   The prediction accuracy rate, AUC value, and F-score of NN are better than those of DNN when Tanh is used as an activation function. However, this result is not apparent when ReLU is used as an activation function.
(3)   NN (DNN) outperforms NN (DNN) with dropout when Tanh is used as an activation function in terms of AUC value and F-score. However, NN (DNN) with dropout outperforms NN (DNN) when ReLU is used as an activation function in terms of AUC value and F-score.

The usability of deep learning has recently been the focus of much attention. Oreski et al. (2012) point out that the majority of studies show that neural networks are more accurate, flexible, and robust than conventional statistical methods when assessing credit risk. However, our results indicate that boosting outperforms the neural network in terms of prediction accuracy, AUC, and F-score. It is also well known that it is not easy to choose appropriate hyper-parameters for neural networks. Thus, neural networks are not always a panacea, especially for relatively small samples. Given this, it is worthwhile to make effective use of other methods such as boosting. Our future work will be to apply a similar analysis to different data in order to check the robustness of our results.

Acknowledgments: We are grateful to the three anonymous referees for their helpful comments and suggestions. An early version of this paper was read at the Workshop of Big Data and Machine Learning. We are grateful to Zheng Zhang and Xiao Jing Cai for helpful comments and suggestions. This research was supported by a grant-in-aid from The Nihon Hoseigakkai Foundation.

Author Contributions: Shigeyuki Hamori conceived and designed the experiments; Minami Kawai, Takahiro Kume, Yuji Murakami and Chikara Watanabe performed the experiments, analyzed the data, and contributed reagents/materials/analysis tools; and Shigeyuki Hamori, Minami Kawai, Takahiro Kume, Yuji Murakami and Chikara Watanabe wrote the paper.

Conflicts of Interest: The authors declare no conflicts of interest. The founding sponsors had no role in the design of the study; in the collection, analyses, or interpretation of data; in the writing of the manuscript, or in the decision to publish the results.

Appendix A. Results of Bayesian Optimization

Table A1. Number of units in middle layer for NN.

Method	Data	Ratio of Training and Test Data (%)	Input Layer	Middle Layer	Output Layer
Tanh	Original	75:25	23	7	2
Tanh	Original	90:10	23	5	2
Tanh with Dropout	Original	75:25	23	14	2
Tanh with Dropout	Original	90:10	23	12	2
ReLU	Original	75:25	23	3	2
ReLU	Original	90:10	23	7	2
ReLU with Dropout	Original	75:25	23	14	2
ReLU with Dropout	Original	90:10	23	19	2
Tanh	Normalized	75:25	23	5	2
Tanh	Normalized	90:10	23	5	2
Tanh with Dropout	Normalized	75:25	23	5	2
Tanh with Dropout	Normalized	90:10	23	10	2
ReLU	Normalized	75:25	23	11	2
ReLU	Normalized	90:10	23	4	2
ReLU with Dropout	Normalized	75:25	23	16	2
ReLU with Dropout	Normalized	90:10	23	12	2

Table A2. Number of units in middle layers for DNN.

Method	Data	Ratio of Training and Test Data (%)	Input Layer	Middle Layer 1	Middle Layer 2	Output Layer
Tanh	Original	75:25	23	5	17	2
Tanh	Original	90:10	23	2	9	2
Tanh with Dropout	Original	75:25	23	9	7	2
Tanh with Dropout	Original	90:10	23	3	11	2
ReLU	Original	75:25	23	4	6	2
ReLU	Original	90:10	23	4	9	2
ReLU with Dropout	Original	75:25	23	13	9	2
ReLU with Dropout	Original	90:10	23	5	20	2
Tanh	Normalized	75:25	23	6	17	2
Tanh	Normalized	90:10	23	4	3	2
Tanh with Dropout	Normalized	75:25	23	9	4	2
Tanh with Dropout	Normalized	90:10	23	3	18	2
ReLU	Normalized	75:25	23	4	6	2
ReLU	Normalized	90:10	23	10	7	2
ReLU with Dropout	Normalized	75:25	23	16	9	2
ReLU with Dropout	Normalized	90:10	23	5	21	2

References

Aksoy, Selim, and Robert M. Haralick. 2001. Feature normalization and likelihood-based similarity measures for image retrieval. *Pattern Recognition. Letters* 22: 563–82. [CrossRef]

Angelini, Eliana, Giacomo di Tollo, and Andrea Roli. 2008. A neural network approach for credit risk evaluation. *Quarterly Review of Economics and Finance* 48: 733–55. [CrossRef]

Boguslauskas, Vytautas, and Ricardas Mileris. 2009. Estimation of credit risks by artificial neural networks models. *Izinerine Ekonomika-Engerrring Economics* 4: 7–14.

Breiman, Leo. 1996. Bagging predictors. *Machine Learning* 24: 123–40. [CrossRef]

Breiman, Leo. 2001. Random forests. *Machine Learning* 45: 5–32. [CrossRef]

Freund, Yoav, and Robert E. Schapire. 1996. Experiments with a new boosting algorithm. Paper presented at the Thirteenth International Conference on Machine Learning, Bari, Italy, July 3–6; pp. 148–56.

Gante, Dionicio D., Bobby D. Gerardo, and Bartolome T. Tanguilig. 2015. Neural network model using back propagation algorithm for credit risk evaluation. Paper presented at the 3rd International Conference on Artificial Intelligence and Computer Science (AICS2015), Batu Ferringhi, Penang, Malaysia, October 12–13; pp. 12–13.

Jayalakshmi, T., and A. Santhakumaran. 2011. Statistical Normalization and Back Propagation for Classification. *International Journal of Computer Theory and Engineering* 3: 83–93.

Khashman, Adnan. 2010. Neural networks for credit risk evaluation: Investigation of different neural models and learning schemes. *Expert Systems with Applications* 37: 6233–39. [CrossRef]

Khemakhem, Sihem, and Younes Boujelbene. 2015. Credit risk prediction: A comparative study between discriminant analysis and the neural network approach. *Accounting and Management Information Systems* 14: 60–78.

Khshman, Adnan. 2009. A neural network model for credit risk evaluation. *International Journal of Neural Systems* 19: 285–94. [CrossRef] [PubMed]

Lantz, Brett. 2015. *Machine Learning with R*, 2nd ed. Birmingham: Packt Publishing Ltd.

LeCun, Yann, Yoshua Bengio, and Geoffrey Hinton. 2015. Deep learning. *Nature* 521: 436–44. [CrossRef] [PubMed]

Oreski, Stjepan, Dijana Oreski, and Goran Oreski. 2012. Hybrid system with genetic algorithm and artificial neural networks and its application to retail credit risk assessment. *Expert Systems with Applications* 39: 12605–17. [CrossRef]

Schapire, Robert E. 1999. A brief introduction to boosting. Paper presented at the Sixteenth International Joint Conference on Artificial Intelligence, Stockholm, Sweden, July 31–August 6; pp. 1–6.

Shapire, Robert E., and Yoav Freund. 2012. *Boosting: Foundations and Algorithms*. Cambridge: The MIT Press.

Sola, J., and Joaquin Sevilla. 1997. Importance of input data normalization for the application of neural networks to complex industrial problems. *IEEE Transactions on Nuclear Science* 44: 1464–68. [CrossRef]

Srivastava, Nitish, Georey Hinton, Alex Krizhevsky, Ilya Sutskever, and Ruslan Salakhutdinov. 2014. Dropout: A simple way to prevent neural networks from overfitting. *Journal of Machine Learning Research* 15: 1929–58.

Yeh, I-Cheng, and Che-hui Lien. 2009. The comparisons of data mining techniques for the predictive accuracy of probability of default of credit card clients. *Expert Systems with Applications* 36: 2473–80. [CrossRef]

Article

Price Discovery and the Accuracy of Consolidated Data Feeds in the U.S. Equity Markets

Brian F. Tivnan [1,2,*], **David Slater** [1], **James R. Thompson** [1], **Tobin A. Bergen-Hill** [1],
Carl D. Burke [1], **Shaun M. Brady** [3], **Matthew T. K. Koehler** [1], **Matthew T. McMahon** [1],
Brendan F. Tivnan [2] **and Jason G. Veneman** [1,*]

[1]   The MITRE Corporation, McLean, VA 22102, USA.; dslater@mitre.org (D.S.); jrthompson@mitre.org (J.R.T.);
      tbergenhill@mitre.org (T.A.B.-H.); cburke@mitre.org (C.D.B.); mkoehler@mitre.org (M.T.K.K.);
      mcmahon@mitre.org (M.T.M.)
[2]   Vermont Complex Systems Center, University of Vermont, Burlington, VT 05405, USA.;
      brendantivnan@cvsdvt.org
[3]   Center for Model-Based Regulation, Davidsonville, MD 21035, USA; sbrady@cmbreg.org
[*]   Corresponding author: btivnan@mitre.org (B.F.T.); veneman@mitre.org (J.G.V.)

Received: 30 September 2018; Accepted: 25 October 2018; Published: 28 October 2018

Abstract: Both the scientific community and the popular press have paid much attention to the speed of the Securities Information Processor—the data feed consolidating all trades and quotes across the US stock market. Rather than the speed of the Securities Information Processor (SIP), we focus here on its accuracy. Relying on Trade and Quote data, we provide various measures of SIP latency relative to high-speed data feeds between exchanges, known as direct feeds. We use first differences to highlight not only the divergence between the direct feeds and the SIP, but also the fundamental inaccuracy of the SIP. We find that as many as 60% or more of trades are reported out of sequence for stocks with high trade volume, therefore skewing simple measures, such as returns. While not yet definitive, this analysis supports our preliminary conclusion that the underlying infrastructure of the SIP is currently unable to keep pace with the trading activity in today's stock market.

Keywords: market microstructure; price discovery; latency

1. Introduction

The scientific community and the popular press have paid much attention to the speed of the Securities Information Processor (SIP)—the data feed consolidating all trade and quote messages across the US stock market—relative to other data services (Tivnan and Tivnan 2016). Here, we address the importance of the SIP.

Elsewhere, we have focused on the importance of the SIP to a key measure of market quality—efficient, price discovery (Tivnan et al. 2017). Here, we focus on extending that analysis to assess the accuracy of the SIP. We use Trade and Quote data to provide various measures of SIP latency relative to direct feeds—the high-speed, data feeds between exchanges. Using first differences, we highlight the fundamental inaccuracy of the SIP. We find that 60% or more of trades are reported out of sequence for stocks with high volume. This disordering of trades skews simple measures, such as returns. While preliminary, this analysis supports our conclusion that the underlying infrastructure of the SIP is currently unable to keep pace with the trading activity in today's U.S. equity markets.

In the sections that follow, we provide an overview of the National Market System and the SIP while adding clarity to the debates surrounding the SIP. We summarize the relevant literature of previous attempts to clarify the role of the SIP within the National Market System, as well as describe our subsequent contribution to this literature. We describe our methods and data in greater detail, followed by a presentation of our findings. We then conclude the paper with a brief discussion of the implications of our findings.

Overview of the National Market System

The National Market System (colloquially known as the "stock market") includes all market centers where investors can buy and sell shares of publicly traded companies. To facilitate the efficient exchange of capital and shares in the National Market System (NMS), each market center is required to publish both the Best Bid (i.e., the highest price at which an investor is willing to pay for a single share of a given stock) and the Best Offer (i.e., the lowest price at which an investor is willing to sell a single share of a given stock), as well as how many shares the investor is willing to sell at that price. Across the entirety of the NMS, the highest bid and the lowest offer comprise what is known as the National Best Bid and Offer (NBBO) and the difference between the Best Bid and Best Offer is known as the spread.

The NBBO reflects a distillation of the order flow across all the stock exchanges comprising the NMS. Figure 1 provides a graphical depiction of the three major datacenters of the NMS, all of which are located in northern New Jersey. Table A1 in the Appendix A also depicts the distribution of the families of exchanges across these datacenters. As depicted in Figure 1, the communications infrastructure connects the datacenters by dedicated, high-speed networks known as Direct Feeds depicted in red and black, as well as by the Security Information Processor depicted in pink. The Direct Feeds provide high-speed communications channels (e.g., faster than 50% of the speed of light (Angel 2014)) where all orders flow between the exchanges. The Securities Information Processor, or SIP, consolidates and distills all the order flow from the Direct Feeds to determine and disseminate the NBBO, as well as report all completed trades. We developed and posted an animation to provide a more illustrative depiction of these interactive dynamics between the direct feeds and the SIP[1].

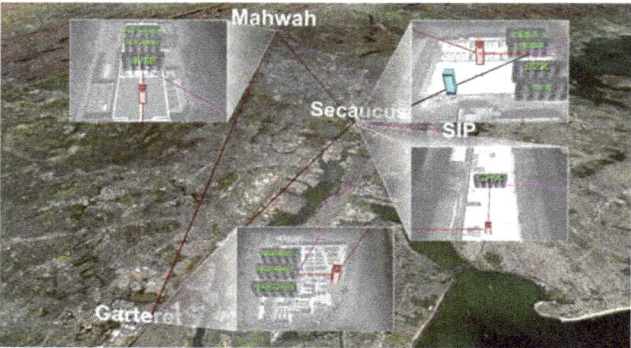

Figure 1. Graphical depiction of the three major market centers in the National Market System (NMS). SIP, Securities Information Processor.

We conclude this overview of the National Market System with a description of the two Trade Reporting Facilities; namely, the NYSE Trade Reporting Facility (NTRF) and the NASDAQ Trade Reporting Facility (QTRF). Both Trade Reporting Facilities consolidate the trade reports from all Alternative Trading Systems (colloquially known as "Dark Pools"). The NTRF consolidates Dark Pool trade reports of NYSE-listed stocks whereas the QTRF consolidates Dark Pool trade reports of NASDAQ-listed stocks.

---

[1]   The MITRE Corporation. "An Example of High Frequency Trader (HFT) Latency Arbitrage." https://www.youtube.com/ watch?v=1ltjnbBaFok&feature=youtu.be. Date of information retrieval: 30 September 2018.

Unlike an exchange, which must display best, local quotes, a Dark Pool is a market center where trading occurs without displaying any local quotes. Prevailing regulations still require that price discovery at Dark Pools are driven by the NBBO—same as at each exchange. While not depicted in Figure 1, we include Dark Pools here in our analysis for completeness, since trade reports from Dark Pools contribute to the overall, message traffic consolidated and disseminated by the SIP.

2. Review of Relevant Literature

There is widespread agreement that Mandelbrot (1963) was one of the first to characterize the dynamic behavior of prices in modern markets; later to be extended by Cont (2001). A related study (Johnson et al. 2012, 2013) identified some anomalous behavior in the dynamics of market prices, which deviated from previous expectations (Mandelbrot 1963; Cont 2001). At the time, however, the resolution of our data prevented us from making any definitive determinations about the causal mechanisms of these behaviors.

Initially in the press and later in his book, Scott Patterson was one of the first to draw attention to the speed discrepancy between the SIP and the direct feeds (Patterson 2012a, 2012b), only later to be followed in 2014 by Michael Lewis' (Lewis 2014) popular book, Flash Boys. Neither of these authors fully explored the implications of the speed discrepancy, instead relying heavily upon the works of financial industry practitioners.

A few industry practitioners were the first to identify the speed discrepancy between that of the SIP and the direct feeds. Arnuk and Saluzzi (2012) were one of the first to highlight these latency discrepancies. Bodek (2013) detailed the sweeping changes instituted by RegNMS, changes which stimulated the technological arms race and the insatiable demand for greater speeds from the direct feeds. Furthermore, Nanex Research (2014a) highlighted the spoils, which can be extracted in specific instances by those market participants so fortunate as to subscribe to the direct feeds.

Scientific contributions to this debate have been preliminary, possibly due to the limited availability of authoritative data within the scientific community. While authoritative datasets exist, subscriptions to them are extraordinarily expensive and therefore largely available only to specialized, market participants along with regulatory agencies.

Ding et al. (2014) provide one of the first scientific analyses of direct feed and SIP latencies. More recently, Bartlett and McCrary (2017) attempted to revise and generalize earlier findings (Nanex Research 2014a) by quantifying the total profits from subscribing to the direct feeds.

One common theme prevails throughout these analyses: The implication that the SIP accurately depicts market dynamics, albeit subject to some latency. We address this limitation of previous studies by highlighting and quantifying the inaccuracies of the SIP.

3. Methods

The implications of ever increasing market speeds can be a difficult topic to understand even for those immersed in market data daily. The following is an attempt to break down some empirical analyses on granular data from US stock markets that illustrate some of the implications from SIP latencies and the subsequent impact on the accuracy of the SIP. We rely on Trade and Quote data spanning the National Market System. More precisely, we purchased the NxCore dataset from Nanex Research for the following periods: The calendar year 2014, and the second and third quarters of 2015.

Many of the subsequent examples stem from market activity on a representative day (i.e., 11 August 2015), which we chose for three reasons. First, 11 August 2015 was a not a noteworthy day in the U.S. equity markets (i.e., the absence of any market-wide events). Second, this representative day closely precedes a notable day in the U.S. equity markets (i.e., 24 August 2015), which is known colloquially as "Manic Monday." Third, there were no announced modifications to the SIP between 11 August and 24 August. Given these three reasons above, it is realistic to assume the same underlying, market infrastructure for both days. Therefore, 11 August 2015 serves as a useful proxy for a representative day in the U.S. equity markets.

We capture both breadth and depth in our analyses. We achieve breadth in two ways. First, we analyzed the entire population of the 7993 unique tickers (i.e., stocks and exchange-traded funds) that printed quotes and trade reports to the SIP on the representative day. The reader will note that an exchange-traded fund (ETF) is a security similar to a mutual fund, but an ETF trades throughout the day in the same manner as a stock. Second, we also closely analyzed SPY (i.e., the SPDR S&P 500 ETF). It is important to note that the SPY is often used as a proxy of the U.S. equity market. Unlike the S P 500 index, which cannot be directly traded, the SPY represents one of the largest and most liquid, market-wide securities. For the SPY, we analyzed price, spread and market crosses. A special case of the spread occurs when the spread becomes negative. Such instances of a negative spread for the NBBO depict a crossed market, or simply *cross* for short. While a small spread indicates general agreement on price across all market participants, a large spread and crosses indicate little agreement on price. Both large spreads and crosses are indicators of inefficient, price discovery.

We also achieve depth of our analysis in a comprehensive manner. Rather than limiting our analyses to any one stock or relying solely on the large-cap stocks that comprise the Dow 30 as in previous studies (Bartlett and McCrary 2017), we chose a convenience sample of 14 stocks. This heterogeneous set of stocks varies on market capitalization, listed exchange and trading volume. This sample ranges from Apple (i.e., stock ticker: AAPL), one of the largest and most actively traded stocks in the world to Acme United Corporation (i.e., stock ticker: ACU), which is a lightly traded, small-cap stock.

Our analyses include some depictions of common descriptive measures of market performance, namely price and trade volume, as well as the monetary value of that trading activity. We then de-construct this market activity by specific exchange and components of the SIP.

We continue our analyses with a focus on the latencies between the direct feeds and the SIP, beginning with simple counts and frequency distributions. We extend this analysis by comparing first differences to highlight the divergence between the direct feeds and the SIP. We conclude with an analysis of these measures for comparison with known market events.

4. Results

As described above, we begin with empirical evidence confirming our focal date as a representative day in the U.S. equity markets. From there, we provide depictions of common descriptive measures of market performance. We then de-construct this market activity by specific exchange and components of the SIP. We then present our analysis of first differences to highlight the divergence between the direct feeds and the SIP. We conclude with an analysis of these measures for comparison with known, market events.

4.1. Representative Day in the U.S. Equity Markets

For simplicity and clarity in the presentation of our analyses, we chose a representative day in the U.S. equity markets (i.e., 11 August 2015) for its distinction from a noteworthy day (i.e., 24 August 2015) within only a two-week span. Figures 2 and 3 provide the empirical evidence to support this distinction. Both figures plot the price, spread and market crosses for SPY.

Figure 2 depicts the market dynamics for SPY on 24 August 2015. Leading up to and through the opening of the market day, the widening spread and frequent crosses indicate a tremendous uncertainty of the price. Even as spreads narrowed and price stabilized throughout the market day, frequent crosses persisted. These are all indicators of inefficient, price discovery.

Figure 3 depicts the market dynamics for SPY on 11 August 2015. Unlike the dynamics of "Manic Monday," Figure 3 reflects a "typical market day." More precisely, spreads remain small throughout the market day and crosses are intermittent yet fleeting while price is largely stable. Moreover, Figure 3 provides no evidence that would lead one to conclude that the underlying, market infrastructure is overwhelmed in any meaningful way on this day.

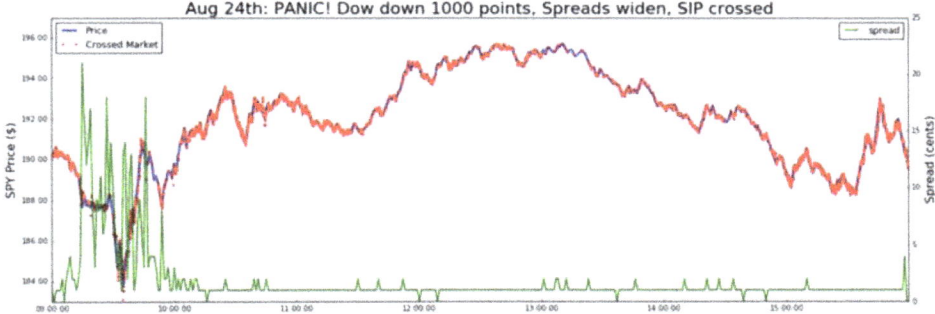

Figure 2. Crosses and Spreads in the SPY on 24 August 2015— "Manic Monday."

Figure 3. Crosses and Spreads in the SPY on 11 August 2015—"typical market day."

4.2. Common, Descriptive Measures of Market Activity

We naturally follow with a time-series depicting the price of a share of Apple over the course of a day. Figure 4 shows the price of Apple, including both pre-market (04:00 to 09:30 hours or 0 to 19,800 seconds in the figures below) and after-hours trading (16:00 to 20:00 hours or 43,200 to 57,600 seconds in the figures below). Figure 4 is typical of the only chart most people see when looking at the stock market. With data at the microsecond level, even in this typical view, one starts to see some anomalous behavior with the spikes at around 44,000 seconds. Those spikes are after-hours trades which, along with pre-market, are not usually shown on popular websites (e.g., Yahoo Finance). This begins to illustrate the complexity dynamics of price behaviors across an entire day, not just during the middle of the day.

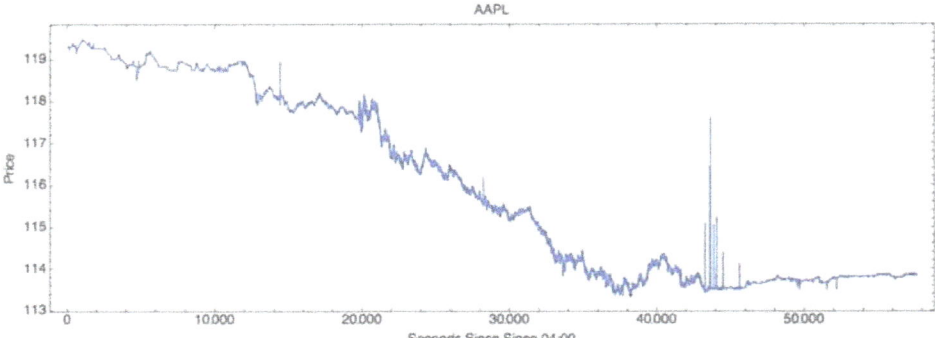

Figure 4. Apple stock price on 11 August 2015 at each second of the day from 04:00 until 20:00.

In Figure 5, we illuminate the interesting dynamics associated with the number of trades per second for a single stock. Here, one will notice the clear difference in activity during pre-market, regular market (09:30–16:00), and after-hours trading (16:00–20:00).

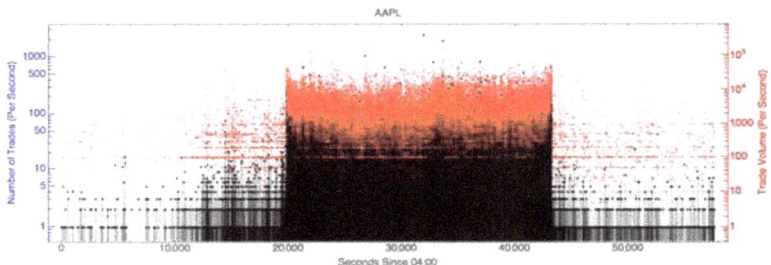

Figure 5. Trades in Apple stock on 11 August 2015 at each second of the day from 04:00 until 20:00.

To get a sense of how much capital is circulating, a look into the number of dollars traded per second in Figure 6 reveals some astounding numbers. Here, one sees that at the highest spike $40 million in Apple stock is traded in one second.

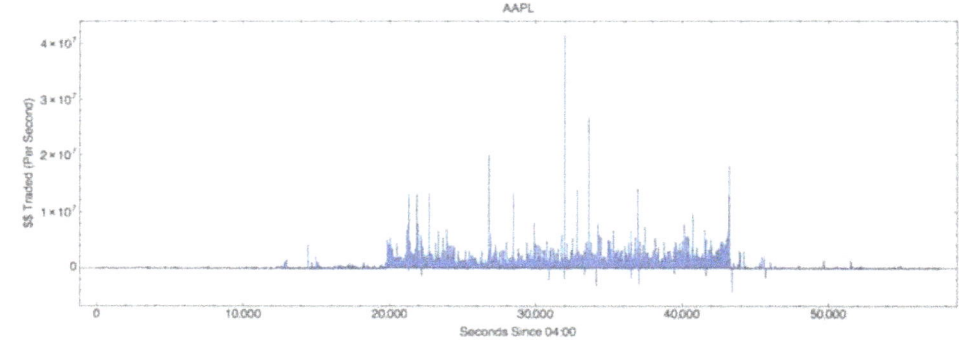

Figure 6. Dollars traded in Apple on 11 August 2015 at each second of the day from 04:00 until 20:00.

To put things in perspective the cumulative traded capital in Figure 7 shows a steady climb to approximately $10 billion traded in a single day for Apple stock. At such a high rate, the $40 million spikes, as seen in Figure 6, hardly register as outliers.

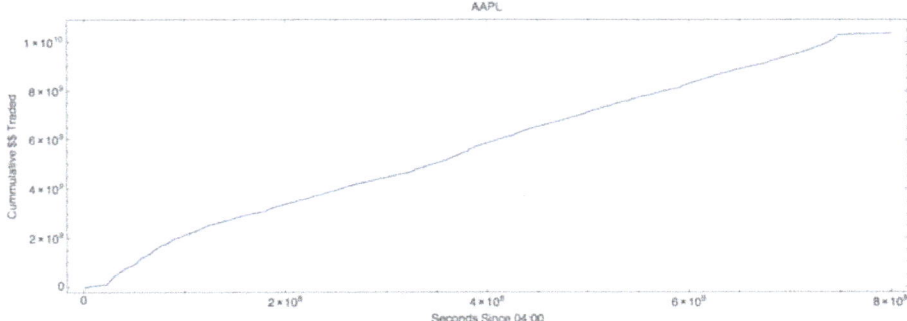

Figure 7. Cumulative dollars traded in Apple stock on 11 August 2015 summed each second from 04:00 until 20:00.

4.3. De-construct Market Activity by Exchange and Components of the SIP

Figure 8 shows how assets are traded at a high volume at the multiple exchanges that comprise the National Market System. The opening and closing hours differ per exchange and are the reason that some lines start late or stop short. The start of regular trading at 09:30 (19,800 seconds since 04:00) is seen in Figure 8 as the sharp increase in volume at all markets at opening time.

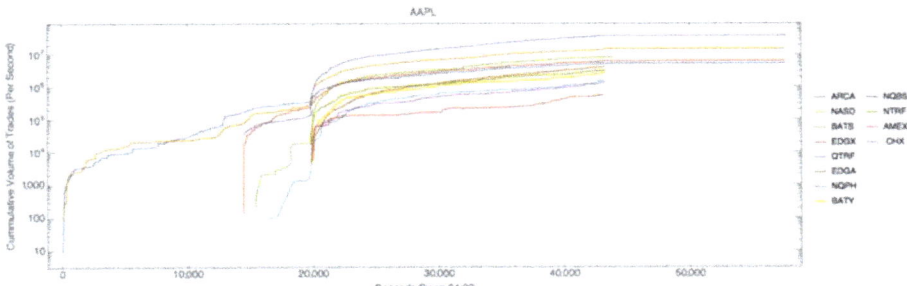

Figure 8. Cumulative trade volume by exchange for Apple stock on 11 August 2015 summed each second from 04:00 until 20:00.

Here, we begin to tie the above financial measures with the concept of bandwidth capacity of the underlying communications networks, it may be more intuitive to think of trade volume and quote lots (a quote lot is typically 100 shares) in terms of messages. A message is defined as an atomic unit of communication that describes a number of shares or lots for a particular asset (e.g., 100 shares of Apple stock). Since there are far more quote messages than there are trade messages (i.e., roughly 10 quote messages for each trade report), the following figures of quote messages per day represent the upper bound of traffic on communication networks.

For simplicity, we have referred to the SIP as a single entity to this point in our analysis. In fact, the SIP is comprised of three, distinct components: SIP A, SIP B and SIP C. The SIPs link "the U.S. markets by processing and consolidating all protected bid/ask quotes and trades from every trading venue into a single, easily consumed data feed (Consolidated Tape Association)." SIP A and B are operated by the Consolidated Tape Association and consolidate market activity for securities listed on New York Stock Exchange (NYSE) on SIP A and securities listed on NYSE ARCA, NYSE MKT, BATS and regional exchanges on SIP B (Consolidated Tape Association). SIP C is operated by NASDAQ for NASDAQ-listed securities (Unlisted Trading Privileges).

In Figure 9, one can again clearly see the opening and closing of the regular market day. Figure 9 shows messages that are recorded at each of the three SIPs. During the market day, there are very few instances that less than 1000 messages per second are printed to the SIPs, while there are times, such as the market open and close, when message traffic exceeds 100,000 messages per second.

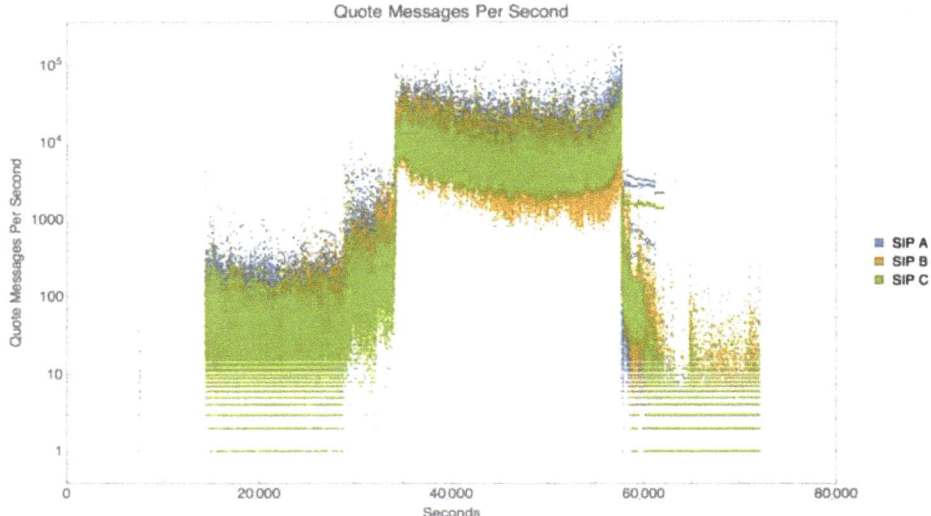

Figure 9. Quote messages by SIP for Apple stock on 11 August 2015 for each second from 04:00 until 20:00.

4.4. Latencies between the Direct Feeds and the SIP

Recall that the SIP exists to unify the market in time via efficient discovery of equity prices. To get a picture of how long it takes for trades to go from being reported at an exchange to being aggregated and recorded by the SIP for all market participants to see, one can look at the SIP latency. Latency is defined here by the timestamp from the SIP minus the timestamp from when the reporting exchange sent the trade or quote information to the SIP. The latency in microseconds for trades at each of the three SIPs for all stocks is shown in Figures 10–12.

From these three figures, one can see that the median, standard deviation and range in latency are similar across each SIP. The median latencies across all SIPs and all exchanges are within 700 μs of each other. From this, one might infer that trade reporting latencies are similar.

While similarities in latency median, standard deviation and range certainly do exist, there are at least two exceptions to these similarities. The first exception is the Chicago Stock Exchange (CHX). It was first reported elsewhere that CHX latencies are outliers from that of the other exchanges, as well as that CHX has limited share of the trading volume despite often contributing to efficient, price discovery (Nanex Research 2014b). Our findings here confirm CHX latencies as outliers. The second exception relates to the NTRF where Dark Pool trades are consolidated for NYSE-listed stocks.

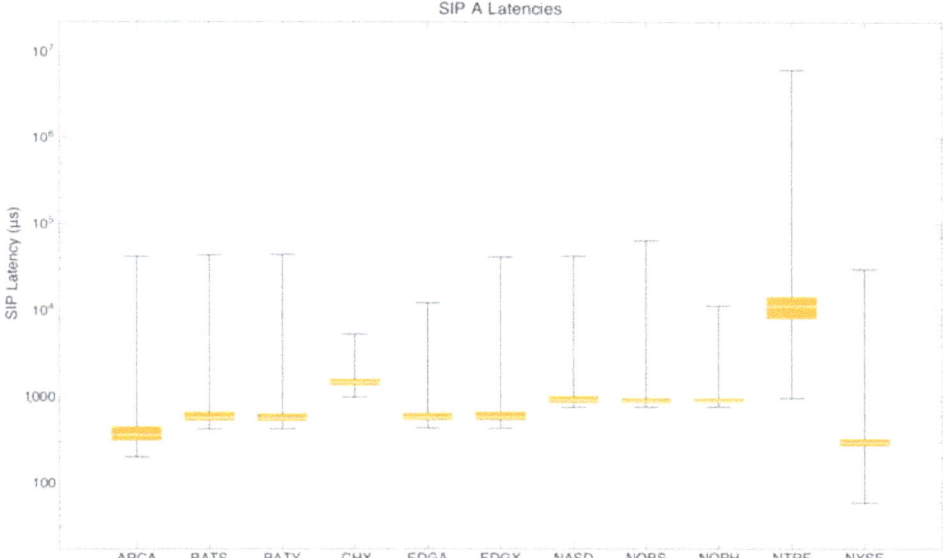

Figure 10. Box plots of latencies for all trades of all stocks traded on 11 August 2015 in microseconds reported by SIP A and separated by exchange.

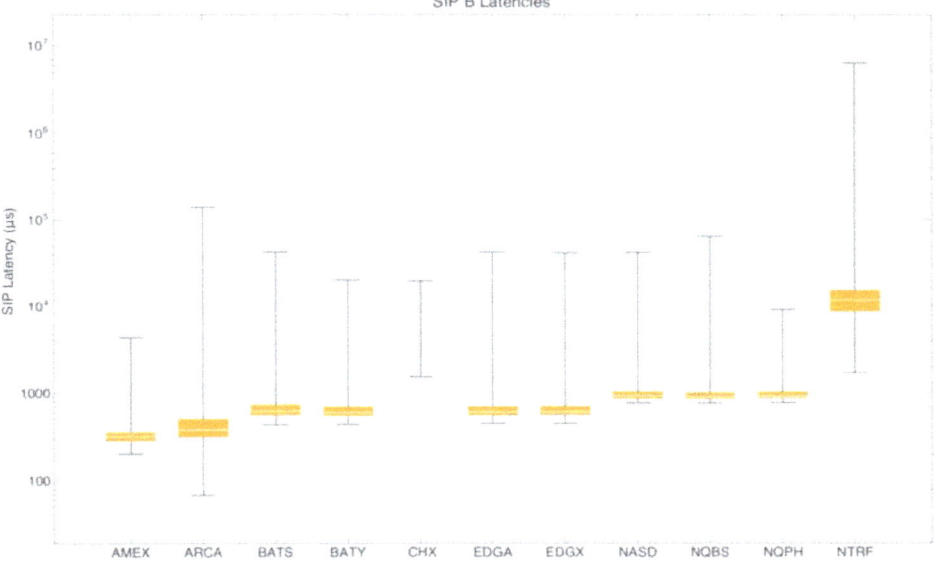

Figure 11. Box plots of latencies for all trades of all stocks traded on 11 August 2015 in microseconds reported by SIP B and separated by exchange.

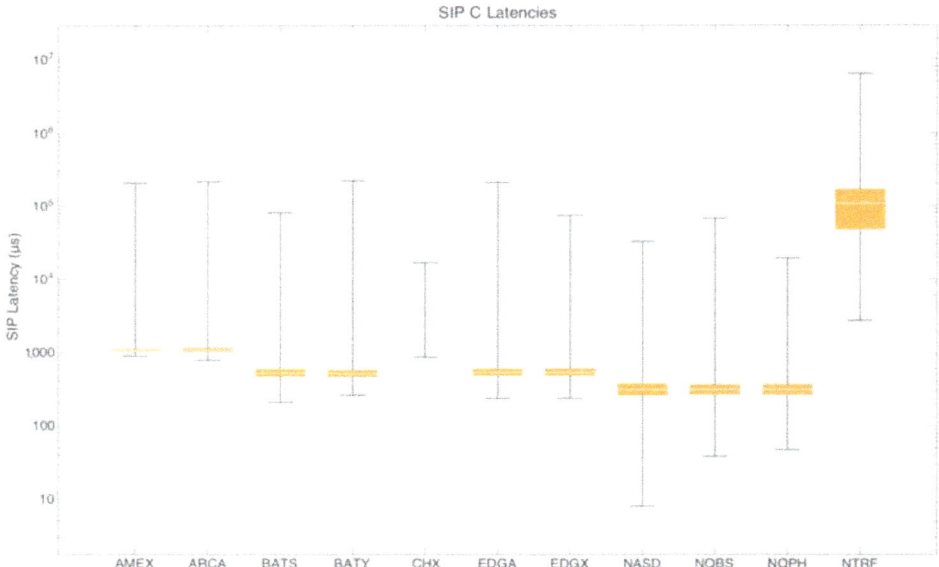

Figure 12. Box plots of latencies for all trades of all stocks traded on 11 August 2015 in microseconds reported by SIP C and separated by exchange.

Looking at latency in more detail, Figure 13 shows the latency in trade reporting for a single stock (i.e., AAPL). Figure 13 presents a far different picture from the SIP latencies and one can see that the latency differs significantly within and between exchanges. The outlier reporting exchange here is QTRF. This clearly shows that the exchanges matter when observing latency.

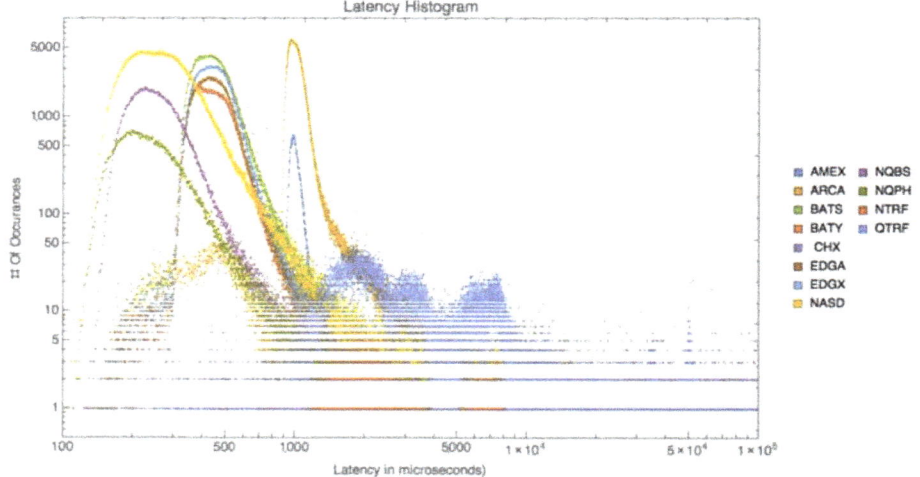

Figure 13. Latency histogram for Apple stock traded on 11 August 2015 by exchange for AAPL (truncated at 10^5 microseconds).

4.5. First Differences Highlight Inaccuracy of the SIP

Figure 14 shows the difference between the best bid and best ask, (i.e., the spread). We generated Figure 14 from the timestamps of the bid and ask quotes as printed to the SIP. This analysis shows that there are a non-trivial number of instances where the spread is negative. Indicative of inefficient price discovery, a negative spread means that one is willing to pay more than a counterparty is willing to sell at that specific time (e.g., buying a soda for $1.05 when the sticker price is only $0.99). This is neither desirable for the buyer nor is it allowed by current market rules (Securities and Exchange Commission), so the SIP might be disseminating inaccurate reports. To assess the accuracy of the SIP, one can look at the spread at each exchange in Figure 15 and see that at any exchange the spread never goes negative. However, instances of a negative spread do occur, particularly a negative spread for the NBBO. Such instances of a negative spread for the NBBO depict a *crossed market*, or simply *cross* for short. For completeness, a spread of zero, known as a *locked* market, depicts another market condition precluded by current market rules. All available orders at the best bid should have been executed against all available orders at the best offer.

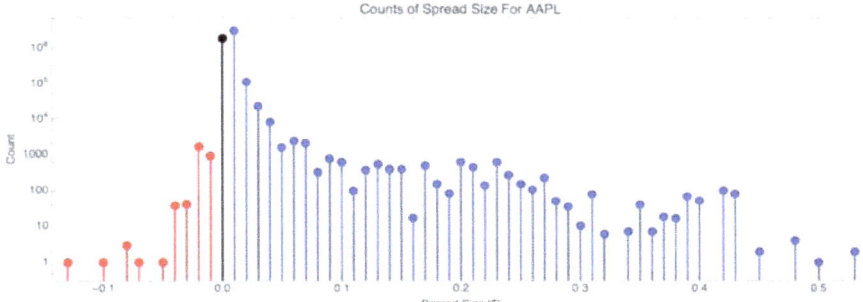

Figure 14. Bid/ask spread in dollars vs. number of occurrences for Apple stock on 11 August 2015.

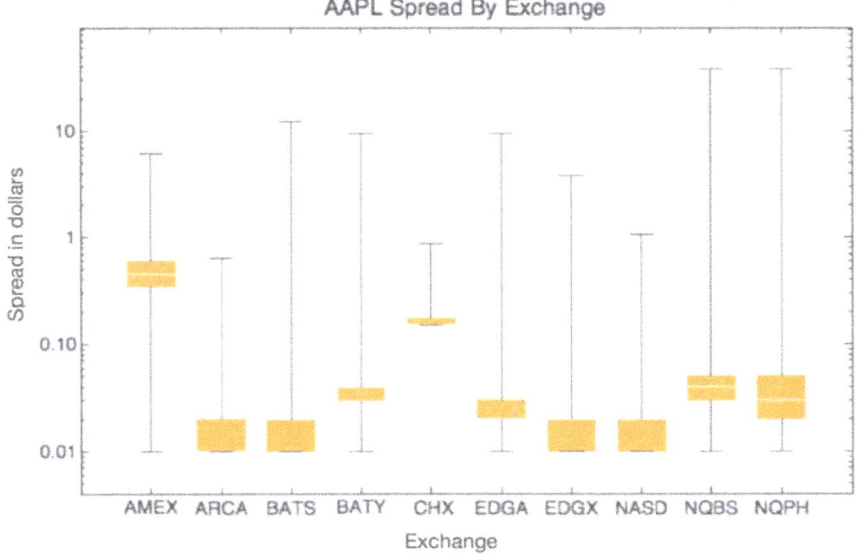

Figure 15. Box plots of spread in dollars for Apple on 11 August 2015 by exchange.

If the SIP appears wrong and the exchanges are never crossed, then this discrepancy may be due to the time it takes for messages to travel from an exchange to the SIP along communications networks. The presence of timing related anomalies indicates the importance of understanding the coupling between the financial markets and communications infrastructure and the implications of how these systems are designed.

These pricing anomalies are present across many stocks (e.g., the component stocks of the Dow 30), but for brevity and space considerations, we limit our treatment here to a convenience sample of 14 stocks listed in Table 1. Some patterns are indicated that give preliminary evidence of a relationship between message traffic and apparent crosses and locks (equal bid and asks which are also disallowed by market rules). If this relationship holds it gives further weight to the importance between finance and communication infrastructure coupling. Figure 16 indicates that as the number of quote messages increases, there is an increasing number of apparent market crossings as seen at the SIP. In Figure 16, the price of the stock is given in the color chart to the right. Stocks that trade for less than one dollar (i.e., penny stocks, blue to blue-green in the figure) operate under different market rules and appear to follow a different relationship between number of messages and crosses. This preliminary result could indicate that market rules also shape the coupling between these infrastructures.

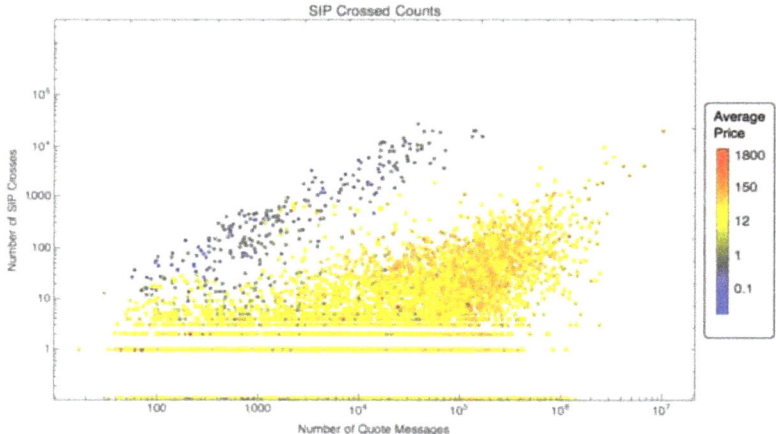

Figure 16. Counts of SIP crosses for all stocks traded on 11 August 2015.

Figure 17 shows the number of times that a stock is apparently locked (i.e., a spread of 0) at the SIP. Figure 17 provides additional evidence that increasing message traffic correlates to more locked stocks.

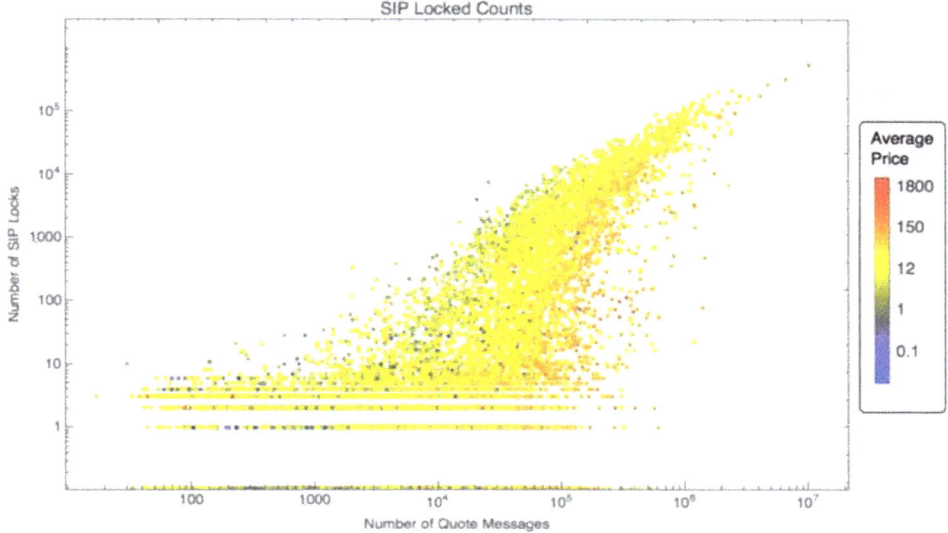

Figure 17. Counts of SIP locks for all stocks traded on 11 August 2015.

The modern financial system relies on efficient and stable communication networks for dissemination of up-to-date information. To get a picture of what can happen in a short time window, one can look at the number of events (trade reports or quote messages) for a stock that occur between the time a trade or quote update is sent to the SIP and the time the SIP reports that update to SIP subscribers—here, we refer to this delay as the latency window. Figure 18 shows that it's very common to see from hundreds to thousands of events occur within this latency window for Apple stock.

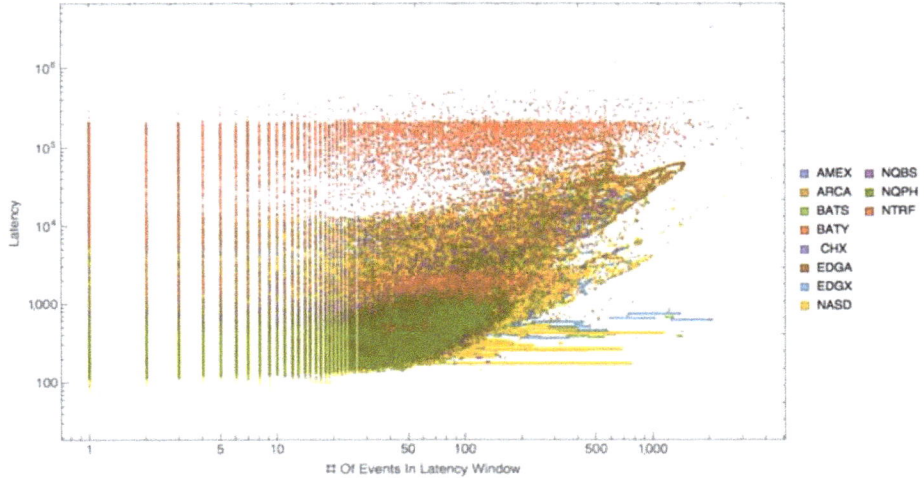

Figure 18. Number of events in latency window for Apple stock on 11 August 2015.

4.6. Crossings Between Order Books Present Arbitrage Opportunities

The appearance of a relationship between the number of apparent market locks and crosses and message (trade report or quote update) volume prompts a deeper look into the number of events within latency windows. Figures 19 and 20 are aligned vertically on the page to reflect time of day along the x axis. In Figure 19, we depict a lightly traded stock (i.e., Second Sight Medical Products, EYES) from our convenience sample to compare with a heavily traded stock (i.e., Apple, AAPL) in Figure 20. In Figure 19, the reader will notice that EYES has limited trading activity before and after the trading day, whereas Figure 20 depicts significant trading before and after hours in AAPL.

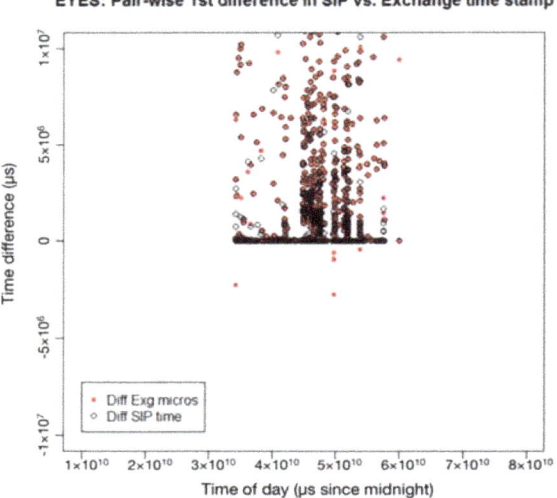

Figure 19. Time difference in SIP vs. exchange time stamp for EYES stock on 11 August 2015.

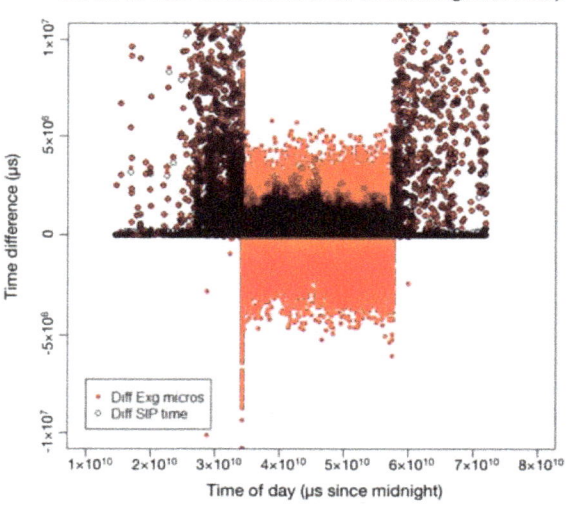

Figure 20. Time difference in SIP vs. exchange time stamp for AAPL stock on 11 August 2015.

In Figure 19, we can see that there are times where the SIP and exchange time do not line up (places where the red and white circles don't line up). For a highly traded stock like AAPL, we see from Figure 20 that there are far more occasions where the difference in time stamps is out of sequence.

A closer analysis of Figures 19 and 20 yields additional insights. Because we sorted by the SIP timestamp using the Precision Time Protocol (Precision Time Protocol), all first differences should be positive. Therefore, all negative differences in the SIP timestamps, as depicted in Figures 19 and 20, indicate that the SIP may often misrepresent the accurate sequence of trades.

We see similar features in a number of stocks across a range of trading volume in Table 1, which shows the total number of trades for a particular asset, and the percentage of those that were reported out of sequence by the SIP. A strong linear trend (slope = 0.66, R-squared = 0.99) exists between the number of trades and the number out of sequence. While additional analyses would be necessary to pinpoint drivers of that trend, such in-depth analyses could prove worthwhile as they might illuminate arbitrage opportunities. These arbitrage opportunities could arise from a crossed market. Recall that a crossed market indicates a negative spread (i.e., a displayed, best bid exceeds a displayed, best offer). If permitted, trading in a crossed market might present opportunities for true arbitrage. As an illustrative example, trading in a crossed market might enable Trader C to purchase an even lot of shares of Apple at $116.00 per share from Trader A and immediately sell the same even lot of Apple shares for $116.02 per share to Trader B. The reader will note that in the absence of Trader C in the market, Traders A and B might be natural counterparties at $116.01 per share of Apple, each experiencing price improvement, which is why trading is halted in crossed markets. To exploit this potential arbitrage opportunity, Trader C must anticipate the crossed market and exploit a latency advantage via a direct-feed connection to the market. While market participants may have the ability to act on these arbitrage opportunities, they may exist for only a very small window of time (e.g., 500 microseconds or less) (Tivnan et al. 2017). These fleeting opportunities for latency arbitrage clearly indicate the ramifications of the tight interdependence between financial markets and the communication networks that connect them.

Table 1. Trades out of sequence for selected stocks on 11 August 2015.

Stock	Percent Out of Sequence	Total Trades	Listing Exchange
AAPL	66.2%	482,578	NASDQ
BAC	50.1%	97,303	NYSE
XOM	43.0%	86,834	NYSE
GOOG	56.3%	69,085	NASDQ
DNR	43.3%	51,185	NYSE
IBM	26.4%	29,960	NYSE
SHAK	27.9%	16,349	NYSE
KLIC	30.3%	3304	NASDQ
GBX	20.6%	2804	NYSE
WBMD	29.9%	2428	NASDQ
EYES	10.3%	1653	NASDQ
BRKA	0.3%	304	NYSE
OHGI	3.8%	286	NASDQ
ACU	0.0%	1	NYSEMKT

5. Conclusions

Above, we uncover clear limitations to the accuracy of the SIP, namely its inability to preserve the correct ordering of trades. Rather than solely relying on a largely homogenous set of stocks (e.g., the components of the Dow 30), we instead opted for a heterogenous set of stocks that varied on market capitalization, listed exchange and trading volume. This heterogeneity yielded convincing evidence that the inaccuracy of the SIP relates to trade volume. Therefore, one can reasonably infer that the physical infrastructure underlying the SIP has finite limitations, which are routinely exceeded for certain stocks.

While the impacts from such SIP inaccuracy could be extensive, we conclude by highlighting two significant implications. First, when the SIP fails to capture the actual order of trades, such inaccuracies will skew stock returns. While a simple measure, returns play a fundamental role in nearly all measures of risk; therefore, the inaccuracies of the SIP uncovered here could reveal extensive limitations for risk management. Finally, given the preponderance of algorithmic trading in today's U.S. equity markets, disordered trades and subsequently skewed returns could result in positive feedback driving markets away from efficient, price discovery.

While convincing, our findings on the accuracy of the SIP are not exhaustive, so we therefore encourage researchers to consider additional dimensions of analysis for future research. A longitudinal study might address the accuracy of the SIP over time. Another study might compare the accuracy of the SIP for component stocks of prevailing market indices (e.g., Dow 30, S P 500 and Russell 3000). Lastly, we suggest that a direct extension of this study of the SIP accuracy of trades includes an analysis of updated quotes.

Author Contributions: Conceptualization, B.F.T. (Brian F. Tivnan), S.M.B., M.T.K.K., M.T.M., D.S., J.R.T., B.F.T. (Brendan F. Tivnan) and J.G.V.; Data curation, B.F.T. (Brian F. Tivnan), D.S., T.A.B.-H. and J.G.V.; Formal analysis, B.F.T. (Brian F. Tivnan), D.S., J.R.T. and M.T.K.K.; Funding acquisition, B.F.T. (Brian F. Tivnan) and S.M.B.; Investigation, M.T.K.K.; Methodology, B.F.T. (Brian F. Tivnan), D.S., J.R.T., Carl Burke, M.T.K.K., M.T.M. and J.G.V.; Project administration, B.F.T. (Brian F. Tivnan) and J.G.V.; Resources, B.F.T. (Brian F. Tivnan) and S.M.B.; Software, D.S., J.R.T., T.A.B.-H., Carl Burke, M.T.K.K. and M.T.M.; Supervision, B.F.T. (Brian F. Tivnan) and J.G.V.; Validation, B.F.T. (Brian F. Tivnan); Visualization, D.S., J.R.T., T.A.B.-H., Carl Burke, M.T.K.K. and B.F.T. (Brendan F. Tivnan); Writing—original draft, B.F.T. (Brian F. Tivnan) and J.G.V.; Writing—review & editing, B.F.T. (Brian F. Tivnan), B.F.T. (Brendan F. Tivnan) and J.G.V.

Funding: The researchers are grateful for external funding which supported the initial phase of this study. B.F.T., D.S., J.R.T., T.A.B-H., C.D.B., S.M.B., M.T.T.K., M.T.M., and J.G.V. were supported by U.S. Department of Homeland Security award #HSHQDC-14-D-00006. The views, opinions and/or findings expressed are those of the authors and should not be interpreted as representing the official views or policies of the Department of Homeland Security or the U.S. Government.

Acknowledgments: The authors gratefully acknowledge the following: Collaborative contributions from Richard Bookstaber, Michael Foley, Christine Harvey, Eric Hunsader, Neil Johnson and Mark Paddrik; helpful insights from Anshul Anand, Chris Danforth, David Dewhurst, Peter Dodds, Jordan Feidler, Andre Frank, Bill Gibson, Frank Hatheway, John Ring, Chuck Schnitzlein, Colin Van Oort, Tom Wilk and attendees at the 2016 International Congress on Agent Computing. The authors' affiliation with The MITRE Corporation is provided for identification purposes only and is not intended to convey or imply MITRE's concurrence with, or support for, the positions, opinions or viewpoints expressed by the authors.

Conflicts of Interest: The authors declare no conflict of interest.

Appendix A

Table A1. Exchanges and Trade Reporting Facilities.

Exchange Family	Exchange Name	Abbreviations	Geographic Location
BATS	BATS	BATS/BZX	Secaucus, NJ
	BATS-Y	BATY/BYX	Secaucus, NJ
	Direct Edge A	EDGA	Secaucus, NJ
	Direct Edge X	EDGX	Secaucus, NJ
Chicago	Chicago Stock Exchange	CHX	Secaucus, NJ
NASDAQ	NASDAQ	NASD	Carteret, NJ
	NASDAQ-Boston	NQBS	Carteret, NJ
	NASDAQ-Philadelphia	NQPH	Carteret, NJ
NYSE	New York Stock Exchange	NYSE	Mahwah, NJ
	New York Stock Exchange—ARCA	ARCA	Mahwah, NJ
	New York Stock Exchange—Market	AMEX/NY-MKT	Mahwah, NJ
SIP	NYSE Trade Reporting Facility	NTRF	Mahwah, NJ
SIP	NASDAQ Trade Reporting Facility	QTRF	Carteret, NJ

References

Angel, James J. 2014. When Finance Meets Physics: The Impact of the Speed of Light on Financial Markets and Their Regulation. *Financial Review* 49: 271–81. [CrossRef]

Arnuk, Salvatore, and Joseph Saluzzi. 2012. *Broken Markets*. Upper Saddle River, New Jersey: FT Press.

Bartlett, Robert P., and Justin McCrary. 2017. How Rigged Are Stock Markets?: Evidence from Microsecond Timestamps. Available online: https://www.nber.org/papers/w22551 (accessed on 30 September 2018).

Bodek, Haim. 2013. *The Problem of HFT: Collected Writings on High Frequency Trading & Stock Market Structure Reform*. Norwalk: Decimus Capital Markets.

Consolidated Tape Association. Available online: https://www.ctaplan.com/index (accessed on 30 September 2018).

Cont, Rama. 2001. Empirical Properties of Asset Returns. *Quantitative Finance* 1: 223–36. [CrossRef]

Ding, Shengwei, John Hanna, and Terrence Hendershott. 2014. How Slow is the NBBO? *A Comparison with Direct Exchange Feeds. Financial Review* 49: 313–32.

Johnson, Neil, Guannan Zhao, Eric Hunsader, Jing Meng, Amith Ravindar, Spencer Carran, and Brian Tivnan. 2012. Financial Black Swans Driven by Ultrafast, Machine Ecology. Available online: https://arxiv.org/abs/1202.1448 (accessed on 30 September 2018).

Johnson, Neil, Guannan Zhao, Eric Hunsader, Hong Qi, Nicholas Johnson, Jing Meng, and Brian Tivnan. 2013. Abrupt Rise of New Machine Ecology Beyond Human Response Time. *Scientific Reports* 3: 2627. [CrossRef] [PubMed]

Lewis, Michael. 2014. *Flash Boys: A Wall Street Revolt*. New York: Norton & Company.

Mandelbrot, Benoit. 1963. *Variation of Certain Speculative Prices*. New York: Springer.

Nanex Research. 2014a. NBBO Misfiring. Available online: http://www.nanex.net/aqck2/4616.html (accessed on 30 September 2018).

Nanex Research. 2014b. Perfect Pilfering. Available online: http://www.nanex.net/aqck2/4661.html (accessed on 30 September 2018).

Patterson, Scott, and Jennifer Strasburg. 2012a. Traders Navigate a Murky New World. *Wall Street Journal*, April 9.

Patterson, Scott. 2012b. *Dark Pools*. New York: Crown Pub.

Precision Time Protocol is "a protocol used to synchronize clocks throughout a computer network". Available online: https://en.wikipedia.org/wiki/Precision_Time_Protocol (accessed on 30 September 2018).

Securities and Exchange Commission. Regulation NMS. Available online: https://www.sec.gov/rules/final/34-51808.pdf (accessed on 30 September 2018).

Tivnan, Brian F., and Brendan F. Tivnan. 2016. Impacts of Market Liquidity and Heterogeneity in the Investor Decision Cycle on the National Market System. Paper presented at SWARMFEST 2016: 20th Annual Meeting on Agent-Based Modeling & Simulation, Burlington, VT, USA, July 31–August 3.

Tivnan, Brian F., Matthew T. K. Koehler, David Slater, Jason Veneman, and Brendan F. Tivnan. 2017. Toward a Model of the U.S. Stock Market: How Important is the Securities Information Processor? Paper presented at the 2017 Winter Simulation Conference, Las Vegas, NV, USA, 3–6 December; Piscataway, NJ, USA: Institute of Electrical and Electronics Engineers, Inc., pp. 1181–92.

Unlisted Trading Privileges. Available online: http://www.utpplan.com/overview (accessed on 30 September 2018).

Article

Expectations for Statistical Arbitrage in Energy Futures Markets

Tadahiro Nakajima [1,2]

[1]   The Kansai Electric Power Company, Incorporated, 6-16, Nakanoshima 3-chome, Kita-Ku, Osaka 530-8270,
     Japan; nakajima.tadahiro@a4.kepco.co.jp; Tel.: +81-6-6441-8821
[2]   Graduate School of Economics, Kobe University, 2-1 Rokkodai-cho Nada-ku, Kobe 657-8501, Japan

Received: 7 December 2018; Accepted: 12 January 2019; Published: 15 January 2019

Abstract: Energy futures have become important as alternative investment assets to minimize the volatility of portfolio return, owing to their low links with traditional financial markets. In order to make energy futures markets grow further, it is necessary to expand expectations of returns from trading in energy futures markets. Therefore, this study examines whether profits can be earned by statistical arbitrage between wholesale electricity futures and natural gas futures listed on the New York Mercantile Exchange. On the assumption that power prices and natural gas prices have a cointegration relationship, as tested and supported by previous studies, the short-term deviation from the long-term equilibrium is regarded as an arbitrage opportunity. The results of the spark-spread trading simulations using historical data from 2 January 2014 to 29 December 2017 show about 30% yield at maximum. This study shows the possibility of generating earnings in energy futures market.

Keywords: cointegration; statistical arbitrage; natural gas; wholesale electricity; futures market; spark spread

1. Introduction

A variety of energy derivatives are listed and actively traded on the New York Mercantile Exchange (NYMEX), the Intercontinental Exchange Futures, and other commodity exchanges. For example, Figure 1 traces the open interests of West Texas Intermediate (WTI) crude oil futures and Henry Hub natural gas futures from the beginning of 1991 to the end of 2016. Both open interests were temporarily stagnated owing to the Lehman shock that preceded the global financial crisis, but in general, they have tended to increase.

Most energy companies in the supply chain of crude oil, natural gas, and power handle extremely large amounts of physical assets. Furthermore, they are exposed to large price fluctuations owing to the geopolitical issues, demand from newly emerging countries, and resource nationalism. Moreover, power futures prices have a very complicated relationship with spot prices and usually contain large forward risk premium, because electricity cannot be stored economically, unlike other commodities, as Haugom et al. (2014, 2018) point out. Therefore, these companies must positively trade energy derivatives in order to hedge their risks even slightly.

Institutional investors hold energy derivatives as alternative investment to benefit from portfolio diversification, because these derivatives have a low correlation with conventional investment, such as stocks, bonds, and foreign currencies. Any entity in any country consumes energy resource, such as crude oil, natural gas, and coal, although they cannot control the price fluctuation risks by themselves. Therefore, there are great expectations of energy derivatives, as most market participants aim to minimize the volatility of return on investment.

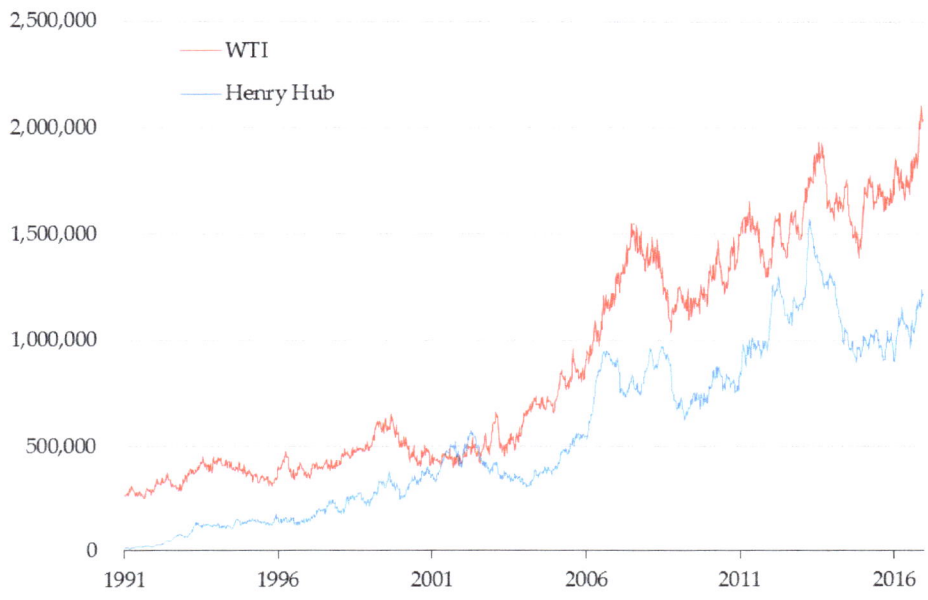

Figure 1. Open interests of WTI futures and Henry Hub futures.

However, the variety of participants is expected to increase, for their own reasons, because energy derivatives trading enables more efficient price formation of the energy types that are the underlying assets. In other words, derivatives trading contributes to more efficient economic resource allocation and maximization of social welfare. Utility companies that handle large amounts of spot positions are expected to expand derivatives trading to earn profit through proprietary trading based on commodity information. Furthermore, traditional financial companies that possess advanced technology developed for and proven in financial markets are expected to increase derivatives trading in order to earn profit by spread trading between various commodity derivatives. It is necessary for a wide and large amount of information that energy companies have to be reflected quickly in each energy price. Moreover, the technology that financial companies possess is necessary to help generate higher efficiency among multiple markets.

Some early studies on this emergent field of statistical arbitrage are as follows. Alexakis (2010) presents the implications of the implementation of statistical arbitrage strategies based on the cointegration relationship between stock indexes in New York, London, Frankfurt, and Tokyo. Mayordomo et al. (2014) examines the statistical arbitrage between credit default swaps and asset swap packages. Focardi et al. (2016) propose an approach based on dynamic factor models of prices to statistical arbitrage and demonstrates the performance empirically by applying the strategies to the stock of companies included in the S&P500. Hain et al. (2018) offers insights into the profitability of convergence trading in European commodity markets. Baviera and Baldi (2018) focus on stop-loss and leverage in statistical arbitrage and apply the new strategy to the spread on Heating Oil and Gas Oil futures. Liu and Su (2018) examine the causality between the returns of gold and silver on the Shanghai Gold Exchange and provide implications for the trading strategies of statistical arbitrage. However, there is no previous research on statistical arbitrage trading among wholesale electricity futures and natural gas futures in the United States (US), to the best of our knowledge.

In general, arbitrage is trading to take advantage of the price difference between two or more markets. In other words, when the same valued items are not the same price at the same time, the arbitrageur can acquire the margin by purchasing the cheaper item and selling the higher-priced one. For instance, spatial arbitrage opportunities occur because gold futures is listed on commodity exchanges around the world and the price varies by exchanges. However, arbitrage opportunities in such similar securities cannot last long, because the price difference is adjusted by arbitrageurs immediately. As another example, statistical arbitrage is possible by taking advantage of the price difference between different securities. Statistical arbitrage is evaluated by quantitative methods. It is conditional on finding and estimating a statistical relationship between multiple securities.

Many previous studies accept the cointegration relationship between electricity prices and natural gas prices. Serletis and Herbert (1999), Emery and Liu (2002), Serletis and Shahmoradi (2006), and Mjelde and Bessler (2009) accept that the regional wholesale electricity index is cointegrated with the natural gas price index in North America. Asche et al. (2006), Joëts and Mignon (2011), Furió and Chuliá (2012), and Freitas and Silva (2015) indicate that there is a cointegration relationship in Europe. Mohammadi (2009) accepts the cointegration hypothesis to examine the relationship between retail power prices and gas prices at wellhead in the US. Gautam and Paudel (2018) examine the demand for power in the residential, commercial, and industrial sectors after the acceptance of cointegration with gas prices.

Therefore, unconditionally accepting the cointegration relationship between natural gas futures prices and wholesale electricity futures prices, we investigate the possibility of profit acquisition in spark-spread trading by regarding the deviation from the long-run equilibrium between these two variables as arbitrage opportunities. The results present profitability by statistical arbitrage trading using a very simple algorithm based on a long-term equilibrium formula between wholesale electricity futures and natural gas futures.

The remainder of this paper is organized as follows. Section 2 explains the methodology adopted. Section 3 describes the data analyzed and used in the simulations. Section 4 presents the results of the analyses and simulations. Section 5 provides a discussion about the results.

2. Methodology

When the cointegration hypothesis between natural gas futures prices and wholesale electricity futures prices is accepted unconditionally, the possibility of earning profit by statistical arbitrage between these two markets is confirmed.

We develop the algorithm under the following two hypotheses. First, long-term equilibrium between gas prices and power prices does not fluctuate dramatically over the short term. Second, these prices do not fully reflect each other on the day. Thereafter, we verify the profitability based on the simulation using historical data.

2.1. Monitoring Prices

As a reference value for transaction candidate date, we monitor daily historical data for three years up to the day before that date. Specifically, we monitor the trend of non-stationarity of both economic variables. We adopt the unit root test developed by Kwiatkowski et al. (1992), the so-called KPSS test. Because the KPSS test, which has a null hypothesis of a stationary, is adequate for monitoring the trend of non-stationarity, while these variables are predicted to have a unit root like the other market variables. Moreover, we examine the stationarity of these variables and the stationarity of the first differences of these variables for the whole period by the augmented Dickey–Fuller (ADF) test and Phillips and Perron (1988) PP test. In addition, we monitor the tendency of the relationship between these prices by the cointegration test proposed by Johansen (1988). We unconditionally accept the cointegration hypothesis between wholesale power futures prices and natural gas futures prices supported by past literature to develop the trading algorithm. Therefore, even if the stationary hypothesis is accepted or the cointegration hypothesis rejected, the cointegration relationship is not denied simply by regarding the results as a power shortage caused by the number of samples or the test methodology. However, to respect the price trend, we attempt to reflect these test results in the trading strategy.

2.2. Estimation of Long-Term Equilibrium Equations

The long-term equilibrium equation estimated at trading candidate date t is

$$E(t) = \alpha(t) \times G(t) + \beta(t) \tag{1}$$

where $E(t)$ and $G(t)$ are futures prices of wholesale electricity and natural gas, respectively; and $\alpha(t)$ and $\beta(t)$ are coefficients estimated by dynamic ordinary least squares (DOLS) using three years up to the day before date t as the sample period. When we estimate the cointegrating vector using DOLS, it is acceptable to determine the orders of lead and lag by minimizing the information criterion. However, the lead values cannot be utilized in a real trading strategy, because these are prices after the trading candidate date. Therefore, the cointegrating vectors are obtained by ordinary least squares estimation of the coefficients of the equation

$$E(t) = \alpha(t) \times G(t) + \beta(t) + \gamma(t) \times (G(t) - G(t-1)) \tag{2}$$

The sampling period is from $t - 3 \times 365$ to $t - 1$, and therefore, we do not use prices after the transaction candidate date.

2.3. Trading

As with ordinary spread trading, this study combines both a long and short position at the same time in gas and power as related futures contracts. In other words, when the price difference is wider than the appropriate level, we sell higher-priced futures and buy lower-priced futures. On the contrary, when the price difference is narrower than the appropriate level, we buy the higher-priced futures and sell the lower-priced futures. The decision on whether the price difference between gas futures and electricity futures is appropriate depends on Equation (1).

The specific procedure is as follows. When

$$E(t) > \alpha(t) \times G(t) + \beta(t) \tag{3}$$

the electricity price is considered high and the gas price low. Therefore, we settle the long position in electricity and take a short position in electricity for

$$E(t)/(E(t) + G(t)) \tag{4}$$

Moreover, we take a long position in gas for

$$G(t)/(E(t) + G(t)) \tag{5}$$

Conversely, when

$$E(t) < \alpha(t) \times G(t) + \beta(t) \tag{6}$$

the electricity price is considered low and the gas price is high. Therefore, we settle the long position in gas and take a short position in gas for

$$G(t)/(E(t) + G(t)) \tag{7}$$

Moreover, we take a long position in electricity for

$$E(t)/(E(t) + G(t)) \tag{8}$$

3. Data

This study employs the PJM Western Hub Real-Time Off-Peak Futures as wholesale power, and the Henry Hub Natural Gas Futures as natural gas from the viewpoint of liquidity and representativeness. Both futures are listed on the NYMEX, which is one of the most efficient commodity exchanges in the world. We use daily data from 2 January 2014 to 29 December 2017, which are obtained from Bloomberg. Shale gas fields developed significantly from 2008 to 2013. At the same time, thermal power generation costs declined. To avoid this structural change, this study uses data from 2014. The long-term equilibrium equation at the trading candidate date is estimated by using three years of observations up to the day before that day. Therefore, the simulation test period is for only one year in 2017.

Table 1 presents the summary statistics of Henry Hub and PJM. Each number of observations is 1007, because the NYMEX was open for 1007 days from 2 January 2014 to 29 December 2017. We reject the hypothesis that both variables are normally distributed by the Jarque–Bera statistics calculated from the skewness and kurtosis. Table 2 presents the results obtained from the KPSS test, ADF test, and PP test. The KPSS test rejects the null hypothesis that these variables are stationary, and accepts the null hypothesis that the first differences of these variables are stationary. Both the ADF test and the PP test accept the null hypothesis that these variables have a unit root, and reject the null hypothesis that the first differences of these variables have a unit root. Moreover, Figure 2 provides the time plots of each variable. Intuitively, it seems that the Henry Hub and PJM are interlocked.

Table 1. Summary statistics.

Statistic	Henry Hub	PJM
Observations	1007	1007
Mean	3.115	24.81
Median	2.925	23.35
Maximum	6.149	36.30
Minimum	1.639	19.20
Standard deviation	0.794	3.879
Skewness	0.777	1.050
Kurtosis	3.283	3.542
Jarque–Bera	104.8 [0.00]	197.4 [0.00]

Note: Values in brackets indicate *p*-values.

Figure 2. Prices of PJM futures and Henry Hub futures.

Table 2. Unit root tests.

Test	Henry Hub	First Differences of Henry Hub	PJM	First Differences of PJM
KPSS	1.724 (0.463) *	0.116 (0.463)	3.176 (0.463) *	0.149 (0.463)
ADF	−2.235 (−2.864)	−32.719 (−2.864) **	−1.627 (−2.864)	−41.267 (−2.864) **
PP	−2.015 (−2.864)	−33.348 (−2.864) **	−1.645 (−2.864)	−41.743 (−2.864) **

Note: Values in parentheses are 5% critical values. * indicates that the stationary hypothesis is rejected at the 5% significance level. ** indicates that the unit root hypothesis is rejected at the 5% significance level.

4. Results of Analyses and Simulations

4.1. Unit Root Tests

Figure 3 presents the KPSS test statistics for 2017. The test statistic on a certain day t is obtained during the sample period from $t - 3 \times 365$ to $t - 1$. The stationary hypotheses of both variables are rejected by all the tests during the period. In other words, while each of these two variables is unit root tested 365 times using approximately 750 samples, we can accept the unit root hypothesis by all KPSS tests.

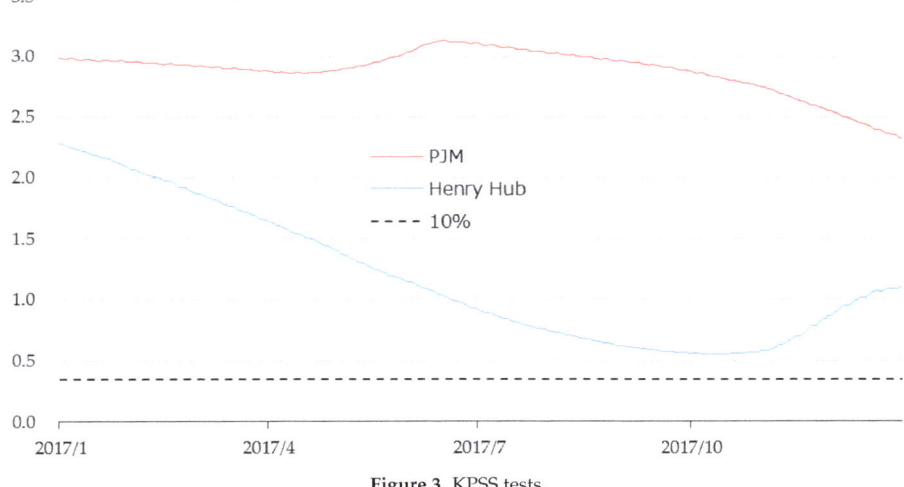

Figure 3. KPSS tests.

4.2. Cointegration Tests

Figure 4a,b present the trace test statistics and maximum eigenvalue test statistics of Johansen (1988) tests in 2017, respectively. As with above unit root tests, each test statistic on a certain day t is obtained during the sample period from $t - 3 \times 365$ to $t - 1$. Figure 4 shows that both trace test results and maximum eigenvalue test results tend to be similar.

In testing for null hypothesis of cointegration, both the trace test and the max eigenvalue test accept the null over the entire period of 2017. Each test with approximately 750 samples is conducted 365 times, and all results accept the null hypothesis.

In testing for the null hypothesis of no cointegration, the null hypothesis cannot be rejected 103 times out of 365 times. We may consider that the relatively small number of samples, the short-term trend of the prices, and the nonlinearity of the real structure cause these results, although these variables are in fact a cointegrating relationship.

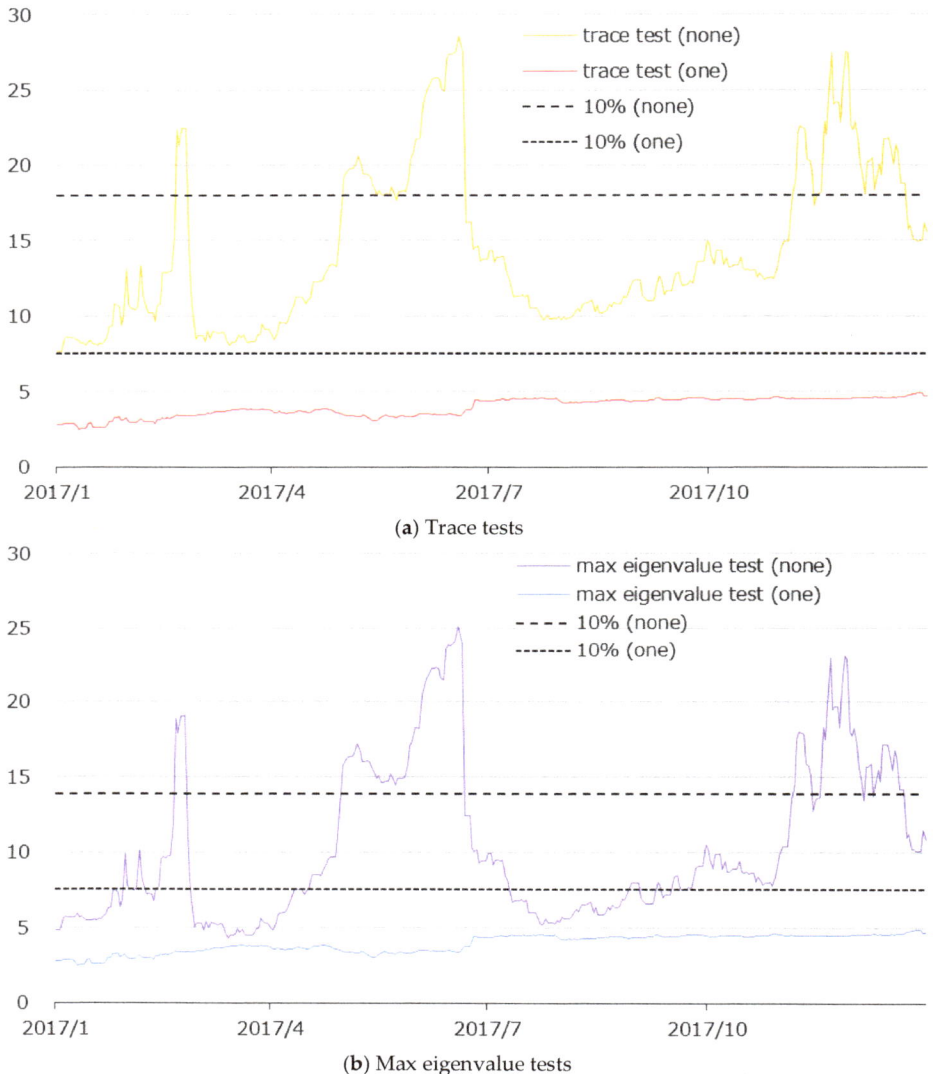

(**a**) Trace tests

(**b**) Max eigenvalue tests

Figure 4. Johansen tests.

4.3. Selection of Trading Dates

The selection of the trading dates depends on the test results related to the relationship between both variables.

First, we define the period when the null hypothesis of no cointegration is rejected by the Johansen (1988) test as period A, and the period that is accepted as period B. Next, the three strategies for trading only in period A, only in period B, and in both periods are defined as conservative, aggressive, and neutral types, respectively. Finally, we simulate these three trading strategies and examine their impact on profitability.

An explanation of each trading strategy and pre-prediction characteristics are shown in Table 3. We refer to period A as a continued tendency for the deviation from the equilibrium to be small and to converge to an equilibrium state in a short time. Therefore, we predict as follows: the conservative type has a disadvantage in that trading opportunities are limited and yield is low.

Table 3. Trading types.

Characteristics	Conservative	Aggressive	Neutral
Trading dates	Dates of rejecting no-cointegration hypothesis	Dates of accepting no-cointegration hypothesis	All opening days
Concept of trading date selection	Only when convergence to equilibrium is expected in a short time	Only when deviation from equilibrium continues	Whenever deviation from equilibrium occurs
Opportunities	Occasionally	Frequently	Always
Yield	Low	High	Medium

We consider that in period B, the large deviation from the equilibrium tends to continue for a long time. Therefore, we forecast that the aggressive type has high yield. The interpretation of the neutral type is a moderation of the conservative type and the aggressive type. The neutral type has an exclusive advantage in that all opening days are trading opportunities, although its return is considered to be average.

There are 251 opening days in 2017 when the current simulation is conducted. As a breakdown, periods A and B comprise 73 days and 178 days, respectively.

4.4. Estimation of Long-Term Equilibrium Equation

Figure 5 provides the time plots of the coefficients of long-term equilibrium Equation (1). These generally change gradually. In other words, the structure seems to change gradually. This study's trading strategy is based on slow structural change and short-term inefficiency, and therefore, we can expect to earn profits unless we hold one position for a long time.

Figure 5. Coefficients of equilibrium equation.

After the simulation, we determine appropriate lead and lag orders based on the Schwarz information criterion in order to estimate the coefficients by DOLS. As a result, we select lead order 0 and lag order 1 in approximately 98% of the simulation period. In other words, Equation (2) is the appropriate equilibrium formula.

4.5. Simulations

Figure 6 provides the observed PJM value and the PJM value estimated from the observed value of the Henry Hub by using daily equilibrium Equation (1). When the estimated PJM is higher than the observed PJM, we interpret this as the Henry Hub being higher than the PJM. Therefore, we take a long position in the PJM and a short position in the Henry Hub. Conversely, when the estimated PJM is lower than the observed PJM, we may consider that the Henry Hub is lower than the PJM is. Therefore, we take a short position in the PJM and a long position in the Henry Hub. The positions were inverted three times in this simulation. In the case of the neutral type, with the whole period as the trading day, we liquidate our position three times.

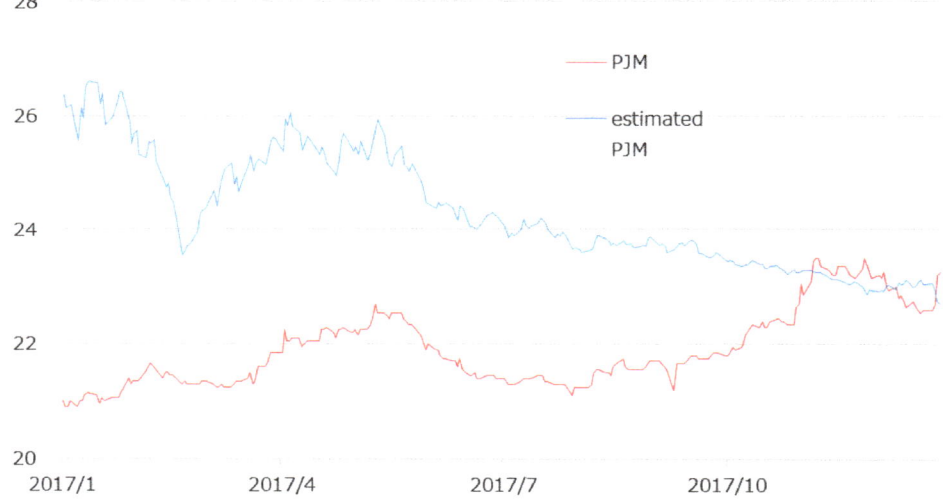

Figure 6. Observed PJM and estimated PJM from observed Henry Hub.

Table 4 presents the results of the simulation. We must take a new position on the selected trading date, and therefore, a cumulative position equals the number of selected trading dates. Before the simulation, we forecast that the yield of the aggressive type is the largest while that of the conservative type is the smallest. Figure 7 provides the time plots of each yield. Each trading strategy has a negative yield for only a very short time. Moreover, all yields have almost the same tendency.

Table 4. Simulation results.

Characteristics	Conservative	Aggressive	Neutral
Cumulative position	73	178	251
Profit	2.363	57.271	14.263
Yield	3.28%	32.81%	5.78%

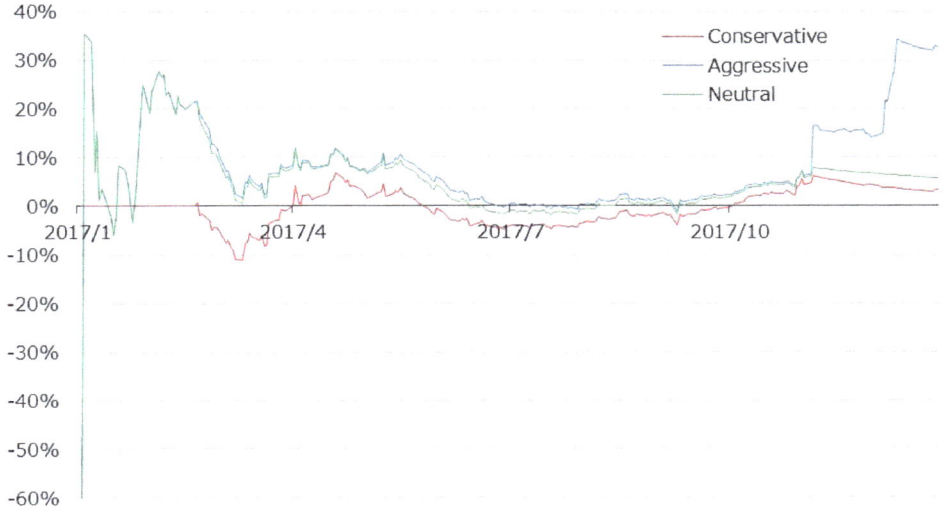

Figure 7. Yield.

5. Discussion

We present profitability by statistical arbitrage trading using a very primitive algorithm based on a long-term equilibrium formula between wholesale electricity futures and natural gas futures.

This study demonstrates the possibility of earning profit by statistical arbitrage between PJM wholesale electricity futures and Henry Hub natural gas futures by trading simulations based on an algorithm using the equilibrium equation estimated daily. From this, we derive the following two hypotheses. First, statistical arbitrage opportunities continue for a relatively long time, because there are not many arbitrage dealers that utilize the long-term equilibrium between these variables. It can be assumed that most traders of these two kinds of futures are energy companies that hedge profits by considering the cost and profit structure, while institutional investors that conduct pair trade among energy derivatives are extremely limited. The second hypothesis is that there is no sudden structural change in the sample period of this study. This is obvious, because the equilibrium equation estimated by the daily data can capture the market structure change. After all, it can be said that there is profitability through daily statistical arbitrage trading, if we can find cointegrated securities without a steep market structure change, earlier than other traders.

However, the problems with the simulation are fourfold, and should be addressed by further study. First, it is insufficient in terms to confirm the robustness of the trading strategy, because the simulation in this study is based on historical data for only one year. In the context of this study, the robustness does not include academic appropriateness of long-run equilibrium between these economic variables, but means practical profitability of the trading strategy, which allows losses within the range specified by the trader. The robustness should be confirmed by Monte Carlo simulation of this trading methodology in data-generating processors or artificial markets that simulate real price fluctuations.

Second, it is expected that the method adopted in this study cannot respond to rapid market structural change. Although the simulations in this sample period, which has a modest market structural change, can show the profitability, it is uncertain whether the change amounts to a deficit or a surplus if prices fluctuate rapidly, like in bubbles or crashes. We may need to develop trading strategies based on the estimation of the spread using high frequency data or an algorithm to detect sudden changes in the market structure to stop trading.

Third, although three kinds of algorithms are tested, these algorithms cannot maximize the returns. The trading strategy for the maximization of returns under appropriate risk management should be able to be developed by changing the sample period to estimate the long-term equilibrium and the position depending on deviation from the long-term equilibrium. This study adopts estimation of long-term equilibrium formula over three years and daily trading with fixed size.

Finally, this study does not consider the constraints of actual exchange at all. In other words, this study assumes the unrealistic conditions in which the contract units are not restricted and trading is possible at the prices of the historical data. Each exchange standardizes the contract specifications for each commodity, and therefore, we cannot adjust the contract units depending on the prices. Furthermore, actual transactions need transaction costs. It is impossible to avoid changing prices owing to own orders. Buying causes price increases, and selling causes price drops. Apart from this, real transactions need real cash, including trading fees. Moreover, this study assumes that traders can constantly and permanently increase their positions. In other words, they can take their positions, which need their infinite credit. These are impossible conditions for risk management.

These realistic tasks on commodity futures trading are unavoidable for practitioners, but tend to be avoided academically. We hope that further study of commodity markets will be promoted from various academic viewpoints.

Funding: This research received no external funding.

Acknowledgments: The author would like to thank Editage (www.editage.jp) for English language editing, and the anonymous reviewers, whose valuable comments helped to improve an earlier version of this paper.

Conflicts of Interest: The author declares no conflict of interest.

References

Alexakis, Christos. 2010. Long-run relations among equity indices under different market conditions: Implications on the implementation of statistical arbitrage strategies. *Journal of International Financial Markets, Institutions and Money* 20: 389–403. [CrossRef]

Asche, Frank, Petter Osmundsen, and Maria Sandsmark. 2006. The UK market for natural gas, oil and electricity: Are the prices decoupled? *The Energy Journal* 27: 27–40. [CrossRef]

Baviera, Raviera, and Tommaso Santagostino Baldi. 2018. Stop-loss and leverage in optimal statistical arbitrage with an application to energy market. *Energy Economics*. forthcoming. [CrossRef]

Emery, Gary W., and Qingfeng Wilson Liu. 2002. An analysis of the relationship between electricity and natural-gas futures prices. *The Journal of Futures Markets* 22: 95–122. [CrossRef]

Focardi, Sergio M., Frank J. Fabozzi, and Ivan K. Mitov. 2016. A new approach to statistical arbitrage: Strategies based on dynamic factor models of prices and their performance. *Journal of Banking & Finance* 65: 134–55. [CrossRef]

Freitas, Carlos J. Pereira, and Patrícia Pereira da Silva. 2015. European Union emissions trading scheme impact on the Spanish electricity price during phase II and phase III implementation. *Utilities Policy* 33: 54–62. [CrossRef]

Furió, Dolores, and Helena Chuliá. 2012. Price and volatility dynamics between electricity and fuel costs: Some evidence for Spain. *Energy Economics* 34: 2058–65. [CrossRef]

Gautam, Tej K., and Krishna P. Paudel. 2018. Estimating sectoral demands for electricity using the pooled mean group method. *Applied Energy* 231: 54–67. [CrossRef]

Hain, Martin, Julian Hess, and Marliese Uhrig-Homburg. 2018. Relative value arbitrage in European commodity markets. *Energy Economics* 69: 140–54. [CrossRef]

Haugom, Erik, Guttorm A. Hoff, Peter Molnár, Maria Mortensen, and Sjur Westgaard. 2014. The forecasting power of medium-term futures contracts. *Journal of Energy Markets* 7: 1–23. [CrossRef]

Haugom, Erik, Guttorm A. Hoff, Peter Molnár, Maria Mortensen, and Sjur Westgaard. 2018. The forward premium in the Nord Pool Power market. *Emerging Markets Finance and Trade* 54: 1793–807. [CrossRef]

Joëts, Marc, and Valérie Mignon. 2011. On the link between forward energy prices: A nonlinear panel cointegration approach. *Energy Economics* 34: 1170–75. [CrossRef]

Johansen, Søren. 1988. Statistical analysis of cointegration vectors. *Journal of Economic Dynamics and Control* 12: 231–54. [CrossRef]

Kwiatkowski, Denis, Peter C. B. Phillips, Peter Schmidt, and Yongcheol Shin. 1992. Testing the null hypothesis of stationarity against the alternative of a unit root. *Journal of Econometrics* 54: 159–78. [CrossRef]

Liu, Guo-Dong, and Chi-Wei Su. 2018. The dynamic causality between gold and silver prices in China market: A rolling window bootstrap approach. *Finance Research Letters*. forthcoming. [CrossRef]

Mayordomo, Sergio, Juan Ignacio Peña, and Juan Romo. 2014. Testing for statistical arbitrage in credit derivatives markets. *Journal of Empirical Finance* 26: 59–75. [CrossRef]

Mjelde, James W., and David A. Bessler. 2009. Market integration among electricity markets and their major fuel source markets. *Energy Economics* 31: 482–91. [CrossRef]

Mohammadi, Hassan. 2009. Electricity prices and fuel costs: Long-run relations and short-run dynamics. *Energy Economics* 31: 503–9. [CrossRef]

Phillips, Peter C., and Pierre Perron. 1988. Testing for a unit root in time series regression. *Biometrika* 75: 335–46. [CrossRef]

Serletis, Apostolos, and John Herbert. 1999. The message in North American energy prices. *Energy Economics* 21: 471–83. [CrossRef]

Serletis, Apostolos, and Akbar Shahmoradi. 2006. Measuring and testing natural gas and electricity markets volatility: Evidence from Alberta's deregulated markets. *Studies in Nonlinear Dynamics & Econometrics* 10: 1341. [CrossRef]

Journal of
Risk and Financial Management

Article

Clarifying the Response of Gold Return to Financial Indicators: An Empirical Comparative Analysis Using Ordinary Least Squares, Robust and Quantile Regressions

Takashi Miyazaki

Japan Center for Economic Research, 1-3-7, Otemachi, Chiyoda-ku, Tokyo 100-8066, Japan;
takashi.miyazaki@jcer.or.jp

Received: 17 December 2018; Accepted: 7 February 2019; Published: 14 February 2019

Abstract: In this study, I apply a quantile regression model to investigate how gold returns respond to changes in various financial indicators. The model quantifies the asymmetric response of gold return in the tails of the distribution based on weekly data over the past 30 years. I conducted a statistical test that allows for multiple structural changes and find that the relationship between gold return and some key financial indicators changed three times throughout the sample period. According to my empirical analysis of the whole sample period, I find that: (1) the gold return rises significantly if stock returns fall sharply; (2) it rises as the stock market volatility increases; (3) it also rises when general financial market conditions tighten; (4) gold and crude oil prices generally move toward the same direction; and (5) gold and the US dollar have an almost constant negative correlation. Looking at each sample period, (1) and (2) are remarkable in the period covering the global financial crisis (GFC), suggesting that investors divested from stocks as a risky asset. On the other hand, (3) is a phenomenon observed during the sample period after the GFC, suggesting that it reflects investors' behavior of flight to quality.

Keywords: gold return; asymmetric dependence; financial market stress; robust regression; quantile regression; structural break; flight to quality

JEL Classification: C12; C21; G11; G15; Q02

---

1. Introduction

Correlations across different asset classes increased during the global financial crisis (GFC) of 2007–2009, and diversification effects did not work when most needed. With the financialization of commodities from the first half to the middle of the 2000s as cross-market linkages increased, many commodity prices plunged along with the stock market crash.[1] This experience makes us recognize the importance of accurately grasping the linkages or contagion between different asset classes, and promote studies that unravel the transmission mechanism and spillover effect between different asset markets (see, e.g., Chudik and Fratzscher 2011; Diebold and Yilmaz 2012; Ehrmann et al. 2011; Guo et al. 2011; Longstaff 2010).

Gold is generally seen as distinct from other traditional assets due to its special character. It is often regarded as a safe haven, especially hedging against the downside risk of stocks or in times of

---

[1] Previous studies that analyze the financialization of commodities and its background include Basu and Gavin (2011); Cheng and Xiong (2014); Domanski and Heath (2007); Silvennoinen and Thorp (2013); Tang and Xiong (2012).

financial turbulence. Academic research on gold as an investment asset has been increasing in recent years (see, for example, O'Connor et al. 2015).

Existing literature that analyze the aspects of gold as a hedge or safety instrument compared with traditional assets include Baur (2011); Baur and Lucey (2010); Baur and McDermott (2010); Cohen and Qadan (2010); Hillier et al. (2006); Hood and Malik (2013); Miyazaki et al. (2012); Miyazaki and Hamori (2013, 2014, 2016, 2018); Piplack and Straetmans (2010); Qadan and Yagil (2012); World Gold Council (2010).

Baur (2011) analyzes the characteristics of gold based on multiple regression. He finds that gold has a hedging function against US dollar depreciation but not against inflation as represented by consumer prices. In addition, he argues that the role of gold as a safety asset is a phenomenon seen more recently. Piplack and Straetmans (2010) examined the tail dependence between US stocks, government bonds, Treasury bills, and gold using the extreme value theory, and conducted statistical tests for flight to quality or flight to liquidity hypotheses. Their empirical results show that gold is, to some extent, effective as a safe asset against the plunge in the values of other assets. Furthermore, there are many existing studies that analyze the properties of commodities including gold as an investment vehicle (e.g., Akram 2009; Batten et al. 2010, 2014; Bhar and Hammoudeh 2011; Chan et al. 2011; Chevallier and Ielpo 2013; Ciner et al. 2013; Erb and Harvey 2006; Gorton and Rouwenhorst 2006; Hammoudeh et al. 2009; Mensi et al. 2013; Sari et al. 2010; Silvennoinen and Thorp 2013, among others). In addition to these studies, Alkhatib and Harasheh (2018); Balcilar et al. (2018); Raza et al. (2018) covers up to more recent sample period during and after the Brexit.

In this study, I use robust and quantile regression techniques to investigate how gold return responds to the changes in various financial indicators, specifically stock return, stock return volatility, financial market stress, crude oil, and the value of the US dollar. In the finance literature involving empirical analyses, there are also many cases where interest is on the tails of the distribution rather than the average (expected value). Quantile regression introduced by Koenker and Bassett (1978) allows us to clarify the relationships between dependent variables and independent variables in the tails of the distributions of data that cannot be captured by only the expected value. Therefore, in recent years in the field of economics and finance, econometricians have come to frequently use quantile regression making it one of the standard tools. Quantile regression is suitable for the purpose of this study in quantifying the role of gold as a hedging function or safety asset.[2] Empirical research using quantile regression include Baur (2013); Baur and Schulze (2005); Bouoiyour et al. (2018); Mensi et al. (2014); Reboredo and Uddin (2016); Reboredo and Uddin (2016) applied quantile regression to analyze the impact of financial stress and policy uncertainty in the US on a wide range of commodity futures prices.

This paper clarifies the role or characteristics of gold as an investment asset, on which, so far, academic research has been relatively scarce in the finance literature. Similar to the motivation of Reboredo and Uddin (2016), this study is also interested in the way gold return responds to a surge in financial market stress, sharp drop in stock prices, and stock market volatility. One novelty of this study is that it considers multiple structural breaks that are endogenously determined. Our empirical results show that the relationship between gold and financial variables mentioned above is not stable and have experienced several structural changes over time. In addition, we provide evidence that gold return rises in response to a plunge in stock prices and a rapid rise in stress in the financial markets, suggesting the role of gold as a safe haven. This result tells us that investors are taking a "flight-to-quality" behavior.

The rest of the paper is organized as follows. In the next section, we briefly outline econometric methodologies used in this paper comprising robust and quantile regression techniques. In addition

---

2   One of the other ways to disentangle the interdependence of data in the tails of the distribution is a method using extreme value theory. Related research includes Hartmann et al. (2004); Piplack and Straetmans (2010); Straetmans et al. (2008).

to presenting data for the analysis, we construct the indicators to measure the level of stress in the financial markets in Section 3. Section 4 presents our major empirical results, while Section 5 concludes.

2. Econometric Methodology

In this section, we outline the robust and quantile regression techniques to be used in this study. While both regression techniques address outliers in the data and asymmetry of distributions, their concepts and approaches are considerably different.

2.1. Robust Regression

The property of an ordinary least squares (OLS) estimator being BLUE (Best Linear Unbiased Estimator) depends on the assumption about the error term. Robust regression is an estimation method for correcting the bias of the OLS estimator caused by the existence of outliers and heteroskedasticity. OLS places equal weights to all observations, whereas robust regression reduces the weights on outliers to mitigate the latter's influence. Robust regression is insensitive to small changes in the sample and distributional assumptions of the data. It is also useful in separating the contribution of the part of the data near the average and the part in the tails.[3]

Among the different variations of weight functions, I choose Bisquare defined as follows.

$$
\begin{cases}
\frac{c^2}{6}\left(1 - \left(1 - \left(\frac{X}{c}\right)^2\right)^3\right), & \text{if } |X| \leq c, \\
\frac{c^2}{6}, & \text{otherwise,}
\end{cases}
\tag{1}
$$

where c is an arbitrary positive tuning constant set to $c = 4.685$ in Bisquare form.[4]

2.2. Quantile Regression

Quantile regression is a method of modeling and estimating the relationship between a dependent variable and independent variables in the tails of the distribution (more specifically, quantile).[5] The distribution of returns of financial assets frequently exhibits the statistical property of heavy tails (see, for example, Cont 2001). If heavy tails and/or asymmetry in the distributions exist, the assumption of normality is not satisfied. Therefore, inference based on classical regression models may lead to misleading conclusions. By utilizing quantile regression, researchers can reveal more accurate dependence structure between variables according to market conditions such as bull or bear markets, and completely know the distribution of returns.

OLS minimizes the sum of squared residuals,

$$
\min_{\alpha, \beta} \sum_{t=1}^{T} (y_t - \alpha - \beta x_t)^2
\tag{2}
$$

whereas quantile regression minimizes the following loss function,

$$
\min_{\alpha(\tau), \beta(\tau)} \sum_{t=1}^{T} \rho_\tau (y_t - \alpha(\tau) - \beta(\tau) x_t)
\tag{3}
$$

---

[3] See Chapter 8 of Fabozzi et al. (2014).

[4] EViews 9.5 is used for the robust regression in this study. For a more detailed technical description, refer to pp. 405-424 in IHS Global Inc. (2016).

[5] For a succinct explanation of quantile regression, I recommend Koenker and Hallock (2001) and Rodriguez and Yao (2017). For more formal treatments, refer to textbooks such as Chapter II.7.2 of Alexander (2008), Chapter 7 of Fabozzi et al. (2014); Hao and Naiman (2007). For nonparametric approach of the quantile regression, see Chao et al. (2012); Franke et al. (2015).

where $\rho_\tau(u)$ is the check function defined as follows.

$$\rho_\tau(u) = u(\tau - 1\{u \le 0\}) = \begin{cases} -(1-\tau)u, & u \le 0 \\ \tau u, & u > 0 \end{cases} \tag{4}$$

where $u = y_t - \alpha(\tau) - \beta(\tau)x_t$, and $\tau \in (0, 1)$ indicates the level of quantile. In particular, if $\tau = 0.5$, that is the median, the quantile regression corresponds to the least absolute deviation method.

In summary, the techniques of robust regression and quantile regression model and estimate the relationships between the dependent variable and independent variables in the center of and in the tails of data distribution, respectively. Resorting to these two regression methods, we can closely shed light on the characteristics of gold return than in previous literature.

3. Data

We adopt the US as a reference market affecting gold price. The US still possesses a dominant influence in the global financial markets, and plays the most important role to transmit financial shocks (see, e.g., Chudik and Fratzscher 2011; Ehrmann et al. 2011). In this study, we focus on the relationships between gold and a variety of financial indicators, specifically stock market return, stock market return volatility, crude oil, the value of the US dollar against major currencies, and general financial market conditions in the US.[6] The sample period covers about past three decades of weekly data from 5 January 1990 to 27 April 2018. Weekly frequency seems to be an appropriate choice to ensure the number of samples and eliminate noise that can occur in daily data. Table 1 displays the data sources. All three financial instruments, namely gold, S&P 500 index and crude oil are spot prices.

Table 1. Data sources.

Variable	Source
Gold price, PM fix (spot)	Bloomberg; originally provided by London Bullion Market Association (LBMA)
S&P 500 Index (spot)	Bloomberg; originally provided by S&P Dow Jones Indices
TED spread	Federal Reserve Economic Database (FRED) of St. Louis Fed
Aaa-10Y spread	Federal Reserve Economic Database (FRED) of St. Louis Fed
Baa-Aaa spread	Federal Reserve Economic Database (FRED) of St. Louis Fed
West Texas Intermediate (WTI) (spot)	Federal Reserve Economic Database (FRED) of St. Louis Fed; originally provided by US Energy Information Administration (EIA)
Trade Weighted US Dollar Index: Major Currencies	Federal Reserve Economic Database (FRED) of St. Louis Fed; originally provided by Board of Governors of the Federal Reserve System (US)

3.1. Measure of Financial Market Stress

Several variables could serve as indicators of financial market conditions. To construct an index to measure the stress level of financial markets, we employ principal component analysis (PCA). Specifically, we apply PCA to the following four interest rate-related variables; Treasury-EuroDollar (TED) spread,[7] credit spread,[8] default spread,[9] and term spread,[10] and set the extracted principal

---

[6] We recognize its relevance, but exclude bond from our analysis since we consider that information in bond market is included, to some extent, in the financial market stress index constructed below. Existing studies explicitly demonstrating the connection of gold with bond include Agyei-Ampomah et al. (2014); Baur and Lucey (2010); Baur and McDermott (2010); Ciner et al. (2013); Miyazaki and Hamori (2016); Piplack and Straetmans (2010).

[7] TED spread is calculated as the spread between the three-month London interbank offered rate based on US dollars and the three-month Treasury bill rate.

[8] Credit spread is calculated as the yield spread between Baa- and Aaa-ranked corporate bonds.

[9] Default spread is calculated as the yield spread between Aaa-ranked corporate bonds and Treasuries with 10-year constant maturities.

[10] Term spread is calculated as the yield spread between Treasuries of 10-year and three-month constant maturities.

components as a measure for the degree of financial market stress.[11] These financial indicators act as liquidity risk, credit risk, default risk, and monetary policy stance or recession risk,[12] respectively. Table 2 reports the results of PCA extracted from the four risk indicators above, and Figure 1 illustrates their evolution. According to Table 2, factor loadings of all financial risk indicators are positive for the first principal component. As seen in Figure 1, the first principal component experiences spikes in the financial turmoil episodes such as failure of long-term capital management (LTCM), dot-com bubble collapse, and Lehman Brothers bankruptcy. From these observational findings, we interpret the first principal component as the degree of general financial market stress and use it as an indicator to measure the tightness of the financial market in the following empirical analysis.

Table 2. Principal component analysis: financial market stress.

	Factor Loadings			
	1st	2nd	3rd	4th
TED	0.088	0.796	0.354	0.483
Aaa-10Y	0.628	−0.068	−0.626	0.458
Baa-Aaa	0.627	0.324	0.079	−0.704
TERM	0.453	−0.507	0.690	0.247
% variance explained	44.18	33.01	14.56	8.26

Notes: This table summarizes the results of the principal component analysis applied to a set of financial risk indicators (TED, Aaa-10Y, Baa-Aaa, and TERM). TED is the spread between the three-month London interbank offered rate based on the US dollars and the three-month Treasury bill rate. Aaa-10Y is the yield spread between Aaa-ranked corporate bonds and Treasuries with 10-year constant maturities. Baa-Aaa is the yield spread between Baa- and Aaa-ranked corporate bonds. TERM is the yield spread between Treasuries of 10-year and three-month constant maturities.

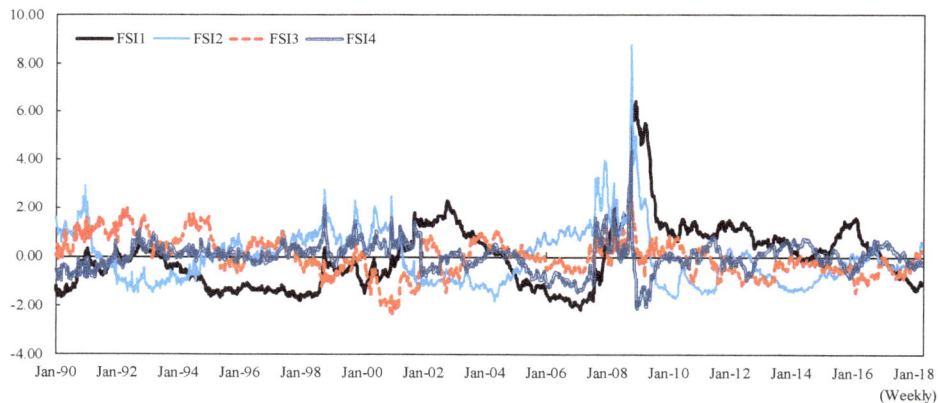

(Weekly)

Panel A. Time series plot of financial stress index

Figure 1. *Cont.*

---

[11] Before carrying out PCA, I standardized to control the variance of these variables. That is, these variables have zero mean and unit variance (standard deviation). Furthermore, according to the augmented Dickey–Fuller test, based on specification without a constant term, the null hypothesis of a unit root for these four variables is rejected at the 1% significance level or higher.

[12] Several existing studies provide evidence that the term spread possesses significant predictive power as a leading indicator of recession. Wheelock and Wohar (2009) is a good survey in this area.

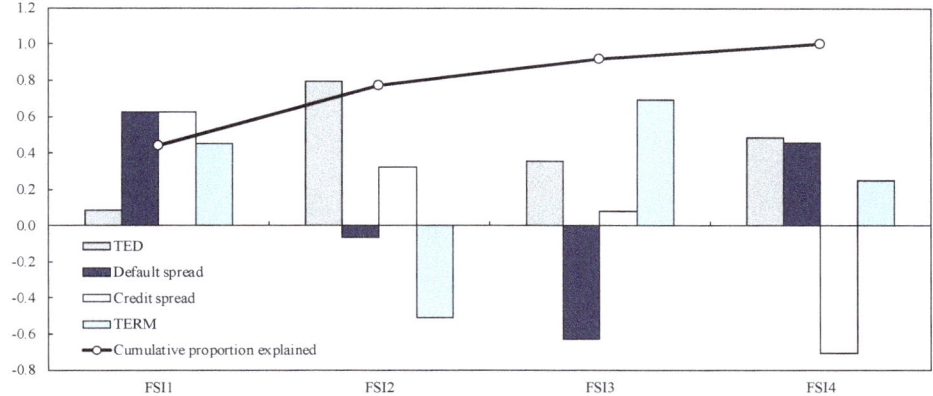

Panel B. Factor loadings and cumulative proportion

Figure 1. FSI1 to FSI4 are the first to fourth principal components obtained by applying principal component analysis to the set of financial risk indicators; TED, Aaa-10Y, Baa-Aaa, and TERM. Here, TED is Ted spread, Aaa-10Y is the yield spread between Aaa-ranked corporate bonds and Treasuries with 10-year constant maturities (default spread), Baa-Aaa is the yield spread between Baa-ranked and Aaa-ranked corporate bonds (credit spread), and TERM is the yield spread between Treasuries of 10-year and three-month constant maturities. We interpret these four principal components as follows. FSI1: Degree of stress in general financial markets. FSI2: Financial tightening in the banking sector or a surge in liquidity risk. FSI3: Monetary policy stance or recession risk. FSI4: Risk premium on corporate bond with a relatively high credit.

3.2. Summary Statistics

The purpose of this study is to examine empirical dependence structure between gold and key financial indicators. We take up five financial indicators considered affecting gold return, namely stock return, stock market volatility, financial market stress, crude oil, and the value of the US dollar. Risk-averse investors demand gold as a hedge against the downside risks of stock market. Gold generally has a low correlation with traditional assets such as stocks and offers an option for an effective diversification investment (World Gold Council 2010). We use S&P 500 Index return and its volatility as a variable representing the stock market conditions. Furthermore, investors demand gold as a safe haven in times of financial turmoil. This phenomenon is an investor behavior generally called "flight to quality." A variable representing the tightness of financial markets is the financial market stress index constructed above. We choose crude oil as a representative commodity belonging to the same asset class as gold, and specifically use the West Texas Intermediate (WTI). Gold is known to be inversely associated with the US dollar since gold functions as a store of value or loss compensation against depreciations in the US dollar (see, for example, Miyazaki and Hamori 2016). We use the trade-weighted US dollar exchange rate as a variable representing the value of the US dollar.

For gold, S&P 500 Index, WTI, and trade-weighted US dollar exchange rate, we transform the series by log-differencing. As for the stock return volatility, we use the square root of the estimates obtained by applying an exponential generalized autoregressive conditional heteroskedasticity (EGARCH) model to the S&P 500 Index return[13]. Because crude oil and gold are priced in dollars, fluctuations in the US dollar rate serve as a common factor in the price fluctuations of both commodities

---

[13] The lag order for both the ARCH and GARCH terms in the EGARCH model is 1, namely, EGARCH (1,1).

(Sari et al. 2010). To eliminate the effect of this common factor in the following empirical analysis, we use as WTI the residuals obtained by regressing WTI on the value of US dollar.

Panels A and B of Table 3 report the descriptive statistics and the correlation matrix of variables used in following empirical analysis. The mean of returns on gold and S&P 500 Index is 0.080 and 0.137, respectively. Since the WTI returns are the residuals regressed to the trade-weighted US dollar exchange rate, its mean is zero. Fluctuations in returns on gold and S&P 500 Index from the standpoint of standard deviation are on the same magnitude, and the return on WTI shows the largest fluctuation. The returns on gold, S&P 500 Index and WTI have negative skewness. Thus, these variables have a heavy left tail in the distribution, meaning they occasionally show a large negative return. Contrarily, the S&P 500 Index return volatility, the financial market stress index, and the trade-weighted US dollar exchange rate have positive skewness. Thus, these variables have a heavy right tail in the distribution, meaning they occasionally show a sharp rise. For all of the time series, kurtosis exceeds three, indicating these variables are leptokurtic. As shown in the Jarque–Bera test statistics and the corresponding p-values, the null hypothesis of normality is strongly rejected for all of time series.

Table 3. Summary statistics.

Panel A: Descriptive Statistics						
	GOLD	**SPX**	**SPVOL**	**FSI1**	**WTI**	**TWEX**
Mean	0.080	0.137	2.048	0.001	0.000	−0.003
Maximum	14.694	11.356	9.885	6.426	25.114	4.342
Minimum	−13.790	−20.084	0.862	−2.136	−18.972	−3.851
Std. Dev.	2.227	2.256	0.867	1.330	4.182	0.946
Skewness	−0.133	−0.753	2.547	1.406	−0.128	0.180
Kurtosis	7.543	9.853	15.000	6.921	6.035	4.064
Jarque–Bera	1274.215	3029.719	10,459.200	1432.904	571.023	77.579
p-value	0.000	0.000	0.000	0.000	0.000	0.000
Num. of obs.	1477	1477	1477	1477	1477	1477
Panel B: Correlation Matrix						
	GOLD	**SPX**	**SPVOL**	**FSI1**	**WTI**	**TWEX**
GOLD	1.000					
SPX	−0.039	1.000				
SPVOL	−0.032	0.029	1.000			
FSI1	0.028	−0.051	0.550	1.000		
WTI	0.113	0.076	−0.077	−0.055	1.000	
TWEX	−0.394	−0.134	0.013	−0.005	0.000	1.000

Notes: Data is weekly frequency. The sample period spans from 12 January 1990, to 27 April 2018. In Panel A, the p-value is the probability that corresponds to the Jarque–Bera test of normality. GOLD denotes the log-differenced gold return. SPX denotes the log-differenced return for the S&P 500 Index. SPVOL denotes the S&P 500 Index return volatility. FSI1 the degree of financial market stress (the first principal component extracted from PCA). WTI denotes the return on West Texas Intermediate (the residual obtained from regressing WTI on TWEX). TWEX denotes the appreciation/depreciation rate of the US dollar against major currencies.

As can be seen in Panel B of Table 3, gold return is weakly negatively correlated with the two variables of the US stock market and is positively correlated with financial market stress and WTI. As expected, gold return has a moderate negative correlation with the US dollar. Not surprisingly, financial market stress and stock market volatility show a positive correlation, suggesting a widespread financial turmoil is likely to be accompanied by a volatile stock market. Somewhat oddly, although it seems that market volatility tends to increase when the stock market declines, the S&P 500 Index return and its volatility show a weak positive correlation. As a matter of course, the correlation coefficient, however, can only capture a symmetric linear relationship between variables.

4. Empirical Results

4.1. OLS and Robust Regression Results

Although the fundamental price of gold is sometimes derived from a convenience yield using futures prices, there is no theoretical model accepted widely like the discounted present value model for stocks. Our model estimated below, therefore, is entirely an empirical model.

The regression equation we estimate is given by,[14]

$$GOLD_t = \beta_0 + \sum_{i=1}^{5} \beta_i GOLD_{t-i} + \beta_6 SPX_t + \beta_7 SPVOL_t + \beta_8 FSI1_t + \beta_9 WTI_t + \beta_{10} TWEX_t + e_t \quad (5)$$

where $GOLD$ is gold return, SPX is S&P 500 Index return, $SPVOL$ is S&P 500 Index return volatility, $FSI1$ is the degree of financial market stress (the first principal component extracted from PCA in the previous section), WTI is return on West Texas Intermediate (the residual obtained from regressing WTI on $TWEX$), $TWEX$ is the appreciation/depreciation rate of the US dollar, β_j ($j = 0, \cdots, 10$) is the parameters to be estimated, and e is the error term.

Before turning to the estimation of the model, we implement a test for structural change developed by Bai and Perron (1998, 2003a, 2003b), which enables us to identify multiple breakpoints. In their test, the number of structural changes considered increases sequentially. Firstly, I test the alternative hypothesis that "the number of structural changes is one" against the null hypothesis of "no structural change." Secondly, If the null hypothesis is rejected, we next test the alternative hypothesis that "the number of structural changes is two" against the null hypothesis that "the number of structural changes is one." More generally, the null hypothesis can be written as "the number of structural changes is m times," and the alternative hypothesis as "the number of structural changes is $m + 1$ times." This procedure is continued until the null hypothesis is accepted. As a result of Bai and Perron (1998, 2003a, 2003b) test, we identified three breakpoints, namely, 2 February 1996, 2 December 2005, and 10 May 2013 (see Table 4). Thus, the whole sample period is divided into four subsample periods.[15]

Table 4. Multiple breakpoint test.

H_0	H_1	Test Statistic	Critical Value	Breakpoint
No break	1 time break	75.49 **	27.03	2/02/1996
1 time break	2 times break	52.16 **	29.24	12/02/2005
2 times break	3 times break	50.21 **	30.45	5/10/2013
3 times break	4 times break	12.92	31.45	

Notes: ** denotes statistical significance at the 5% and 1% levels.

Figure 2 depicts the behavior of gold price together with the structural breakpoints (break dates are exhibited by solid vertical lines). What kind of economic reasons can be given as a background to the structural breakpoints identified in these periods? A possible explanation for the first structural break date is an adoption of "strong dollar policy" led by Robert Rubin, United States Secretary of the Treasury. Gold prices are closely linked to changes in the value of the US dollar. With this policy, US dollar appreciated and the gold price declined. The second structural breakpoint is connected with the development of financialization of commodities. This trend promoted to strengthen the correlation among various asset classes as mentioned in Introduction. Among the three structural breaks, the second break date, 2 December 2005, approximately coincides with the one found by

---

[14] Taking into account the autocorrelation of the residuals, we include the autoregressive term up to five lags. For the sake of brevity, we do not explicitly mention the autoregressive term in the empirical analysis below.

[15] The null hypothesis of "no structural break" is also rejected in the Chow test which designated jointly and beforehand three structural breakpoints identified by Bai and Perron (1998, 2003a, 2003b) test as a candidate of structural breakpoints. Therefore, these structural breakpoints identified above have robustness.

Miyazaki and Hamori (2014).[16] The last structural breakpoint can be attributed to the emergence of anticipation that the loosening monetary policy in the US, specifically Quantitative Easing program 3, implemented after the GFC, is going to shrink. This anticipation has caused an appreciation of the US dollar, and has led gold prices, which has been boomed since the GFC, turned to fall.

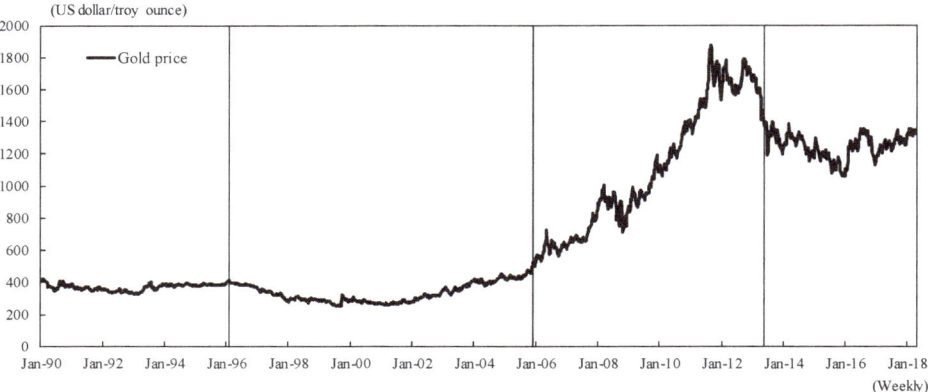

Figure 2. The solid vertical lines in the figure represent the break dates specified by applying Bai and Perron (1998, 2003a, 2003b) method.

Table 5 summarizes the estimation results based on OLS and robust regression. The OLS and robust regression results are roughly similar. In the full sample period, the results of the significance test for coefficients are the same except for the constant term. In both OLS and robust regression, gold return has a negative correlation with the S&P 500 Index return, but in the robust regression the estimate drops to about half of OLS. Thus, it seems that the estimate by OLS has a bias caused by outliers. In fact, turning to the results of the two tests (Breusch–Pagan–Godfrey and White) for heteroskedasticity reported at the bottom of panel A in Table 5, the null hypothesis of no heteroskedasticity is strongly rejected. Therefore, the robust regression provides us with more reliable results than those of the OLS. The gold return is positively associated with crude oil return. This relation indicates that both prices tend to move toward the same direction, suggesting that investors perhaps regard these two commodities as belonging to the same asset class. The coefficient for the value of US dollar is close to one in absolute terms, indicating that gold return moves nearly in a one-to-one negative correlation with the value of the US dollar.

---

[16] Miyazaki and Hamori (2014) demonstrate that there is a cointegrating relation with regime shift between gold and the three financial variables, namely US short-term interest rates, US dollar, and S&P 500 Index based on daily data. They identify a structural break date on 13 December 2005.

Table 5. OLS and robust regression results.

Dependent Variable: GOLD

A. Full Sample: 2/16/1990–4/27/2018
Number of Observations: 1472

	OLS		Robust regression	
	Coefficient	S.E.	Coefficient	S.E.
SPX	−0.099 **	0.036	−0.055 **	0.020
SPVOL	−0.101	0.111	−0.099	0.063
FSII	0.096	0.058	0.078	0.041
WTI	0.065 **	0.015	0.046 **	0.011
TWEX	−0.962 **	0.082	−0.892 **	0.048
Constant	0.312	0.231	0.302 *	0.136
Adj R^2	0.186		0.263	

Breusch–Pagan–Godfrey test
$\chi^2(10)$ 0.000
White test
$\chi^2(65)$ 0.000

B. First Sample: 2/16/1990–1/26/1996
Number of Observations: 311

	OLS		Robust regression	
	Coefficient	S.E.	Coefficient	S.E.
SPX	−0.228 **	0.045	−0.182 **	0.047
SPVOL	−0.367 *	0.165	−0.672 **	0.146
FSII	0.145	0.120	0.160	0.113
WTI	0.090 **	0.019	0.083 **	0.018
TWEX	−0.155	0.105	−0.151	0.079
Constant	0.744 *	0.324	1.240 **	0.265
Adj R^2	0.126		0.232	

Breusch–Pagan–Godfrey test
$\chi^2(10)$ 0.136
White test
$\chi^2(65)$ 0.000

C. Second Sample: 2/02/1996–11/25/2005
Number of Observations: 513

	OLS		Robust regression	
	Coefficient	S.E.	Coefficient	S.E.
SPX	0.004	0.028	−0.011	0.026
SPVOL	−0.115	0.099	−0.183 *	0.093
FSII	0.148	0.076	0.201 **	0.066
WTI	0.015	0.016	0.018	0.014
TWEX	−0.850 **	0.091	−0.870 **	0.070
Constant	0.344	0.227	0.460 *	0.226
Adj R^2	0.200		0.338	

Breusch–Pagan–Godfrey test
$\chi^2(10)$ 0.001
White test
$\chi^2(65)$ 0.006

D. Third sample: 12/02/2005–5/03/2013
Number of observations: 388

	OLS		Robust regression	
	Coefficient	S.E.	Coefficient	S.E.
SPX	−0.267 **	0.078	−0.177 **	0.049
SPVOL	−0.063	0.249	0.157	0.149
FSII	0.045	0.127	−0.109	0.092
WTI	0.154 **	0.032	0.129 **	0.030
TWEX	−1.573 **	0.182	−1.513 **	0.129
Constant	0.437	0.513	0.060	0.322
Adj R^2	0.316		0.401	

Breusch–Pagan–Godfrey test
$\chi^2(10)$ 0.000
White test
$\chi^2(65)$ 0.000

E. Fourth sample: 5/10/2013–4/27/2018
Number of observations: 260

	OLS		Robust regression	
	Coefficient	S.E.	Coefficient	S.E.
SPX	−0.126	0.069	−0.095	0.065
SPVOL	0.222	0.163	0.092	0.210
FSII	−0.062	0.139	−0.049	0.164
WTI	−0.052	0.027	−0.046	0.029
TWEX	−1.131 **	0.130	−1.102 **	0.117
Constant	−0.329	0.297	−0.116	0.361
Adj R^2	0.299		0.381	

Breusch–Pagan–Godfrey test
$\chi^2(10)$ 0.007
White test
$\chi^2(65)$ 0.181

Notes: S.E. stands for standard error. For the OLS regression, the standard errors are adjusted by using the Newey–West (1987) method. Adj R^2 for robust regression shows adjusted R^2_W proposed by Renaud and Victoria-Feser (2010). * and ** denote statistical significance at the 5% and 1% levels, respectively.

Then, we turn to the results of each subsample period. In the first sample, besides the returns on the S&P 500 Index and WTI, the stock return volatility is estimated significantly. However, its sign is negative and is opposite to the expected sign, whereas a significant relationship with the US dollar has disappeared. Breusch–Pagan–Godfrey and White tests present mixed evidence for heteroskedasticity, that is, the former cannot reject homoskedasticity hypothesis, while the latter reject the hypothesis. Therefore, we cannot clearly determine which of the OLS and robust regression results are reliable. In any case, however, estimated coefficients do not differ greatly in magnitude.

The second sample period has the largest number of observations among the four subsamples, and the OLS and robust regression results show some differences. In the OLS estimation, only the US dollar is significant, while in robust regression, stock return volatility is still negative and significant, and the rise in financial market stress works to push the gold return up significantly. The latter is consistent with the expected sign. Both of two tests for heteroskedasticity reject the null hypothesis, suggesting that employing robust regression is adequate.

In the third and fourth subsamples, we find no noticeable difference when comparing both estimation results. Although the results of the third sample period are similar to the those of the full sample, the coefficients for the stock return, WTI, and US dollar are approximately two or three times larger than those in the full sample. This finding implies that the connection between gold and the financial variables has strengthened during this period, consistent with the financialization of commodities. Both of two tests for heteroskedasticity reject the null hypothesis, indicating that resorting to robust regression is suitable.

For the fourth sample period, only the coefficient on the US dollar is negative and significant. Two tests for heteroskedasticity lead us to different conclusions, respectively, similar to the first sample period. Although neither is significant, there are some differences in estimated coefficient of S&P 500 Index volatility and constant term, between two methods.

In the following subsection, we present the results using quantile regression to explore the relationship in the tails of the distribution that cannot be captured by OLS and robust regressions.

4.2. Quantile Regression Results

4.2.1. Full Sample Period

Our quantile regression model corresponding to Equation (5) is given by,

$$
\begin{aligned}
GOLD(\tau)_t = \beta_0(\tau) + \sum_{i=1}^{5} \beta_i(\tau)GOLD_{t-i} + \beta_6(\tau)SPX_t + \beta_7(\tau)SPVOL_t + \beta_8(\tau)FSI1_t \\
+ \beta_9(\tau)WTI_t + \beta_{10}(\tau)TWEX_t + e_t
\end{aligned}
\tag{6}
$$

where τ indicates the quantile level. Each coefficient takes a different estimate according to the quantile level. By looking at each of the subsample periods, we can examine the change in the conditional joint distribution between gold return and each of financial indicators over time.

I present the estimation results for seven quantiles from 0.05 to 0.95 in Table 6. To compare the results visually, Figure 3 graphically illustrates all the quantile processes.

Table 6. Quantile process.

	Quantiles						
	0.05	**0.10**	**0.25**	**0.50**	**0.75**	0.90	0.95
SPX^{full}	−0.062	−0.034	−0.007	−0.074 **	−0.088 **	−0.149 **	−0.183 **
	(0.059)	(0.057)	(0.044)	(0.026)	(0.022)	(0.053)	(0.040)
SPX^1	−0.076	−0.166 *	−0.262 **	−0.179 *	−0.155 *	−0.227 *	−0.197
	(0.083)	(0.075)	(0.070)	(0.070)	(0.073)	(0.112)	(0.129)
SPX^2	0.144 *	0.149 **	0.013	−0.012	−0.012	0.014	0.023
	(0.073)	(0.055)	(0.046)	(0.032)	(0.029)	(0.056)	(0.137)
SPX^3	−0.061	−0.163	−0.082	−0.167	−0.337 **	−0.304 **	−0.222 **
	(0.087)	(0.108)	(0.068)	(0.089)	(0.085)	(0.065)	(0.072)
SPX^4	−0.244	−0.267 **	−0.133	−0.087	0.034	−0.076	−0.060
	(0.174)	(0.102)	(0.116)	(0.075)	(0.097)	(0.101)	(0.081)
SPVOL^{full}	−0.313	−0.325 *	−0.302 *	−0.040	0.068	0.300	0.420 *
	(0.232)	(0.155)	(0.125)	(0.089)	(0.083)	(0.198)	(0.174)
SPVOL^1	−0.716 **	−0.785 **	−0.845 **	−0.564	−0.202	0.508	0.924
	(0.207)	(0.267)	(0.246)	(0.290)	(0.293)	(0.446)	(1.179)
SPVOL^2	−0.406 **	−0.352	−0.230	−0.139	−0.104	0.044	0.189
	(0.149)	(0.248)	(0.187)	(0.112)	(0.117)	(0.310)	(0.323)
SPVOL^3	−0.549	−0.951 **	−0.378	0.116	0.382	0.593	0.341
	(0.343)	(0.238)	(0.195)	(0.370)	(0.269)	(0.306)	(0.375)
SPVOL^4	0.060	0.162	0.248	0.045	0.089	0.135	−0.050
	(0.492)	(0.288)	(0.206)	(0.215)	(0.231)	(0.364)	(0.283)
FSI1^{full}	−0.195	−0.196 *	−0.071	0.061	0.226 **	0.251 **	0.272 *
	(0.114)	(0.094)	(0.065)	(0.054)	(0.059)	(0.094)	(0.112)
FSI1^1	−0.232	−0.160	0.168	0.057	0.101	0.300	0.202
	(0.271)	(0.257)	(0.138)	(0.127)	(0.141)	(0.293)	(0.519)
FSI1^2	−0.144	0.164	0.142	0.156	0.180*	0.305	0.315
	(0.199)	(0.117)	(0.104)	(0.086)	(0.087)	(0.172)	(0.320)
FSI1^3	0.138	0.219	−0.026	−0.120	−0.068	−0.088	−0.034
	(0.325)	(0.159)	(0.107)	(0.124)	(0.127)	(0.168)	(0.250)
FSI1^4	−0.754	−0.620 *	−0.545 **	0.040	0.330	0.771 **	0.742 **
	(0.413)	(0.246)	(0.163)	(0.175)	(0.185)	(0.271)	(0.199)
WTI^{full}	0.122 **	0.100 **	0.071 **	0.043 **	0.035 **	0.064 **	0.052
	(0.032)	(0.023)	(0.020)	(0.014)	(0.013)	(0.020)	(0.027)
WTI^1	0.134 **	0.114 **	0.067 *	0.078 **	0.080 **	0.110 **	0.171
	(0.032)	(0.035)	(0.033)	(0.026)	(0.024)	(0.039)	(0.104)
WTI^2	0.001	0.001	−0.008	0.021	0.034 *	0.006	0.046
	(0.036)	(0.036)	(0.023)	(0.016)	(0.014)	(0.028)	(0.047)
WTI^3	0.326 **	0.217 **	0.159 **	0.113	0.144 **	0.132 **	0.080
	(0.095)	(0.051)	(0.041)	(0.059)	(0.039)	(0.048)	(0.050)
WTI^4	−0.010	−0.017	−0.059	−0.053	−0.058	−0.081	−0.149 **
	(0.080)	(0.049)	(0.040)	(0.034)	(0.051)	(0.107)	(0.055)
TWEX^{full}	−0.919 **	−0.961 **	−1.001 **	−0.958 **	−0.837 **	−0.858 **	−0.844 **
	(0.099)	(0.122)	(0.084)	(0.068)	(0.066)	(0.092)	(0.118)
TWEX^1	−0.170	−0.204	−0.067	−0.150	−0.159	−0.180	−0.255
	(0.188)	(0.145)	(0.092)	(0.099)	(0.100)	(0.132)	(0.190)
TWEX^2	−0.644 **	−0.891 **	−0.791 **	−0.917 **	−0.833 **	−0.858 **	−1.046 **
	(0.128)	(0.117)	(0.096)	(0.095)	(0.108)	(0.137)	(0.286)
TWEX^3	−1.452 **	−1.591**	−1.551**	−1.661 **	−1.320 **	−1.103 **	−0.916 **
	(0.363)	(0.257)	(0.163)	(0.192)	(0.210)	(0.212)	(0.260)
TWEX^4	−1.323 **	−1.445 **	−1.349 **	−1.167 **	−1.082 **	−0.773*	−0.637 **
	(0.237)	(0.245)	(0.156)	(0.160)	(0.164)	(0.317)	(0.211)
Constant^{full}	−2.254 **	−1.491 **	−0.371	0.204	1.021 **	1.750 **	2.320 **
	(0.470)	(0.304)	(0.242)	(0.176)	(0.182)	(0.372)	(0.374)
Constant^1	−0.899 *	−0.390	0.851 *	0.966 *	1.125*	1.037	1.034
	(0.371)	(0.547)	(0.407)	(0.474)	(0.518)	(0.811)	(1.851)
Constant^2	−1.592 **	−0.956	−0.330	0.393	1.162 **	1.757 **	2.348 **
	(0.385)	(0.524)	(0.453)	(0.265)	(0.293)	(0.622)	(0.755)
Constant^3	−2.699 **	−0.589	−0.118	−0.045	1.157	1.943 **	3.243 **
	(0.776)	(0.462)	(0.370)	(0.702)	(0.595)	(0.623)	(0.832)
Constant^4	−2.792 **	−2.255 **	−1.379 **	0.013	0.905 *	2.035 **	2.831 **
	(0.756)	(0.504)	(0.376)	(0.390)	(0.382)	(0.767)	(0.574)

Notes: The superscript letters "full," "1," "2," "3," and "4" represent the periods for the full sample, first sample, second sample, third sample, and fourth sample, respectively. The numbers in parentheses below each coefficient estimate are the standard errors. * and ** denote statistical significance at the 5% and 1% levels, respectively.

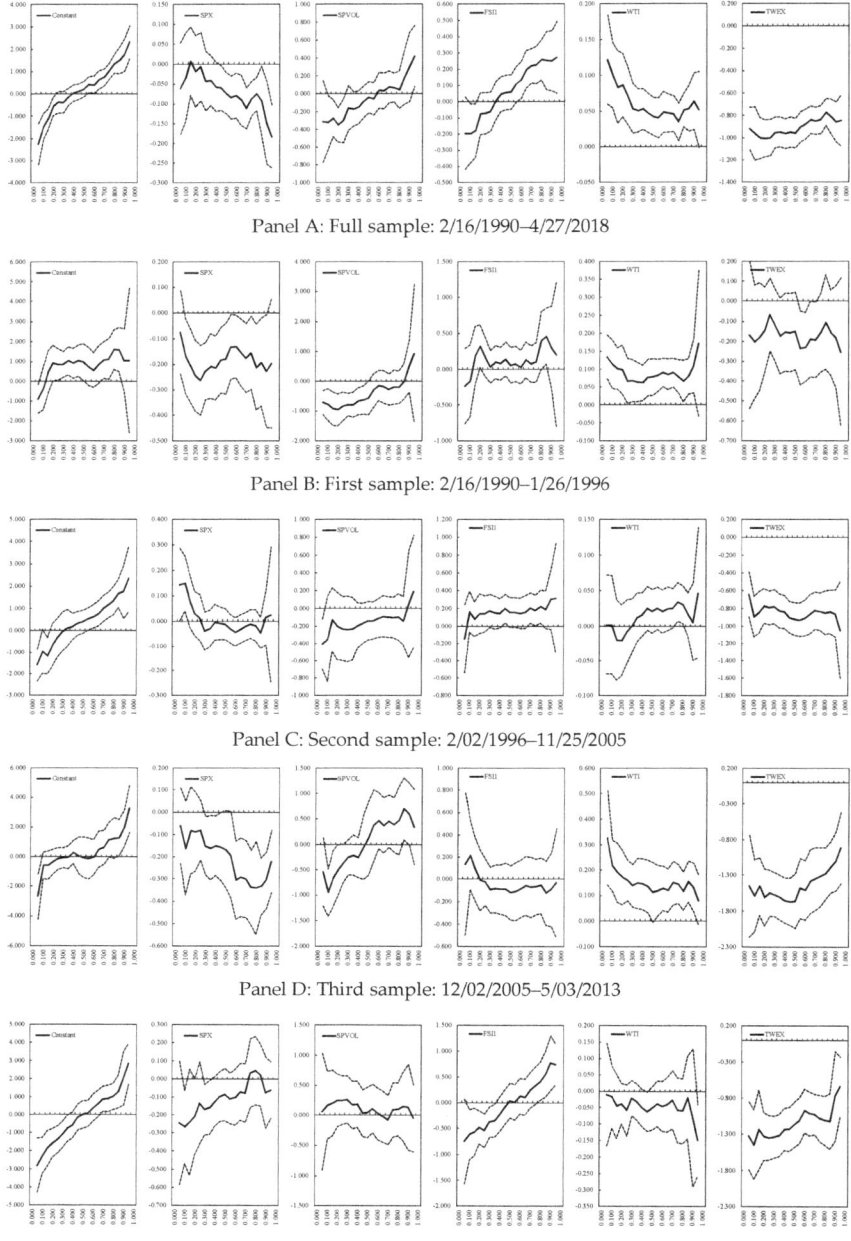

Panel A: Full sample: 2/16/1990–4/27/2018

Panel B: First sample: 2/16/1990–1/26/1996

Panel C: Second sample: 2/02/1996–11/25/2005

Panel D: Third sample: 12/02/2005–5/03/2013

Panel E: Fourth sample: 5/10/2013–4/27/2018

Figure 3. This graph illustrates the quantile process of gold return. For each panel, from left to right, we show the evolutions of coefficient on constant term, S&P 500 index return, S&P 500 Index return volatility, financial market stress, crude oil return, and the appreciation/depreciation rate of the trade-weighted US dollar. The dotted lines in the figure represent the 95% confidence intervals.

As shown in Panel A of Figure 3, Gold return is negatively correlated with the S&P 500 Index return and is significantly negative from the intermediate quantiles to the upper quantiles. The higher the quantile, the larger the coefficient increases in absolute value. The result means that gold return would rise largely when the stock return falls. However, the slope equality test at the lower and upper quantiles based on the Wald test cannot reject the null hypothesis of equality at 5% significance level, implying that dependence structures do not differ across quantile levels. Looking at the relationship with the stock return volatility, the estimated coefficient is negative for lower quantiles and positive for upper quantiles, implying that the gold return responds to the stock return volatility asymmetrically. The result that gold return rises as the stock market volatility increases is considered to reflect the investor behavior of divesting from stocks as a risky asset and demanding gold as a safety asset. Applying the Wald test, we can reject the slope equality hypothesis at 5% significance level, suggesting that dependence structures are different across quantile levels. Analogous to stock return volatility, for the financial market stress, the estimated coefficient is negative for the lower quantiles and positive for the upper quantiles, indicating asymmetric response of gold return to the degree of financial market stress. The Wald test clearly rejects the null hypothesis of equality at 1% significance level again. In other words, when the general financial market tightens, gold returns rise, and this result reflects the flight-to-quality behavior of investors.

Regarding the relationships with crude oil and the value of the US dollar, no noticeable difference is found from the results using OLS and robust regression. That is, the coefficient is significantly positive from lower to upper quantiles for crude oil, whereas it is significantly negative from lower to upper quantiles for the US dollar. The latter result is consistent with the findings of Miyazaki and Hamori (2016).

In summary, quantile regression allows us to clarify the responses of gold return on stock returns, stock market volatility, and financial market tightness in the tails of the distribution. Such relationships were not captured by OLS and robust regressions. In the following, we present detailed results for each subsample period.

4.2.2. Subsample Periods

For every explanatory variable, the confidence intervals are widened at the upper quantiles. Gold return shows a constantly negative correlation with the S&P 500 Index return and with crude oil, regardless of quantile level. Gold return is negatively correlated with the stock return volatility at the lower quantiles. There is no remarkable relationship between gold return and financial market tightness and between gold return and the value of US dollar.

As in the first sample period, the confidence intervals are widened at the upper quantiles for every explanatory variable. We can observe a significant negative correlation between gold return and the value of the US dollar from the lower to the upper quantile, but no notable relationship is found for other explanatory variables.

Our third sample period covers the outbreak of the GFC. As seen in Figure 3, the results for this period are similar to those in the full sample period. The correlation between returns of gold and stock market is significantly negative from the intermediate quantiles to the upper quantiles. The negative coefficient tends to become larger as the quantile increases. Unlike the full sample period, however, the Wald test during this sample period rejects the null hypothesis of equality at the 5% significance level, indicating that dependence structures differ across quantile values. Likewise, for the relationship with the stock market volatility, we can observe a similar pattern to those in the whole sample. That is, the coefficient is negative in lower quantiles positive in the upper quantiles. However, the result of the Wald test shows that the null hypothesis of equality cannot be rejected marginally at the 5% significance level (p-value = 0.057). Thus, we obtain partial evidence that flight to quality of investors from stock as a risky asset to gold as a safety asset had occurred.[17] Similar arguments can be applied to crude oil and the value of US dollar. In other words, gold return is constantly and positively correlated with crude oil irrespective of quantile level and is negatively associated with the US dollar throughout the quantiles. Surprisingly, gold return does not respond significantly to the degree of general financial market stress throughout the quantiles.

Finally, we confirm the results in the sample period after the GFC. At the lower quantiles, gold return is negatively associated with the stock return. Meanwhile, we find no noticeable relation between gold return and stock return volatility and between gold return and crude oil. For the US dollar, similar to other subsample periods except the first one, there is a significant negative correlation from the lower quantiles to upper quantiles. A noteworthy feature in this sample period is that asymmetry is found in association with financial market risk; the coefficient is negative in the lower quantiles and positive in the upper quantiles. This result tells us that as the general financial market tightens, gold return rises. The Wald test also strongly reinforces this result. That is, the null hypothesis of equality is rejected at the 1% significance level. Thus, we can say that the flight to quality and the demand for gold as a safe haven by investors are phenomena that emerged recently. This finding is consistent with Baur (2011), but the findings of this study refer to a much later phenomenon.[18]

5. Conclusions

In this study, we investigate how gold returns respond to changes in financial variables such as stock returns and financial market conditions. In particular, in order to elaborate the behavior in the tails of the distribution, we use quantile regression to confirm that gold return exhibits an asymmetric response depending on the quantile level. Specifically, according to our empirical results, gold return rises when; (1) stock return falls, (2) stock market volatility increases, and (3) the general financial market tightens. Findings (1) and (2) are remarkable in the sample period covering the GFC and (3) is prominent in the sample after the GFC to the present. Furthermore, gold return shows almost constant positive correlation with crude oil, and negative correlation with the value of the US dollar. These results provide useful implications for portfolio selection of individual investors, risk management of financial institutions, and policymakers aiming for financial stability.

The analysis in this paper can be extended by explicitly incorporating the correlation with stock returns into the model, as in Connolly et al. (2005). They analyze the relationships between returns on stocks and bonds under a regime-switching framework. Furthermore, performing out-of-sample forecasting and evaluation of goodness of fit is also an important issue.[19] Additionally, it is worth extending the model in this paper to predictive regression. Another way of extending of our analysis is to model the dependence structure by using copula or extreme value theory, which is now widely applied in the empirical finance literature. We leave these promising extensions for future research.

Funding: This research received no external funding.

Acknowledgments: I would like to thank two anonymous referees, whose insightful comments and suggestions helped to improve an earlier draft of this paper.

Conflicts of Interest: The author declares no conflict of interest.

References

Agyei-Ampomah, Sam, Dimitrios Gounopoulos, and Khelifa Mazouz. 2014. Does gold offer a better protection against losses in sovereign debt bonds than other metals? *Journal of Banking & Finance* 40: 507–21.

---

[17] See also Miyazaki and Hamori (2013). They show that there exists a unilateral causality in not only the mean but the variance from stock return to gold return in the sample period post subprime crisis.

[18] Although we do not dwell in the main text on the details of the results using FSI2, FSI3, and FSI4 as a financial stress index, all results are available from the author upon request.

[19] I would like to thank an anonymous referee for raising this point.

Akram, Q. Farooq. 2009. Commodity prices, interest rates and the dollar. *Energy Economics* 31: 838–51. [CrossRef]

Alkhatib, Akram, and Murad Harasheh. 2018. Performance of Exchange Traded Funds during the Brexit referendum: An event study. *International Journal of Financial Studies* 6: 64. [CrossRef]

Alexander, Carol. 2008. *Market Risk Analysis: Practical Financial Econometrics (Vol. II)*. Hoboken: Wiley.

Bai, Jushan, and Pierre Perron. 1998. Estimating and testing linear models with multiple structural changes. *Econometrica* 66: 47–78. [CrossRef]

Bai, Jushan, and Pierre Perron. 2003a. Computation and analysis of multiple structural change models. *Journal of Applied Econometrics* 18: 1–22. [CrossRef]

Bai, Jushan, and Pierre Perron. 2003b. Critical values for multiple structural change tests. *The Econometrics Journal* 6: 72–78. [CrossRef]

Balcilar, Mehmet, Zeynel Abidin Ozdemir, and Huseyin Ozdemir. 2018. *Dynamic Return and Volatility Spillovers among S&P 500, Crude Oil and Gold*. Discussion Paper 15–46. Famagusta: Eastern Mediterranean University, Department of Economics.

Basu, Parantap, and William T. Gavin. 2011. What explains the growth in commodity derivatives? *Federal Bank of St. Louis Review* 93: 37–48. [CrossRef]

Batten, Jonathan A., Cetin Ciner, and Brian M. Lucey. 2010. The macroeconomic determinants of volatility in precious metals markets. *Resources Policy* 35: 65–71. [CrossRef]

Batten, Jonathan A., Cetin Ciner, and Brian M. Lucey. 2014. Which precious metals spill over on which, when and why? Some evidence. *Applied Economics Letters* 22: 466–73. [CrossRef]

Baur, Dirk G. 2011. Explanatory mining for gold: Contrasting evidence from simple and multiple regressions. *Resources Policy* 36: 265–75. [CrossRef]

Baur, Dirk G. 2013. The structure and degree of dependence: A quantile regression approach. *Journal of Banking & Finance* 37: 786–98.

Baur, Dirk G., and Niels Schulze. 2005. Coexceedances in financial markets—A quantile regression analysis of contagion. *Emerging Markets Review* 6: 21–43. [CrossRef]

Baur, Dirk G., and Brian M. Lucey. 2010. Is gold a hedge or a safe haven? An analysis of stocks, bonds and gold. *Financial Review* 45: 217–29. [CrossRef]

Baur, Dirk G., and Thomas K. McDermott. 2010. Is gold a safe haven? International evidence. *Journal of Banking & Finance* 34: 1886–98.

Bhar, Ramaprasad, and Shawkat Hammoudeh. 2011. Commodities and financial variables: Analyzing relationships in a changing regime environment. *International Review of Economics & Finance* 20: 469–84.

Bouoiyour, Jamal, Refk Selmi, and Mark Wohar. 2018. Measuring the response of gold prices to uncertainty: An analysis beyond the mean. In *Economic Modelling*. Amsterdam: Elsevier, in press.

Chan, Kam Fong, Sirimon Treepongkaruna, Robert Brooks, and Stephen Gray. 2011. Asset market linkages: Evidence from financial, commodity and real estate assets. *Journal of Banking & Finance* 35: 1415–26.

Chao, Shih-Kang, Wolfgang K. Härdle, and Weining Wang. 2012. *Quantile Regression in Risk Calibration*. SFB 649 Discussion Paper 2012-006. Berlin: Humboldt-Universität.

Cheng, Ing-Haw, and Wei Xiong. 2014. Financialization of commodity markets. *Annual Review of Financial Economics* 6: 419–41. [CrossRef]

Chevallier, Julien, and Florian Ielpo. 2013. Volatility spillovers in commodity markets. *Applied Economics Letters* 20: 1211–27. [CrossRef]

Chudik, Alexander, and Marcel Fratzscher. 2011. Identifying the global transmission of the 2007–2009 financial crisis in a GVAR model. *European Economic Review* 55: 325–39. [CrossRef]

Ciner, Cetin, Constantin Gurdgiev, and Brian M. Lucey. 2013. Hedges and safe havens: An examination of stocks, bonds, gold, oil, and exchange rates. *International Review of Financial Analysis* 29: 202–11. [CrossRef]

Cohen, Gil, and Mahmod Qadan. 2010. Is gold still a shelter to fear? *American Journal of Social and Management Sciences* 1: 39–43. [CrossRef]

Connolly, Robert, Chris Stivers, and Licheng Sun. 2005. Stock market uncertainty and the stock-bond return relation. *Journal of Financial and Quantitative Analysis* 40: 161–94. [CrossRef]

Cont, Rama. 2001. Empirical properties of asset returns: Stylized facts and statistical issues. *Quantitative Finance* 1: 223–36. [CrossRef]

Diebold, Francis X., and Kamil Yilmaz. 2012. Better to give than to receive: Predictive directional measurement of volatility spillovers. *International Journal of Forecasting* 28: 57–66. [CrossRef]

Domanski, Dietrich, and Alexandra Heath. 2007. Financial investors and commodity markets. *BIS Quarterly Review* 3: 53–67.

Ehrmann, Michael, Marcel Fratzscher, and Roberto Rigobon. 2011. Stocks, bonds, money markets, and exchange rates: Measuring international financial transmission. *Journal of Applied Econometrics* 26: 948–74. [CrossRef]

Erb, Claude B., and Campbell R. Harvey. 2006. The strategic and tactical value of commodity futures. *Financial Analysts Journal* 62: 69–97. [CrossRef]

Fabozzi, Frank J., Sergio M. Focardi, Svetlozar T. Rachev, and Bala G. Arshanapalli. 2014. *The Basics of Financial Econometrics: Tools, Concepts, and Asset Management Applications*. Hoboken: John Wiley & Sons, Inc.

Franke, Jürgen, Peter Mwita, and Weining Wang. 2015. Nonparametric estimates for conditional quantiles of time series. *AStA Advances in Statistical Analysis* 99: 107–30. [CrossRef]

Gorton, Gary, and K. Geert Rouwenhorst. 2006. Facts and fantasies about commodity futures. *Financial Analysts Journal* 62: 47–68. [CrossRef]

Guo, Feng, Carl R. Chen, and Ying Sophie Huang. 2011. Markets contagion during financial crisis: A regime-switching approach. *International Review of Economics & Finance* 20: 95–109.

Hammoudeh, Shawkat, Ramazan Sari, and Bradley T. Ewing. 2009. Relationships among strategic commodities and with financial variables: A new look. *Contemporary Economic Policy* 27: 251–64. [CrossRef]

Hao, Lingxin, and Daniel Q. Naiman. 2007. *Quantile Regression*. Quantitative Applications in the Social Sciences, No. 149. Thousand Oaks: SAGE Publications, Inc.

Hartmann, Philipp, Stefan Straetmans, and C. G. de Vries. 2004. Asset market linkages in crisis periods. *Review of Economics and Statistics* 86: 313–26. [CrossRef]

Hillier, David, Paul Draper, and Robert Faff. 2006. Do precious metals shine? An investment perspective. *Financial Analysts Journal* 62: 98–106. [CrossRef]

Hood, Matthew, and Farooq Malik. 2013. Is gold the best hedge and a safe haven under changing stock market volatility? *Review of Financial Economics* 22: 47–52. [CrossRef]

IHS Global Inc. 2016. *EViews 9 User's Guide II*. California: IHS Global Inc.

Koenker, Roger, and Gilbert Bassett Jr. 1978. Regression quantiles. *Econometrica* 46: 33–50. [CrossRef]

Koenker, Roger, and Kevin F. Hallock. 2001. Quantile regression. *Journal of Economic Perspectives* 15: 143–56. [CrossRef]

Longstaff, Francis A. 2010. The subprime credit crisis and contagion in financial markets. *Journal of Financial Economics* 97: 436–50. [CrossRef]

Mensi, Walid, Makram Beljid, Adel Boubaker, and Shunsuke Managi. 2013. Correlations and volatility spillovers across commodity and stock markets: Linking energies, food, and gold. *Economic Modelling* 32: 15–22. [CrossRef]

Mensi, Walid, Shawkat Hammoudeh, Juan C. Reboredo, and Duc K. Nguyen. 2014. Do global factors impact BRICS stock markets? A quantile regression approach. *Emerging Markets Review* 19: 1–17. [CrossRef]

Miyazaki, Takashi, and Shigeyuki Hamori. 2013. Testing for causality between the gold return and stock market performance: Evidence for "gold investment in case of emergency". *Applied Financial Economics* 23: 27–40. [CrossRef]

Miyazaki, Takashi, and Shigeyuki Hamori. 2014. Cointegration with regime shift between gold and financial variables. *International Journal of Financial Research* 5: 90–97. [CrossRef]

Miyazaki, Takashi, and Shigeyuki Hamori. 2016. Asymmetric correlations in gold and other financial markets. *Applied Economics* 48: 4419–25. [CrossRef]

Miyazaki, Takashi, and Shigeyuki Hamori. 2018. The determinants of a simultaneous crash in gold and stock markets: An ordered logit approach. *Annals of Financial Economics* 13: 1850004. [CrossRef]

Miyazaki, Takashi, Yuki Toyoshima, and Shigeyuki Hamori. 2012. Exploring the dynamic interdependence between gold and other financial markets. *Economics Bulletin* 32: 37–50.

O'Connor, Fergal A., Brian M. Lucey, Jonathan A. Batten, and Dirk G. Baur. 2015. The financial economics of gold—A survey. *International Review of Financial Analysis* 41: 186–205. [CrossRef]

Piplack, Jan, and Stefan Straetmans. 2010. Comovements of different asset classes during market stress. *Pacific Economic Review* 15: 385–400. [CrossRef]

Qadan, Mahmod, and Joseph Yagil. 2012. Fear sentiments and gold price: Testing causality in-mean and in-variance. *Applied Economics Letters* 19: 363–66. [CrossRef]

Raza, Syed Ali, Nida Shah, and Muhammad Shahbaz. 2018. Does economic policy uncertainty influence gold prices? Evidence from a nonparametric causality-in-quantiles approach. *Resources Policy* 57: 61–68. [CrossRef]

Reboredo, Juan C., and Gazi Salah Uddin. 2016. Do financial stress and policy uncertainty have an impact on the energy and metals markets? A quantile regression approach. *International Review of Economics & Finance* 43: 284–98.

Renaud, Olivier, and Maria-Pia Victoria-Feser. 2010. A robust coefficient of determination for regression. *Journal of Statistical Planning and Inference* 140: 1852–62. [CrossRef]

Rodriguez, Robert N., and Yonggang Yao. 2017. *Five Things You Should Know about Quantile Regression.* Paper SAS525–2017. Cary: SAS Institute Inc.

Sari, Ramazan, Shawkat Hammoudeh, and Ugur Soytas. 2010. Dynamics of oil price, precious metal prices, and exchange rate. *Energy Economics* 32: 351–62. [CrossRef]

Silvennoinen, Annastiina, and Susan Thorp. 2013. Financialization, crisis, and commodity correlation dynamics. *Journal of International Financial Markets, Institutions & Money* 24: 42–65.

Straetmans, Stefan T. M., Willem F. C. Verschoor, and Christian C. P. Wolff. 2008. Extreme US stock market fluctuations in the wake of 9/11. *Journal of Applied Econometrics* 23: 17–42. [CrossRef]

Tang, Ke, and Wei Xiong. 2012. Index investment and the financialization of commodities. *Financial Analysts Journal* 68: 54–74. [CrossRef]

Wheelock, David C., and Mark E. Wohar. 2009. Can the term spread predict output growth and recessions? A survey of the literature. In *Federal Reserve Bank of St.* Louis Review 91. St. Louis: Federal Reserve Bank.

World Gold Council. 2010. *Gold: Hedging against Tail Risk.* London: World Gold Council.

Journal of
Risk and Financial Management

Article

Testing for Causality-In-Mean and Variance between the UK Housing and Stock Markets

Yuki Toyoshima

Shinsei Bank, Limited, 4-3, Nihonbashi-muromachi 2-chome, Chuo-ku, Tokyo 103-8303, Japan;
Yuki.Toyoshima@shinseibank.com

Received: 24 March 2018; Accepted: 6 April 2018; Published: 26 April 2018

Abstract: This paper employs the two-step procedure to analyze the causality-in-mean and causality-in-variance between the housing and stock markets of the UK. The empirical findings make two key contributions. First, although previous studies have indicated a one-way causal relation from the housing market to the stock market in the UK, this paper discovered a two-way causal relation between them. Second, a causality-in-variance as well as a causality-in-mean was detected from the housing market to the stock market.

Keywords: causality-in-variance; cross-correlation function; housing and stock markets

JEL Classification: C22; E44; G11

1. Introduction

Although major financial institutions experienced the subprime mortgage crisis and Lehman Brothers went out of business, the market for real estate has grown steadily in the last decade. As indicated in Figure 1, the UK is one of the largest markets in the world, followed by the US, Japan, Australia, and France. In addition, since the UK decided to withdraw from the European Union ("Brexit"), based on a referendum conducted on 23 June 2016, market participants and macroeconomic policymakers have focused more on its impact on the UK real estate market. Therefore, examining the relation between the UK real estate and other financial markets is useful for both practitioners and academic researchers. Many previous empirical studies have explored the relation between the real estate and stock markets. Regarding this relation, we need to understand the following two effects. First, researchers who support the "wealth effect" claim that households benefiting from unanticipated gains in stock prices tend to increase housing demand. Second, researchers who support the "credit price effect" claim that an increase in real estate prices can stimulate economic activity and the future profitability of companies by raising the value of collateral and reducing the cost of borrowing for both companies and households. Thus, identifying the direction of causality between the real estate and stock markets as well as the number of lags is essential.

As mentioned above, many previous empirical studies have analyzed the relation between the real estate and stock markets (e.g., Gyourko and Keim (1992); Ibbotson and Siegel (1984); Ibrahim (2010); Kapopoulos and Siokis (2005); Lin and Fuerst (2014); Liow (2006); Liow (2012); Liow and Yang (2005); Louis and Sun (2013); Okunev and Wilson (1997); Okunev et al. (2000); Quan and Titman (1999); Su (2011); and Tsai et al. (2012)). To the best of our knowledge, no studies have analyzed the causality-in-variance between the real estate and stock markets. As indicated by Ross (1989), volatility provides useful data on the flow of information. For institutional investors such as banks, life insurance companies, hedge funds, and pension funds, deeper knowledge of spillover mechanisms for volatility can be useful for diversifying investments and hedge risk.

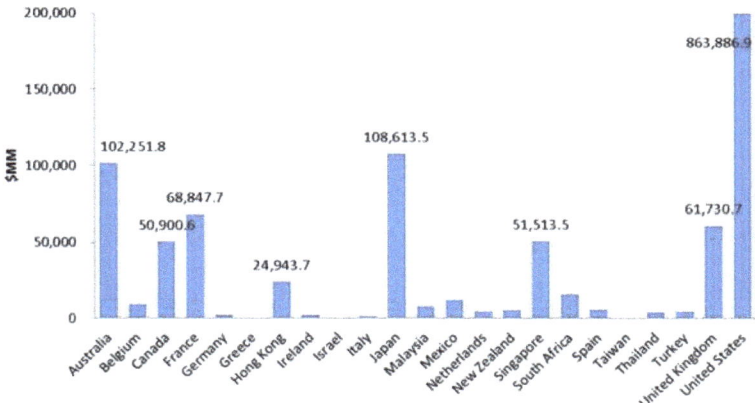

Figure 1. Market capitalization of the S&P Global REIT (Real Estate Investment Trust) Index in August 2016. *Data Source*: S&P Capital IQ.

Table 1 summarizes the previous studies. Academic research on the relation between the real estate and stock markets has been undertaken since the 1980s. In this research, almost all studies have focused on the cointegration relation between the two markets. In recent years, not only a linear cointegration method but also a nonlinear cointegration method has been undertaken (e.g., Liow and Yang (2005); Okunev et al. (2000); Su (2011); and Tsai et al. (2012)). Using data from four major Asian countries (Japan, Hong Kong, Singapore, and Malaysia), Liow and Yang (2005) analyzed the relation between the securitized real estate and stock markets. Moreover, they conducted a fractional cointegration analysis of two asset markets. Furthermore, they revealed that fractional cointegration exists between the securitized real estate and stock markets of Hong Kong and Singapore. Okunev et al. (2000) examined the dynamic relation between the US real estate and S&P 500 stock index from 1972 to 1998 by conducting both linear and nonlinear causality tests. While the linear test results generally indicate a unidirectional relation from the real estate market to the stock market, nonlinear causality tests indicate a strong unidirectional relation from the stock market to the real estate market. Su (2011) used a nonparametric rank test to empirically investigate the long-run nonlinear equilibrium relation within Western European countries. Nonlinear causality test results demonstrated that unidirectional causality from the real estate market to the stock market exists in the Germany, the Netherlands, and the UK. Unidirectional causality from the stock market to the real estate market was observed in Belgium and Italy, and feedback effects were discovered in France, Spain, and Switzerland. Tsai et al. (2012) used nonlinear models to analyze the long-term relation between the US housing and stock markets. Empirical results demonstrated that the wealth effect between the stock and housing markets is more significant when the stock price outperforms the housing price by an estimated threshold level.

This paper uses the cross-correlation function (CCF) approach developed by Cheung and Ng (1996) to examine the causal relation between the housing and stock markets in the UK. This empirical technique has been widely applied in the examination of stock, fixed income, and commodities markets, business cycles, and derivatives.[1] While the test of Granger causality techniques examines the causality-in-mean, the CCF approach detects both the causality-in-mean and causality-in-variance.[2]

---

[1] Some examples include studies by Hamori (2003), Alaganar and Bhar (2003), Bhar and Hamori (2005, 2008), Hoshikawa (2008), Nakajima and Hamori (2012), Miyazaki and Hamori (2013), Tamakoshi and Hamori (2014), and Toyoshima and Hamori (2012).

[2] See Hafner and Herwartz (2008) and Chang and McAleer (2017a) for the causality-in-variance analysis using multivariate GARCH models.

The CCF approach can detect the direction of causality as well as the number of leads/lags involved.[3] Furthermore, it permits flexible specification of the innovation process and nondependence on normality.[4]

Table 1. Summaries of previous studies.

Authors	Empirical Technique	Country	Principal Results
Gyourko and Keim (1992)	Market regression model	the US	Lagged equity REIT and stock return are predictors of property index.
Ibbotson and Siegel (1984)	Correlation, Regression	the US	Low correlation between the real estate and stocks, bonds is found.
Ibrahim (2010)	VAR model, Granger causality tests	Thailand	Unidirectional causality from stock prices to house prices is found.
Kapopoulos and Siokis (2005)	VAR model, Granger causality tests	Greece	Unidirectional causality from stock prices to house prices is found.
Lin and Fuerst (2014)	Johansen, Gregory-Hansen ,Nonlinear cointegration tests	9 Asian countries	Market segmentation is observed in China, Japan, Thailand, Malaysia, Indonesia and South Korea.
Liow (2006)	ARDL cointegration tests	Singapore	Contemporaneous long-term relationship between the stock market, residential and office property prices is found.
Liow (2012)	Asymmetric DCC model	8 Asian countries	Conditional real estate-stock correlations are time varying and asymmetric in some cases.
Liow and Yang (2005)	FIVEC model, VEC model	4 Asian countries	FIVECM improves the forecasting performance over conventional VECM models.
Louis and Sun (2013)	Fama–MacBeth procedure	the US	Firms' long-term abnormal stock returns are negatively related to past growth in housing prices.
Okunev and Wilson (1997)	Cointegration tests	the US	Weak and nonlinear relationship between the stock and real estate markets is found.
Okunev et al. (2000)	Linear and nonlinear causality tests	the US	Strong uni-directional relationship from the stock market to the real estate market is found in nonlinear causality test.
Quan and Titman (1999)	Cross-sectional regression	17 countries	Positive relation between real estate values and stock returns is found.
Su (2011)	TEC model, Non-parametric rank test	8 Western European countries	Unidirectional causality from the real estate markets to the stock market is found in the Germany, Netherlands and the UK.
Tsai et al. (2012)	M-TAR cointegration model	the US	Threshold cointegration relationship between the housing market and the stock market is found.

The remainder of this paper is organized as follows. The next section presents the CCF approach. In the following sections, we discuss the data, descriptive statistics, and results of the unit root tests and provide a description of the autoregressive-exponential generalized autoregressive conditional heteroskedasticity (AR-EGARCH) specification. Thereafter, we present the empirical results and discuss the findings. Finally, a summary and conclusion are presented in the closing section.

2. Empirical Techniques

Following Cheung and Ng (1996), suppose there are two stationary and ergodic time series, X_t and Y_t. When $I_{1,t}$, $I_{2,t}$, and I_t are three information sets defined by $I_{1,t} = (X_t, X_{t-1}, \ldots)$, $I_{2,t} = (Y_t, Y_{t-1}, \ldots)$, and $I_t = (X_t, X_{t-1}, \ldots, Y_t, Y_{t-1}, \ldots)$, Y is said to cause X in the mean if

$$E[X_t|I_{1,t-1}] \neq E[X_t|I_{t-1}]. \tag{1}$$

---

[3] One purpose of this paper is to detect the number of leads/lags, so we do not adopt Hong (2001) approach.
[4] See also Hamori (2003).

Similarly, X is said to cause Y in the mean if

$$E[Y_t|I_{2,t-1}] \neq E[Y_t|I_{t-1}]. \tag{2}$$

Feedback effect in the mean occurs if Y causes X in the mean and X causes Y in the mean. On the other hand, Y is said to cause X in the variance if

$$E\left[(X_t - \mu_{X,t})^2|I_{1,t-1}\right] \neq E\left[(X_t - \mu_{X,t})^2|I_{t-1}\right], \tag{3}$$

where $\mu_{X,t}$ denotes the mean of X_t conditioned on $I_{1,t-1}$. Similarly, X is said to cause Y in the variance if

$$E\left[(Y_t - \mu_{Y,t})^2|I_{2,t-1}\right] \neq E\left[(Y_t - \mu_{Y,t})^2|I_{t-1}\right], \tag{4}$$

where $\mu_{Y,t}$ denotes the mean of Y_t conditioned on $I_{2,t-1}$. Feedback effect in the variance occurs if X causes Y in the variance and Y causes X in the variance.

We impose the following structure in Equation (1) through Equation (4) to detect causality-in-mean and causality-in-variance. Suppose X_t and Y_t are written as

$$X_t = \mu_{X,t} + \sqrt{h_{X,t}}\varepsilon_t, \tag{5}$$

$$Y_t = \mu_{Y,t} + \sqrt{h_{Y,t}}\zeta_t, \tag{6}$$

where $\{\varepsilon_t\}$ and $\{\zeta_t\}$ are two independent white noise processes with zero mean and unit variance.

For the causality-in-mean test, we have the standardized innovation as follows:

$$u_t = (X_t - \mu_{X,t})^2/h_{X,t} = \varepsilon_t^2, \tag{7}$$

$$v_t = (Y_t - \mu_{Y,t})^2/h_{Y,t} = \zeta_t^2, \tag{8}$$

with ε_t and ζ_t being the standardized residuals. Since these residuals are unobservable, we use their estimates. Next, using their estimates, we calculate the sample cross-correlation of the squared standardized residual series, $r_{uv}(k)$, and the sample cross-correlation caluculated using the standardized residual series, $r_{\varepsilon\zeta}(k)$, at time lag k.

The quantities $r_{\varepsilon\zeta}(k)$ and $r_{uv}(k)$ are used to detect causality-in-mean and causality-in-variance, respectively, using the CCF approach.

First, we can detect the null hypothesis that there is no causality-in-mean using the following CCF statistic:

$$CCF = \sqrt{T} \cdot r_{\varepsilon\zeta}(k). \tag{9}$$

If the CCF test statistic is below the critical value calculated using the standard normal distribution, then we cannot reject the null hypothesis.

Second, we can detect the null hypothesis that there is no causality-in-variance using the test statistic, which is given by

$$CCF = \sqrt{T} \cdot r_{uv}(k). \tag{10}$$

If the CCF test statistic is below the critical value calculated using the standard normal distribution, then we cannot reject the null hypothesis.

The CCF approach is divided into two steps. First, we estimate univariate time-series models that consider the time variant conditional means and conditional variances. In this paper, we adopt the AR-EGARCH formulation.[5] Second, from the estimated AR-EGARCH model, we calculate the

---

5   See Nelson (1991).

standardized residuals of estimated model and calculate the series of standardized squared residuals by conditional variances. As mentioned above, we use the CCF of these standardized residuals to test the null hypotheses of no causality-in-mean and no causality-in-variance.

3. Data, Descriptive Statistics, and Results of an Augmented Dickey–Fuller Test

We employ monthly data on the UK housing and stock markets from January 1991 to August 2016. This sample period was chosen based on the availability of data obtained from *The Nationwide Building Society*.[6]

Table 2 presents the descriptive statistics for the monthly change rate in stock and housing prices. As indicated in Figure 2, the volatility of the stock market is higher than that of the housing market. The measure for skewness and kurtosis, Jarque–Bera statistics, are used to detect whether the housing and the stock monthly change rates are normally distributed.[7] The Jarque–Bera statistics reject normality at a 10% significance level in both variables.

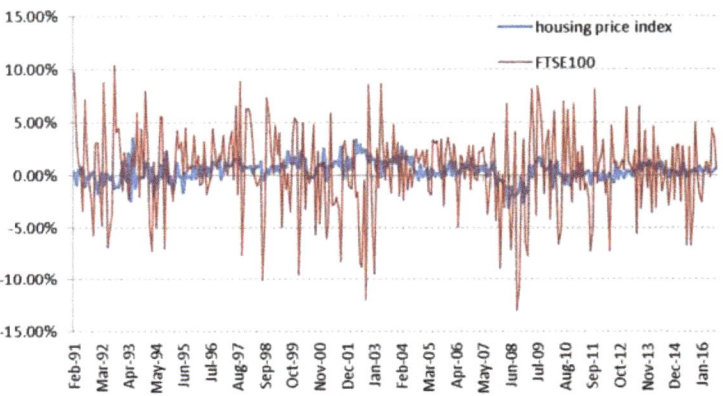

Figure 2. Rates of change in the stock and housing indexes. *Data Source*: Nationwide Building Society, Yahoo Finance.

Table 2. Descriptive Statistics: Rates of change in the stock and housing indexes.

Statistics	Housing	Stock
Sample Size	307	307
Mean	0.4421%	0.4527%
Std. Dev.	0.9544%	4.0076%
Skewness	−0.2221	−0.4557
Kurtosis	1.1434	0.5011
Maximum	3.4912%	10.3952%
Minimum	−3.1084%	−13.0247%
Jarque-Bera	19.2472	13.8362
Probability	0.0066%	0.0990%

Table 3 indicates the results of the Augmented Dickey–Fuller test. The results reveal that, while the null hypothesis that the variables have a unit root is accepted in both variables in the level, the null hypothesis is rejected at the first difference.

---

[6] We obtained the data from the URL below: http://www.nationwide.co.U.K./about/house-price-index/download-data#tab: Downloaddata.

[7] See Jarque and Bera (1987).

Table 3. Results of an augmented Dickey–Fuller test.

Variable		Auxuliary Model		
		Const	Const & Trend	None
housing	Level	−0.2988	−2.3811	1.5701
	First difference	−4.5065 ***	−4.5019 ***	−3.8047 ***
stock	Level	−1.8598	−2.2418	0.7945
	First difference	−17.3975 ***	−17.4146 ***	−17.2370 ***

Notes: *** indicates significance at 1%.

4. Estimation of an AR-EGARCH Model

The first step of the CCF approach is to model the monthly change rates in the housing and stock prices. We estimate the AR(k)-EGARCH(p,q) model as follows:

$$y_t = a_0 + \sum_{i=1}^{k} a_i y_{t-i} + b_0 Crisis_t + \varepsilon_t, \quad \varepsilon_{t/t-1} \sim N(0, \sigma_t^2), \tag{11}$$

$$Crisis_t = \begin{cases} 0 & (t = Jan\ 91, \ldots, May\ 07) \\ 1 & (t = Jun\ 07, \ldots, Aug16) \end{cases}, \tag{12}$$

$$log(\sigma_t^2) = \omega + \sum_{i=1}^{q} (\alpha_i |Z_{t-i}| + \gamma_i Z_{t-i}) + \sum_{i=1}^{p} \beta_i log(\sigma_{t-i}^2), \tag{13}$$

where $z_t = \varepsilon_t / \sigma_t$. Note that the left-hand side of Equation (13) is the log of the conditional variance. Using the log form of the EGARCH(p,q) model, it is possible to guarantee the non-negativity constraints without imposing the constraints of the coefficients.[8] By including the term z_{t-i}, the EGARCH(p,q) model reflects the asymmetric effect of positive and negative shocks. If $\gamma_i > 0$ then $z_{t-1} = \varepsilon_{t-1} / \sigma_{t-1}$ is positive. The persistence of shocks to the conditional variance is given by $\sum_{i=1}^{p} \beta_i$.

Equation (11), which is the conditional mean, is formulated as an autoregressive model of order k. To determine the optimal lag length k for each variables, we use the Schwartz–Bayesian Information Criterion (SBIC).[9]. The SBIC is also applied in Equation (13) to determine the optimal lag length p and q.[10]

Table 4 presents the estimates for the AR(k)-EGARCH(p,q) model. Regarding the standard error, this paper accepts the robust standard error developed by Bollerslev and Wooldridge (1992). First, the EGARCH(1,1) model is chosen for both variables. While all parameters of the EGARCH model in the monthly change rate in the stock price are significant, all parameters excluding γ_1 in the monthly change rate in the housing price are significant at the conventional significance levels.

Furthermore, Table 4 reports the estimates of the coefficient β_1, which measures the degree of volatility persistence. We find that β_1 is significant at conventional significance levels, and the value of β_1 is close to 1. These estimates lead to the conclusion that the persistence in shocks to volatility is relatively large. Table 2 also indicates the diagnostics of the empirical results of the AR-EGARCH model. While $Q(24)$ is a test statistic for the null hypothesis that there is no autocorrelation up to order 24 for standardized residuals, $Q^2(24)$ is a test statistic for the null hypothesis that there is no autocorrelation up to order 24 for standardized residuals squared.[11] These tables show that both statistics are statistically significant at 5% level for all cases. Thus, the null hypothesis that there is no autocorrelation up to order 24 for standardized residuals and the standardized residuals squared is accepted. These results empirically support the formulation of the AR-EGARCH model.

---

[8] The EGARCH model suffers from a number of fundamental problems, including the lack of regularity conditions and hence the absence of any asymptotic properties. See McAleer and Hafner (2014) and Chang and McAleer (2017b) for details.

[9] See Schwarz (1978).

[10] We selected the final models from EGARCH(1,1), EGARCH(1,2), EGARCH(2,1), and EGARCH(2,2).

[11] See Ljung and Box (1978).

Table 4. AR-EGARCH (autoregressive-exponential generalized autoregressive conditional heteroskedasticity) model.

Parameters	Housing		Stock	
	AR(3)-EGARCH(1,1)		AR(1)-EGARCH(1,1)	
	Estimate	SE	Estimate	SE
a_0	0.0021 ***	(0.0007)	0.0088 ***	(0.0024)
a_1	0.0321	(0.061)	−0.0791	(0.0602)
a_2	0.4095 ***	(0.0518)		
a_3	0.2522 ***	(0.0582)		
b_0	−0.0011	(0.0007)	−0.007 *	(0.0037)
ω	−0.4465 *	(0.2485)	−1.3275 ***	(0.4386)
α_1	0.2362 ***	(0.0818)	0.3162 ***	(0.1148)
γ_1	−0.0074	(0.0476)	−0.1191 *	(0.0614)
β_1	0.9741 ***	(0.0224)	0.8365 ***	(0.058)
Log Likelihood	1074.4320		571.2161	
SBIC	−6.8994		−3.6025	
Q(24)	35.4320		11.6550	
P-value	0.0620		0.9840	
$Q^2(24)$	0.0000		19.3240	
P-value	0.0000		0.7350	

Notes: ***, * indicate significance at 1% and 10%, respectively. $Q(24)$ and $Q^2(24)$ are the Ljung–Box (LB) statistics with 24 lags for the standardized residuals and their squares. In addition, we checked the lag of LB statistics from 1 to 24.

5. Testing for Causality-In-Variance

The second step is to detect causality-in-mean and causality-in-variance, using the calculated sample cross-correlations. Table 4 indicates the empirical results. Lags are measured in months, which range from 1 to 24. For example, in the case of "housing and stock $(-k)$," the significance of positive lags implies that the causal direction is from the stock market to the housing market.

Table 5 presents significance lags causality for both cases. First, in the case of "housing and stock $(-k)$," the causality-in-mean exists in lag 6 and the causality-in-variance exists in lags 5 and 9. Second, in the case of "housing and stock $(+k)$," the causality-in-mean exists in lags 21 and the causality-in-variance exists in lags 4 and 12. The above results provide two interesting findings. First, although Su (2011) indicated a one-way causal relation from the housing market to the stock market in the UK, this paper discovered a two-way causal relation between them. This supports the idea that both a wealth effect and a credit price effect exist between the housing and stock markets. Second, both causality-in-mean and causality-in-variance are detected from the housing market to the stock market. This finding has never been referred to in previous studies and it is useful for both practitioners and academic researchers.

Table 5. Cross-correlation for levels and squares of the standardized residuals.

Lag k	Housing and Stock $(-k)$		Housing and Stock $(+k)$	
	Mean	Variance	Mean	Variance
1	−0.0271	0.0067	0.0011	0.0320
2	−0.0262	0.0549	0.0651	−0.0196
3	−0.0675	0.0259	0.0363	−0.0358
4	0.0037	0.0589	0.0709	0.0920 *
5	−0.0390	0.1460 ***	0.0322	−0.0423
6	0.1366 ***	−0.0407	−0.0797	0.0530
7	0.0016	0.0007	−0.0380	0.0256
8	−0.0386	0.0050	0.0105	−0.0298
9	0.0410	0.1444 ***	−0.0114	−0.0154
10	0.0375	0.0101	0.0179	0.0630

Table 5. *Cont.*

Lag k	Housing and Stock $(-k)$		Housing and Stock $(+k)$	
	Mean	Variance	Mean	Variance
11	0.0269	0.0238	−0.0132	0.0012
12	−0.0728	0.0150	−0.0204	0.1879 ***
13	−0.0695	−0.0248	−0.0084	0.0257
14	−0.0648	0.0234	−0.1309	0.0503
15	−0.0835	0.0087	−0.0859	−0.0555
16	−0.0120	−0.0113	−0.0087	−0.1055
17	0.0301	0.0263	−0.0620	−0.0064
18	−0.0497	0.0383	−0.0341	0.0603
19	−0.0406	0.0092	−0.0573	0.0592
20	−0.0200	0.0175	0.0051	0.0288
21	−0.0161	−0.0574	0.0944 **	0.0129
22	−0.0141	−0.0669	−0.0235	0.0560
23	−0.0868	−0.0501	0.0720	0.0092
24	−0.1098	−0.0152	−0.0469	−0.0259

Notes: ***, **, * indicate significance at 1%, 5%, and 10%, respectively.

6. Conclusions

This paper analyzes the causality-in-mean and causality-in-variance between the UK stock and housing markets using monthly data from January 1991 to August 2016. A CCF approach developed by Cheung and Ng (1996) and a causality-in-variance test applied to financial market prices are used as tests (Cheung and Ng 1996). The empirical findings make two key contributions. First, although Su (2011) showed a one-way causal relation from the housing market to the stock market in the UK, this paper discovered a two-way causal relation between them. Thus, both a wealth effect and a credit price effect exist between the housing and stock markets. This paper also detected a causality-in-mean and causality-in-variance from the housing market to the stock market. This point has never been referred to in previous studies and is useful for both practitioners and academic researchers.

Acknowledgments: We would like to thank three anonymous reviewers, whose valuable comments helped to improve an earlier version of this paper.

Conflicts of Interest: The author declares no conflict of interest.

References

Alaganar, V. T., and Ramaprasad Bhar. 2003. An International Study of Causality-in-Variance: Interest Rate and Financial Sector Returns. *Journal of Economics and Finance* 27: 39–55. [CrossRef]

Bhar, Ramaprasad, and Shigeyuki Hamori. 2005. Causality in Variance and the Type of Traders in Crude Oil Futures. *Energy Economics* 27: 527–39. [CrossRef]

Bhar, Ramaprasad, and Shigeyuki Hamori. 2008. Information Content of Commodity Futures Prices for Monetary Policy. *Economic Modelling* 25: 274–83. [CrossRef]

Bollerslev, Tim, and Jeffrey. M. Wooldridge. 1992. Quasi-Maximum Likelihood Estimation and Inference in Dynamic Models with Time Varying Covariances. *Econometric Reviews* 11: 143–72. [CrossRef]

Chang, Chia-Lin, and Michael McAleer. 2017a. A simple test for causality in volatility. *Econometrics* 5: 15. [CrossRef]

Chang, Chia-Lin, and Michael McAleer. 2017b. The correct regularity condition and interpretation of asymmetry in EGARCH. *Economics Letters* 161: 52–55. [CrossRef]

Cheung, Yin-Wong, and Lilian K. Ng. 1996. A Causality-in-Variance Test and Its Applications to Financial Market Prices. *Journal of Econometrics* 72: 33–48. [CrossRef]

Gyourko, Joseph, and Donald B. Keim. 1992. What Does the Stock Market Tell Us about Real Estate Returns? *Journal of the American Real Estate Finance and Urban Economics Association* 20: 457–86. [CrossRef]

Hafner, Christian M., and Helmut Herwartz. 2008. Testing for Causality in Variance Using Multivariate GARCH Models. *Annals of Economics and Statistics* 89: 215–41. [CrossRef]

Hamori, Shigeyuki. 2003. *An Empirical Investigation of Stock Markets: The CCF Approach*. Dordrecht: Kluwer Academic Publishers.

Hong, Yongmiao. 2001. A Test for Volatility Spillover with Application to Exchange Rates. *Journal of Econometrics* 103: 183–224. [CrossRef]

Hoshikawa, Takeshi. 2008. The Causal Relationships between Foreign Exchange Intervention and Exchange Rate. *Applied Economics Letters* 15: 519–22. [CrossRef]

Ibbotson, Roger G., and Laurence B. Siegel. 1984. Real Estate Returns: A Comparison with Other Investments. *Real Estate Economics* 12: 219–42. [CrossRef]

Ibrahim, Mansor H. 2010. House Price-Stock Price Relations in Thailand: An Empirical Analysis. *International Journal of Housing Markets and Analysis* 3: 69–82. [CrossRef]

Jarque, Carlos M., and Anil K. Bera. 1987. Test for Normality of Observations and Regression Residuals. *International Statistical Review* 55: 163–72. [CrossRef]

Kapopoulos, Panayotis, and Fotios Siokis. 2005. Stock and Real Estate Prices in Greece: Wealth versus Credit-Price Effect. *Applied Economics Letters* 12: 125–28. [CrossRef]

Lin, Pin-te, and Franz Fuerst. 2014. The Integration of Direct Real Estate and Stock Markets in Asia. *Applied Economics* 46: 1323–34. [CrossRef]

Liow, Kim Hiang, and Haishan Yang. 2005. Long-Term Co-Memories and Short-Run Adjustment: Securitized Real Estate and Stock Markets. *The Journal of Real Estate Finance and Economics* 31: 283–300. [CrossRef]

Liow, Kim Hiang. 2006. Dynamic Relationship between Stock and Property Markets. *Applied Financial Economics* 16: 371–76. [CrossRef]

Liow, Kim Hiang. 2012. Co-Movements and Correlations Across Asian Securitized Real Estate and Stock Markets. *Real Estate Economics* 40: 97–129. [CrossRef]

Ljung, Greta M., and George E. P. Box. 1978. On a Measure of Lack of Fit in Time Series Models. *Biometrika* 66: 265–70. [CrossRef]

Louis, Henock, and Amy X. Sun. 2013. Long-Term Growth in Housing Prices and Stock Returns. *Real Estate Economics* 41: 663–708. [CrossRef]

McAleer, Michael, and Christian M. Hafner. 2014. A one line derivation of EGARCH. *Econometrics* 2: 92–97. [CrossRef]

Miyazaki, Takashi, and Shigeyuki Hamori. 2013. Testing for causality between the gold return and stock market performance: Evidence for gold investment in case of emergency. *Applied Financial Economics* 23: 27–40. [CrossRef]

Nakajima, Tadahiro, and Shigeyuki Hamori. 2012. Causality-in-Mean and Causality-in-Variance among Electricity Prices, Crude Oil Prices, and Yen-US Dollar Exchange Rates in Japan. *Research in International Business and Finance* 26: 371–86. [CrossRef]

Nelson, Daniel B. 1991. Conditional Heteroskedasticity in Asset Returns: A New Approach. *Econometrica* 59: 347–70. [CrossRef]

Okunev, John, and Patrick J. Wilson. 1997. Using Nonlinear Tests to Examine Integration between Real Estate and Stock Markets. *Real Estate Economics* 25: 487–503. [CrossRef]

Okunev, John, Patrick Wilson, and Ralf Zurbruegg. 2000. The Causal Relationship between Real Estate and Stock Markets. *Journal of Real Estate Finance and Economics* 21: 251–61. [CrossRef]

Quan, Daniel C., and Sheridan Titman. 1999. Do Real Estate Prices and Stock Prices Move Together? An International Analysis. *Real Estate Economics* 27: 183–207. [CrossRef]

Ross, Stephen A. 1989. Information and Volatility: No-Arbitrage Martingale Approach to Timing and Resolution Irrelevancy. *Journal of Finance* 44: 1–17. [CrossRef]

Su, Chi-Wei. 2011. Non-Linear Causality between the Stock and Real Estate Markets of Western European Countries: Evidence from Rank Tests. *Economic Modelling* 28: 845–51. [CrossRef]

Schwarz, Gideon. 1978. Estimating the Dimension of a Model. *Annals of Statistics* 6: 461–64. [CrossRef]

Tsai, I-Chun, Cheng-Feng Lee, and Ming-Chu Chiang. 2012. The Asymmetric Wealth Effect in the U.S. Housing and Stock Markets: Evidence from the Threshold Cointegration Model. *Journal of Real Estate Finance and Economics* 45: 1005–20. [CrossRef]

Tamakoshi, Go, and Shigeyuki Hamori. 2014. Causality-in-variance and causality-in-mean between the Greek sovereignbond yields and Southern European banking sector equity returns. *Journal of Economics and Finance* 38: 627–42. [CrossRef]

Toyoshima, Yuki, and Shigeyuki Hamori. 2012. Volatility Transmission of Swap Spreads among the United States, Japan, and the United Kingdom: A Cross-Correlation Function Approach. *Applied Financial Economics* 22: 849–62. [CrossRef]

Journal of
Risk and Financial
Management

Article

Modeling the Dependence Structure of Share Prices among Three Chinese City Banks

Guizhou Liu, Xiao-Jing Cai and Shigeyuki Hamori *

Graduate School of Economics, Kobe University, 2-1, Rokkodai, Nada-Ku, Kobe 657-8501, Japan;
liuguizhou0402@gmail.com (G.L.); cai_xiaojing@people.kobe-u.ac.jp (X.-J.C.)
*   Correspondence: hamori@econ.kobe-u.ac.jp

Received: 23 August 2018; Accepted: 28 September 2018; Published: 29 September 2018

Abstract: We study the dependence structure of share price returns among the Beijing Bank, Ningbo Bank, and Nanjing Bank using copula models. We use the normal, Student's t, rotated Gumbel, and symmetrized Joe-Clayton (SJC) copula models to estimate the underlying dependence structure in two periods: one covering the global financial crisis and the other covering the domestic share market crash in China. We show that Beijing Bank is less dependent on the other two city banks than Nanjing Bank, which is dependent on the other two in share price extreme returns. We also observe a major decrease of dependency from 2007 to 2018 in three one-to-one dependence structures. Interestingly, contrary to recent literatures, Ningbo Bank and Nanjing Bank tend to be more dependent on each other in positive returns than in negative returns during the past decade. We also show the dynamic dependence structures among three city banks using time-varying copula.

Keywords: city banks; dependence structure; copula

1. Introduction

Research on the co-movement among financial asset returns has tended to focus more on tail dependence rather than linear correlation, as the former can capture the dependence structure in a period with extreme events (boom or crash). The dependence structure has been studied using many financial time series data, such as international share market indices, exchange rates, and bond yields; other non-financial data, such as oil and gold prices, have also been proven to be highly related to the tail dependence of financial markets. Furthermore, research on tail dependence has shown that for most financial asset returns, there is more dependence during a crash than during boom periods (see, for example, (Ang and Chen 2002)). Potential asymmetric characteristics exist in the tail dependence structure. For instance, as shown first by Patton (2006), some exchange rate returns exhibit asymmetric tail dependence. These results relating to tail dependence aroused our interest in the asymmetry in tail dependence.

In financial asset returns, tail dependence may change over time. As shown by Patton (2006), the tail dependence of DM (Deutsche mark)–USD (US dollar) and YEN (Japanese yen)–USD potentially changes over time, especially before and after the introduction of the Euro. Similarly, the exchange rate returns reflect not only the financial market, but the consideration and behavior of the three central banks (such as motivating exports), especially before and after the introduction of the Euro. In this study, we considered time-varying copula models to further capture the change of tail dependence over time.

Little attention has been paid to the dependence structure among the share prices of city banks in China. Share price returns are based on the prediction of not only macroeconomic variables, but also profitability and risks, which are highly dependent on banking industry policies, bank strategies, local investment opportunities and risks, inter-bank lending, and inter-bank bond markets. The risks can be passed from one bank to another, as indicated by tail dependence. The other banks, which include the big four state-owned commercial banks, have large branches all over the country; these banks tend to have a more stable dependence structure and similar share price movements than city banks. Each city bank only has branches in the major cities and its own city where business first started. The dependence structure of city banks changes more obviously than that of the major banks. Beijing Bank, Ningbo Bank, and Nanjing Bank were the earliest listed city banks in the Chinese share market and have the largest data sample.

To investigate the underlying changes in dependence structure among the three city banks, we considered separating the sample and comparing the dependence strength in two distinct periods, as well as introducing time-varying copula models. The first step was to decide the proper separation of timing. In the past decade, the Chinese share market (Main Board) has experienced two large declines, one in the 2008 global financial crisis, and the other in the second half of 2015. The shares of the three banks saw a large decline of more than 75% after being listed in the summer of 2007. All share prices reached close to the initial public offering (IPO) prices in the subsequent eight years. However, the prices shrank again to half in only two months during the domestic stock market crash. We separated the total sample at the start of the domestic stock market crash in June 2015.

This study makes two contributions. First, unlike most previous studies, we used copula models on the city banks' share price returns. Many scholars have used copula functions to capture the dependence structure and extend the models to asymmetric and time-varying ones, mostly on aggregate variables. Dependence structures have been widely discussed in terms of exchange rates (Patton 2006), carbon dioxide commission prices in international energy markets (Marimoutou and Soury 2015), oil prices and stock market indices (Sukcharoen et al. 2014), precious metal prices (Reboredo and Ugolini 2015), and international stock markets (Luo et al. 2011). Most of the studies using copula models were based on aggregate variables. Our study sheds new light on the dependence structures among minor city banks based on various types of copula models. The second contribution is that we examined the changes in dependence structure of the daily share price returns between the Beijing Bank, Ningbo Bank, and Nanjing Bank. Furthermore, the total sample was separated into two parts: (1) From 19 September 2007 to 4 June 2015, which covered the global financial crisis, and (2) from 12 June 2015 to 21 May 2018, which covered the domestic share market crash. Constant copula models were used on the total sample and two distinct periods to compare the change in overall correlation and tail dependence. Moreover, time-varying copula models were used to verify the changes in dependence structure, mainly in tail dependence.

We present our conclusions in four parts. First, the share price returns of the Ningbo Bank and Nanjing Bank had a higher dependency than the group of Ningbo Bank and Beijing Bank and the group of Nanjing Bank and Ningbo Bank. Second, a major decrease of dependence was found among the three city banks. However, the dependency of Ningbo Bank on Nanjing Bank seemed to be more consistent from 2008 to 2015 than the other two groups. Third, and most importantly, the joint increase of the share prices of Ningbo Bank and Nanjing Bank happened more frequently than the joint decrease, which will shed new light on the research about financial assets price co-movement. Fourth, to better demonstrate the potential changes over time, the coefficients and figures of innovation were given in the rotated Gumbel and Student's t copula model (both in generalized autoregressive score [GAS]). The outcome of using the time-varying model suggested similar results in the constant copula models. Tail dependence rose rapidly in the beginning of period 1 and dropped in period 2.

The structure of the remaining paper is as follows: In Section 2, we introduce the basic methodology applied in this study, including the marginal distribution models, the fundamental copula theory, and several copula functions. In Section 3, we first introduce the data sample and the descriptive statistics, followed by the empirical results in constant and time-varying copula models. We discuss the dependence structure between Beijing Bank, Ningbo Bank, and Nanjing Bank in the total sample and in two distinct periods. In Section 4, we summarize our conclusions.

2. Empirical Methodology

This section begins with a discussion about the specific models for estimating the marginal distribution, including the flexible skewed t and empirical distribution function (EDF). We then discuss the copula theory and some constant and time-varying copula models.

2.1. Models for Marginal Distributions

To model the dependence structure among the three city banks, we first had to model the conditional marginal distributions. Before modeling the marginal distributions, we documented the log-difference of the share prices of the three city banks as daily returns. We modeled the time series data with possible time-dependent conditional mean and variance. Orders of the ARMA model and standard GARCH (1,1) model developed by Bollerslev (1987) were selected according to the Bayesian Information Criterion (BIC). The mean and variance models can be written in the forms given below. We denoted a given variable of daily returns as Y_t and the returns shocks as ε_t. The standardized residual, η_t had a constant conditional distribution, where the mean was zero and variance was one. $\hat{\mu}_i$ represents the estimated mean part of series i.

$$Y_t = c_y + \sum_{i=1}^{p} \phi_{i,y} Y_{t-i} + \sum_{j=1}^{q} \theta_{j,y} \varepsilon_{t-j} + \varepsilon_t, \ \varepsilon_t = \sqrt{h_t} \eta_t, \ \eta_t \sim iid(0,1) \tag{1}$$

$$h_t = \omega + \beta h_{t-1} + \alpha \varepsilon_{t-1}^2, \ \hat{\eta}_{i,t} = (Y_{i,t} - \hat{\mu}_i)/\sqrt{\hat{h}_{i,t}}, \ i = 1,2,3 \tag{2}$$

It is a well-known fact that most financial time series data have fat tails and do not follow normal distribution (Fama 1965). To better capture the possible fat tails feature, a Student's t distribution is recommended (Bollerslev 1987). We assumed that the term η_t followed a Student's t distribution rather than a normal distribution. After estimating the marginal mean and variance models, we needed to model the distribution of estimated standardized residuals. We denoted the distribution function as F_i. Following Patton (2013), we considered parametric and non-parametric models in modeling the distribution of the standardized residuals in each financial data series. In the non-parametric model, we estimated F_i in EDF:

$$\hat{F}_i(\eta) \equiv \frac{1}{T+1} \sum_{t=1}^{T} 1\{\hat{\eta}_{i,t} \le \eta\}, \ i = 1,2,3 \tag{3}$$

In the parametric model, we followed the simple and flexible skewed t distribution developed by Hansen (1994). There are two parameters in this model: the first one is the skewness parameter, $\lambda \in (-1,1)$, and the second is the degrees of freedom parameter, $\nu \in (2,\infty)$; the two parameters control the degree of asymmetry and the fat tail feature. This model has many features. The distribution is a skewed normal distribution when $\nu \longrightarrow \infty$, a standardized Student's t distribution when $\lambda = 0$, and a $N(0,1)$ when $\lambda = 0$, $\nu \longrightarrow \infty$. In empirical study, the condition $\nu \longrightarrow \infty$ occurs when ν is larger than some level. After estimating the parametric model using the simple and flexible skewed t distribution, we carried out the goodness of fit (GoF) test on this result.

2.2. Constant Copula Models

We first describe the copula theory before analyzing the dependence structure. A key concept was presented by Sklar (1959), who indicated that joint distribution (**F**) in n dimensions could be decomposed into the corresponding n univariate marginal distributions (F_i) and copula function ($C : [0,1]^n \longrightarrow [0,1]$) with n dimensions. Based on this foundation, another copula interpretation, the probability integral transformation (i.e., $U_i \equiv F_i(X_i)$) indicated by Casella and Berger (1990), has become popular in copula theory. After the transformation, variable U_i has a uniform $f(0,1)$ distribution that is unrelated to the original distribution F_i when F_i is continuous. After a vector of probability integral transformation $\mathbf{U} \equiv [U_1, U_2, \cdots, U_n]$ is obtained, C becomes a joint distribution function with uniform $f(0,1)$ distribution. Various copula models have been used to capture the dependence structure between time series data. However, the normal copula model cannot capture the tail dependence because the tail dependence is assumed to be zero. Other forms of copula such as the Gumbel and Clayton functions, can obtain tail dependence coefficients. Although the Gumbel (Clayton) copula can only obtain a non-zero (zero) upper tail dependence coefficient and a zero (non-zero) lower tail dependence coefficient, it can be further developed to the rotated-Gumbel (rotated-Clayton) to obtain the reverse tail dependence coefficient. We started with the selection of (constant) copula functions based on the rank of log-likelihood values. Normal, rotated-Gumbel, Student's t, and SJC copula functions were selected, and all were used in a bivariate case. We assumed that u_1 and u_2 were in the uniform distribution $[0,1]$. Each copula model is briefly introduced below:

The normal copula function can be written as Equation (4), where θ is a linear correlation parameter and ϕ is a univariate standard normal distribution:

$$C(u_1, u_2) = \int_{-\infty}^{\phi^{-1}(u_1)} \int_{-\infty}^{\phi^{-1}(u_2)} \frac{1}{2\pi\sqrt{1-\theta^2}} exp(-\frac{s^2 - 2\theta st + t^2}{2(1-\theta^2)}) dsdt \qquad (4)$$

The Student's t copula function can be defined as Equation (5), with v representing the degrees of freedom and $t_v^{-1}(\cdot)$ being the inverse of a standard Student's t distribution:

$$C(u_1, u_2) = \int_{-\infty}^{t_v^{-1}(u_1)} \int_{-\infty}^{t_v^{-1}(u_2)} \frac{1}{2\pi\sqrt{1-\theta^2}} (1 + \frac{s^2 - 2\theta st + t^2}{v(1-\theta^2)})^{-\frac{v+2}{v}} dsdt \qquad (5)$$

The Gumbel copula (Gumbel 1960), concentrates on the upper tail dependence with zero lower tail dependence. It can be written in Equation (6) with parameter γ. In fact, there is abundant evidence indicating that financial asset returns tend to have joint negative extremes (dramatic falls) more often than joint positive extremes (sharp increases) (Patton 2006). Therefore, the rotated Gumbel function might be more practical than the Gumbel copula, where parameter γ is often calculated by denoting a new series as $u_1' = 1 - u_1$ and $u_2' = 1 - u_2$, and the lower tail dependence will be $2 - 2^{1/\gamma}$.

$$C(u_1, u_2) = exp\{-[(-lnu_1)^\gamma + (-lnu_2)^\gamma]^{1/\gamma}\}, \; \gamma \in (1, +\infty) \qquad (6)$$

We considered the modified Clayton copula developed by Joe (1997), rather than the Clayton copula. We refer to the transformed copula as the Joe–Clayton copula (Patton 2006). The Joe–Clayton copula can be written in Equation (7), with $\tau^U \in (0,1)$ and $\tau^L \in (0,1)$ representing the upper and lower tail dependence, respectively. The parameters are $\kappa = 1/log_2(2 - \tau^U)$ and $\gamma = -1/log_2(\tau^L)$.

$$C_{JC}(u_1, u_2|\tau^U, \tau^L) = 1 - (1 - \{[1 - (1 - u_1)^\kappa]^{-\gamma} + [1 - (1 - u_2)^\kappa]^{-\gamma} - 1\}^{-1/\gamma})^{1/\kappa} \qquad (7)$$

As indicated by Patton (2006), asymmetry may still exist when the upper and lower tail dependence strengths are equal in the Joe–Clayton copula. Owing to this major problem, we followed the modification proposed by Patton (2006), which is denoted as the SJC copula:

$$C_{SJC}(u_1, u_2|\tau^U, \tau^L) = 0.5(C_{JC}(u_1, u_2|\tau^U, \tau^L) + C_{JC}(1 - u_1, 1 - u_2|\tau^L, \tau^U) + u_1 + u_2 - 1) \qquad (8)$$

2.3. Time-Varying Copula Models

For analyzing the time-varying dependence strength, we considered using the rotated Gumbel and Student's t copula models with the generalized autoregressive score (GAS) model introduced by Creal et al. (2013). In this model, a parameter δ_t is denoted as the time-varying copula parameter. The score of the likelihood in the copula is written as $I_t^{-1/2}s_t$. Specifically, in the rotated Gumbel copula model, the parameter $\delta_t = h^{-1}(f_t)$ can be defined as $\delta_t = 1 + \exp(f_t)$ because the parameter should be larger than one. In the Student's t copula model, the parameter can be defined as $\delta_t = (1 - \exp\{-f_t\})/(1 + \exp\{-f_t\})$ to obtain the dependence parameter between -1 and 1.

$$f_t = h(\delta_t) \leftrightarrow \delta_t = h^{-1}(f_t) \tag{9}$$

$$where, \ f_{t+1} = \omega + \beta f_t + \alpha I_t^{-1/2} s_t$$

$$s_t \equiv \frac{\partial}{\partial \delta} log\boldsymbol{c}(U_{1t}, U_{2t}; \delta_t), I_t \equiv E_{t-1}\left[s_t s_t'\right] = I(\delta_t)$$

3. Data and Empirical Results

3.1. Summary Statistics and Marginal Distributions

Our data contained the share price returns (based on adjusted prices) of three city banks in China: Beijing Bank, Ningbo Bank, and Nanjing Bank. The share prices and returns of these three city banks are shown in Figures 1 and 2. We chose these banks not only because they are among the top five city banks in China, but also because they have stronger market liquidity in the Main Board share market, compared to that of other city banks. The share price data collected from IPOs in 2007 provided abundant data samples that covered the global financial crisis in 2008, as well as the China share market crash in late 2015. We observed large declines in share prices and high variances in returns during the global financial crisis in 2008 and the domestic stock market crash in 2015. To explore the dependence structure among these three banks, we formed three combinations: Beijing Bank and Ningbo Bank were Group 1, Beijing Bank and Nanjing Bank were Group 2, and Ningbo Bank and Nanjing Bank were Group 3.

We computed the return rates of interest using the log-difference method with the n.a. values and outliers deleted. We reported all relevant analyses in the total sample, first period sample, and second period sample. The total sample ranged from 19 September 2007 to 21 May 2018. The first period from 19 September 2007 to 4 June 2015 covered the 2008 global financial crisis. The second period from 15 June 2015 to 21 May 2018 covered the domestic stock market crash from 12 June 2015 to 19 February 2016. Descriptive statistics and the marginal distribution coefficients are given in Tables 1 and 2, respectively.

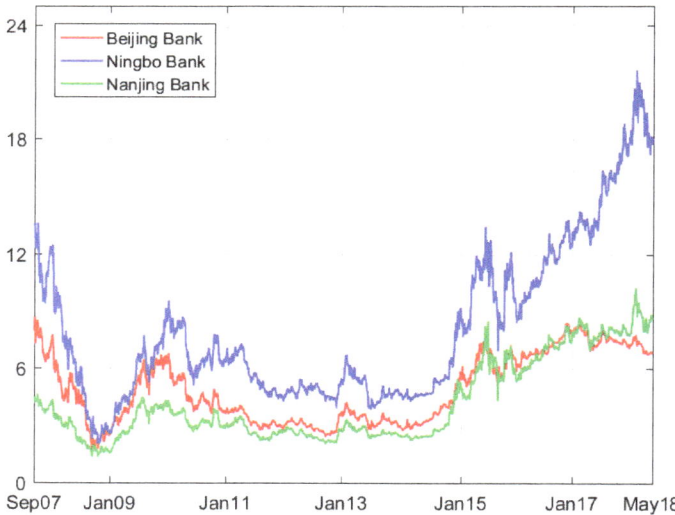

Figure 1. Daily share prices of the Beijing Bank, Ningbo Bank, and Nanjing Bank from 19 September 2007 to 21 May 2018.

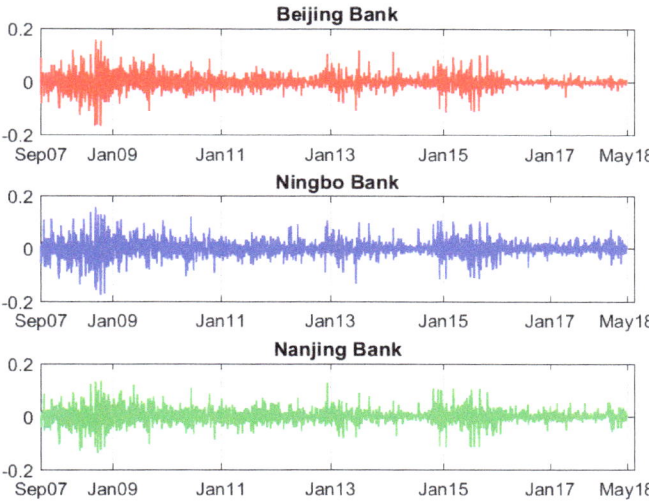

Figure 2. Daily returns of the Beijing Bank, Ningbo Bank, and Nanjing Bank from 19 September 2007 to 21 May 2018.

Table 1. Descriptive statistics of share price returns.

	Mean	S.E.	Min	Max	Skewness	Kurtosis	Jarque–Bera
				Beijing Bank			
Total	0.0001	0.0273	−0.1679	0.1584	−0.0347	11.4668	3075.041
Period 1	0.0003	0.0301	−0.1679	0.1584	−0.0380	10.1996	1320.999
Period 2	−0.0004	0.0180	−0.1119	0.1022	−0.1274	18.1298	4121.534
				Ningbo Bank			
Total	0.0002	0.0309	−0.1773	0.1586	−0.0743	10.2697	1877.701
Period 1	0.0003	0.0331	−0.1773	0.1586	−0.0274	9.7959	1079.081
Period 2	−0.0001	0.0242	−0.1144	0.1037	−0.4137	10.6811	632.7394
				Nanjing Bank			
Total	0.0004	0.0274	−0.1387	0.1335	0.0340	10.0755	1709.185
Period 1	0.0006	0.0289	−0.1387	0.1335	0.1903	9.3543	853.2647
Period 2	−0.0002	0.0231	−0.1158	0.1054	−0.8319	13.0402	1465.303

Notes: Period 1 ranges from 19 September 2007 to 4 June 2015 and period 2 ranges from 15 June 2015 to 21 May 2018. Observations of the total sample, first period, and second period were 2469, 1797, and 672, respectively. The table displays the basic summary statistics of the total sample, first period sample, and second period sample. As usual, financial asset returns show skewness around zero and kurtosis larger than three, indicating a non-normal distribution. The Jarque–Bera test statistics are reported, all of which stayed significant at 1%, indicating a non-normal distribution.

Table 2. Marginal distribution parameters estimation result.

	Total		Period 1		Period 2	
			Beijing Bank Mean Model			
φ_0	-6×10^{-5}	(0.0003)	−0.0001	(0.0005)	−0.0002	(0.0003)
φ_1	−0.0584 ***	(0.0192)	−0.0667 ***	(0.0227)	−1.5568 ***	(0.0168)
φ_2					−1.2535 ***	(0.0154)
φ_3					−0.6816 ***	(0.0239)
φ_4	—	—	—	—	−0.0164	(0.0206)
θ_1					1.5119 ***	(0.0001)
θ_2					1.0736 ***	(0.0002)
θ_3					0.5416 ***	(0.0007)

Table 2. *Cont.*

	Total		Period 1		Period 2	
	Beijing Bank Variance model					
ω	0.0000	—	0.0000	—	0.0000	—
α	0.0669 ***	(0.0200)	0.0607 ***	(0.0139)	0.1553 ***	(0.0451)
	0.9321 ***	(0.0196)	0.9376 ***	(0.0139)	0.8435 ***	(0.0368)
ν	4.6502 ***	(0.4315)	4.7860 ***	(0.5694)	3.1771 ***	(0.3759)
	Skewed t density					
λ	0.0272		0.0208		−0.0005	
ν	4.5413		4.5336		3.2202	
	Ljung–Box test					
$Q(20)$	6.8882	(0.9970)	4.7600	(0.9998)	28.4805	(0.0985)
$Q^2(20)$	23.6720	(0.2570)	16.5393	(0.6827)	19.6328	(0.4811)
	GoF tests on skewed t distribution model (p value)					
KS	0.96		0.99		0.99	
CvM	0.95		0.99		0.99	
	Ningbo Bank Mean model					
φ_0	0.0003	(0.0004)	0.0003	(0.0005)	0.0005	(0.0005)
φ_1					1.4112 ***	(0.0300)
φ_2					−1.6308 ***	(0.0293)
φ_3					1.3830 ***	(0.0307)
φ_4	—	—	—	—	−0.6112 ***	(0.0165)
θ_1					−1.4267 ***	(0.0120)
θ_2					1.5598 ***	(0.0326)
θ_3					−1.3749 ***	(0.0162)
θ_4					0.5695 ***	(0.0044)
	Variance model					
ω	0.0000	—	0.0000	—	0.0000	—
α	0.0564 ***	(0.0187)	0.0462 ***	(0.0074)	0.1148 ***	(0.0397)
	0.9426 ***	(0.0191)	0.9528 ***	(0.0071)	0.8366 ***	(0.0508)
ν	4.3642 ***	(0.4138)	4.4861 ***	(0.5291)	4.1153 ***	(0.6908)
	Skewed t density					
λ	0.0241		0.0061		0.0161	
ν	4.2382		4.3157		4.3207	
	Ljung–Box test					
$Q(20)$	22.2234	(0.3285)	13.2727	(0.8654)	20.1693	(0.4474)
$Q^2(20)$	24.9517	(0.2033)	19.9116	(0.4635)	22.6349	(0.3071)
	GoF tests on skewed t distribution model (p value)					
KS	0.89		0.88		0.44	
CvM	0.97		0.94		0.22	
	Nanjing Bank Mean model					
φ_0	0.0002	(0.0004)	0.0001	(0.0004)	0.0001	(0.0001)
φ_1			0.3352	(0.3948)	−0.0700 ***	(3×10^{-5})
φ_2					−0.0381 ***	(1×10^{-5})
φ_3			—	—	−0.0996 ***	(3×10^{-5})
φ_4	—	—			0.9056 ***	(0.0002)
θ_1			−0.4203	(0.3801)	0.0627 ***	(3×10^{-5})
θ_2					−0.0162 ***	(3×10^{-5})
θ_3			—	—	0.0386 ***	(2×10^{-5})
θ_4					−0.9260 ***	(0.0002)
	Variance model					
ω	0.0000	—	0.0000	—	0.0000	—
α	0.0682 ***	(0.024)	0.0504 **	(0.0205)	0.1769 ***	(0.0627)
β	0.9308 ***	(0.0257)	0.9486 ***	(0.0226)	0.8068 ***	(0.0517)
ν	4.2478 ***	(0.3742)	4.2761 ***	(0.4511)	3.3927 ***	(0.5039)

Table 2. *Cont.*

	Total		Period 1		Period 2	
	Nanjing Bank Skewed t density					
λ	0.0327		0.0346		0.0077	
ν	4.1747		4.1871		3.4216	
	Ljung–Box test					
$Q(20)$	8.7088	(0.9860)	11.3141	(0.9377)	26.2620	(0.1573)
$Q^2(20)$	22.0430	(0.3382)	18.9296	(0.5264)	20.0537	(0.4546)
	GoF tests on skewed t distribution model (*p* value)					
KS	0.66		0.79		0.37	
CvM	0.87		0.84		0.31	

Notes: The table summarizes the coefficients of the ARMA model for each bank's share returns, and standard GARCH (1,1) for all three share price return residuals. Period 1 ranges from 19 September 2007 to 4 June 2015 and period 2 ranges from 15 June 2015 to 21 May 2018. For each parameter, standard errors are reported in parentheses with *** and ** representing the significance levels of 1% and 5%, respectively. In all GARCH models, ω was estimated to be zero and thus standard residuals are not reported. We estimated the skewness parameter λ and a degrees of freedom parameter ν in the skewed t model. $Q(20)$ statistics and *p*-values were given under the null hypothesis of the Ljung–Box test, so that no autocorrelation existed in standardized residuals up to lags 20, with $Q^2(20)$ representing the test on squared standardized residuals up to lags 20. All results from the Ljung–Box test showed that the squared standardized residuals in each estimation model of the three bank shares in the total sample and two distinct samples had no significant evidence of autocorrelation up to lags 20. All insignificant p-values in the KS and CvM test (goodness of fit test, GOF) indicated that we failed to reject the null hypothesis, which states that the skewed t model can well specify the distribution of standardized residuals in all share price returns.

3.2. Constant Copula Results

We used four copula models in the constant parameter case. The normal copula model, although unable to detect the tail dependence, can obtain the correlation coefficient to compare the strength of correlation in each period. The rotated Gumbel copula model, providing a higher likelihood than the normal copula, can obtain information about the lower tail dependence. Owing to this feature, we selected the rotated Gumbel copula model to capture the dependence structure changes in the joint decreases of share prices. The Student's t copula model has the highest likelihood value and can capture tail dependence, although the lower and upper dependences are set to be equal. The SJC copula model combines the merits of the Student's t copula and rotated Gumbel copula because it can detect potentially different dependence in both tails. In parametric distribution, the SJC copula has the least standard errors among all models.

There were several findings among the three groups based on results in Tables 3–5. First, Group 3 (Ningbo Bank and Nanjing Bank) and Group 1 (Beijing Bank and Ningbo Bank) showed the highest and lowest dependence coefficients among the three groups. This rank of dependency suggested that Beijing Bank was less dependent on the other two banks than Nanjing Bank, which was dependent on the other two banks, and that Ningbo Bank was more dependent on Nanjing Bank than on Beijing Bank. Second, Group 1 and Group 2 (Beijing Bank and Ningbo Bank) similarly showed much higher dependence in period 1 than period 2. For instance, in the rotated Student's t copula model, the dependence coefficient ($g_T(\hat{\rho}, \hat{v})$) in Groups 1 and 2 dropped 66% and 42% from period 1 to period 2, respectively. However, the dependence coefficient in Group 3 dropped only 21%. Third, the lower tail dependence was evidently higher than the upper tail dependence in the SJC copula model for Groups 1 and 2, but not for Group 3. It has been documented that the Beijing Bank share price tends to fall more frequently than rising together with the Ningbo Bank and Nanjing Bank. The probability of share prices going up was slightly higher than that of falling down together for the Ningbo Bank and Nanjing Bank group. In all groups, the Student's t copula model had the highest value of log-likelihood, followed by the SJC copula model and the rotated Gumbel copula model.

Table 3. Constant copula models in Group 1, consisting of the Beijing Bank and Ningbo Bank.

	Total		Period 1		Period 2	
	Parametric	**Semi**	**Parametric**	**Semi**	**Parametric**	**Semi**
	Normal copula					
$\hat{\rho}$	0.7669	0.7662	0.8237	0.8228	0.5817	0.5795
S.E.	(0.0135)	(0.0104)	(0.011)	(0.0108)	(0.0369)	(0.0266)
$\log \mathcal{L}$	1094.03	1091.71	1019.28	1015.47	139.17	137.49
	Rotated Gumbel copula					
$\hat{\gamma}$	2.1976	2.2310	2.5492	2.5686	1.6066	1.6043
S.E.	(0.0819)	(0.0393)	(0.0875)	(0.0582)	(0.0891)	(0.0530)
$\hat{\tau}^L$	0.6292	0.6356	0.6875	0.6902	0.4605	0.4596
$\log \mathcal{L}$	1107.79	1111.69	1031.20	1029.37	135.62	134.72
	Student's t copula					
$\hat{\rho}$	0.7684	0.7731	0.8268	0.8281	0.5759	0.5800
S.E.	(0.0145)	(0.008)	(0.011)	(0.0085)	(0.0368)	(0.0255)
$\hat{\upsilon}^{-1}$	0.2793	0.2970	0.2807	0.2897	0.1458	0.1496
S.E.	(0.0286)	(0.028)	(0.0401)	(0.0331)	(0.0560)	(0.0405)
$g_T(\hat{\rho}, \hat{\upsilon})$	0.4766	0.4930	0.5424	0.5495	0.1847	0.1923
$\log \mathcal{L}$	1192.44	1192.73	1100.10	1097.01	144.47	142.93
	SJC copula					
$\hat{\tau}^L$	0.5964	0.6090	0.6697	0.6748	0.3998	0.4039
S.E.	(9×10^{-16})	(0.0143)	(1×10^{-15})	(0.0136)	(5×10^{-17})	(0.0373)
$\hat{\tau}^U$	0.5815	0.5937	0.6567	0.6633	0.3623	0.3736
S.E.	(9×10^{-16})	(0.0167)	(1×10^{-15})	(0.0173)	(1×10^{-16})	(0.0451)
$\log \mathcal{L}$	1156.34	1161.0939	1073.60	1074.64	145.01	143.32

Notes: In this table, we report the maximum likelihood estimation and standard errors in parentheses. "Parametric" and "Semi" represent the parametric and semi-parametric models, respectively. Period 1 ranges from 19 September 2007 to 4 June 2015 and period 2 ranges from 15 June 2015 to 21 May 2018. Lower tail dependence of the rotated Gumbel copula was calculated by $\hat{\tau}^L = 2 - 2^{1/\hat{\gamma}}$. Both tail dependences in the Student's t copula were calculated in $g_T(\hat{\rho}, \hat{\upsilon}) = 2 \times F_{student}(-\sqrt{(\hat{\upsilon}+1)\frac{\hat{\rho}-1}{\hat{\rho}+1}}, \hat{\upsilon}+1)$.

Table 4. Constant copula models in Group 2, consisting of the Beijing Bank and Nanjing Bank.

	Total		Period 1		Period 2	
	Parametric	**Semi**	**Parametric**	**Semi**	**Parametric**	**Semi**
	Normal copula					
$\hat{\rho}$	0.8119	0.8115	0.8564	0.8556	0.6487	0.6422
S.E.	(0.0128)	(0.0083)	(0.0105)	(0.0084)	(0.0271)	(0.0311)
$\log \mathcal{L}$	1328.56	1326.63	1187.93	1183.38	183.89	178.64
	Rotated Gumbel copula					
$\hat{\gamma}$	2.4486	2.4967	2.8528	2.8799	1.8240	1.8076
S.E.	(0.0926)	(0.0482)	(0.1002)	(0.0638)	(0.0822)	(0.0673)
$\hat{\tau}^L$	0.6728	0.6800	0.7250	0.7279	0.5377	0.5326
$\log \mathcal{L}$	1347.26	1351.38	1209.54	1207.97	196.85	190.97
	Student's t copula					
$\hat{\rho}$	0.8126	0.8176	0.8601	0.8613	0.6551	0.6563
S.E.	(0.0129)	(0.0066)	(0.0099)	(0.0065)	(0.0264)	(0.0264)
$\hat{\upsilon}^{-1}$	0.2616	0.2838	0.2841	0.2945	0.2370	0.2393
S.E.	(0.0329)	(0.0267)	(0.0334)	(0.0325)	(0.0592)	(0.0500)
$g_T(\hat{\rho}, \hat{\upsilon})$	0.5127	0.5334	0.5877	0.5951	0.3429	0.3459
$\log \mathcal{L}$	1424.53	1427.29	1269.65	1266.36	207.44	202.25
	SJC copula					
$\hat{\tau}^L$	0.6559	0.6687	0.7204	0.7266	0.5184	0.5109
S.E.	(1×10^{-15})	(0.0147)	(8×10^{-16})	(0.0129)	(5×10^{-16})	(0.0305)
$\hat{\tau}^U$	0.6147	0.6322	0.6786	0.6846	0.4114	0.4228
S.E.	(4×10^{-16})	(0.0154)	(8×10^{-16})	(0.027)	(4×10^{-16})	(0.0488)
$\log \mathcal{L}$	1378.74	1389.56	1229.00	1230.85	201.73	195.47

Notes: In this table, we report the maximum likelihood estimation and standard errors in parentheses. "Parametric" and "Semi" represent the parametric and semi-parametric models, respectively. Period 1 ranges from 19 September 2007 to 4 June 2015 and period 2 ranges from 15 June 2015 to 21 May 2018. Lower tail dependence of the rotated Gumbel copula was calculated as $\hat{\tau}^L = 2 - 2^{1/\hat{\gamma}}$. Both tail dependences in the Student's t copula were calculated in $g_T(\hat{\rho}, \hat{\upsilon}) = 2 \times F_{student}(-\sqrt{(\hat{\upsilon}+1)\frac{\hat{\rho}-1}{\hat{\rho}+1}}, \hat{\upsilon}+1)$.

Table 5. Constant copula models in Group 3, consisting of the Ningbo Bank and Nanjing Bank.

	Total		Period 1		Period 2	
	Parametric	**Semi**	**Parametric**	**Semi**	**Parametric**	**Semi**
	Normal copula					
$\hat{\rho}$	0.8461	0.8451	0.8714	0.8705	0.7376	0.7347
S.E.	(0.0090)	(0.0072)	(0.0081)	(0.0068)	(0.0253)	(0.0214)
$\log \mathcal{L}$	1552.99	1546.23	1279.92	1274.06	264.24	260.76
	Rotated Gumbel copula					
$\hat{\gamma}$	2.7077	2.7167	2.9071	2.9372	2.1190	2.0990
S.E.	(0.0876)	(0.0530)	(0.1260)	(0.0605)	(0.1431)	(0.0872)
$\hat{\tau}^L$	0.7083	0.7094	0.7307	0.7338	0.6130	0.6087
$\log \mathcal{L}$	1539.47	1534.07	1251.24	1247.42	269.94	264.34
	Student's t copula					
$\hat{\rho}$	0.8483	0.8492	0.8701	0.8719	0.7480	0.7479
S.E.	(0.0091)	(0.0059)	(0.0128)	(0.0055)	(0.0251)	(0.0182)
$\hat{v}^{-1}$	0.2620	0.2702	0.2283	0.2407	0.2769	0.2648
S.E.	(0.0310)	(0.0280)	(0.0404)	(0.0333)	(0.0594)	(0.0441)
$g_T(\hat{\rho}, \hat{v})$	0.5582	0.5646	0.5659	0.5776	0.4549	0.4460
$\log \mathcal{L}$	1650.47	1643.97	1332.23	1328.24	292.83	285.36
	SJC copula					
$\hat{\tau}^L$	0.6806	0.6839	0.7102	0.7160	0.5611	0.5570
S.E.	(1×10^{-14})	(0.0130)	(1×10^{-16})	(0.0123)	(1×10^{-15})	(0.0390)
$\hat{\tau}^U$	0.6912	0.6993	0.7183	0.7281	0.5739	0.5769
S.E.	(9×10^{-15})	(0.0120)	(5×10^{-16})	(0.0108)	(9×10^{-16})	(0.0287)
$\log \mathcal{L}$	1604.25	1605.73	1304.74	1309.07	282.73	275.45

Notes: In this table, we report the maximum likelihood estimation and standard errors in parentheses. "Parametric" and "Semi" represent the parametric and semi-parametric models, respectively. Period 1 ranges from 19 September 2007 to 4 June 2015 and period 2 ranges from 15 June 2015 to 21 May 2018. Lower tail dependence of the rotated Gumbel copula was calculated in $\hat{\tau}^L = 2 - 2^{1/\hat{\gamma}}$. Both tail dependences in the Student's t copula were calculated in $g_T(\hat{\rho}, \hat{v}) = 2 \times F_{student}(-\sqrt{(\hat{v}+1)\frac{\hat{\rho}-1}{\hat{\rho}+1}}, \hat{v}+1)$.

3.3. Time-Varying Copula Results

The difference in dependence strengths between period 1 and period 2 suggested that there may be changes in tail dependence. To illustrate possible time-varying tail dependence, we constructed the rotated Gumbel copula (in GAS) and the Student's t copula (in GAS) in a time-dependent model. The estimated parameters of the three groups are reported in Tables 6–8, respectively. The six innovation graphs of tail dependence provide visually understandable results (Figures 3–8). The innovation in the semi-parametric models are reported.

Table 6. Time-varying copula models in Group 1 (Beijing Bank and Ningbo Bank).

	Total		Period 1		Period 2	
	Parametric	**Semi**	**Parametric**	**Semi**	**Parametric**	**Semi**
	Rotated Gumbel copula (GAS)					
$\hat{\omega}$	0.0019	0.0021	0.0259	0.0302	−0.0837	−0.0833
S.E.	(0.0155)	(0.0001)	(0.0072)	(0.0043)	(0.0004)	(0.0543)
$\hat{\alpha}$	0.0650	0.0593	0.0832	0.0905	0.0630	0.0675
S.E.	(0.0622)	(0.0018)	(0.0199)	(0.0176)	(0.0012)	(0.0569)
$\hat{\beta}$	0.9892	0.9906	0.9447	0.9369	0.8355	0.8397
S.E.	(0.0014)	(0.0005)	(0.0143)	(0.0061)	(0.0327)	(0.1143)
$\log \mathcal{L}$	1185.62	1187.58	1053.58	1050.44	136.41	135.64
	Student's t copula (GAS)					
$\hat{\omega}$	0.0218	0.0213	0.1012	0.1004	0.0192	0.0300
S.E.	(0.0018)	(0.0018)	(2×10^{-9})	(0.0036)	(0.0296)	(0.0038)
$\hat{\alpha}$	0.0634	0.0632	0.0740	0.0724	0.0261	0.0516
S.E.	(0.0052)	(0.0102)	(4×10^{-8})	(0.0109)	(0.0139)	(0.0202)
$\hat{\beta}$	0.9897	0.9896	0.9584	0.9585	0.9843	0.9764
S.E.	(5×10^{-6})	(6×10^{-7})	(4×10^{-7})	(1×10^{-7})	(0.0228)	(0.0123)
$\hat{v}^{-1}$	0.2174	0.2185	0.2413	0.2447	0.1590	0.1687
S.E.	(0.0219)	(0.0285)	(0.0314)	(0.0338)	(0.0479)	(0.0442)
$\log \mathcal{L}$	1273.17	1271.04	1117.50	1114.18	146.96	145.95

Notes: In this table, we report the maximum likelihood estimation and standard errors in parentheses. "Parametric" and "Semi" represent the parametric and semi-parametric models, respectively. Period 1 ranges from 19 September 2007 to 4 June 2015 and period 2 ranges from 15 June 2015 to 21 May 2018.

Table 7. Time-varying copula models in Group 2 (Beijing Bank and Nanjing Bank).

	Total		Period 1		Period 2	
	Parametric	**Semi**	**Parametric**	**Semi**	**Parametric**	**Semi**
	Rotated Gumbel copula (GAS)					
$\hat{\omega}$	0.0180	0.0177	0.1313	0.1390	-0.0282	-0.0230
S.E.	(0.0022)	(0.0026)	(0.0018)	(0.6113)	(0.0478)	(0.1966)
$\hat{\alpha}$	0.1271	0.1234	0.2225	0.2159	0.1131	0.1018
S.E.	(0.0169)	(0.0220)	(0.0214)	(0.2863)	(0.1006)	(0.0790)
$\hat{\beta}$	0.9556	0.9556	0.7855	0.7816	0.7877	0.8301
S.E.	(2×10^{-5})	(2×10^{-5})	(0.0036)	(0.8849)	(0.2617)	(0.8756)
$\log \mathcal{L}$	1426.91	1425.74	1247.19	1243.53	219.16	214.94
	Student's t copula (GAS)					
$\hat{\omega}$	0.1015	0.1001	0.5077	0.2921	0.1339	0.1192
S.E.	(0.0584)	(0.0043)	(4×10^{-8})	(0.0089)	(0.1118)	(0.0084)
$\hat{\alpha}$	0.1364	0.1316	0.2103	0.1620	0.1105	0.0849
S.E.	(0.0627)	(0.0190)	(0.0298)	(0.0290)	(0.0374)	(0.0203)
$\hat{\beta}$	0.9568	0.9580	0.8080	0.8898	0.9201	0.9287
S.E.	(0.0258)	(5×10^{-6})	(7×10^{-6})	(4×10^{-6})	(0.0649)	(8×10^{-6})
$\hat{v}^{-1}$	0.1986	0.2175	0.2266	0.2246	0.2060	0.2034
S.E.	(0.0367)	(0.0212)	(0.0334)	(0.0336)	(0.0396)	(0.0444)
$\log \mathcal{L}$	1513.26	1513.64	1309.93	1306.48	229.49	224.16

Notes: In this table, we report the maximum likelihood estimation and standard errors in parentheses. "Parametric" and "Semi" represent the parametric and semi-parametric models, respectively. Period 1 ranges from 19 September 2007 to 4 June 2015 and period 2 ranges from 15 June 2015 to 21 May 2018.

Table 8. Time-varying copula models in Group 3 (Ningbo Bank and Nanjing Bank).

	Total		Period 1		Period 2	
	Parametric	**Semi**	**Parametric**	**Semi**	**Parametric**	**Semi**
	Rotated Gumbel copula (GAS)					
$\hat{\omega}$	0.0163	0.0157	0.0398	0.0478	0.0102	0.0074
S.E.	(0.0007)	(0.0021)	(0.0005)	(0.0017)	(0.0043)	(0.0024)
$\hat{\alpha}$	0.0848	0.0804	0.0857	0.0855	0.1216	0.1228
S.E.	(0.0138)	(0.0278)	(0.0210)	(0.0257)	(0.0747)	(0.0269)
$\hat{\beta}$	0.9712	0.9727	0.9388	0.9291	0.9526	0.9461
S.E.	(0.0014)	(0.0012)	(0.0008)	(0.0014)	(0.0560)	(0.0030)
$\log \mathcal{L}$	1595.39	1586.46	1270.49	1264.77	287.67	280.34
	Student's t copula (GAS)					
$\hat{\omega}$	0.0748	0.0746	0.1383	0.1446	0.0364	0.0477
S.E.	(0.0031)	(0.0034)	(0.0050)	(0.0003)	(0.0142)	(0.0057)
$\hat{\alpha}$	0.0991	0.0993	0.0923	0.0929	0.1047	0.1016
S.E.	(0.0205)	(0.0253)	(0.0430)	(0.0223)	(0.0205)	(0.0344)
$\hat{\beta}$	0.9706	0.9707	0.9490	0.9472	0.9815	0.9762
S.E.	(4×10^{-6})	(1×10^{-5})	(3×10^{-5})	(0.0017)	(0.0073)	(8×10^{-7})
$\hat{v}^{-1}$	0.2252	0.2252	0.2255	0.2278	0.2460	0.1939
S.E.	(0.0239)	(0.0392)	(0.0391)	(0.0343)	(0.0382)	(0.0437)
$\log \mathcal{L}$	1713.66	1704.27	1356.18	1350.24	309.03	301.51

Notes: In this table, we report the maximum likelihood estimation and standard errors in parentheses. "Parametric" and "Semi" represent the parametric and semi-parametric models, respectively. Period 1 ranges from 19 September 2007 to 4 June 2015 and period 2 ranges from 15 June 2015 to 21 May 2018.

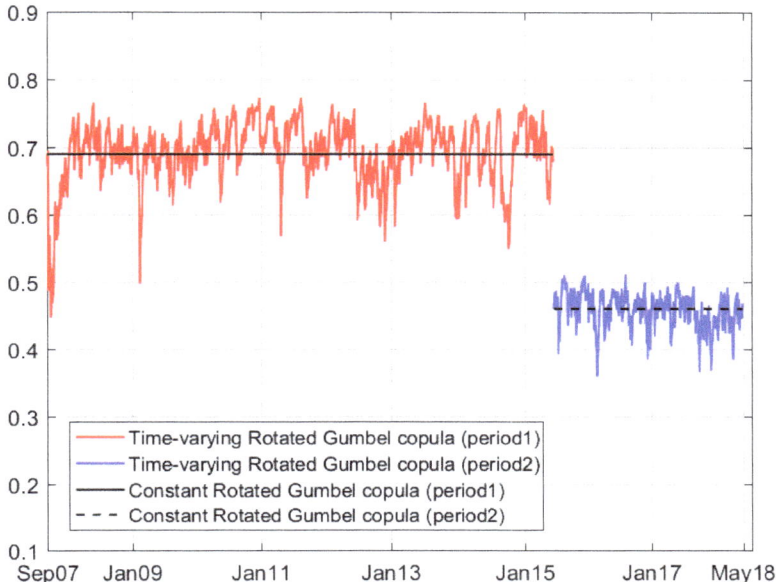

Figure 3. Time-varying and constant tail dependence in the Rotated Gumbel copula for Group 1 (Beijing Bank and Ningbo Bank). Period 1 ranges from 19 September 2007 to 4 June 2015 and period 2 ranges from 15 June 2015 to 21 May 2018.

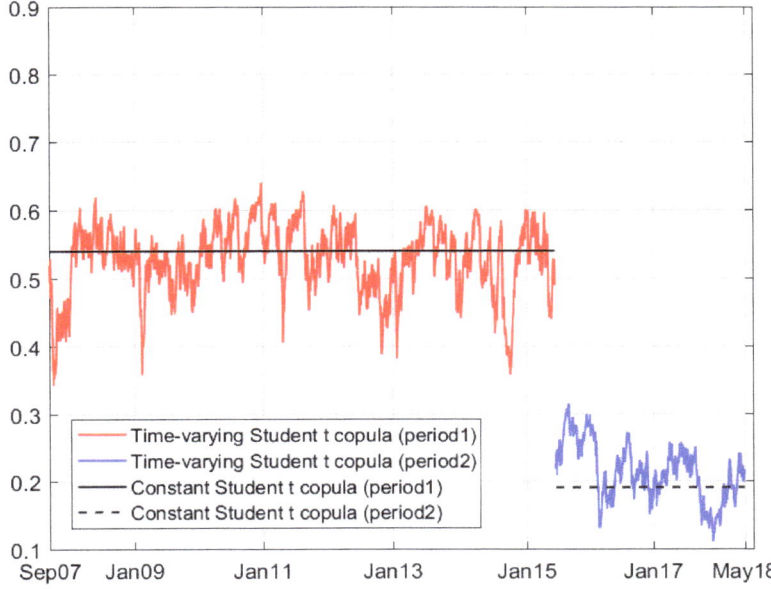

Figure 4. Time-varying and constant tail dependence in the Student's t copula for Group 1 (Beijing Bank and Ningbo Bank). Period 1 ranges from 19 September 2007 to 4 June 2015 and period 2 ranges from 15 June 2015 to 21 May 2018.

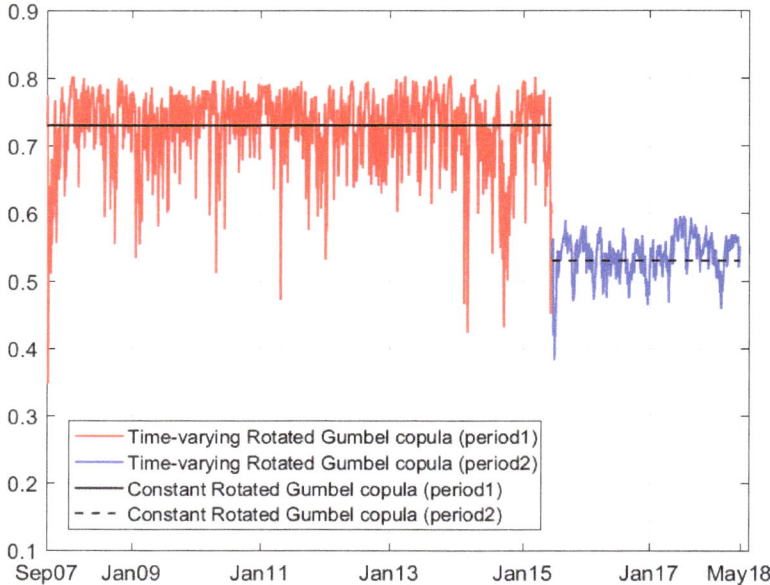

Figure 5. Time-varying and constant tail dependence in the Rotated Gumbel copula for Group 2 (Beijing Bank and Nanjing Bank). Period 1 ranges from 19 September 2007 to 4 June 2015 and period 2 ranges from 15 June 2015 to 21 May 2018.

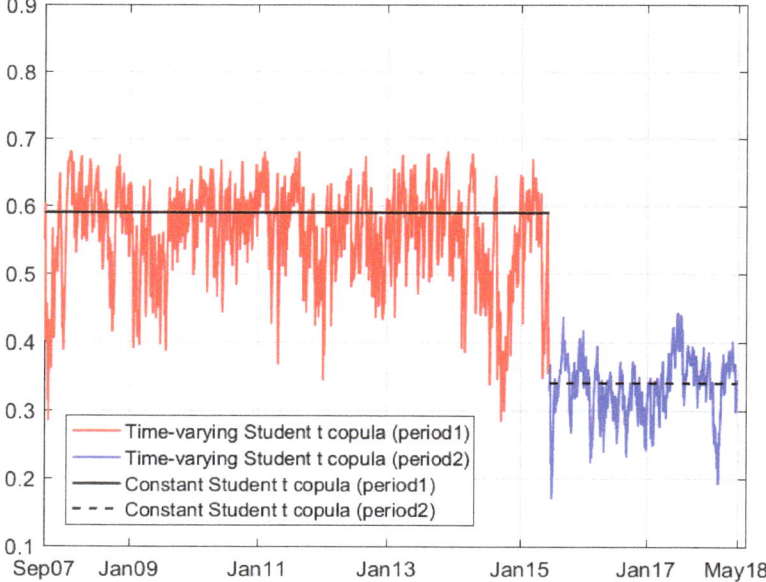

Figure 6. Time-varying and constant tail dependence in the Student's t copula for Group 2 (Beijing Bank and Nanjing Bank). Period 1 ranges from 19 September 2007 to 4 June 2015 and period 2 ranges from 15 June 2015 to 21 May 2018.

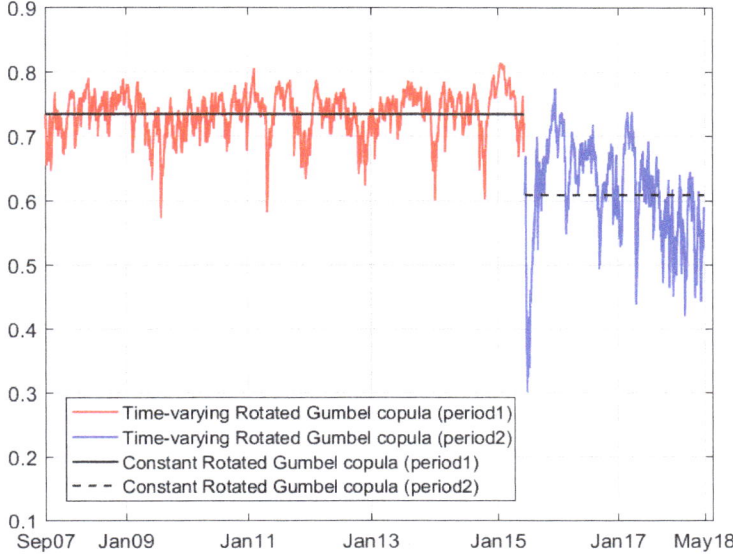

Figure 7. Time-varying and constant tail dependence in the Rotated Gumbel copula for Group 3 (Ningbo Bank and Nanjing Bank). Period 1 ranges from 19 September 2007 to 4 June 2015 and period 2 ranges from 15 June 2015 to 21 May 2018.

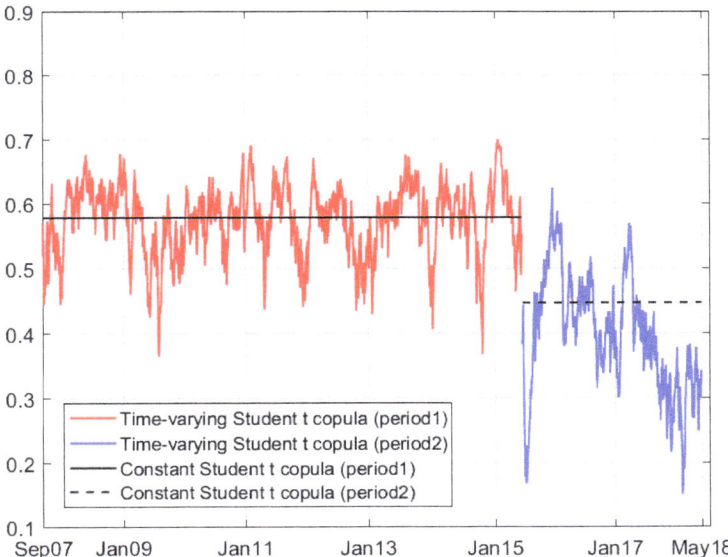

Figure 8. Time-varying and constant tail dependence in the Student's t copula for Group 3 (Ningbo Bank and Nanjing Bank). Period 1 ranges from 19 September 2007 to 4 June 2015 and period 2 ranges from 15 June 2015 to 21 May 2018.

In the group of Beijing Bank and Ningbo Bank, lower tail dependence indicated by the rotated Gumbel copula (GAS) model reached the highest level of 0.75 in less than six months. Until the end of period 1, the lower tail dependence maintained a level at around 0.69, which was the tail dependence captured by the constant rotated Gumbel copula model. In period 2, the lower tail dependence fluctuated at around the level of 0.46, which was much lower than the one in period 1. In the case of the Student's t copula (GAS) model, the innovation was similar to the one in the rotated Gumbel copula (GAS) model. The tail dependence in period 2 was less than half of the one in period 1.

In the group consisting of Beijing Bank and Nanjing Bank, the lower tail dependence indicated by the rotated Gumbel copula (GAS) model appeared rather random after the global financial crisis, but stayed around the 0.72 level, followed by a decrease in period 2. In the Student's t copula model, we obtained the tail dependence in period 1 in the range of around 0.59. In period 2, the dependence strength decreased to 0.34.

In the group of Ningbo Bank and Nanjing Bank, lower tail dependence indicated by the rotated Gumbel copula (GAS) model appeared rather stable after the global financial crisis and stayed around the 0.71 level, followed by a slight decrease in period 2. In the Student's t copula model, we obtained a tail dependence in period 1 that ranged around 0.56. In period 2, the dependence strength decreased to 0.45.

3.4. Goodness-of-Fit Tests

The Kolomogorov–Smirnov (KS) and Cramer–von Mises (CvM) methods are frequently used in goodness-of-fit tests in copula models. In Tables 9 and 10, we present the p-value results in the goodness-of-fit test for each constant copula model in the parametric and semi-parametric cases. The normal copula, rotated Gumbel copula, and the student's t copula passed the tests in the parametric case; in the semi-parametric case, the normal copula and rotated Gumbel copula models did not pass the tests in the majority of the groups and periods, and the student's t copula model was rejected in one test at the 5% level and in five tests at the 10% level. The SJC copula model passed the KS and CvM tests in all periods and groups, in both the parametric and semi-parametric cases. In the KS and CvM tests for time-varying copula models, the process requires the Rosenblatt transform. The two time-varying copula models passed the goodness-of-fit test in all cases (Tables 11 and 12).

Table 9. Goodness-of-fit test in the constant copula (parametric case).

	Total		Period 1		Period 2	
	KS_C	CvM_C	KS_C	CvM_C	KS_C	CvM_C
Normal copula						
Group 1	0.92	0.97	0.96	0.98	0.99	0.94
Group 2	0.80	0.95	0.93	0.96	0.99	0.98
Group 3	0.82	0.96	0.93	0.94	0.38	0.33
Rotated Gumbel copula						
Group 1	0.95	0.93	0.97	0.95	0.98	0.94
Group 2	0.91	0.95	0.95	0.91	0.99	0.97
Group 3	0.87	0.92	0.92	0.93	0.26	0.21
Student's t copula						
Group 1	0.96	0.98	0.97	0.99	0.99	0.97
Group 2	0.80	0.96	0.92	0.96	0.99	0.98
Group3	0.88	0.97	0.94	0.96	0.34	0.30
SJC copula						
Group1	0.94	0.95	0.95	0.96	0.99	0.99
Group2	0.81	0.91	0.80	0.88	0.99	0.99
Group3	0.86	0.95	0.89	0.89	0.49	0.43

Notes: In this table, we report the p-values of the Kolomogorov–Smirnov (KS_C) and Cramer–von Mises (CvM_C) goodness-of-fit tests for the constant copula models in the parametric case, based on 500 simulations. The subscript C indicates that the test was carried out on the empirical copula of the standardized residuals. Group 1 refers to the group of Beijing Bank and Ningbo Bank. Group 2 refers to the group of Beijing Bank and Nanjing Bank. Group 3 refers to the group of Ningbo Bank and Nanjing Bank. Period 1 ranges from 19 September 2007 to 4 June 2015 and period 2 ranges from 15 June 2015 to 21 May 2018. p-values less than 0.05 are shown in bold.

Table 10. Goodness-of-fit test in constant copula (semi-parametric case).

	Total		Period 1		Period 2	
	KS_C	CvM_C	KS_C	CvM_C	KS_C	CvM_C
	Normal copula					
Group1	0.17	**0.01**	0.14	**0.00**	0.91	0.61
Group2	0.09	**0.01**	**0.02**	**0.00**	0.22	0.24
Group3	0.07	**0.01**	0.09	**0.04**	0.15	**0.02**
	Rotated Gumbel copula					
Group1	**0.00**	**0.00**	**0.00**	**0.00**	0.12	**0.00**
Group2	**0.00**	**0.00**	**0.00**	**0.00**	0.13	**0.00**
Group3	**0.00**	**0.00**	**0.00**	**0.00**	**0.00**	**0.00**
	Student's t copula					
Group1	0.62	0.54	**0.04**	0.10	0.88	0.70
Group2	0.48	0.50	0.05	0.07	0.58	0.63
Group3	0.17	0.29	0.44	0.23	0.50	0.10
	SJC copula					
Group1	0.99	0.99	0.99	0.99	0.99	0.99
Group2	0.99	0.99	0.99	0.99	0.99	0.99
Group3	0.99	0.99	0.99	0.99	0.99	0.99

Notes: In this table, we report the p-values of the Kolomogorov–Smirnov (KS_C) and Cramer–von Mises (CvM_C) goodness-of-fit tests for the constant copula models in the semi-parametric case, based on 500 simulations. The subscript C indicates that the test was carried out on the empirical copula of the standardized residuals. Group 1 refers to the group of Beijing Bank and Ningbo Bank. Group 2 refers to the group of Beijing Bank and Nanjing Bank. Group 3 refers to the group of Ningbo Bank and Nanjing Bank. Period 1 ranges from 19 September 2007 to 4 June 2015 and period 2 ranges from 15 June 2015 to 21 May 2018. p-values less than 0.05 are shown in bold.

Table 11. Goodness-of-fit test in time-varying copula (parametric case).

	Total		Period 1		Period 2	
	KS_R	CvM_R	KS_R	CvM_R	KS_R	CvM_R
	Rotated Gumbel copula (GAS)					
Group 1	0.99	0.99	0.99	0.99	0.97	0.96
Group 2	0.99	0.99	0.99	0.88	0.99	0.99
Group 3	0.99	0.99	0.97	0.97	0.80	0.69
	Student's t copula (GAS)					
Group 1	0.99	0.99	0.99	0.99	0.99	0.99
Group 2	0.99	0.99	0.98	0.99	0.99	0.99
Group 3	0.99	0.99	0.96	0.97	0.92	0.81

Notes: In this table, we report the p-values of the Kolomogorov–Smirnov (KS_R) and Cramer–von Mises (CvM_R) goodness-of-fit tests for the time-varying copula models in the parametric case, based on 100 simulations. The subscript R indicates that the test was carried out on the empirical copula of the Rosenblatt transform of the residuals. Group 1 refers to the group of Beijing Bank and Ningbo Bank. Group 2 refers to the group of Beijing Bank and Nanjing Bank. Group 3 refers to the group of Ningbo Bank and Nanjing Bank. Period 1 ranges from 19 September 2007 to 4 June 2015 and period 2 ranges from 15 June 2015 to 21 May 2018.

Table 12. Goodness-of-fit test in time-varying copula (semi-parametric case).

	Total		Period 1		Period 2	
	KS_R	CvM_R	KS_R	CvM_R	KS_R	CvM_R
	Rotated Gumbel copula (GAS)					
Group 1	0.81	0.99	0.24	0.97	0.09	0.33
Group 2	0.83	0.99	0.98	0.99	0.47	0.44
Group 3	0.85	0.99	0.93	0.99	0.93	0.88
	Student's t copula (GAS)					
Group 1	0.63	0.59	0.39	0.40	0.66	0.57
Group 2	0.99	0.89	0.66	0.67	0.96	0.96
Group 3	0.58	0.80	0.50	0.60	0.61	0.62

Notes: In this table, we report the p-values of the Kolomogorov–Smirnov (KS_R) and Cramer–von Mises (CvM_R) goodness-of-fit tests for the time-varying copula models in the semi-parametric case, based on 100 simulations. The subscript R indicates that the test was carried out on the empirical copula of the Rosenblatt transform of the residuals. Group 1 refers to the group of Beijing Bank and Ningbo Bank. Group 2 refers to the group of Beijing Bank and Nanjing Bank. Group 3 refers to the group of Ningbo Bank and Nanjing Bank. Period 1 ranges from 19 September 2007 to 4 June 2015 and period 2 ranges from 15 June 2015 to 21 May 2018.

4. Conclusions

In this study on the share price returns of three city banks, we investigated the potential dependence structure. We used copula models rather than the usual linear correlation to capture the detailed tail dependence. We used various copula models to estimate the underlying dependence in extreme periods. The Student's t, SJC, and rotated Gumbel copula models could specify the tail dependence with higher log-likelihood values better than the other copula models. Furthermore, by extending the Student's t and rotated Gumbel copula models to the GAS and time-varying models, we could obtain more information about the innovation of changes in tail dependence.

Unlike most of the literature using copula models, we focused on the tail dependence of the share price returns of city banks rather than aggregate variables, such as share markets indices and exchange rates. The tail dependence may be dependent on profitability, own risks, inter-bank business, and outside influence. Although city banks fall in the same sector in share markets, they may have diverse returns due to different strategies or business behaviors. During and after a stock market crash, the city banks may have diverse reactions, which supports our assumption that there may be a different level of dependence between two banks during two periods.

We found diverse dependence structures among the three groups of city banks. First, the tail dependence was higher between the share price returns of Ningbo Bank and Nanjing Bank, than that of the other two combinations. Beijing Bank was less dependent on the other two city banks, and Nanjing Bank was dependent on the other two. Ningbo Bank was more dependent on Nanjing Bank, than on Beijing Bank. Second, we observed a major break in the three dependence structures. Beijing Bank became much less dependent on the other two banks during the 2015 domestic share market crash, than during the 2008 financial crisis. However, the dependency of Nanjing Bank on Ningbo Bank did not change as much as that of the other two combinations from 2008 to 2015. Third, the share prices of Ningbo Bank and Nanjing Bank had a slightly higher possibility of increasing than decreasing together. This was different from recent studies on financial asset price co-movement, which often suggest that financial assets tend to have more dependence in price crashes than in booms.

The share price returns of Ningbo Bank were found to be more similar to that of Nanjing Bank, compared to that of Beijing Bank. This observation of the share price extreme returns of three city banks reconfirmed our research results in the copula models. Risk-avoiding behavior is a possible cause of the decrease in tail dependence. It is recommended that for city commercial banks, strategies such as obtaining superior assets and involving less risky inter-bank business be adopted, and that for the central bank, reasonable capital liquidity and supervision should be ensured to create a healthier inter-bank market. Nowadays, the majority of local Chinese companies are experiencing low profit margins. The central and local governments should help boost the domestic economy, under both fiscal and monetary policies, and avoid the crisis from happening in the real economy, which may transmit to banking systems.

Author Contributions: S.H. conceived and designed the experiments; G.L. performed the experiments, analyzed the data, and contributed reagents/materials/analysis tools; G.L., X.-J.C., and S.H. wrote the paper.

Funding: This research was funded by JSPS KAKENHI Grant Number 17K18564 and (A) 17H00983.

Acknowledgments: We are grateful to three anonymous referees for their helpful comments and suggestions. We are also grateful to the participants of The SIBR 2018 Hong Kong Conference on Interdisciplinary Business & Economics Research for helpful comments.

References

Ang, Andrew, and Joseph Chen. 2002. Asymmetric correlations of equity portfolios. *Journal of Financial Economics* 63: 443–94. [CrossRef]

Bollerslev, Tim. 1987. A conditionally heteroskedastic time series model for speculative prices and rates of return. *The Review of Economics and Statistics* 69: 542–47. [CrossRef]

Casella, G., and Roger L. Berger. 1990. *Statistical Inference*. Belmont: Duxbury Press.

Creal, D., Siem Jan Koopman, and André Lucas. 2013. Generalized autoregressive score models with applications. *Journal of Applied Econometrics* 28: 777–95. [CrossRef]

Fama, Eugene F. 1965. The behavior of stock-market prices. *The Journal of Business* 38: 34–105. [CrossRef]

Gumbel, Emil J. 1960. Bivariate exponential distributions. *Journal of the American Statistical Association* 55: 698–707. [CrossRef]

Hansen, Bruce E. 1994. Autoregressive conditional density estimation. *International Economic Review*, 705–30. [CrossRef]

Joe, Harry. 1997. *Multivariate Models and Multivariate Dependence Concepts*. Boca Raton: CRC Press.

Luo, W., Robert D. Brooks, and Param Silvapulle. 2011. Effects of the open policy on the dependence between the Chinese 'A' stock market and other equity markets: An industry sector perspective. *Journal of International Financial Markets, Institutions and Money* 21: 49–74. [CrossRef]

Marimoutou, Vêlayoudom, and Manel Soury. 2015. Energy markets and CO_2 emissions: Analysis by stochastic copula autoregressive model. *Energy* 88: 417–29. [CrossRef]

Patton, Andrew J. 2006. Modelling asymmetric exchange rate dependence. *International Economic Review* 47: 527–56. [CrossRef]

Patton, Andrew J. 2013. Copula methods for forecasting multivariate time series. In *Handbook of Economic Forecasting*. New York: Elsevier, vol. 2, pp. 899–960. [CrossRef]

Reboredo, Juan C., and Andrea Ugolini. 2015. Downside/upside price spillovers between precious metals: A vine copula approach. *The North American Journal of Economics and Finance* 34: 84–102. [CrossRef]

Sklar, Abe. 1959. Fonctions de répartition à n dimensions et leurs marges. *Publications de l'Institut de Statistique de l'Université de Paris* 8: 229–31.

Sukcharoen, Kunlapath, Tatevik Zohrabyan, David Leatham, and Ximing Wu. 2014. Interdependence of oil prices and stock market indices: A copula approach. *Energy Economics* 44: 331–39. [CrossRef]

Journal of
Risk and Financial Management

Article

Bank Credit and Housing Prices in China: Evidence from a TVP-VAR Model with Stochastic Volatility

Xie He, Xiao-Jing Cai and Shigeyuki Hamori *

Graduate School of Economics, Kobe University, 2-1, Rokkodai, Nada-Ku, Kobe 657-8501, Japan;
kakyo1515@gmail.com (X.H.); cai_xiaojing@people.kobe-u.ac.jp (X.-J.C.)
* Correspondence: hamori@econ.kobe-u.ac.jp

Received: 2 November 2018; Accepted: 11 December 2018; Published: 15 December 2018

Abstract: Housing prices in China have been rising rapidly in recent years, which is a cause for concern for China's housing market. Does bank credit influence housing prices? If so, how? Will the housing prices affect the bank credit system if the market collapses? We aim to study the dynamic relationship between housing prices and bank credit in China from the second quarter of 2005 to the fourth quarter of 2017 by using a time-varying parameter vector autoregression (VAR) model with stochastic volatility. Furthermore, we study the relationships between housing prices and housing loans on the demand side and real estate development loans on the supply side, separately. Finally, we obtain several findings. First, the relationship between housing prices and bank credit shows significant time-varying features; second, the mutual effects of housing prices and bank credit vary between the demand side and supply side; third, influences of housing prices on all kinds of bank credit are stronger than influences in the opposite direction.

Keywords: housing price; bank credit; housing loans; real estate development loans; TVP-VAR model

1. Introduction

The importance of the link between the housing market and macroeconomic activity in China has been proven with plenty of evidence in the literature (e.g., Hong 2014; Cai and Wang 2018). Over the last decade, the real estate market has made a significant contribution to the Chinese macroeconomy. As shown in Figure 1, the real estate industry contributions to GDP and the tertiary industry have been maintained at over 5% and 12%, respectively. Meanwhile, one drastic decline was observed in 2008 due to the global financial crisis. That crisis was directly caused by the decline of the US GDP in the third quarter of 2008, which did not revive until the first quarter of 2010. It was triggered by a sharp decline in housing prices after the collapse of the property bubble, leading to mortgage delinquencies, foreclosures, and the devaluation of housing-related securities.

After the marketization of real estate in China, which began with the reform of the housing system in 1979, housing prices have shown an increasing trend, especially into the 21st century. In particular, from the first quarter of 2005 to the third quarter of 2017, the real housing price increased rapidly from 2923 Yuan/m^2 to 5424 Yuan/m^2. On the other hand, the amount of real medium- and long-term loans in China increased nearly 6.5 times over the same period. Meanwhile, the variation in housing prices and bank credit showed significant consistency. Thus, in order to avoid suffering the same fate as the US, i.e., the collapse of a real estate bubble affecting the whole Chinese economy, the relationship between housing market activity and bank credit is noteworthy.

In fact, many empirical studies have investigated the relationship between housing prices and credit. That bank credit and the housing price have a mutual effect is supported by plenty of evidence in the literature. For instance, Collyns and Senhadji (2002) found that the growth of bank credit has had a certain contemporaneous effect on residential property prices in four East Asian countries: Hong Kong,

Korea, Singapore, and Thailand. They concluded that bank lending contributed significantly to the real estate bubble in Asia prior to the 1997 East Asian crisis. The findings of Mora (2008) prove that bank lending is a possible explanation for the Japanese real estate boom during the 1980s. Gimeno and Carrascal (2010) found that credit had a positive causality on the housing price in Spain when the credit aggregate departed from its long-run level. Gerlach and Peng (2005) examined the relationship between property prices and bank lending in Hong Kong, and their results suggest that the development of property prices influences bank lending.[1]

Figure 1. The Chinese real estate industry contributions to the tertiary industry and GDP in billions of Yuan. Source: China Statistics Bureau.

Davis and Zhu (2011) argued that the effect of commercial property prices on credit is stronger than the reverse. More importantly, their research showed that because bank credit affects both the property buyer and the developer, when bank credit is extended, it may boost demand and stimulate an increase in housing prices. Credit has a positive effect on commercial property prices in the short run. Meanwhile, the extension of bank credit may also finance new construction, and housing prices will finally adjust downwards through an improvement in supply. However, because of the lags in supply, the negative effect will only be felt in the long term.

Based on this perspective, this study makes two contributions. First, we not only observe the relationship between the housing price and bank credit in market as a whole but also divide the market into two parts: the demand side and the supply side. We intend to quantify the different relationships between housing prices and bank credit on these two fronts. Hence, this paper compares three different variable sets from the market as a whole, and from the demand and supply sides of the housing market.

The second contribution is that unlike most previous studies which were based on the simple vector autoregression (VAR) model, we adopt the time-varying parameter VAR (TVP-VAR) model with stochastic volatility which delivers more accurate empirical results. The simple VAR model has an obvious limitation: linear coefficients are time-invariant. However, in reality, the economic structure and the relationships among economic variables are more complicated and change over time, which means that the linear and time-invariant features of a simple VAR model are unrealistic.

---

[1] Yuan and Hamori (2014) analyzed the crowding out effect of affordable and unaffordable housing in China.

However, the TVP-VAR model can circumvent this problem perfectly. As stated by Nakajima (2011), "The TVP-VAR model enables us to capture the possible time-varying nature of the underlying structure in the economy in a flexible and robust manner". Moreover, stochastic volatility, which also influences the data generating process of economic variables and was originally proposed by Black (1976), may cause misspecification if it is ignored during analysis. Nakajima (2011) estimated the TVP regression model with stochastic volatility and constant volatility for a given set of simulated data, finding that the estimation result of the model with stochastic volatility was closer to the true value. Tian and Hamori (2016) use a time-varying structural vector auto-regression model with stochastic volatility to study the financial shock transmission mechanism. For this reason, we also incorporate stochastic volatility into the TVP-VAR model. On the other hand, due to the intractability of the likelihood function, stochastic volatility makes the estimation difficult. To circumvent this problem, we also use Markov chain Monte Carlo (MCMC) methods in the context of a Bayesian inference to estimate the model.

In this paper, our empirical results are presented in three parts. First, we find that the relationship between housing prices and bank credit has significant time-varying features. Second, the mutual effect between housing prices and bank credit varies on both the demand side and the supply side. Third, the influences of housing prices on all kinds of bank credit are stronger than influences in the opposite direction.

The remainder of the article is organized as follows. Section 2 presents a theoretical analysis of the interaction effect between bank credit and housing prices based on references. Section 3 introduces the model specifications. Section 4 discusses the data and the identification procedure. Section 5 shows the empirical results of each set of variables, and Section 6 presents the conclusions.

2. Theoretical Analysis of the Interaction Effect between Bank Credit and Housing Prices

Bank credit is considered to influence the housing market. Although bank credit is considered to have a positive effect on housing prices in general, in fact, the effect should not be understood as a whole, as it not only depends on the objects of bank credit—both the supply side of housing and the demand side—but it also depends on time. The effect of bank credit on housing prices may differ because of differences in influences on the two sides of the housing market. In addition, the different periods and lengths of time will also change the effect.

On the demand side, there is no doubt that housing loans are the main way for general consumers to buy houses. As housing loans expand, the demand for housing will also increase. This demand is not only for personal use but also for investment. In China, property is considered to be a good investment due to its ability to increase in value. Once housing loans can be obtained easily, speculative demand for property can also be stimulated with the help of bank funds, especially in the short term, because the supply of housing is inelastic, so prices will increase as a result of influences from the demand side.

On the supply side, the long-term and the short-term effects of real estate development loan[2] on housing prices are different. In China, real estate development loans are the main source of capital for constructors. According to calculations by Qin and Yao (2012), from 1998 to 2010, the average annual proportion of capital gained directly by banks from real estate development investment was more than 20.78%, while if the capital gained indirectly by banks, such as from down payments and personal mortgages, is also counted[3], this proportion is more than 66.81%. Thus, it is not difficult to see how important bank credit is to the constructors. In fact, since the marketization of real estate in China, the housing market in China has always been a seller's market in which the constructors have more bargaining power than the buyers. Meanwhile, in the short term, bank credit can relieve the financial

---

[2] In this paper, real estate development loan refers to the loan that bank issues to the borrower to finance construction of real estates and supportive facilities.
[3] In China, the presale of commercial residential houses allows developers to use the capital that consumers borrow from the bank for construction.

pressure of constructors, further enhancing their bargaining power and pushing up housing prices. However, in the long term, high real estate development also leads to a high supply of housing, and after the 2008 financial crisis, a high investment in the housing market led to a "high inventory" problem in China. In October 2016, the number of residential houses for sale hit another historical high. Many cities in China that have a high inventory of housing face huge pressure to reduce their numbers of unsold homes. Thus, high real estate loans will also make housing prices decrease in the long term because of oversupply in the long term, as concluded by Davis and Zhu (2011).

On the other hand, the growth of housing prices also has a strong effect on bank credit. In periods when housing prices continue to rise, banks are likely to underestimate the risk of credit on real estate development, causing them to expand their credit supply to the real estate industry.

For general consumers, based on research by Goodhart and Hofmann (2008) and other references, the growth of housing prices will mainly affect housing loans in three ways: the wealth effect, the collateral effect, and the expectation effect. First, the growth of housing prices via the wealth effect makes individuals willing to get more credit from the bank. Under the life cycle model of household consumption, a permanent increase in housing wealth can increase both household spending and borrowing if individuals want to smooth consumption over their life cycles. Second, since property is a general collateral item, a growth in housing prices can also increase the collateral value of individuals which can lead to lenders getting credit from the bank more easily. Third, the expectation effect explains that if housing prices begin to rise, consumers will anticipate that they will keep increasing, which encourages them to get a bigger housing loan to purchase property as soon as possible.

For the constructors, rises in housing prices can increase their expected investment return in real estate development, which will inevitably encourage them to expand their investment scale and attract new companies to enter the field. Since bank credit is the most important source of capital for the constructors, credit demand will significantly increase.

3. Time-Varying Parameter VAR Model with Stochastic Volatility

This paper follows Nakajima (2011) for the time-varying TVP-VAR model with stochastic volatility[4]. Consider the time varying structural VAR model

$$A_t y_t = B_{0t} + B_{1t} y_{t-1} + \cdots + B_{st} y_{t-s} + u_t, \quad t = s+1, \ldots n, \tag{1}$$

where y_t is a $k \times 1$ vector of observed variables, B_{0t} is an $k \times 1$ vector of the intercept term, $A_t, c_t, B_{1t}, \ldots, B_{st}$ are $k \times k$ matrices of time varying coefficients. The disturbance u_t is a $k \times 1$ time-varying structural shock, and it is assumed that $u_t \sim N(0, \Sigma_t \Sigma_t)$, where

$$\Sigma_t = \begin{pmatrix} \sigma_{1,t} & 0 & \cdots & 0 \\ 0 & \sigma_{2,t} & \ddots & \vdots \\ \vdots & \ddots & \ddots & 0 \\ 0 & \cdots & 0 & \sigma_{k,t} \end{pmatrix}$$

The simultaneous relations of the structural shock are specified by recursive identification, assuming that A_t is lower-triangular. Meanwhile, it is important to note that A_t is allowed to vary over time, which implies that an innovation to the i-th variable has a time invariant effect on the j-th variable:

---

[4]   Hereafter, for simplicity, we use the "TVP-VAR model" to indicate the model with stochastic volatility.

$$
A_t = \begin{pmatrix} 1 & 0 & \cdots & 0 \\ a_{21,t} & \ddots & \ddots & \vdots \\ \vdots & \ddots & \ddots & 0 \\ a_{k1,t} & \cdots & a_{kk-1,t} & 1 \end{pmatrix}
$$

Thus, Equation (1) can be rewritten as the following reduced form VAR model:

$$
y_t = C_{0t} + C_{1t}y_{t-1} + \cdots + C_{st}y_{t-s} + A_t^{-1} \sum_t \varepsilon_t, \quad \varepsilon_t \sim N(0, I_k), \tag{2}
$$

where $C_{it} = A_t^{-1}B_{it}$, for $i = 0, \ldots, s$. By stacking the elements in the rows of C_i's to a vector ς_t ($k^2(s+1) \times 1$ vector), the model can be written as follows:

$$
y_t = X_t\varsigma_t + A_t^{-1} \sum_t \varepsilon_t. \tag{3}
$$

$$
X_t = I_k \otimes (1, y'_{t-1}, \cdots, y'_{t-s}), \, t = s+1, \cdots, n
$$

where $\otimes$ denotes the Kronecker product. Meanwhile, following Primiceri (2005), $a_t = (a_{21}, a_{31}, a_{32}, a_{41}, \cdots, a_{k,k-1})'$ is a stacked vector of the lower-triangular elements, assuming ς_t, A_t, and $\sum_t$ all change over time.

If the variance is assumed to be constant while the coefficients are time-varying, it will cause the estimate parameters to be biased, because the possibility of volatility variation is ignored (Nakajima, 2011). To avoid this misspecification, stochastic volatility is also incorporated into the TVP-VAR model. It is assumed that the log-volatility is $h_t = (h_{1t}, \cdots, h_{kt})'$, $h_{jt} = \log \sigma_{jt}^2$, and for $j = 1, \cdots, k$, $t = s+1, \ldots, n$, it is also modeled to follow a random walk. The variances (σ_{jt}^2) are assumed to evolve as geometric random walks belonging to the class of models known as stochastic volatility.[5]

The dynamics of the model's time varying parameters in (3) and the stochastic volatility are specified as follows:

$$
\begin{matrix} \varsigma_{t+1} = \varsigma_t + u_{\varsigma t}, \\ a_{t+1} = a_t + u_{at}, \\ h_{t+1} = h_t + u_{ht}, \end{matrix} \quad \begin{pmatrix} \varepsilon_t \\ u_{\varsigma t} \\ u_{at} \\ u_{ht} \end{pmatrix} \sim N \left(0, \begin{pmatrix} I & O & O & O \\ O & \Sigma_{\varsigma} & O & O \\ O & O & \Sigma_a & O \\ O & O & O & \Sigma_h \end{pmatrix} \right), \tag{4}
$$

for $t = s+1, \cdots, n$, where $\varsigma_{s+1} \sim N(\mu_{\varsigma_0}, \Sigma_{\varsigma_0})$, $a_{s+1} \sim N(\mu_{a_0}, \Sigma_{a_0})$ and $h_{s+1} \sim N(\mu_{h_0}, \Sigma_{h_0})$.

Moreover, in this paper, we also make two assumptions that follow Nakajima (2011) and need to be stated. First, the assumption of a lower-triangular matrix for A_t is the recursive identification for the VAR system. Second, for simplicity, we assume that Σ_a and Σ_h are diagonal matrices.

4. Data and Settings

Table 1 shows all variables in our model. In out paper we use a four-variable TVP-VAR model to estimate the quarterly seasonally-adjusted data from the second quarter of 2005 to the fourth quarter of 2017 in China[6]. Furthermore, we estimated three different sets of variables. The first set was defined as $y_t = (IR_t, GDP_t, BC_t, HP_t)$, the second is $y_t = (IR_t, GDP_t, HL_t, HP_t)$, and the third is

---

5   Here, we use the log-normal SV model, which was originally proposed by Taylor (1986). The simplest model can also be
    defined: $y_t = \gamma \exp\left(\frac{h_t}{2}\right)$, $h_{t+1} = \phi h_t + \eta_t$, $\eta_t \sim NID\left(0, \sigma_\eta^2\right)$, $t = 0, \ldots, n-1$, $\gamma > 0$. For more details on the statistical
    aspects of ARCH and stochastic volatility, see Shephard (1996). Yang and Hamori (2018) compared the performances of the
    GARCH and SV models to analyze international agricultural commodity prices.
6   Because of the availability of data, we started the sample period in the second quarter of 2005.

$y_t = (IR_t, GDP_t, DL_t, HP_t)$, where IR refers to the logarithmic growth of the Inter Bank Offered Rate (IBOR) as the interest rate variable; GDP refers to the logarithmic growth of the real GDP; BC refers to the logarithmic growth of the real medium and long term loans as the bank credit variable and reflects credit in the whole market; HP refers to the logarithmic growth of the real price of housing; HL refers to the logarithmic growth of housing loans and reflects credit on the demand side; and DL refers to the logarithmic growth of real estate development loans and reflects credit on the supply side.

Table 1. Model Variables.

Variable	Data	Data Source
Housing Prices (HP)	The logarithmic growth of real price of housing	CEIC database
Interest Rate (IR)	The logarithmic growth of the Inter Bank Offered Rate (IBOR)	CEIC database
GDP	The logarithmic growth of real GDP	CEIC database
Bank Credit (BC)	The logarithmic growth of real medium- and long-term loan	CEIC database
Housing Loan (HL)	The logarithmic growth of housing loan	CEIC database
Real Estate Development Loan (DL)	The logarithmic growth of real estate development loan	CEIC database

The variables were all sourced from the China Entrepreneur Investment Club (CEIC) database[7].

In the first set of variables, we intended to study the relationship between bank credit and housing prices. The reason we chose the medium and long term loans as the variables of bank credit was because they influence both property buyers and developers.

In the second and third sets of variables, we wanted to study the relationship between bank credit and the housing price on the supply side and the demand side separately. For this reason, we chose housing loans for the demand side and real estate development loans for the supply side.

In addition, the cycle of bank credit can be significantly influenced by the interest rate. McQuinn and O'Reilly (2008) also showed the importance of interest rates not only in determining the housing price, but also in reflecting the availability of credit. Hence, we added the interest rate into the model as well. As the lending or mortgage rates in China are strictly regulated, IBOR is a better indicator of demand and supply in all financial markets. For this reason, the interest rate data used in this paper refers to the Inter Bank Offered Rate. Meanwhile, in consideration of the influence of macroeconomics, GDP was also added into our model.

The housing price represents the average price of commercial property in China.

Table 2 presents the descriptive statistics for the logarithmic growth of variables in the model. The Jarque–Bera statistics, which are used to detect whether the logarithmic growth of variables is normally distributed, rejected normality at a 5% significance level in all variables. Figure 2 plots the logarithmic growth of bank credit and housing prices.

Meanwhile, before the estimation, it was necessary to perform unit root tests to ensure the stationarity of data. As presented in Table 3, all variables in the model were tested for stationarity using the Augmented Dickey–Fuller (ADF), Phillips–Perron (PP) and Dickey Fuller GLS (DF-GLS) tests. The ADF test was proposed in 1981 and has become the most popular of the many competing tests. The PP test is an alternative unit root testing approach of the ADF test which was proposed in 1988. The DF-GLS test was proposed in 1992 and is considered an improved version of the ADF test. Many studies use many different methods simultaneously to test for stationarity (e.g., Mwabutwa et al. 2016), to make their results more convincing. All of the tests shown in Table 3 demonstrate that the variables were stationary at all levels. Subsequently, we were able to build a stable constant parameter VAR model to obtain the lags of the TVP-VAR, which were based on application of the Schwarz criterion to the stable constant parameter VAR for all sets of variables.

---

[7] The CEIC database belongs to CEIC Data Company Ltd., whose headquarters are in Hong Kong. This company compiles and updates economic and financial data series such as banking statistics, construction, and properties for economic research on emerging and developed markets, especially in China.

Table 2. Descriptive statistics.

	HP	IR	GDP	BC	HL	DL
Sample Size	51	51	51	51	51	51
Mean	0.5890	−0.6814	1.0724	1.5791	1.9800	1.7245
Std. Dev.	1.2609	8.4497	0.9204	0.9286	0.9912	1.4552
Skewness	−0.3381	−0.0905	−0.5015	1.6381	0.9906	2.1208
Kurtosis	4.7143	5.0809	5.4204	6.0717	3.7497	13.9351
Maximum	3.6529	23.7312	2.7776	4.5034	4.8360	8.9988
Minimum	−3.7025	−26.2599	−1.6036	−0.0115	0.3222	−1.9866
Jarque–Bera	7.2166	9.2712	14.5874	42.8576	9.5353	292.3303
Probability	0.0271	0.0097	0.0006	0.0000	0.0085	0.0000

Figure 2. The logarithmic growth of bank credit and housing prices.

Table 3. Testing for stationarity.

Variables	ADF	PP	DF-GLS
	Level	Level	Level
HP	−4.3138 ***	−7.3650 ***	−7.3510 ***
IR	−3.4648 **	−3.1574 **	−3.4111 ***
GDP	−6.5760 ***	−6.5925 ***	−5.0991 ***
BC	−2.8507 *	−2.9110 *	−2.7068 ***
HL	−8.7130 ***	−8.5561 ***	−7.2918 ***
DL	−4.7565 ***	−4.8917 ***	−4.7964 ***

Notes: To employ the unit root test, we used the intercepts of all variables; the symbols ***, **, and * denote significance at the 1%, 5%, and 10% levels, respectively. ADF: Augmented Dickey–Fuller; PP: Phillips–Perron; DF-GLS: Dickey Fuller GLS.

Finally, before starting the MCMC simulation, the following priors were assumed for the *i*-th diagonals of the covariance matrices, which is in accordance with Nakajima (2011):

$$\left(\sum_\varsigma\right)^{-2}_i \sim Gamma(40, 0.02), \quad \left(\sum_\alpha\right)^{-2}_i \sim Gamma(40, 0.02), \quad \left(\sum_h\right)^{-2}_i \sim Gamma(40, 0.02).$$

For the initial state of the time-varying parameter, rather flat priors are set; $\mu_{\beta_0} = \mu_{a_0} = \mu_{h_0} = 0$, and $\Sigma_{\beta_0} = \Sigma_{a_0} = \Sigma_{h_0} = 10 \times I$.

5. Empirical Results

This paper estimated the TVP-VAR model using a simulation by drawing M = 20,000 samples with the Markov Chain Monte Carlo (MCMC) algorithm and discarding the initial 2000 samples in the burn-in period.

5.1. Bank Credit and Housing Prices

Table 4 shows the estimated results of selected parameters in the TVP-VAR model for the first set of variables: (IR, GDP, BC, HP). The table shows the posterior mean, posterior standard deviation, 95 percent interval, and the Geweke (1992) convergence diagnostics (CD) of the i-th diagonal elements of $(\Sigma_\varsigma)_i$, $(\Sigma_a)_i$ and $(\Sigma_h)_i$, as well as the inefficient factors computed by using MCMC sampling. In the estimated results, all Geweke values were less than the 5% significance level based on the convergence diagnostics of 1.96 in the first set of variables, indicating acceptance of the null hypothesis of convergence to the posterior distribution. Meanwhile, the inefficient factors were rather low, which implies that the number of efficient samples used for the parameters and stated variables were sufficient, the minimum being approximately M/100 = 200.

Figure 3 illustrates the sample auto-correlation, sample paths, and the posterior densities of the parameters for the first set of variables. The sample auto-correlations in the first row of each figure all decreased quickly and ranged slightly around the 0 level, suggesting that most samples had low auto-correlation. Also, the sample paths in the second row in each figure were all very stable, indicating that the samples produced from the MCMC method were efficient.

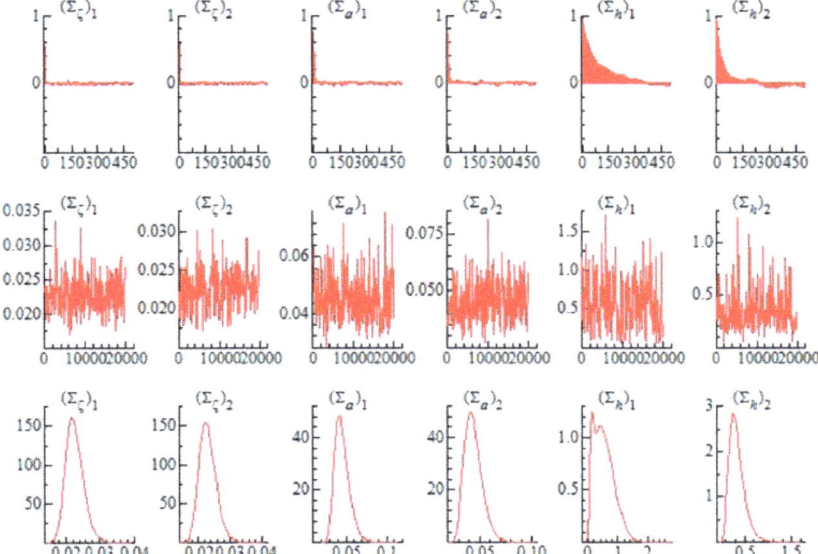

Figure 3. Estimation results of parameters in the TVP-VAR model (bank credit–housing prices). Notes: The figure shows sample auto-correlations (**top**), sample paths (**middle**), and posterior densities (**bottom**). In the top figures, the x-axis is the sample auto-correlation, and the y-axis is the lag; in the middle figures, the x-axis is the sampled value, and the y-axis is the iteration; in the bottom figure, the x-axis is the probability density, and the y-axis is the sampled value. The estimates of Σ_ς and Σ_a are multiplied by 100.

The Impulse Response Function is considered a useful tool to show the dynamic movements simulated by running the VAR model. For this reason, we performed an impulse response analysis based on the TVP-VAR model. Moreover, for comparison, the results of the standard VAR model, whose parameters are all-invariant, are also shown in Figure 4.

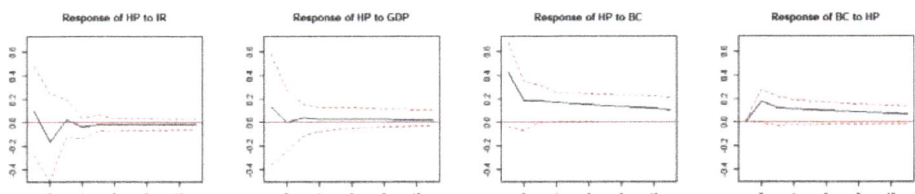

Figure 4. Impulse response based on the standard TVP model for IR, GDP BC, and HP. Notes: This shows the impulse response based on the standard VAR model for the variable set (IR, GDP, BC, HP); the solid line refers to the posterior mean, and the dotted line refers to 95% credible intervals.

In Figure 4, although the impulse responses of housing prices to interest rates were negative in only a few quarters, they were statistically insignificant with 95% confidence intervals throughout the measurement period. The impulse responses of housing prices to GDP were only slightly positive but were also statistically insignificant. Meanwhile, the impulse responses of housing prices to bank credit were positive throughout the measurement period, and they were only statistically insignificant within the first three quarters. In contrast, the impulse responses of bank credit to housing prices also stayed positive for the whole time period and were statistically significant. The standard VAR model showed a positive mutual effect between housing prices and bank credit, but it also cast doubt on the effects of interest rate and GDP on housing prices.

On the other hand, Figure 5 shows the time-varying impulse responses based on the TVP-VAR model, they are drawn in a time-series manner by showing the size of impulses for each quarter, half a year, and year. As shown in Figure 5, remarkably, all of the impulse responses have varied significantly over time. The impulse response of housing price to interest rate in each quarter remained positive until 2009, and was negative thereafter. Meanwhile, the responses for half-year and yearly changes were inverse and remained at a low level. This implies that the housing price can also be controlled by the interest rate, as shown by David (2013), but only in the short term. The quarterly and yearly impulse responses of housing prices to GDP were negative throughout the measurement period and the half-year responses only turned positive a few times.

Table 4. Estimation of selected parameters in the time-varying parameter TVP-VAR model (bank credit–housing prices).

	Mean	St. Dev	95%L	95%U	Geweke	Inef.
$(\Sigma_\varsigma)_1$	0.0227	0.0026	0.0183	0.0286	0.2150	3.9600
$(\Sigma_\varsigma)_2$	0.0230	0.0027	0.0185	0.0290	0.3410	2.8200
$(\Sigma_a)_1$	0.0453	0.0092	0.0310	0.0667	0.0230	8.3900
$(\Sigma_a)_2$	0.0444	0.0086	0.0309	0.0641	0.0930	11.4500
$(\Sigma_h)_1$	0.5335	0.3378	0.0752	1.2870	0.1080	125.3200
$(\Sigma_h)_2$	0.3431	0.1722	0.1036	0.7669	0.6420	63.5400

Notes: This is the estimation result of selected parameters in the TVP-VAR model for the variable set (IR, GDP, BC, HP). It shows that the means, standard deviations, the 95% credible intervals (upper and lower), the Geweke (1992) convergence diagnostics, and the number of inefficient samples are part of the diagonal elements of the covariance matrices; the estimates of Σ_ς and Σ_a are multiplied by 100.

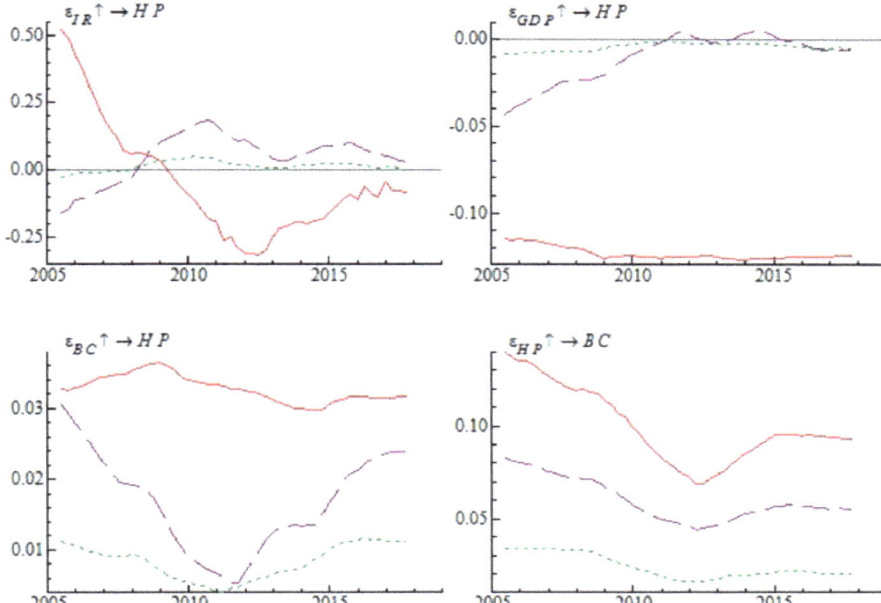

Figure 5. Impulse response for three different horizons. Notes: This shows the impulse response of the TVP-VAR model for the variable set of (IR, GDP, BC, HP); HP represents housing prices, BC represents bank credit, and IR represents the interest rate; the solid line refers to the time-varying impulse responses for each quarter; the dashed line refers to half-year responses; and the dotted line refers to yearly responses.

We can see that both the impulse responses of the housing price to bank credit and the reverse were positive throughout the sample period, which proves that although the mutual effect between housing price and bank credit may vary between the different sides, in the market as a whole, the mutual effect was still positive throughout the sample period in China.

In addition, we can also notice that the effect of the housing price on bank credit was stronger than the influence of bank credit on the housing price. This also implies that the banking and credit system will be greatly affected if the housing price begins to fluctuate wildly.

5.2. Housing Loans and Housing Prices

Table 5 shows the estimated results of the selected parameters in the TVP-VAR model for the second set of variables: (IR, GDP, HL, HP). In the estimated results, all Geweke values were less than the 5% significance level based on the convergence diagnostics of 1.96 in the first set of variables, indicating acceptance of the null hypothesis of convergence to the posterior distribution. Meanwhile, the number of inefficient factors was rather low, which implies that the number of efficient samples for the parameters and stated variables was sufficient, the minimum being approximately M/100 = 200.

Figure 6 illustrates the sample auto-correlation, sample paths, and posterior densities of the parameters for the second set of variables. The sample auto-correlation shown in the first row of each figure decreased quickly and ranged around the 0 level, suggesting that most samples had low auto-correlation. Also, the sample paths shown in the second row of each figure were all very stable, indicating that the samples produced from the MCMC method were efficient.

Figure 7 shows the impulse response functions based on the standard VAR model for the second variable set (IR, GDP, HL, HP). In Figure 7, the impulse responses of housing prices to the interest rate and the impulse responses of housing prices to the GDP are similar to those presented in Section 5.1. Meanwhile, the impulse responses of housing prices to housing loans were positive throughout the sample period but were statistically insignificant at the 95% confidence interval for the first four quarters. In the opposite direction, the impulse responses of housing loans to housing prices were positive and statistically significant throughout the measurement period.

Table 5. Estimation of selected parameters in the TVP-VAR model (housing loans–housing prices).

	Mean	St. Dev	95%L	95%U	Geweke	Inef.
$(\Sigma_\varsigma)_1$	0.0228	0.0027	0.0184	0.0287	0.3550	4.5000
$(\Sigma_\varsigma)_2$	0.0230	0.0027	0.0185	0.0289	0.5260	3.2000
$(\Sigma_a)_1$	0.0445	0.0088	0.0308	0.0650	0.5580	10.3100
$(\Sigma_a)_2$	0.0505	0.0108	0.0336	0.0754	0.4100	12.0700
$(\Sigma_h)_1$	0.4923	0.3177	0.0858	1.1984	0.2590	103.9000
$(\Sigma_h)_2$	0.4434	0.2130	0.1547	0.9810	0.2930	78.8900

Notes: (i) These are the estimation results of selected parameters in the TVP-VAR model for the variable set (IR, GDP, HL, HP). The means, standard deviations, the 95% credible intervals (upper and lower), the Geweke (1992) convergence diagnostics, and the number of inefficient samples are shown; (ii) $(\Sigma_\varsigma)_i$, $(\Sigma_a)_j$, $(\Sigma_h)_k$ are part of the diagonal elements of the covariance matrices; (iii) the estimates of Σ_ς and Σ_a are multiplied by 100.

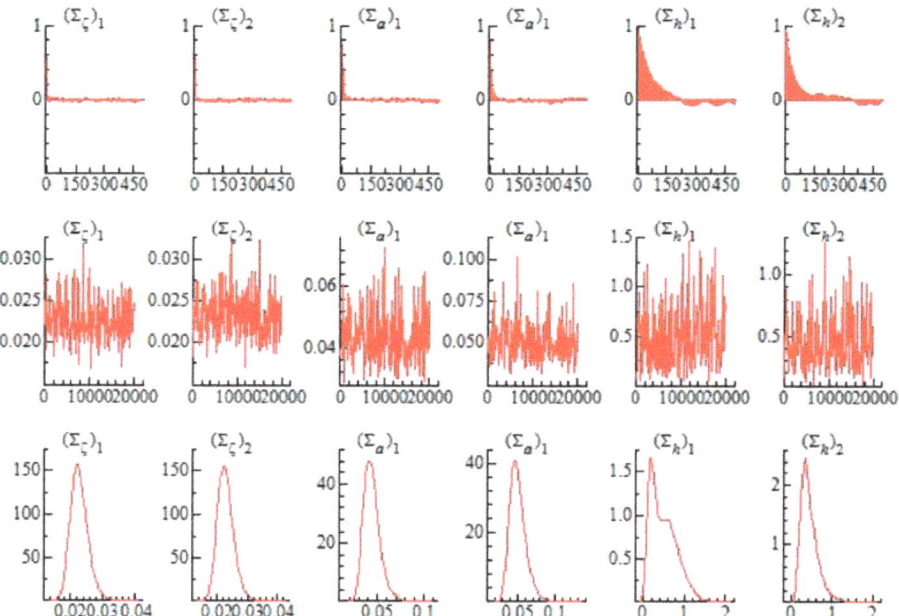

Figure 6. Estimation results of parameters in the TVP-VAR model (housing loans–housing prices). Notes: The figure shows sample auto-correlations (**top**), sample paths (**middle**), and posterior densities (**bottom**); in the top figures, the *x*-axis is the sample auto-correlation, and the *y*-axis is the lag; in the middle figures, the *x*-axis is the sampled value, and the *y*-axis is the iteration; in the bottom figure, the *x*-axis is the probability density, and the *y*-axis is the sampled value; the estimates of Σ_ς and Σ_a are multiplied by 100.

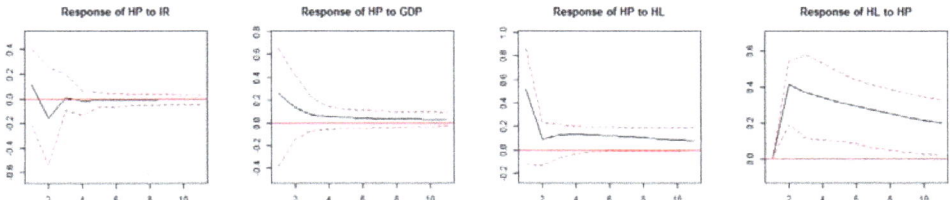

Figure 7. Impulse response based on the standard TVP model for (IR, GDP HL, HP). Notes: This shows the impulse response based on the standard VAR model for the variable set (IR, GDP, BC, HP); the solid line refers to posterior mean, and the dotted line refers to 95% credible intervals.

For comparison, the results of time-varying impulse responses based on TVP-VAR model are shown in Figure 8. They also show the significant time-varying features in each impulse response. Figure 8 shows that the impulse responses of the housing prices and housing loans to the interest rate had a similar variation to that shown in Figure 5. Meanwhile, the impulse response of housing prices to housing loans was positive for the half-year and yearly measurements, and for quarterly measurements in most periods; however, it turned negative after 2013 which implies that in that period, housing prices could not be controlled by housing loans in the short term. In contrast, housing prices also showed a positive effect on housing loans throughout the sample period which coincides with the theory that a growth in housing prices will affect the housing loans via the wealth effect, the collateral effect, and the expectation effect.

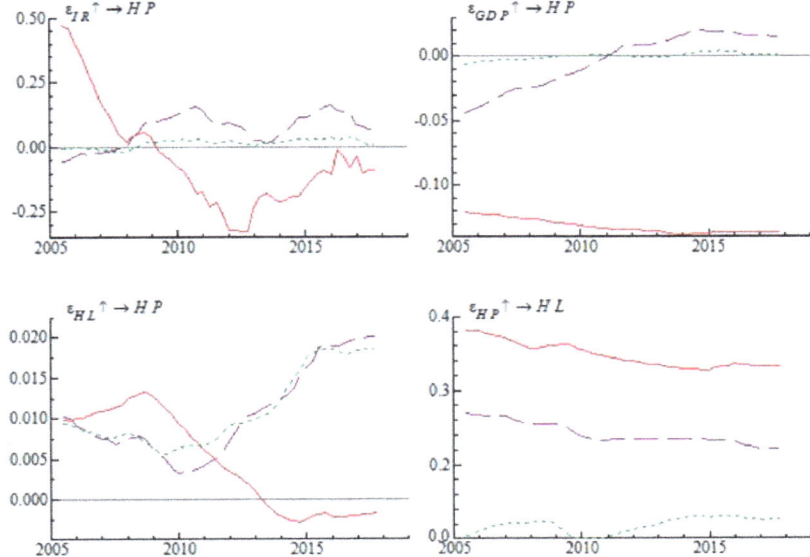

Figure 8. Impulse response for three different horizons. Notes: This shows the impulse response of the TVP-VAR model for the variable set of (IR, GDP, HL, HP); HP represents the housing price, HL represents housing loans, and IR represents the interest rate; the solid line refers to time-varying impulse responses for each quarter; the dashed line refers to half-year responses; and the dotted line refers to yearly responses.

In addition, the effect of housing prices on housing loans was stronger than the influence of housing loans on housing prices.

5.3. Real Estate Development Loan and Housing Prices

Table 6 shows the estimated results of selected parameters in the TVP-VAR model for the third set of variables: (IR, GDP, DL, HP). In the estimated results, all Geweke values were less than the 5% significance level based on the convergence diagnostics of 1.96 in the first set of variables, indicating acceptance of the null hypothesis of convergence to the posterior distribution. Meanwhile, the number of inefficient factors was rather low, which implies that the number of efficient samples for the parameters and stated variables was sufficient, the minimum being approximately M/100 = 200.

Table 6. Estimation of selected parameters in the TVP-VAR model (real estate development loans–housing prices).

	Mean	St. Dev	95%L	95%U	Geweke	Inef.
$(\Sigma_\varsigma)_1$	0.0228	0.0026	0.0183	0.0284	0.4130	2.9400
$(\Sigma_\varsigma)_2$	0.0230	0.0027	0.0184	0.0291	0.3460	4.6700
$(\Sigma_a)_1$	0.0462	0.0096	0.0316	0.0686	0.1720	19.6300
$(\Sigma_a)_2$	0.0599	0.0157	0.0373	0.0971	0.2420	14.9100
$(\Sigma_h)_1$	0.4279	0.2924	0.0743	1.1305	0.5250	138.0900
$(\Sigma_h)_2$	0.4495	0.2496	0.1159	1.1173	0.9050	107.8300

Notes: This table shows the estimation results of selected parameters in the TVP-VAR model for the variable set (IR, GDP, DL, HP). Tt shows means, standard deviations, the 95% credible intervals (upper and lower), the Geweke (1992) convergence diagnostics, and the number of inefficient samples; $(\Sigma_\varsigma)_i$, $(\Sigma_a)_j$, $(\Sigma_h)_k$ are part of the diagonal elements of the covariance matrices; the estimates of Σ_ς and Σ_a are multiplied by 100.

Figure 9 illustrates sample auto-correlations, sample paths, and the posterior densities of the parameters for the third set of variables. The sample auto-correlations shown in the first row in each figure all decreased quickly and ranged around the 0 level, suggesting that most samples had low auto-correlation. Also, the sample paths shown in the second row in each figure were all very stable, indicating that the samples produced from the MCMC method were efficient.

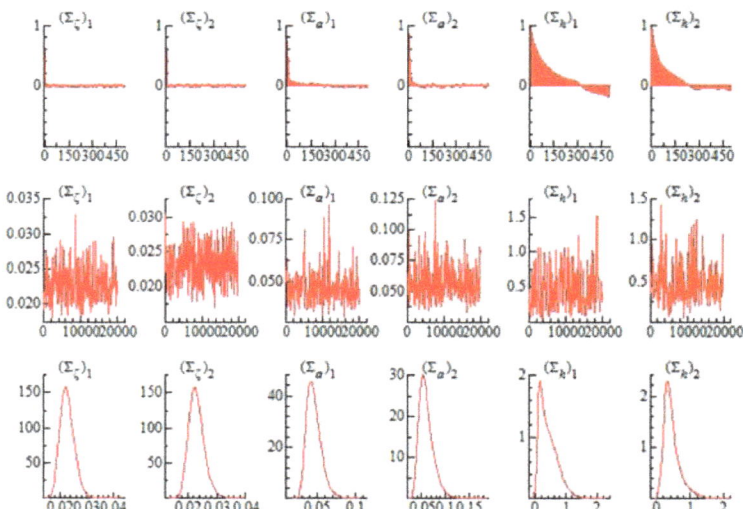

Figure 9. Estimation results of parameters in the TVP-VAR model (real estate development loans–housing prices). Notes: The figure shows sample auto-correlations (**top**), sample paths (**middle**), and posterior densities (**bottom**); in the top figures, the *x*-axis is the sample auto-correlation, and the *y*-axis is the lag; in the middle figures, the *x*-axis is the sampled value, and the *y*-axis is the iteration; in the bottom figures, the *x*-axis is the probability density, and the *y*-axis is the sampled value; the estimates of Σ_ς and Σ_a are multiplied by 100.

Figure 10 shows the impulse response functions based on the standard VAR model for the third variable set (IR, GDP, DL, HP). In Figure 10, it can be seen that the impulse responses of housing prices to real estate development loan were positive but statistically insignificant at the 95% confidence interval within the first three quarters. Meanwhile, it is also interesting to note that the impulse responses of real estate development loans to housing prices were slightly positive but statistically insignificant over all periods.

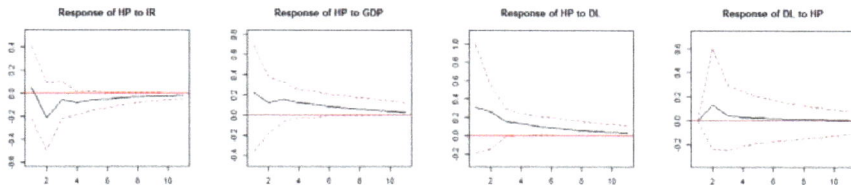

Figure 10. Impulse response based on the standard TVP model for (IR, GDP DL, HP). Notes: This shows the impulse response based on the standard VAR model for the variable set (IR, GDP, DL, HP); the solid line refers to the posterior mean; and the dotted line refers to the 95% credible intervals.

Figure 11 shows the time-varying responses for the third set of variables (IR, GDP, DL, HP), in which we can also see the significant time-varying features in each impulse response. The time-varying impulse response function showed negative responses of real estate development loans to the housing prices over all periods. Although this seems to not coincide with the theoretical analysis in Section 2, there is a possibility that if housing prices continue to rise, real development loans will not expand and may even reduce under government regulation. The impulse responses of the housing price to real estate development loans were also negative over the short-term, half-year and yearly periods. Meanwhile, in the short term, positive responses were seen for one quarter before the middle of 2017. This supports the economic theory that the effects of real estate development loan vary in different periods.

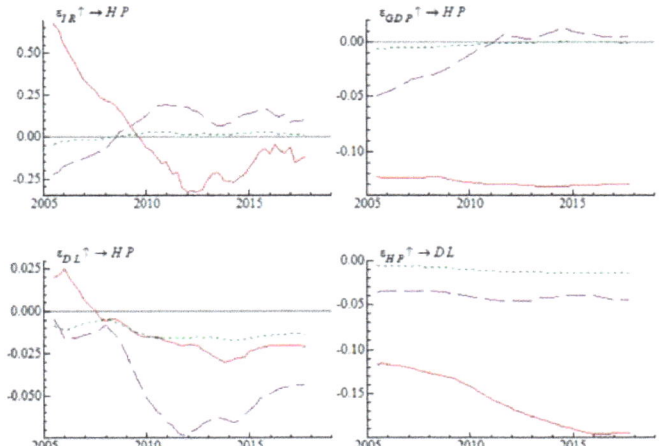

Figure 11. Impulse response for three different horizons. Notes: This shows the impulse response of the TVP-VAR model for the variable set of (IR, GDP, DL, HP); HP represents the housing price, DL represents real estate development loans, and IR represents the interest rate; the solid line refers to time-varying impulse responses for each quarter, the dashed line refers to half-year responses, and the dotted line refers to yearly responses.

In addition, we can see that the effect of housing prices on real estate development loans was also stronger than the effect in the opposite direction.

6. Conclusions

The limitation of the VAR model is that it cannot capture possible non-linearity or time variation in the lag structure of the model, and it also cannot capture possible heteroscedasticity of the shocks and non-linearity in the simultaneous relations among the variables of the model. Meanwhile, the TVP-VAR model with stochastic volatility is so flexible and robust that it can capture possible changes in the underlying structure of the economy. For this reason, in accordance with following Nakajima (2011), we used the TVP-VAR model with stochastic volatility to study the dynamic relationship between bank credit and housing prices in China from 2005Q2 to 2007Q4. Moreover, in order to study how bank credit affects buyers and developers, we also performed the same estimation for housing loans and real estate development loans. Finally, we obtained the following findings.

Firstly, the relationships between housing prices, bank credit, housing loans, and real estate development loans showed significant time-varying features, meaning that they change in different periods.

Secondly, the mutual effect between housing prices and bank credit varied between the different sides. In the market as a whole, the mutual effect over the whole sample period in China was shown to be positive. On the demand side, the mutual effect between housing prices and housing loans was also positive in most measured periods. However, we still saw that the effect of housing loans on housing prices for each quarter was negative in some years which casts doubt on the controllability of the housing loans control channel which is intended to control housing prices in the short term. On the demand side, the effect of housing prices was shown to be negative which seems to not coincide with the theoretical analysis in Section 2, but there is a possibility that is influenced by government regulation. In the opposite direction, the effect of real estate development loans on housing prices was shown to be negative in the long term, half-year and yearly periods, but positive for the short-term, quarterly, and some yearly periods, which coincides with the theoretical analysis.

Finally, it is also interesting to note that influences of housing prices on all kinds of bank credit are stronger than those in the opposite direction. This implies that the People's Bank of China should pay attention to the risk that a housing price collapse would have effects on the bank credit system.

Based on the TVP-VAR with stochastic volatility, we identified the time-varying effects of bank credit on housing prices and the reverse in the Chinese housing market. Furthermore, we found different time-varying relationships between these two factors on the demand side and the supply side. Nevertheless, we did not find evidence of, or observe, any reasons why a time-varying effect happened during this period. This could be a future study direction.

Author Contributions: S.H. conceived and designed the experiments; X.H. performed the experiments, analyzed the data, and contributed reagents/materials/analysis tools; X.H., X.-J.C., and S.H. drafted the manuscript.

Funding: This research was supported by JSPS KAKENHI Grant Number 17K18564 and (A) 17H00983.

Acknowledgments: We are grateful to the three anonymous referees for their helpful comments and suggestions.

Conflicts of Interest: The authors declare no conflicts of interest. The founding sponsors had no role in the design of the study, in the collection, analyses, or interpretation of data, in the writing of the manuscript, or in the decision to publish the results.

References

Black, Fischer. 1976. Studies of Stock Market Volatility Changes. In *Proceedings of the 1976 Meetings of the Business and Economic Statistics Section*. Washington DC: American Statistical Association, pp. 177–81.

Cai, Weina, and Sen Wang. 2018. The Time-Varying Effects of Monetary Policy on Housing Prices in China: An Application of TVP-VAR Model with Stochastic Volatility. *International Journal of Business Management* 13: 149–57. [CrossRef]

Collyns, Charles, and Abdelhak Senhadji. 2002. *Lending Booms, Real Estate, and The Asian Crisis*. IMF Working Paper. Washington DC: IMF, pp. 1–46. Available online: https://ssrn.com/abstract=879360 (accessed on 10 September 2018).

Davis, E. Philip, and Haibin Zhu. 2011. Bank lending and commercial property cycles: Some cross-country evidence. *Journal of International Money and Finance* 30: 1–21. [CrossRef]

David, Nissim Ben. 2013. Predicting housing prices according to expected future interest rate. *Applied Economics* 45: 3044–48. [CrossRef]

Geweke, John. 1992. Evaluating the Accuracy of Sampling-Based Approaches to the Calculation of Posterior Moments. In *Bayesian Statistics 4*. Edited by José-Miguel Bernardo, James O. Berger, Alexander Philip Dawid and Adrian Frederick Melhuish Smith. Oxford: Oxford University Press, pp. 169–93.

Gerlach, Stefan, and Wensheng Peng. 2005. Bank Lending and Property Prices in Hong Kong. *Journal of Banking & Finance* 29: 461–81. [CrossRef]

Goodhart, Charles, and Boris Hofmann. 2008. House Prices, Money, Credit and the Macroeconomy. *Oxford Review of Economic Policy* 24: 180–205. Available online: https://EconPapers.repec.org/RePEc:oup:oxford:v:24:y:2008:i:1:p:180-205 (accessed on 20 October 2018). [CrossRef]

Gimeno, Ricardo, and Carmen Martínez Carrascal. 2010. The relationship between house prices and house purchase loans: The Spanish case. *Journal of Banking & Finance* 34: 1849–55. [CrossRef]

Hong, Liming. 2014. The Dynamic Relationship between Real Estate Investment and Economic Growth: Evidence from Prefecture City Panel Data in China. *IERI Procedia* 7: 2–7. [CrossRef]

McQuinn, Kieran, and Gerard O'Reilly. 2008. Assessing the role of income and interest rates in determining house prices. *Economic Modelling* 25: 377–90. [CrossRef]

Mwabutwa, Chance, Nicola Viegi, and Manoel Bittencourt. 2016. Evolution of Monetary Policy Transmission Mechanism in Malawi: A TVP-VAR Approach. *Journal of Economic Development* 41: 33–55.

Mora, Nada. 2008. The Effect of Bank Credit on Asset Prices: Evidence from the Japanese Real Estate Boom during the 1980s. *Journal of Money, Credit and Banking* 40: 57–87. Available online: https://www.jstor.org/stable/25096240 (accessed on 19 September 2018). [CrossRef]

Nakajima, Jouchi. 2011. *Time-Varying Parameter VAR Model with Stochastic Volatility: An Overview of Methodology and Empirical Applications*. IMES Discussion Paper Series, 11-E-09; Tokyo: Institute for Monetary and Economic Studies, Bank of Japan.

Primiceri, Giorgio. 2005. Time Varying Structural Vector Autoregressions and Monetary Policy. *The Review of Economic Studies* 72: 821–52. [CrossRef]

Qin, Lin, and Yimin Yao. 2012. A Study of the Relationship between Bank Credit and Real Estate Prices. *Comparative Economic & Social Systems* 2: 188–202. (In Chinese)

Shephard, Neil. 1996. Statistical Aspects of ARCH and Stochastic Volatility. In *Time Series Models in Econometrics, Finance and Other Fields*. London: Chapman & Hall, pp. 1–67.

Taylor, Stephen J. 1986. *Modelling Financial Time Series*. Chichester: John Wiley.

Tian, Shuairu, and Shigeyuki Hamori. 2016. Time-Varying Price Shock Transmission and Volatility Spillover in Foreign Exchange, Bond, Equity, and Commodity Markets: Evidence from the United States. *North American Journal of Economics and Finance* 38: 163–71. [CrossRef]

Yuan, Nannan, and Shigeyuki Hamori. 2014. Crowding-out effects of affordable and unaffordable housing in China, 1999–2010. *Applied Economics* 46: 4318–33. [CrossRef]

Yang, Lu, and Shigeyuki Hamori. 2018. Modeling the dynamics of international agricultural commodity prices: A comparison of GARCH and stochastic volatility models. *Annals of Financial Economics* 13: 1–20. [CrossRef]

Journal of
Risk and Financial Management

Article

Is Window-Dressing around Going Public Beneficial? Evidence from Poland

Joanna Lizińska * and **Leszek Czapiewski**

Department of Corporate Finance, Poznań University of Economics and Business, al. Niepodległości 10,
61-875 Poznań, Poland; leszek.czapiewski@ue.poznan.pl
* Correspondence: joanna.lizinska@ue.poznan.pl; Tel.: +48-61-854-3862

Received: 13 December 2018; Accepted: 18 January 2019; Published: 21 January 2019

Abstract: The informativeness of financial reports has been of a great importance to both investors and academics. Earnings are crucial for evaluating future prospects and determining company value, especially around milestone events such as initial public offerings (IPO). If investors are misled by manipulated earnings, they could pay too high a price and suffer losses in the long-term when prices adjust to real value. We provide new evidence on the relationship between earnings management and the long-term performance of IPOs as we test the issue with a methodology that has not been applied so far for issues in Poland. We use a set of proxies of earnings management and test the long-term IPO performance under several factor models (CAPM, and three extensions of the Fama-French model). Aggressive IPOs perform very poorly later and earn severe negative stock returns up to three years after going public. The difference in returns in accrual quantiles is statistically significant in almost half of methodology settings. The results seem to suggest that investors might not be able to discount pre-IPO abnormal accruals and could be overoptimistic. Once the true earnings performance is revealed over time, the market makes downward price corrections.

Keywords: earnings management; earnings manipulation; earnings quality; initial public offering; IPO; asset pricing model

---

1. Introduction

Financial statements are a very important source of information for stakeholders. Businesses are expected to follow numerous accounting standards and rules in the process of recording activities and transactions properly. Managers are given discretion to some extent in reporting a company' situation. Managerial discretion in reporting has both benefits and disadvantages. Managers should use their unique knowledge to make financial statements more informative. However, managers may also use their judgment in reporting to mislead other stakeholders. Following a high information asymmetry between issuers and investors of initial public offering (IPO) companies at the time of the going public, investors rely heavily on financial statements. Simultaneously, IPO firms have an opportunity to manage earnings as usually little is known about market newcomers. They also have incentives to do so as the moment of going public is a very important event that attracts a lot of attention.

The key objective of this research is to assess whether the long-term performance of initial public offerings in Poland differs systematically according to the magnitude of around-the-issue earnings management. Previously published studies on Polish IPOs reported results using the event-time approach, according to the buy-and-hold abnormal returns (BHAR) or cumulative abnormal returns (CAR). They have been both very popular measures of the long-term performance. Fama (1998) and other researchers (Barber and Lyon 1997; Lyon et al. 1999; Jegadeesh and Karceski 2009) point out the deficiencies of the event-time approach such as skewness bias, violations in cross-sectional independence, or re-balancing bias. Our study is the first one that discusses the relationship between earnings management and the long-term IPO performance in Poland with the alternative methodology, namely the calendar-time portfolio approach. The method that we apply is mentioned by many researchers as mitigating many statistical problems arising in long-term event studies. Given the general lack of evidence on explanations of long-term abnormal returns with the calendar-time portfolio based on the opportunistic earnings management behavior for the Polish capital market, this is the area where this study contributes to the existing literature as it provides international insights into the discussion. Poland is an important area of economic growth in Europe which inclines academics to address many financial issues and makes possible conclusions important. The results of the long-term implications of earnings management for IPOs in Poland are not obvious. First, it is because of the theoretical background that is briefly summarized in the paper. Second, Poland has different characteristics to other markets. This country has undertaken a long journey of economic liberalization since the transition of its economy. During the period we examine, it has been classified as an emerging market by all of the leading agencies. Just recently, though, it has been ranked by FTSE Russell as a developed market. The uniqueness of studies on an emerging market that transforms into a developed economy, is a strong and motivating argument for taking empirical research. This is the only way to uncover mechanisms of capital markets based on the fact that direct comparison with US-centered research is limited. Although Poland is the eighth largest economy in the European Union (EU) and the largest among Central and Eastern European countries in the EU, Polish companies' capitalization is much smaller in comparison to US stock markets. It has deep consequences for a methodology of empirical research as many methodological solutions have been proposed for the US, which is an incomparably larger market. Applying these solutions to much smaller markets encounters numerous practical problems. This paper is one of the pieces of the research stream that touches the uniqueness of less-developed economies and faces the difficulty of methodological issues for small capital markets. All of these arguments taken together make the research on the long-term implications of earnings management for Polish IPOs challenging and contributing to the existing literature. Under the overoptimism hypothesis, we expect that the greater the earnings management level around the time of the issue, the larger the long-term price correction.

Both earnings management and abnormal long-term market performance of IPOs cannot be measured directly so they are observed with proxies. We proxy for earnings management using discretionary accruals. Factor regressions produce intercepts for rolling IPO portfolios that proxy for abnormal long-term performance. As alternative methodologies suffer from different types of biases as well as have their strong points, we provide a broad set of robustness checks. Accruals are estimated as the difference between real accruals and non-discretionary accruals where the latter are estimated using the cross-sectional industry-year regressions under the Jones model (Jones 1991), the modified Jones model (Dechow et al. 1995), the McNichols model (McNichols 2000), and Ball–Shivakumar model (Ball and Shivakumar 2006). We also apply a broad set of asset pricing models to assess the long-term performance. Empirically, we start with the Capital Asset Pricing Model (Sharpe 1964; Lintner 1969), and extend the analysis of long-term abnormal performance with estimating monthly risk premiums under three multifactor models: the Fama-French three-factor model (Fama and French 1993), the Carhart four-factor model (Carhart 1997), and the latest innovation—namely, the Fama-French five-factor model (Fama and French 2015, 2016).

Our results show strong long-term underperformance of initial public offerings in Poland using the calendar-time portfolio approach. Alphas are statistically and economically significant for both low- and high-accrual IPO firms. Both, conservative and aggressive IPO companies experience a relative decline in market value in the long run. The magnitude of IPO negative returns is sensitive to the methodology, but it does not change the conclusions about long-term IPO underperformance. Annualized abnormal returns range from −8.2% to −13.7% for conservative IPO companies, whereas the span for aggressive IPO companies is from −12.1% up to even −20.5%. Importantly, we report that more conservative IPO firms outperform firms that managed their earnings more aggressively. The average difference between quantiles totals 5.9 percentage points annually, and it ranges from 2.0

percentage points annually up to even 10.4 percentage points per year. Average annualized alphas for conservative IPO firms equals −10.2%, whereas it is −16.1% for aggressive IPO firms. The average abnormal returns are much more negative for the aggressive IPO companies and this difference is statistically significant in almost half of methodology settings. The rest of the paper is organized as follows. Section 2 gives a brief discussion of the existing literature. Section 3 briefly describes the data sources, details earnings management proxies and methods of the long-run performance measures. Section 4 contains descriptive statistics and a short risk premium presentation. Section 5 presents evidence on the explanatory power of earnings management for the long-term abnormal performance and offers tests for robustness of results. Section 6 discusses the empirical results in the light of the existing comparable evidence on other markets and outlines future research. The last section concludes the paper.

2. Brief Theoretical Background

The question of earnings management has not been constrained solely to equity issues. Proxies of earnings management have been applied to a broad set of issues in finance which argues for the importance of earnings management for many company activities (Healy 1985; Liberty and Zimmerman 1986; McNichols and Wilson 1988; Jones 1991; Pourciau 1993; DeFond and Jiambalvo 1994; Gaver et al. 1995; Holthausen et al. 1995; Perry and Williams 1994; Teoh et al. 1998b).

The choice whether to manage or not to manage earnings when a firm is planning to sell its shares to the market for the first time is not obvious. The issue of earnings management relates to two opposite hypotheses. The first one is connected with the opportunism of IPO issuers. The second theory relates to the expected enhanced reporting quality of public companies together with regulatory limits on discretion, penalties for misreporting, or greater external monitoring.

Analyzing the importance of earnings to investors, Sloan (1996) suggests that the cash flow component may be underweighted and the accrual component may be overweighted. If an IPO firm engages in increasing earnings around going public and investors are not able to recognize the true information content of earnings as indicators of future prospects, they will raise stock prices at issue. In the long-term, when the real performance is revealed and information asymmetries between the issuer and its investors are lower, the market is expected to adjust the IPO prices down. This is one of the possible explanations for the long-term underperformance observed for the US IPOs, as well as other developed markets or emerging markets.

Reported earnings consist of cash flows and accruals. Accruals are defined as accounting adjustments to cash flows. If earnings are artificially boosted around going public, it is much easier to proceed with the accrual part than with real cash changes, which justifies accruals as a measure of earnings manipulation. According to different ideas behind the income statement and cash flow statement, earnings usually differ from cash flows. Following this, accruals appear as a natural consequence of this. However, not all the accruals have the same degree of managerial discretion. This inclines us toward decomposing accruals, as in Jones (1991). Some accruals are normal to company activities or are exposed to limited managerial discretion. They are non-discretionary components (normal or expected accruals). The discretionary part of accruals (abnormal accruals) proxies for the earnings manipulation level as these accruals are considered to have been the 'managed' part of the earnings.

Previous papers suggest that IPO companies manage their earnings for the moment of going public, and usually conclude that companies managing their accruals aggressively also experience strong long-term underperformance (Teoh et al. 1998a; DuCharme et al. 2001; Roosenboom et al. 2003; Chen et al. 2005; Pastor-Llorca and Poveda-Fuentes 2011; Ahmad-Zaluki et al. 2011; Xie 2001; Chan et al. 2001). However, Beneish (1998) questions systematic investor valuation errors based on inflated earnings. Along the same lines, Ball and Shivakumar (2005), Ball and Shivakumar (2006) and Ball and Shivakumar (2008) argue in favor of more conservative reporting by public companies.

The research on the links between earnings management and subsequent IPO performance in Poland is scant. Lizińska and Czapiewski (2018a) used the buy-and-hold approach and reported that more aggressive IPOs performed poorly in the long run. However, the difference in the long-term abnormal returns between firms with lower and higher discretionary accruals was not robust in all settings of methodology. Lizińska and Czapiewski (2018b) combined earnings quality around going public with the long-term price behavior and tested the puzzle with OLS regressions based on the BHAR approach. Robustness tests allowed for a conclusion that the long-term buy-and-hold abnormal returns of initial public offerings completed before the peak of the crisis were negatively related to earnings management around IPO date.

3. Sources of Data and Methodology

The research sample covers initial public offerings listed on the Warsaw Stock Exchange (WSE) from January 2002 to December 2014. We include only offerings from the main equity market, and those without prior quotation on alternative markets. The sample covers only issues with a new common stock issuance. Delisted companies are included both in the IPO sample and in the benchmark sample. Initial public offerings are restricted to the non-financial industry.

The data are derived from Notoria Serwis, the official site of the WSE and InfoStrefa.com. Market returns for companies are based on adjusted close prices and they include dividends, splits and pre-emptive rights. The list of IPOs ends in 2014 but the market data cover a longer period as it was necessary to calculate long-term adjusted returns.

The aim of the research relates to the extent to which earnings management is related to the subsequent long-term abnormal market performance of IPO firms in Poland. As none of this can be observed directly, we rely on proxies. Both, the estimates of earnings management and long-term performance have been much debated in the literature. We do not aim to expand the methodology in this research, but apply a broad set of methodology settings derived from the existing literature. The empirical modelling encompasses five time-consuming steps: earnings management proxy estimation, ranking of IPOs according to aggressive or conservative earnings management, risk premiums estimation for a set of asset pricing models, estimation of the measure of long-term risk-adjusted IPO performance according to the calendar-time portfolio approach in accrual quantiles, and estimation of an equivalent regression of the difference in intercepts between the aggressive and conservative IPOs.

In this research, the level of earnings manipulation is estimated with accrual-based methods. It is much easier to manage profits with the accrual part of earnings than with real cash changes. It is a strong argument to use accruals as a measure of earnings manipulation. We run cross-sectional regressions for every industry and every year to assess the non-discretionary part of accruals (*NDACC*). In the next step, we relate them to real accruals to get the discretionary part (*DACC*), which is an earnings manipulation estimator. Real accruals reflect the accounting meaning of adjustments and are composed of non-cash current assets change, change in current liabilities, and depreciation. A prerequisite for running industry-year regression is a minimum industry size of five companies. An embargo of two years is imposed on an IPO firm which excludes each IPO from the benchmark group for other IPO companies during this period. Cross-sectional regressions allow us to incorporate changes in economic conditions that affect a particular industry. Accruals, as well as their components, are scaled with lagged assets (A) to reduce heteroscedasticity in residuals for accruals and their components (Ronen and Yaari 2008).

We use set of accrual-based earnings management proxies. First, we use the Jones model (Jones 1991) which assumes that the level of expected accruals is largely determined by gross property, plant, and equipment (*PPE*) and change in revenues (ΔREV) as in the following equation

$$NDACC_{it}^J = \alpha_{i1}\left(\frac{1}{A_{i,t}}\right) + \alpha_{i2}\Delta REV_{i,t} + \alpha_{i3}PPE_{i,t} + \varepsilon_{i,t}. \tag{1}$$

Dechow et al. (1995) extended the Jones model and proposed a modified version. They included the change in trade receivables (ΔREC) to account for the possibility of credit sales manipulation by inducing sales in certain periods without real money inflows. Thus, increases in trade receivables are excluded from the change in revenues as in the equation

$$NDACC_{it}^{mJ} = \alpha_{i1}\left(\frac{1}{A_{i,t}}\right) + \alpha_{i2}(\Delta REV_{i,t} - \Delta REC_{i,t}) + \alpha_{i3}PPE_{i,t} + \varepsilon_{i,t}. \tag{2}$$

We also consider other improvements to the Jones model. The Dechow and Dichev (2002) model, in the version proposed by McNichols (2000), considers extensions of the Jones model by current, past, and future cash flow from operating activities (*CFO*)

$$NDACC_{it}^{McN} = \alpha_{i1}\left(\frac{1}{A_{i,t}}\right) + \alpha_{i2}CFO_{i,t-1} + \alpha_{i3}CFO_{i,t} + \\ +\alpha_{i4}CFO_{i,t+1} + \alpha_{i5}\Delta REV_{i,t} + \alpha_{i6}PPE_{i,t} + \varepsilon_{i,t} \tag{3}$$

Ball and Shivakumar (2006) incorporate timely loss recognition in the accruals estimation process. They include *DCFO* which is 1 if the change in cash flows is less than zero, and 0 otherwise, and a book value of fixed assets (*FASSET*)

$$NDACC_{it}^{BS} = \alpha_{i1}\left(\frac{1}{A_{i,t}}\right) + \alpha_{i5}\Delta REV_{i,t} + FASSET_{i,t} + \alpha_{i3}CFO_{i,t} + \alpha_{i3}DCFO_{i,t} \\ +\alpha_{i3}CFO_{i,t} \cdot \alpha_{i3}DCFO_{i,t} + \varepsilon_{i,t} \tag{4}$$

In the next research step, we rank initial public offerings by discretionary accruals into two quantiles: conservative for the smallest abnormal accruals (C) and aggressive for largest discretionary accruals (A) as in Ahmad-Zaluki et al. (2011). The ranks are given independently for each of the earnings management proxies. Next, portfolios of aggressive or conservative IPO are constructed on the basis of IPOs that went public in the past 36 months, with monthly rebalancing.

In the main research step, we estimate the long-term abnormal performance across accrual quantiles. Long-term risk-adjusted performance of IPOs is estimated according to a calendar-time portfolio approach. Given the concerns about proper measure, we use a variety of methodological settings. Thus, we deliver a broad set of robustness checks. We use the explanation for the cross-section of average returns steaming from the capital asset pricing model (Sharpe 1964; Lintner 1969), Fama and French (1993) three-factor model, the Carhart (1997) four-factor model, and the Fama and French (2015) five-factor model (CAPM, 3FF, 4C, and 5FF, hereafter).

The first model used in the study is the CAPM. Jensen's alpha is given by the relationship between excess return and beta

$$R_t^P - R_t^F = \alpha + \beta\left(R_t^M - R_t^F\right) + \varepsilon_t^P, \tag{5}$$

where R_t^P is the calendar time portfolio return, R_t^F is the risk-free rate calculated with WIBOR, R_t^M is the monthly market return based on the stock market index (Warsaw Stock Index, WIG), and ε_t^P is the error term.

Next, the estimate of alpha is derived from the Fama and French (1993) three-factor model

$$R_t^P - R_t^F = \alpha + \beta_M\left(R_t^M - R_t^F\right) + \beta_{SMB}SMB_t + \beta_{HML}HML_t + \varepsilon_t^P, \tag{6}$$

where SMB_t is the difference in returns between portfolios of small and big companies, and HML_t is the average return on the two value portfolios minus the average return on the two growth portfolios.

As an additional check, an intercept is estimated according to the Carhart (1997) four-factor model as in

$$R_t^P - R_t^F = \alpha + \beta_{RM}\left(R_t^M - R_t^F\right) + \beta_{SMB}SMB_t + \beta_{HML}HML_t + \beta_{WML}WML_t, \tag{7}$$

where WML_t is the average return on the two high prior return portfolios minus the average return on the two low prior return portfolios.

The last measure of abnormal performance is the intercept in the Fama and French (2015) five-factor model

$$R_t^P - R_t^F = \alpha + \beta_{RM}\left(R_t^M - R_t^F\right) + \beta_{SMB}SMB_t + \beta_{HML}HML_t + \beta_{RMW}RMW_t + \beta_{CMA}CMA_t, \quad (8)$$

where RMW_t is the average return on the two robust operating profitability portfolios minus the average return on the two weak operating profitability portfolios, and CMA_t is the average return on the two conservative investment portfolios minus the average return on the two aggressive investment portfolios.

We estimate monthly risk premiums for factor models by monthly intervals. Each monthly regression produces an intercept (alpha) which serves us as the abnormal long-term performance measure. Testing intercepts in accrual quantiles, allows us to discuss the relationship between the long-term abnormal IPO performance in Poland and the extent of earnings management proxied by discretionary accruals. Finally, we again run equivalent monthly factor regressions of the difference in alphas between aggressive and conservative initial public offerings. We estimate these regressions in all of the methodology settings to check the robustness of the results.

4. Descriptive Statistics and Risk Premiums

IPO activity fluctuated highly during the sample period. The peak number of initial public offerings in 2007 just before the financial crisis was followed by an enormous drop in equity issuance in the following years. Although the market conditions started to recover with the beginning of 2009, and Warsaw Stock Exchange Index (WIG Index) quotations improved substantially, IPO activity remained relatively weak. The illustration of these changes is included in Figure 1.

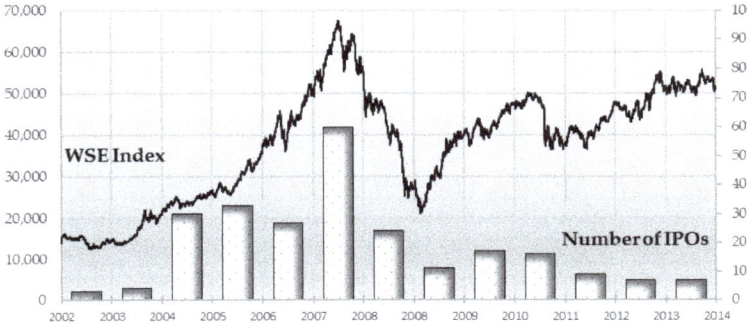

Figure 1. IPO activity and market situation.

The changes in the general situation on the WSE also resulted in changes in risk premiums. We illustrate these changes with Figure 2, where part (a) presents changes of the risk market premium (*RMP*), part (b) describes the performance of small stocks relative to big stocks (*SMB*, small-minus-big risk premium), part (c) illustrates the performance of value stocks relative to growth stocks (*HML*, high-minus-low risk premium), part (d) presents the momentum factor (*WML*, winners-minus-losers risk premium), part (e) is connected with the profitability factor (*RMW*, robust-minus-weak risk premium), and part (f) reflects the investment factor (*CMA*, conservative-minus-aggressive risk premium).

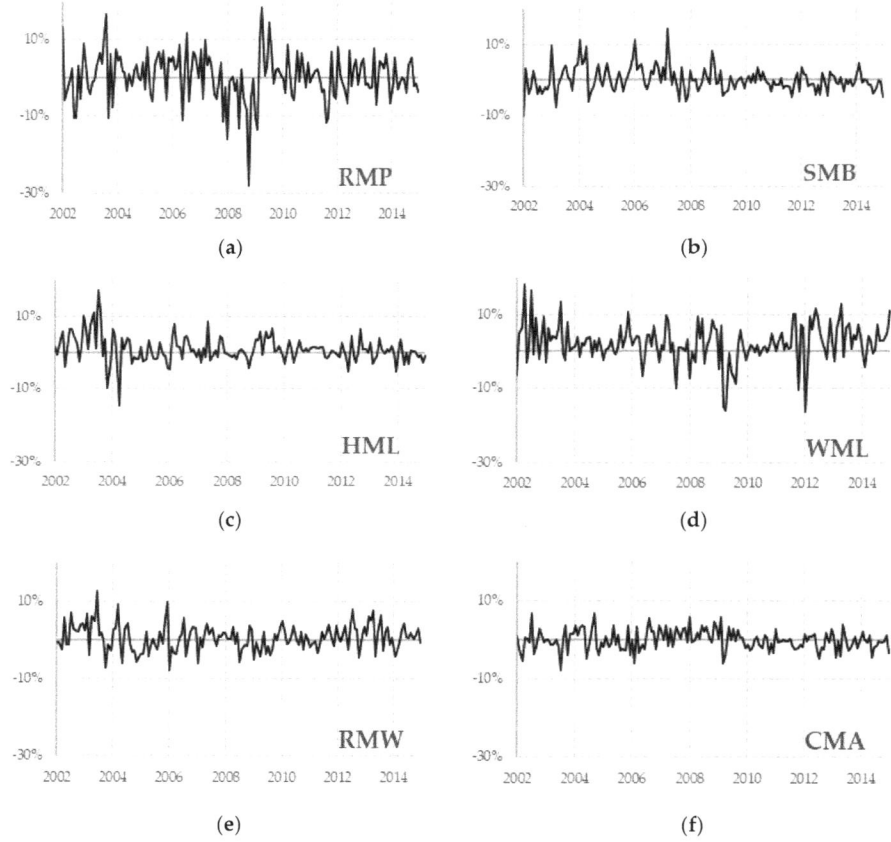

Figure 2. Risk premiums.

Descriptive statistics are detailed in Table 1. Prior to the initial public offering, the sample firms have much lower assets in comparison to other non-financial companies listed on the WSE. While the difference measured with the mean is not so pronounced, the difference in the median values is really huge, as IPO companies were 20 times smaller than already listed non-financial companies. When we look at the median values, IPO firms almost doubled their total assets on average in the year of going public. Significant differences in size between IPO firms and already listed firms are also reported for revenues. IPO companies used the leverage to a similar extent before going public as already listed non-financial companies. However, after additional equity issuance, the leverage of IPO companies dropped substantially. IPO companies were also much more profitable around going public. Net and operating profitability before going public was substantially higher in comparison to average profitability of already listed non-financial companies. A drop in profitability of assets and equity in the year of going public is not a surprise. An additional equity financing received at IPO rarely converted into earnings immediately in the same year and probably had long-term consequence for profitability. The high relative profitability of IPO firms could be a result of high accruals around going public. If earnings are overstated above cash flows, questions about the long-term market implications of around-the-issue earnings manipulation arise.

Table 1. Descriptive statistics.

Company Characteristics		Mean		Median	
		IPO	WSE *	IPO	WSE *
Total assets (mln PLN)	Y-1	757 mln	1.095 mln	66 mln	1.171 mln
Total assets (mln PLN)	Y0	906 mln	1.226 mln	113 mln	1.223 mln
Revenues (mln PLN)	Y-1	544 mln	985 mln	95 mln	995 mln
Revenues (mln PLN)	Y0	635 mln	1.095 mln	124 mln	1.103 mln
Leverage	Y-1	56.1%	55.9%	58.1%	51.6%
Leverage	Y0	39.3%	53.3%	39.4%	51.6%
Return on assets	Y-1	13.0%	3.7%	8.3%	4.8%
Return on assets	Y0	8.6%	4.0%	6.8%	6.5%
Return on equity	Y-1	30.8%	3.0%	22.0%	16.0%
Return on equity	Y0	15.2%	9.2%	11.8%	15.7%
Operating return on assets	Y-1	16.6%	6.7%	11.2%	8.1%
Operating return on assets	Y0	10.6%	6.8%	8.6%	8.2%
Operating return on equity	Y-1	42.7%	10.6%	32.8%	19.2%
Operating return on equity	Y0	19.0%	16.4%	14.9%	19.2%

Note: * only for non-financial companies listed on the Warsaw Stock Exchange.

5. Earnings Manipulation and Calendar-Time Portfolio Returns: Empirical Results

We examine whether the long-term performance of IPOs in Poland differs systematically according to the magnitude of earnings management. We rank IPOs by their abnormal accruals and test long-term market performance. We repeat the multi-step procedure in sixteen alternative methodology settings of the calendar-time portfolio approach.

IPOs are partitioned into accrual quantiles using the median value of discretionary accruals. We use the Jones model, the modified Jones model, the McNichols model, and the Ball–Shivakumar model (Tables 2–5, respectively). Factor regressions are estimated each month for 36-month rolling portfolios in IPO quantiles based on four accrual methods (independently). A low level of abnormal accruals proxies for conservative earnings management (C) and high level of abnormal accruals represents aggressive IPO issuers (A).

Next, we estimate factor regressions on conservative and aggressive accrual IPO quantiles, separately. For robustness, we apply the CAPM model, the Fama-French three-factor model, the Carhart four-factor model, and the Fama-French five-factor model (CAPM, 3FF, 4C, and 5FF, respectively). The dependent variable is a portfolio return in excess of the risk-free rate. Intercepts in calendar-time portfolio regressions for IPO quantiles are interpreted as a monthly measure for long-term abnormal performance. The detailed results of factor regressions according to four models are presented sequentially in four contiguous pairs (for conservative and aggressive IPOs) columns in Panel A of Tables 2–5. The annualized abnormal returns for the conservative and aggressive IPO issuers are illustrated on Figure 3. The results of the estimation of an equivalent regression of the difference in intercepts between the aggressive and conservative IPOs are detailed in Panel B of Tables 2–5.

In this section, we provide robustness check of empirical testing of the relationship between the level of abnormal accruals and the long-term risk-adjusted returns. Intercepts are statistically and economically significant for both low- and high-accrual IPO firms. Both, conservatively and aggressively earnings managed companies experience a relative decline in market value in the long run. Even if the magnitude of IPO long-term underperformance is sensitive to the methodology, it does not change the fact of negative returns in the prevailing number of methodology settings. The intercepts are statistically and economically significant for both low- and high-accrual IPO firms in all of the settings, except for accruals based on the Jones model in the conservative quantile.

Table 2. Calendar-time portfolio regressions according to the Jones model.

	CAPM (C)	CAPM (A)	3FF (C)	3FF (A)	4C (C)	4C (A)	5FF (C)	5FF (A)
Panel A: Calendar-Time Portfolio Regressions for the Conservative and Aggressive Portfolio								
Intercept	−0.006	−0.013 ***	−0.007 *	−0.016 ***	−0.007 *	−0.012 ***	−0.009 **	−0.017 ***
	(−1.566)	(−2.955)	(−1.971)	(−3.954)	(−1.691)	(−2.748)	(−2.439)	(−4.438)
RMP	0.803 ***	0.925 ***	0.774 ***	0.856 ***	0.773 ***	0.821 ***	0.719 ***	0.782 ***
	(13.063)	(13.407)	(13.200)	(13.347)	(12.769)	(12.727)	(12.440)	(12.704)
SBM			0.537 ***	0.581 ***	0.560 ***	0.603 ***	0.699 ***	0.764 ***
			(4.759)	(4.712)	(4.786)	(4.838)	(5.939)	(6.095)
HML			0.190	0.589 ***	0.147	0.470 ***	0.357 **	0.779 ***
			(1.300)	(3.689)	(0.987)	(2.959)	(2.340)	(4.795)
WML					−0.053	−0.221 ***		
					(−0.730)	(−2.844)		
RMW							0.102	0.024
							(0.844)	(0.185)
CMA							−0.528 ***	−0.716 ***
							(−3.458)	(−4.401)
p-value for F	0.000	0.000	0.000	0.000	0.000	0.000	0.000	0.000
adj. R^2	0.588	0.600	0.650	0.678	0.648	0.693	0.684	0.725
Panel B: Equivalent Regressions of the Difference between the Conservative and Aggressive Portfolio Returns								
α(A)−α(C)		−0.007 **		−0.009 **		−0.005		−0.008 **
p-value		0.036		0.012		0.109		0.018

Note: *t*-statistic is in parentheses. *, **, *** indicate significance at the 10, 5, and 1 percent levels, respectively.

Table 3. Calendar-time portfolio regressions for year in quantiles according to the modified Jones model.

	CAPM (C)	CAPM (A)	3FF (C)	3FF (A)	4C (C)	4C (A)	5FF (C)	5FF (A)
Panel A: Calendar-Time Portfolio Regressions for the Conservative and Aggressive Portfolio								
Intercept	−0.007 *	−0.012 ***	−0.008 **	−0.014 ***	−0.007 *	−0.011 **	−0.009 **	−0.016 ***
	(−1.784)	(−2.652)	(−2.215)	(−3.549)	(−1.712)	(−2.513)	(−2.616)	(−4.061)
RMP	0.799 ***	0.942 ***	0.770 ***	0.876 ***	0.760 ***	0.849 ***	0.711 ***	0.806 ***
	(13.071)	(13.573)	(13.171)	(13.504)	(12.694)	(12.846)	(12.403)	(12.828)
SBM			0.529 ***	0.583 ***	0.564 ***	0.598 ***	0.684 ***	0.774 ***
			(4.713)	(4.676)	(4.874)	(4.680)	(5.856)	(6.046)
HML			0.202	0.547 ***	0.144	0.440 ***	0.362 **	0.745 ***
			(1.387)	(3.383)	(0.976)	(2.709)	(2.393)	(4.489)
WML					−0.093	−0.189 **		
					(−1.291)	(−2.367)		
RMW							0.059	0.072
							(0.492)	(0.549)
CMA							−0.564 ***	−0.677 ***
							(−3.718)	(−4.073)
p-value for F	0.000	0.000	0.000	0.000	0.000	0.000	0.000	0.000
adj. R^2	0.588	0.606	0.649	0.678	0.653	0.686	0.686	0.720
Panel B: Equivalent Regressions of the Difference between the Conservative and Aggressive Portfolio Returns								
α(A)−α(C)		−0.005		−0.006 *		−0.004		−0.007 *
p-value		0.109		0.053		0.160		0.053

Note: *t*-statistic is in parentheses. *, **, *** indicate significance at the 10, 5, and 1 percent levels, respectively.

Table 4. Calendar-time portfolio regressions for year in quantiles according to the McNichols model.

	CAPM (C)	CAPM (A)	3FF (C)	3FF (A)	4C (C)	4C (A)	5FF (C)	5FF (A)
Panel A: Calendar-Time Portfolio Regressions for the Conservative and Aggressive Portfolio								
Intercept	−0.009 **	−0.011 **	−0.010 **	−0.013 ***	−0.008 **	−0.010 **	−0.011 ***	−0.015 ***
	(−2.147)	(−2.579)	(−2.602)	(−3.388)	(−2.010)	(−2.463)	(−3.065)	(−4.032)
RMP	0.897 ***	0.827 ***	0.865 ***	0.771 ***	0.853 ***	0.749 ***	0.795 ***	0.710 ***
	(13.995)	(12.905)	(14.025)	(12.749)	(13.478)	(12.139)	(13.342)	(12.103)
SBM			0.533 ***	0.529 ***	0.562 ***	0.549 ***	0.704 ***	0.729 ***
			(4.498)	(4.551)	(4.598)	(4.605)	(5.792)	(6.098)
HML			0.229	0.463 ***	0.163	0.374 **	0.422 ***	0.663 ***
			(1.488)	(3.075)	(1.049)	(2.466)	(2.681)	(4.283)
WML					−0.106	−0.156 **		
					(−1.396)	(−2.105)		
RMW							0.057	0.141
							(0.459)	(1.155)
CMA							−0.678 ***	−0.572 ***
							(−4.304)	(−3.691)
p-value for F	0.000	0.000	0.000	0.000	0.000	0.000	0.000	0.000
adj. R^2	0.621	0.582	0.673	0.652	0.675	0.659	0.716	0.696
Panel B: Equivalent Regressions of the Difference between the Conservative and Aggressive Portfolio Returns								
α(A)−α(C)		−0.002		−0.003		−0.002		−0.003
p-value		0.304		0.212		0.332		0.176

Note: *t*-statistic is in parentheses. *, **, *** indicate significance at the 10, 5, and 1 percent levels, respectively.

Table 5. Calendar-time portfolio regressions for year in quantiles according to the Ball–Shivakumar model.

	CAPM (C)	CAPM (A)	3FF (C)	3FF (A)	4C (C)	4C (A)	5FF (C)	5FF (A)
Panel A: Calendar-time portfolio regressions for the conservative and aggressive portfolio								
Intercept	−0.008 *	−0.012 ***	−0.009 **	−0.015 ***	−0.008 *	−0.012 ***	−0.010 ***	−0.016 ***
	(−1.810)	(−2.953)	(−2.222)	(−3.965)	(−1.737)	(−2.908)	(−2.632)	(−4.526)
RMP	0.851 ***	0.884 ***	0.818 ***	0.822 ***	0.809 ***	0.797 ***	0.750 ***	0.762 ***
	(12.922)	(13.584)	(12.790)	(13.790)	(12.296)	(13.148)	(12.020)	(13.140)
SBM			0.515 ***	0.611 ***	0.543 ***	0.629 ***	0.683 ***	0.794 ***
			(4.186)	(5.334)	(4.276)	(5.375)	(5.371)	(6.718)
HML			0.237	0.511 ***	0.179	0.409 ***	0.428 **	0.683 ***
			(1.488)	(3.441)	(1.106)	(2.742)	(2.594)	(4.460)
WML					−0.092	−0.177 **		
					(−1.163)	(−2.421)		
RMW							0.060	0.095
							(0.462)	(0.787)
CMA							−0.659 ***	−0.565 ***
							(−3.995)	(−3.683)
p-value for F	0.000	0.000	0.000	0.000	0.000	0.000	0.000	0.000
adj. R^2	0.582	0.607	0.632	0.692	0.634	0.700	0.675	0.729
Panel B: Equivalent regressions of the difference between the conservative and aggressive portfolio returns								
α(A)−α(C)		−0.005		−0.006 *		−0.004		−0.006 *
p-value		0.120		0.071		0.173		0.071

Note: *t*-statistic is in parentheses. *, **, *** indicate significance at the 10, 5, and 1 percent levels, respectively.

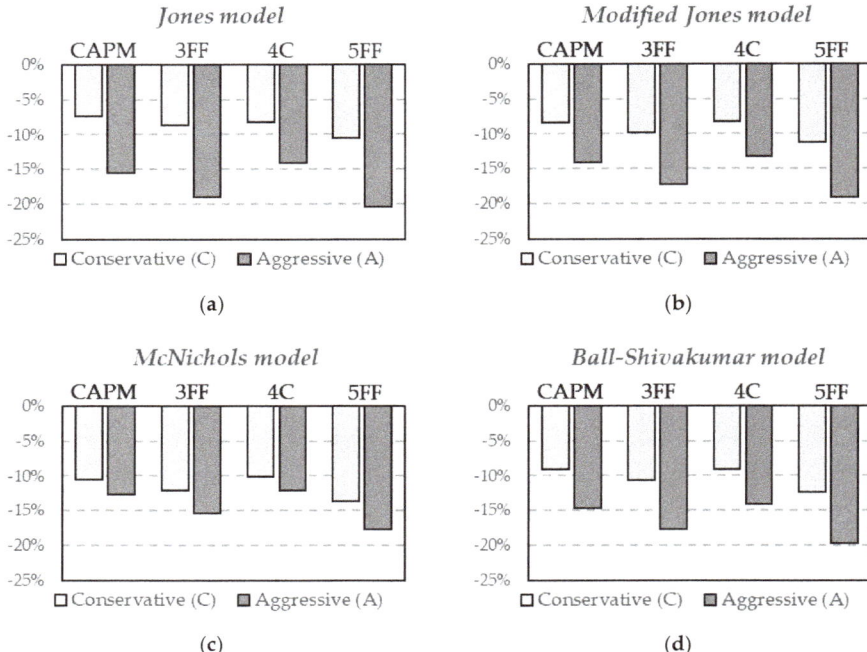

Figure 3. Annualized alphas for conservative and aggressive accrual quantiles according to the Jones model (**a**), the modified Jones model (**b**), the McNichols model (**c**), and the Ball-Shivakumar model (**d**).

More conservative IPO firms outperform more aggressive firms. The average difference between quantiles totals 5.9 percentage points annually and it ranges from 2.0 percentage points annually up to even 10.4 percentage points per year. Conservative IPO firms experience less severe average underperformance in the long-tun proxied with an intercept in factor regression and calendar-time approach. The average annualized intercepts for low-accrual IPOs range from −8.2% up to −13.7% with average underperformance of −10.2%. Otherwise, companies managing their earnings more aggressively report much more negative returns after going public. High-accrual companies earn large negative stock returns. The poor long-term performance of aggressive IPO companies ranges from −12.1% up to as much as −20.5% annually with an average annualized intercept totaling −16.1%. Severe long-term abnormal returns of aggressive IPOs are robust to asset pricing model choices. The difference in the abnormal long-term performance is statistically significant in almost half of 16 methodology settings (four ways of IPOs partitioning based on alternative accrual models and four alternative factor regressions).

6. Discussion of Empirical Results and Future Research

The IPO long-term anomaly and the accrual anomaly have been an important stream of research in financial management. Many previous studies reported that earnings are managed around IPO (Aharony et al. 1993; Friedlan 1994; Teoh and Wong 1997; Teoh et al. 1998a, 1998c). Contrary to that, Ball and Shivakumar (2008) showed that public firms report more conservatively. Armstrong et al. (2015) concluded that IPO companies are not systematically opportunistic. Much of the existing literature reports significant long-term IPO underperformance with some studies dissecting the long-term IPO anomaly with an accrual-based explanation for other, mostly developed, markets. A negative relationship between discretionary accruals and subsequent stock returns was found in several studies (DuCharme et al. 2001; Chan et al. 2001; Xie 2001). Teoh et al. (1998a) found a difference in performance between aggressive and conservative firms and reported that more conservative firms outperformed more aggressive firms in the long-term. They concluded that the long-term returns range from −2.23 percent to +0.94 percent per year for conservative IPOs. For aggressive IPOs, annualized intercepts imply a long-term underperformance of −6.85 percent to −10.73 percent per year. The last study is especially important in discussing our results as it was also based on the calendar-time portfolio approach. However, they tested the issue for US IPOs.

Taking together our results from the broad set of methodology settings, the conclusions about the severe underperformance of aggressive IPOs are consentaneous and robust to methodology. The results on the difference between conservative and aggressive IPOs based on a broad set of robustness checks of the calendar-time portfolio approach seem to support the conclusion about the negative relationship between around-the-issue earnings management and subsequent long-term performance of IPOs. The annualized differences in alphas between conservative and aggressive initial public offerings in Poland are economically significant in all of the cases and they are statistically significant in almost half of 16 methodology settings. However, in some settings the difference is not statistically significant so the evidence on the explanatory power of earnings management for the long-term IPO returns in Poland may be perceived as not undisputable.

The results for Poland may be specific to some extent. First, the sample period includes substantial changes of the capital market. This country has been classified as an emerging market by all of the leading agencies. Just recently, though, Poland has been ranked by FTSE Russell as a developed market. Ongoing improvements in Poland's capital markets infrastructure and steady economic progress were the key points of the decision. Simultaneously, Poland is still perceived as an emerging market by other agencies. Poland is an important area of economic growth in Europe. Poland's economy was the only one in the European Union to avoid a recession through the last global financial crisis from 2008–2009. It has been one of the largest economies in Europe. In the same time, Polish companies' capitalization as well as the number of equities listed on the exchange is much smaller in comparison to US or other developed stock markets.

An important fact is that Poland has different characteristics to other markets. First, a simple comparison to results for emerging markets is difficult because of the process of recent development in Poland. Second, a direct comparison to US-centered research or studies focused on other developed markets is also limited. Finally, one of the key fundamentals of capital market development are corporate governance mechanisms which are crucial for its growth and stability (Brown et al. 2011; Krishnan et al. 2011; Hong et al. 2016). The area of corporate governance and corporate social responsibility as an extension of earnings management problem could be developed in future studies. The research on earnings manipulation around going public could also be broadened by the analysis of the role of insiders and institutional holdings in earnings manipulation around equity issues (Darrough and Rangan 2005; Wu and Yang 2018).

An important and pervasive issue in empirical corporate finance is endogeneity. It is mainly connected with the problem of correlation between explanatory variables and the error term in a regression. We do not apply a traditional regression model with earnings management as an explanatory variable and the subsequent long-term IPO performance as dependent variable. We use a different methodology which tests abnormal returns for IPO quantiles distinguished depending on the level of earnings management. Hence, the methods like instrumental variables, difference-in-difference method, or regression discontinuity design (Roberts and Whited 2005; Li 2016) have no direct application in our study. Another issue is the problem of endogenous events. We follow Dahlquist and Jong (2008) who demonstrate that the calendar-time approach is not biased and does not suffer from the problems of traditional measures of abnormal returns, even in small samples. They also report that it is unlikely that the endogeneity of clustering of IPOs explains the long-term underperformance. The problem of testing endogenous events (not only IPOs) for small capital markets like Warsaw Stock Exchange in Poland, could be developed in a separate study in the future to continue the discussion of Schultz (2003), Viswanathan and Wei (2008), or Ang and Zhang (2015).

The issue of earnings management around initial public offerings is such a broad area of financial management that this study was not able to answer all of the arising questions. Hence, the empirical research could be extended in the future also in another way. One of the challenging directions of future research is connected with real activities manipulation around the date of going public. Influencing the level of abnormal discretionary expenses and sales-based items is an example of real activities manipulation. As the information set about market newcomers is usually limited, testing real activities manipulation is not an easy task, especially for relatively small exchanges and those that have been classified as emerging markets for a long time. There exist studies where the real activities manipulation has been tested in other settings, not especially connected with initial public offerings (Graham et al. 2005; Roychowdhury 2006; Cohen and Zarowin 2010; Kothari et al. 2016). Earnings management through real activities around IPO has been discussed in a limited setting so far (Alhadab and Clacher 2018; Wongsunwai 2013). This study could also be continued by analyzing the trade-off decision between real and accrual-based earnings manipulation (Zang 2012; Kothari et al. 2016). Another contributing research question would be to test whether IPO companies in Poland that managed accruals might have incentives to switch to real activities manipulation activities (Gunny 2010). Possible conclusions based on real activities management around going public would be important for both investors and academics. The possible future research directions connected with empirical testing of real activities management could help shed new light on possible consequences for the long-term market IPO valuation.

7. Conclusions

We provide new evidence on the relationship between around-the-issue earnings management and the long-term performance of initial public offerings (IPO) in Poland. We test this issue with a methodology that has not hitherto been applied for equities listed on the Warsaw Stock Exchange (WSE). The study gives international insights in the area of financial management, where country-specific factors may influence managers' decisions to manipulate earnings.

The results of testing the long-term implications of earnings management are important both for investors and academics. The informativeness of financial reports has always been of a great importance to investors. Earnings quality is an important practical concern during the whole life of companies, but it is of enormous importance around important company events such as going public, when little is usually known about a company. As the information about earnings is key in evaluating the future prospects of a company and determining its value, managers have incentives to manage earnings for that moment. If buyers are misled by artificially inflated earnings, they could pay too high a price at IPO and suffer losses in the long-term when prices adjust to the real value of the market newcomers.

Accrual quantiles are built using a set of alternative proxies of earnings management. The industry-year cross-sectional regressions are run for each IPO according to four models: the Jones model, the modified Jones model, the McNichols model, and Ball–Shivakumar model. The long-term performance is tested in 36-month rolling IPO portfolios under four asset pricing models: the CAPM, the Fama-French three-factor model, the Carhart four-factor model, and the Fama-French five-factor model. The magnitude of IPO negative returns is sensitive to the methodology, but this does not change the conclusions about long-term IPO underperformance. Both conservative and aggressive companies experience a relative decline in market value in the long run. However, we report more severe long-term performance for accrual-aggressive IPO issuers, as the annualized abnormal returns range from -12.1% up to even -20.5%, whereas the span is -8.2% to -13.7% for conservative IPO companies. The average annualized intercepts for low-accrual IPOs is -10.2%. The poor long-term performance of aggressive IPO companies is much more pronounced, as the average annualized intercept totals -16.1%. This results for accrual quantiles are robust with respect to alternative accrual model specifications, and to alternative abnormal returns measures based on a set of factor models. The average difference in returns between quantiles totals 5.9 percentage points annually, and ranges from 2.0 percentage points annually even up to 10.4 percentage points. Aggressive IPO companies experience more negative abnormal returns and this difference is economically significant in all of the cases. It is also statistically significant in almost half of methodology settings. The interpretation of such results could be as follows. Investors were not able to discount the pre-IPO use of abnormal accruals. Following this, they were overoptimistic about the future prospects of the company. Once the true earnings performance is revealed over the course of time, they make downward price corrections resulting in the negative long-term performance.

Author Contributions: The authors contributed equally to the research and writing of the manuscript.

Funding: Financial support for this paper from the National Science Centre, Poland is gratefully acknowledged (the number of the research project 2015/19/D/HS4/01950).

Acknowledgments: We would like to thank three anonymous referees.

Conflicts of Interest: The authors declare no conflict of interest. The funders had no role in the design of the study; in the collection, analyses, or interpretation of data; in the writing of the manuscript, or in the decision to publish the results.

References

Aharony, Joseph, Chan-Jane Lin, and Martin P. Loeb. 1993. Initial Public Offerings, Accounting Choices, and Earnings Management. *Contemporary Accounting Research* 10: 61–81. [CrossRef]

Ahmad-Zaluki, Nurwati A., Kevin Campbell, and Alan Goodacre. 2011. Earnings management in Malaysian IPOs: The East Asian crisis, ownership control, and post-IPO performance. *International Journal of Accounting* 46: 111–37. [CrossRef]

Alhadab, Mohammad, and Iain Clacher. 2018. The impact of audit quality on real and accrual earnings management around IPOs. *British Accounting Review* 50: 442–61. [CrossRef]

Ang, James S., and Shaojun Zhang. 2015. Evaluating Long-Horizon Event Study Methodology. In *Handbook of Financial Econometrics and Statistics*. Edited by Cheng-Few Lee and John C. Lee. New York: Springer, pp. 383–411.

Armstrong, Chris, George Foster, and Daniel J. Taylor. 2015. Abnormal accruals in newly public companies: Opportunistic misreporting or economic activity? *Management Science* 62: 1316–38. [CrossRef]

Ball, Ray, and Lakshmanan Shivakumar. 2005. Earnings quality in UK private firms: Comparative loss recognition timeliness. *Journal of Accounting and Economics* 39: 83–128. [CrossRef]

Ball, Ray, and Lakshmanan Shivakumar. 2006. The Role of Accruals in Asymmetrically Timely Gain and Loss Recognition. *Journal of Accounting Research* 44: 207–42. [CrossRef]

Ball, Ray, and Lakshmanan Shivakumar. 2008. Earnings quality at initial public offerings. *Journal of Accounting and Economics* 45: 324–49. [CrossRef]

Barber, Brad M., and John D. Lyon. 1997. Detecting long-run abnormal stock returns: The empirical power and specification of test statistics. *Journal of Financial Economics* 43: 341–72. [CrossRef]

Beneish, Messod D. 1998. Discussion of "Are accruals during initial public offerings opportunistic?". *Review of Accounting Studies* 3: 209–21. [CrossRef]

Brown, Philip, Wendy Beekes, and Peter Verhoeven. 2011. Corporate governance, accounting and finance: A review. *Accounting & Finance* 51: 96–172. [CrossRef]

Carhart, Mark M. 1997. On Persistence in Mutual Fund Performance. *Journal of Finance* 52: 57–82. [CrossRef]

Chan, Konan, Louis K. Chan, Narasimhan Jegadeesh, and Josef Lakonishok. 2001. Earnings quality and stock returns. *National Bureau of Economic Research*. [CrossRef]

Chen, Ken Y., Kuen-Lin Lin, and Jian Zhou. 2005. Audit quality and earnings management for Taiwan IPO firms. *Managerial Auditing Journal* 20: 86–104. [CrossRef]

Cohen, Daniel A., and Paul Zarowin. 2010. Accrual-based and real earnings management activities around seasoned equity offerings. *Journal of Accounting and Economics* 50: 2–19. [CrossRef]

Dahlquist, Magnus, and Frank de Jong. 2008. Pseudo Market Timing: A Reappraisal. *Journal of Financial and Quantitative Analysis* 43: 547. [CrossRef]

Darrough, Masako, and Srinivasan Rangan. 2005. Do Insiders Manipulate Earnings When They Sell Their Shares in an Initial Public Offering? *Journal of Accounting Research* 43: 1–33. [CrossRef]

Dechow, Patricia M., and Ilia D. Dichev. 2002. The Quality of Accruals and Earnings: The Role of Accrual Estimation Errors. *Accounting Review* 77: 35–59. [CrossRef]

Dechow, Patricia M., Richard G. Sloan, and Amy P. Sweeney. 1995. Detecting Earnings Management. *Accounting Review* 70: 193–225. Available online: http://www.jstor.org/stable/248303 (accessed on 16 May 2015).

DeFond, Mark L., and James Jiambalvo. 1994. Debt covenant violation and manipulation of accruals. *Journal of Accounting and Economics* 17: 145–76. [CrossRef]

DuCharme, Larry L., Paul H. Malatesta, and Stephan E. Sefcik. 2001. Earnings Management: IPO Valuation and Subsequent Performance. *Journal of Accounting, Auditing & Finance* 16: 369–96. [CrossRef]

Fama, Eugene F. 1998. Market efficiency, long-term returns, and behavioral finance. *Journal of Financial Economics* 49: 283–306. [CrossRef]

Fama, Eugene F., and Kenneth R. French. 1993. Common risk factors in the returns on stocks and bonds. *Journal of Financial Economics* 33: 3–56. [CrossRef]

Fama, Eugene F., and Kenneth R. French. 2015. A five-factor asset pricing model. *Journal of Financial Economics* 116: 1–22. [CrossRef]

Fama, Eugene F., and Kenneth R. French. 2016. Dissecting Anomalies with a Five-Factor Model. *Review of Financial Studies* 29: 69–103. [CrossRef]

Friedlan, John M. 1994. Accounting Choices of Issuers of Initial Public Offerings. *Contemporary Accounting Research* 11: 1–31. [CrossRef]

Gaver, Jennifer J., Kenneth M. Gaver, and Jeffrey R. Austin. 1995. Additional evidence on bonus plans and income management. *Journal of Accounting and Economics* 19: 3–28. [CrossRef]

Graham, John R., Campbell R. Harvey, and Shiva Rajgopal. 2005. The economic implications of corporate financial reporting. *Journal of Accounting and Economics* 40: 3–73. [CrossRef]

Gunny, Katherine A. 2010. The Relation Between Earnings Management Using Real Activities Manipulation and Future Performance: Evidence from Meeting Earnings Benchmarks. *Contemporary Accounting Research* 27: 855–88. [CrossRef]

Healy, Paul M. 1985. The effect of bonus schemes on accounting decisions. *Journal of Accounting and Economics* 7: 85–107. [CrossRef]

Holthausen, Robert W., David F. Larcker, and Richard G. Sloan. 1995. Annual bonus schemes and the manipulation of earnings. *Journal of Accounting and Economics* 19: 29–74. [CrossRef]

Hong, Bryan, Zhichuan Li, and Dylan Minor. 2016. Corporate Governance and Executive Compensation for Corporate Social Responsibility. *Journal of Business Ethics* 136: 199–213. [CrossRef]

Jegadeesh, Narasimhan, and Jason Karceski. 2009. Long-run performance evaluation: Correlation and heteroskedasticity-consistent tests. *Journal of Empirical Finance* 16: 101–11. [CrossRef]

Jones, Jennifer J. 1991. Earnings Management During Import Relief Investigations. *Journal of Accounting Research* 29: 193–228. [CrossRef]

Kothari, Stephen P., Natalie Mizik, and Sugata Roychowdhury. 2016. Managing for the Moment: The Role of Earnings Management via Real Activities versus Accruals in SEO Valuation. *Accounting Review* 91: 559–86. [CrossRef]

Krishnan, C. N. V., Vladimir I. Ivanov, Ronald W. Masulis, and Ajai K. Singh. 2011. Venture Capital Reputation, Post-IPO Performance, and Corporate Governance. *Journal of Financial and Quantitative Analysis* 46: 1295–333. [CrossRef]

Li, Frank. 2016. Endogeneity in CEO power: A survey and experiment. *Investment Analysts Journal* 45: 149–62. [CrossRef]

Liberty, Susan E., and Jerold L. Zimmerman. 1986. Labor union contract negotiations and accounting choices. *Accounting Review* 61: 692–712.

Lintner, John. 1969. The Valuation of Risk Assets and the Selection of Risky Investments in Stock Portfolios and Capital Budgets: A Reply. *The Review of Economics and Statistics* 51: 222–24. [CrossRef]

Lizińska, Joanna, and Leszek Czapiewski. 2018a. Earnings Management and the Long-Term Market Performance of Initial Public Offerings in Poland. In *Finance and Sustainability: Proceedings from the Finance and Sustainability Conference, Wroclaw 2017*. Edited by Agnieszka Bem, Karolina Daszyńska-Żygadło, Taťána Hajdíková and Péter Juhász. Springer Proceedings in Business and Economics. Cham: Springer International Publishing, vol. 62, pp. 121–34.

Lizińska, Joanna, and Leszek Czapiewski. 2018b. Towards Economic Corporate Sustainability in Reporting: What Does Earnings Management around Equity Offerings Mean for Long-Term Performance? *Sustainability* 10: 4349. [CrossRef]

Lyon, John D., Brad M. Barber, and Chih-Ling Tsai. 1999. Improved Methods for Tests of Long-Run Abnormal Stock Returns. *Journal of Finance* 54: 165–201. [CrossRef]

McNichols, Maureen F. 2000. Research design issues in earnings management studies. *Journal of Accounting and Public Policy* 19: 313–45. [CrossRef]

McNichols, Maureen F., and G. Peter Wilson. 1988. Evidence of Earnings Management from the Provision for Bad Debts. *Journal of Accounting Research* 26: 1. [CrossRef]

Pastor-Llorca, María J., and Francisco Poveda-Fuentes. 2011. Earnings Management and the Long-Run Performance of Spanish Initial Public Offerings. In *Initial Public Offerings (IPO): An International Perspective of IPOs*. Edited by Greg N. Gregoriou. Quantitative Finance. Burlington: Elsevier Science, pp. 81–112.

Perry, Susan E., and Thomas H. Williams. 1994. Earnings management preceding management buyout offers. *Journal of Accounting and Economics* 18: 157–79. [CrossRef]

Pourciau, Susan. 1993. Earnings management and nonroutine executive changes. *Journal of Accounting and Economics* 16: 317–36. [CrossRef]

Roberts, Michael R., and Toni M. Whited. 2005. Endogeneity in empirical corporate finance. *Handbook of the Economics of Finance* 2: 493–572. [CrossRef]

Ronen, Joshua, and Varda Yaari. 2008. *Earnings Management: Emerging Insights in Theory, Practice, and Research*. Springer Series in Accounting Scholarship. New York: Springer.

Roosenboom, Peter, Tjalling van der Goot, and Gerard Mertens. 2003. Earnings management and initial public offerings: Evidence from the Netherlands. *International Journal of Accounting* 38: 243–66. [CrossRef]

Roychowdhury, Sugata. 2006. Earnings management through real activities manipulation. *Journal of Accounting and Economics* 42: 335–70. [CrossRef]

Schultz, Paul. 2003. Pseudo Market Timing and the Long-Run Underperformance of IPOs. *Journal of Finance* 58: 483–517. [CrossRef]

Sharpe, William F. 1964. Capital asset prices: A theory of market equilibrium under conditions of risk. *Journal of Finance* 19: 425–42. [CrossRef]

Sloan, Richard G. 1996. Do stock prices fully reflect information in accruals and cash flows about future earnings? *Accounting Review* 71: 289–315.

Teoh, Siew Hong, Ivo Welch, and Tak J. Wong. 1998a. Earnings Management and the Long-Run Market Performance of Initial Public Offerings. *Journal of Finance* 53: 1935–74. [CrossRef]

Teoh, Siew Hong, Ivo Welch, and Tak J. Wong. 1998b. Earnings management and the underperformance of seasoned equity offerings. *Journal of Financial Economics* 50: 63–99. [CrossRef]

Teoh, Siew Hong, Tak J. Wong, and Gita R. Rao. 1998c. Are Accruals during Initial Public Offerings Opportunistic? *Review of Accounting Studies* 3: 175–208. [CrossRef]

Teoh, Siew Hong, and Tak J. Wong. 1997. Analysts' Credulity about Reported Earnings and Overoptimism in New Equity Issues. *SSRN Electronic Journal*. [CrossRef]

Viswanathan, S., and Bin Wei. 2008. Endogenous Events and Long-Run Returns. *Review of Financial Studies* 21: 855–88. [CrossRef]

Wongsunwai, Wan. 2013. The Effect of External Monitoring on Accrual-Based and Real Earnings Management: Evidence from Venture-Backed Initial Public Offerings. *Contemporary Accounting Research* 30: 296–324. [CrossRef]

Wu, Ching-Chih, and Tung-Hsiao Yang. 2018. Insider Trading and Institutional Holdings in Seasoned Equity Offerings. *Journal of Risk and Financial Management* 11: 53. [CrossRef]

Xie, Hong. 2001. The Mispricing of Abnormal Accruals. *Accounting Review* 76: 357–73. [CrossRef]

Zang, Amy Y. 2012. Evidence on the Trade-Off between Real Activities Manipulation and Accrual-Based Earnings Management. *Accounting Review* 87: 675–703. [CrossRef]

Article

Effect of Corporate Governance on Institutional Investors' Preferences: An Empirical Investigation in Taiwan

Su-Lien Lu [1,*] and Ying-Hui Li [2]

[1] International Bachelor Degree Program in Finance, National Pingtung University of Science and Technology, Neipu Pingtung 912, Taiwan
[2] Graduate Institute of Finance, National Pingtung University of Science and Technology, Neipu Pingtung 912, Taiwan; lydia@mail.npust.edu.tw
* Correspondence: lotus-lynn@mail.npust.edu.tw

Received: 31 December 2018; Accepted: 10 February 2019; Published: 14 February 2019

Abstract: This study discusses the institutional investors' shareholding base on corporate governance system in Taiwan. The sample was 4760 Taiwanese companies from 2005 to 2012. Then, this study established six hypotheses to investigate the effects of corporate governance on institutional investors' shareholdings. The panel data regression model and piecewise regression model were adopted to determine whether six hypotheses are supported. For sensitive analysis, additional consideration was given on the basis of industrial category (electronics or nonelectronics), and the 2008–2010 global financial crises. This study discovered that a nonlinear relationship exists between the domestic institutional investors' shareholdings. The managerial ownership ratio and blockholder ownership ratio have positive effects both on domestic and foreign institutional investors. However, domestic and foreign institutional investors have distinct opinions regarding independent director ratios. Finally, the corporate governance did not improve institutional investors' shareholdings during financial crisis periods; instead, they paid more attention to firm profits or other characteristics.

Keywords: institutional investors' shareholdings; panel data model; piecewise regression model; global financial crisis

---

1. Introduction

The Cadbury Report (Cadbury 1992) was first produced by the Committee on the Financial Aspects of Corporate Governance (Cadbury Committee), which provided the definition of corporate governance as the "system by which companies are directed and controlled", voluntary adoption of the governance best practices and the "comply or explain" principle (Shan and Napier 2014). The Cadbury Report (Cadbury 1992) has proven important influences on development of corporate governance codes worldwide.

The 1997 Asian financial crisis severely affected the economies of Southeast Asia because of the exit of foreign capital after property assets collapsed; this was a consequence of the lack of corporate governance mechanisms in these countries. After the 1997 financial crisis in Asia, there are series of corporate fraud cases and distressed debt broke out in Taiwan. The Taiwanese government has been propagating the importance of corporate government to corporations since 1998.

In the United States, the 2001 Enron and Xerox cases led Congress to legislate the Sarbanes–Oxley Act to reinforce corporate governance in the United States. Therefore, corporate governance has become a crucial subject garnering increased political interest. The passing of the law restored the accuracy and reliability of financial information and established a series of requirements that affected U.S. corporate governance and influenced similar laws in multiple countries, including Taiwan.

In 2006, Taiwanese government were legislated the Company Law and Securities and Exchange Act to empower corporate governance principles. Company Law is the regulation for corporate governance, including the operations of shareholders' meetings, board of directors and supervisors. On 11 January 2006, amendments to the Securities and Exchange Act were announced independent directors and audit committees as well as to strength the function, structure and operations of a company's board of directors.

In 1999, the World Bank stated that corporate governance comprises internal and external aspects. Internal corporate governance, which involves monitoring activities and then taking corrective action to accomplish organizational goals, facilitates internal monitoring by the board of directors. By contrast, external corporate governance involves externally monitoring manager behavior by including an independent third party (i.e., an external auditor). Thus, corporate governance is a system of law and sound approaches by which corporations are directed and controlled, focusing on internal and external corporate structures to monitor the actions of management and directors.

Jensen and Meckling (1976) discussed conflicts of interest between various contracting parties, including shareholders, corporate managers and debt holders. They found that agency costs generated by the existence of debt and outside equity, which is the sum of monitoring costs, bonding costs and residual loss. Fama and Jensen (1983) indicated corporate governance mechanisms are designed to reduce inefficiencies and eliminate agency costs.

Traditionally, institutional investors are passive owners and their growth will weaken governance and exacerbate agency problems (Bebchuk et al. 2017). However, institutional investors are active owners through proxy voting and behind-the-scenes engagement with management (Carleton et al. 1998; McCahery et al. 2016; Appel et al. 2016). Thus, institutional investors with widespread holdings may benefit firms.

Aggarwal et al. (2005) suggested that obtaining high-quality accounting information enables foreign investors to monitor and protect their investments and efficiently allocate capital. La Porta et al. (1997, 1998, 2000) indicated the necessity for strong investor protection laws and improved corporate governance mechanisms that protect and attract outside investors. Elsewhere, Leuz et al. (2003) discovered that the quality of the information available for outside investors is also high in countries with strong investor protection laws; thus, the implementation of improved corporate governance mechanisms can attract institutional investors.

A substantial amount of research has explored the influence of corporate governance attributes on corporate performance and has suggested that corporate governance variables significantly influence firm performance. However, the relationship between corporate governance attributes and the investment preferences of institutional investors has seldom been discussed. This study contributes to the literature by analyzing the relationship between the shareholding preferences of institutional investors and corporate governance. This study establishes six hypotheses to investigate the shareholding preferences of domestic and foreign institutional investors based on corporate governance mechanisms, including managerial ownership, independent directors, blockholder ownership, pledge stock ratios and CEO duality. Then, the panel data regression model and piecewise regression model are used to determine whether these hyphotheses are supported. The empirical results reveal that corporate governance variables have dissimilar effects on the investment preferences of domestic and foreign institutional investors, such as independent director ratio and pledge stock ratio. Moreover, a nonlinear relationship exists between the shareholding preferences of institutional investors and managerial ownership.

The remainder of this paper is organized as follows: Section 2 provides empirical designs, including hypotheses and definition of variables; Section 3 describes the details of the model, Section 4 describes the data sample; Section 5 presents an analysis of the empirical results, and Section 6 presents our conclusion.

2. Empirical Design

2.1. Hypotheses Development

Jensen and Meckling (1976) argued that managers are incentivized to seek pecuniary and nonpecuniary benefits at the expense of shareholder wealth. Managers divert progressively fewer firm resources to nonvalue-maximizing activities when their equity stakes increase, because they must bear an increasing fraction of agency costs associated with their expropriation activities. Therefore, managerial ownership may affect firm performance, which affects the shareholding preferences of institutional investors. This study infers that managerial ownership has a positive relation with institutional investors' shareholdings and establishes Hypothesis 1 as follows.

Hypothesis 1 (H1): *The larger managerial ownership ratio, the higher institutional investors' shareholdings.*

However, the correlation between managerial ownership and firm performance is inconsistent. McConnell and Servaes (1990); Keasey et al. (1994) and Chen (2006) have all reported a bell-shaped relationship between managerial ownership and firm performance. Conversely, Morck et al. (1988); Hermalin and Weisbach (1991); Mudambi and Nicosia (1998); Griffith (1999); Short and Keasey (1999); De Miguel et al. (2004); Florackis (2005) and Mura (2007) have observed a cubic relationship. Davies et al. (2005) and Florackis et al. (2009) have reported a quintic relationship. As a result, there is a nonlinear relationship between managerial ownership and institutional investors' shareholdings and Hypothesis 2 was formulated as follows:

Hypothesis 2 (H2): *The relationship between managerial ownership ratio and institutional investors' shareholdings is nonlinear.*

The shareholding structure of a company can be divided into two categories, blockholder and nonblockholder, based on the percentage of shares owned. Because a high proportion of blockholder ownership provides an excellent opportunity for management to optimize the company value, blockholder ownership may affect the participation of institutional investors. Driffield et al. (2007) revealed that the effects of blockholder ownership on company value are significant and positive in four East Asian countries. However, several studies have suggested that high blockholder ownership may divert management action and harm minority shareholders; for example, Morck et al. (1988); Prowse (1993); Shleifer and Vishny (1997) and Minguez-Vera and Martin-Ugedo (2007) have determined that blockholder effects tend to be negatively associated with firm performance. In summary, this study inferred that the higher blockholder ownership, the higher the institutional investors' shareholdings. Hypothesis 3 was established as follows.

Hypothesis 3 (H3): *The higher blockholder ownership ratio, the greater institutional investors' shareholdings.*

The accounting scandals occurred primarily because of financial reporting fraud, including nondisclosure and deliberate falsification. To reduce this risk and enhance the perceived integrity of financial reports, the financial reports of a corporation must be audited by an independent external auditor, who issues a report that accompanies the financial statements. A board includes internal and external directors. Fama and Jensen (1983) asserted that internal directors are likely to collude with managers and make decisions against shareholders by exploiting their superior position and the information that they can access. By contrast, external directors act as supervisors to eliminate problems because of their neutral position. Beasley (1996) demonstrated that firms with independent directors have low scandal rates. If outside directors are independent and professionally capable, they can objectively make decisions and effectively monitor managers. Weisbach (1988), Rosenstein and Wyatt (1997) and Huson et al. (2001) have all reported that if a high ratio of independent directors are hired, firm performance improves. Thus, Hypothesis 4 was formulated as follows:

Hypothesis 4 (H4): *The higher independent directors ratio, the higher institutional investors' shareholdings.*

Generally, directors can collateralize their shares and further purchase stocks to manipulate stock prices or enhance their power. Because the collateralized shares are closely related to share prices, the value of the collateralized shares depreciates when share prices slump. Consequently, shareholders who collateralize their shares may prey on small shareholders or hurt the company. Kao et al. (2004) revealed that financial distress is closely related to high share ratios pledged by directors. Yeh and Lee (2002) indicated that the higher the ratio of collateralized shares, the less favorable the firm's performance. Additionally, Chiou et al. (2002) discovered that if the proportion of shares collateralized by a board of directors is high, the directors may be distracted from operating the business (because the fluctuation of stock prices is closely related to their finances), which leads to poor firm performance. Therefore, Hypothesis 5 was formulated as follows:

Hypothesis 5 (H5): *The higher the collateralized shares by directors, the lower institutional investor' shareholdings.*

The CEO is simultaneously the chairperson of the board, a practice that is common in the United States. From 1999 to 2003, a dual CEO leadership structure was applied in multiple firms that originally comprised nondual structures. This trend partially stemmed from several high-profile cases involving companies with dual CEO structures. However, the empirical evidence is inconsistent regarding which leadership structure is more beneficial for firm performance. For example, Fama and Jensen (1983) and Jensen (1993) have reported that CEO duality may increase the expenses of an agency because the ability of the board is hindered. Moreover, the weakening of a board's ability to minimize the expenses of an agency can result in poor corporate performance (Jensen and Meckling 1976; Fama and Jensen 1983; Patton and Baker 1987). Daily and Dalton (1993); Pi and Timme (1993) and Dahya et al. (1996) have all similarly suggested that CEO duality negatively affects the performance of a firm. However, U.S. regulators and investors are increasingly recommending against the separation of CEO and chairperson duties. Stoeberl and Sherony (1985) have suggested that dividing CEO and chairperson of the board duties may increase information-sharing costs, which can increase the communication costs of firm-specific information, decision-making processes, and other activities that are already inefficient. Assigning blame for poor company performance may also be more difficult with two leaders than when there is only one. In the United Kingdom, Dahya et al. (2009) argued that the separation of CEO and chairperson of the board duties cannot improve firm performance. Elsewhere, Boyd (1995) and Dahya and Travlos (2000) have documented a positive association between CEO duality and firm performance. Although the specific effects remain unknown, it is clear that CEO duality influences firm performance, which affects the shareholdings of institutional investors. Accordingly, Hypothesis 6 were formulated as follows:

Hypothesis 6 (H6): *The higher CEO duality, the lower institutional investors' shareholdings.*

2.2. Variables Definitions

The shareholding preference of institutional investors (RELWEIGHT) was measured by the weight of their shareholding relative to their weight in the market. According to Zhang et al. (2009), the shareholding preference of institutional investors can be presented as:

$$RELWEIGHT_{it}^{j} = \frac{W_{it}^{F,j} - W_{it}^{M}}{W_{it}^{M}}, \, j = 1, 2; i = 1, \ldots, N; t = 1, \ldots, T \tag{1}$$

where $j = 1$ and $j = 2$ represent domestic and foreign institutional investors, respectively; i denotes the firm; t is the sample period from January 2005 to December 2012; and W_{it}^{M} is the weight of firm i in the market in period t. The expression $W_{it}^{F,j}$ is the ratio of institutional investors' shareholdings for firm i in the market, and is defined by Zhang et al. (2009) as:

$$W_{it}^{F,j} = \frac{INSTU_{it}^{j} \times MV_{it}}{\sum_{i=1}^{N} INSTU_{it}^{j} \times MV_{it}} \tag{2}$$

where $INSTU_{it}^{j}$ is the ratio of domestic or foreign shareholding of firm i in period t, and MV_{it} is the market value of firm i in period t.

3. Model

The data presented in this paper include time series and cross-sectional data that constitute a panel data model that refers to data sets consisting of multiple observations on each sampling unit. Panel data analysis was applied to investigate the investment preferences of domestic and foreign investors; this study also applied traditional ordinary least squares (OLS) for comparison.

Because the effects of managerial ownership on corporate performance represent a nonlinear relationship, managerial ownership and institutional investors' shareholdings may also be in a nonlinear relationship. Therefore, this paper establishes two models. The first is constructed by assuming a linear relationship between investment preference and managerial ownership, whereas the second model is a piecewise regression model constructed by assuming that three cutting points exist in a managerial ownership ratio. The first regression model is presented as

$$
\begin{aligned}
REALWEIGHT_{i,t}^{j} \\
= \beta_0 + \beta_1 MANAGER_{i,t-1} + \beta_3 INDEP_{i,t-1} + \beta_4 PLEDGE_{i,t-1} \\
+ \beta_5 DUAL_{i,t-1} + \beta_6 LNTA_{i,t-1} + \beta_7 SYSTEMRISK_{i,t-1} + \beta_8 EPS_{i,t-1} \\
+ \nu_t
\end{aligned}
\tag{3}
$$

where

RELWEIGHT: institutional investors' shareholdings.

$MANAGER_{i,t-1}$: managerial ownership ratio of firm i in period $t-1$.

$BLOCK_{i,t-1}$: blockholder ownership of firm i in period $t-1$. This variable is measured by percentage in the top 5% by individual holding company and nonindividual nonholding company.

$INDEP_{i,t-1}$: independent director ratio of firm i in period $t-1$.

$PLEDGE_{i,t-1}$: pledge stock ratio of firm i in period $t-1$.

$DUAL_{i,t-1}$: a dummy variable to measure whether the CEO is the chair of the board. This variable is equal to 1 if the CEO is also the chair of the board; otherwise, it is 0.

$LNTA_{i,t-1}$: the firm scale of firm i in period $t-1$, which is measured by taking the natural log of total assets.

$SYSTEMRISK_{i,t-1}$: the system risk of firm i in period $t-1$.

$EPS_{i,t-1}$: earning per share of firm i in period $t-1$. This variable is measured as

EPS = (Net Income − Preferred Dividends)/Weighted Average Number of Common Shares Outstanding

Notably, Equation (3) has three control variables: LNTA, SYSTEMRISK, and EPS. LNTA is the natural log of total assets that is used to control the influence of firm scale measures on the shareholding preferences of institutional investors (Falkenstein 1996; Choe et al. 1999; Dahlquist and Robertsson 2001; Gompers and Metrick 2001; Ng and Wang 2004). EPS is the proxy of firm performance used to control the influence of firm performance measures on the shareholding preferences of institutional investors (Faccio and Lasfer 1999). Finally, SYSTEMRISK is the market risk of sample firms, used to control the influence of market risk measures on the shareholding preferences of institutional investors (Li 2002; Cao et al. 2007).

Morck et al. (1988) have demonstrated that managerial ownership is a crucial factor in regression analyses of firm performance. However, Morck et al. (1988); McConnell and Servaes (1990) and Holderness et al. (1999) have all discovered a substantial, inverse U-shaped relationship between managerial ownership and firm performance. Therefore, we considered managerial ownership to be crucial and nonmonotonical when evaluating the shareholdings of institutional investors. On the basis of Davies et al. (2005) and Zhang et al. (2009), we subsequently modified Equation (3) to a piecewise regression model as follows:

$$
\begin{aligned}
RELWEIGHT_{i,t}^{j} \\
= \beta_0 + \beta_1 MANAGER_{i,t-1} \\
+ \beta_2 (MANAGER_{i,t-1} - 10\%) \times a_1 \\
+ \beta_3 (MANAGER_{i,t-1} - 20\%) \times a_2 \\
+ \beta_4 (MANAGER_{i,t-1} - 30\%) \times a_3 + \beta_5 BLOCK_{i,t-1} \\
+ \beta_6 INDEP_{i,t-1} + \beta_7 PLEDGE_{i,t-1} + \beta_8 DUAL_{i,t-1} \\
+ \beta_9 LNTA_{i,t-1} + \beta_{10} SYSTEMRISK_{i,t-1} + \beta_{11} EPS_{i,t-1} \\
+ \nu_t
\end{aligned}
\tag{4}
$$

where

$$
a_1 = \begin{cases} 1, & if \ MANAGER_{i,t-1} \geq 10\% \\ 0, & if \ MANAGER_{i,t-1} < 10\% \end{cases}
$$

$$
a_2 = \begin{cases} 1, & if \ MANAGER_{i,t-1} \geq 20\% \\ 0, & if \ MANAGER_{i,t-1} < 20\% \end{cases}
$$

$$
a_3 = \begin{cases} 1, & if \ MANAGER_{i,t-1} \geq 30\% \\ 0, & if \ MANAGER_{i,t-1} < 30\% \end{cases}
$$

The definitions of other variables are defined in Equation (3).

4. Data

For the sample period from January 2005 to December 2012, this study collected 4760 samples from 18 industries selected from among Taiwan's listed companies.[1] The sample period include the 2007–2008 global financial crisis and apply the subsample period for sensitive analysis. These monthly data obtained from the Taiwan Economic Journal (TEJ). However, this study excluded several industries, such as the financial and security industries, because of the sensitive nature of their business; incomplete data were also excluded.

5. Empirical Results and Analysis

5.1. Descriptive Statistics

Table 1 presents the descriptive statistics of the institutional investors' shareholdings, corporate variables and control variables. The mean of the managerial ownership ratio was 22.89%. However, the maximal value of the managerial ownership ratio was 89.24%, which was observed in the electronics

---

[1] According to regulatory framework of corporate governance, which is shown by corporate governance center of Taiwan Stock Exchange, the Taiwan Stock Exchange (TWSE) and Taipei Exchange (TPEx) specified their criteria for the review of securities listings in 2002. "An IPO company must set up an independent director and meet certain qualifications. Furthermore, regulations, such as 'Corporate Governance Best Practice Principles', 'Code of Practice for Corporate Social Responsibility', and 'Code of Practice for Integrity Management' were subsequently announced for domestic enterprises to follow. These will guide enterprises in strengthening their sense of corporate governance and social responsibility, establishing a consensus on integrity management, constructing a corporate governance culture, and creating mutual values." (http://cgc.twse.com.tw/).

industry. The average of the independent director ratio was 7.77%, and the maximum and minimum were 60% and 0%, respectively. The Taiwanese corporate governance law of 2006 mandated that a public limited company must have a board of directors with at least three directors and two supervisors.[2] The listing regulations stipulate that a company applying for listing for the first time must have no fewer than five directors and must reserve certain positions for independent directors and supervisors.[3] Because the law was enacted in 2006, several sample firms were not affected by the law and the minimum of the independent director shareholdings ratio was 0%.

Table 1. Descriptive statistics.

Variable		Mean	Median	Standard Deviation	Minimum	Maximum
RELWEIGHT	Domestic	−0.069	−0.186	0.607	−1.000	2.667
	Foreign	−0.440	−0.620	0.563	−1.000	2.667
MANAGER (%)		22.892	19.940	13.597	0.000	89.240
BLOCK (%)		19.565	17.600	11.849	0.000	69.66
INDEP (%)		7.765	0.000	13.865	0.000	60.000
PLEDGE (%)		12.696	0.000	20.245	0.000	98.050
LNTA (thousand dollar)		15.995	15.814	1.411	11.119	21.438
SYSTEMRISK (%)		0.877	0.915	0.485	−5.274	10.248
EPS (dollar)		1.831	1.275	3.725	−52.320	73.320
DUAL		–	–	–	0.000	1.000

Note: RELWEIGHT is the preference of institutional investors' shareholding, including domestic and foreign. MANAGER is the managerial ownership ratio. BLOCK is the blockholder ownership ratio. INDEP is the independent director ratio. PLEDGE is the stock pledge ratio. LNTA is firm scale. SYSTEMRISK is the system risk. EPS is the earning per share. DUAL is the CEO duality. DUAL is dummy variable and this variable is equal to 1 if the CEO is also the chair of the board; otherwise, it is 0.

The average stock pledge ratio was 12.07%, but the maximum was 98.05%, which is seven times that of the minimal value. Notably, this variable was higher during the financial crisis of 2007–2008, which numerous economists consider to be the most detrimental financial crisis since the U.S. Great Depression in the 1930s.

This study also discovered that the volatility of the electronics industry is higher than that of other industries, and that this industry had the maximal values for both the managerial ownership and stock pledge ratios[4].

Table 2 displays the correlations among the studied corporate governance variables, control variables, and shareholding preferences of domestic and foreign institutional investors. Domestic and foreign institutional investors were determined to have dissimilar perspectives on system risk and independent directors. Notably, although foreign institutional investors abided by the 2006 law that requires first-time listing firms to have no fewer than five directors and to reserve certain seats for independent directors and supervisors, they did not consider independent directors capable of efficiently monitoring managers. By contrast, the domestic institutional investors recognized the function of the independent directors. Thus, the directions of correlation for the independent directors were inconsistent. The foreign institutional investors perceived system risk, whereas the domestic institutional investors did not. If the system risk was high, foreign institutional investors may have decreased their shareholdings; therefore, they most likely followed the law because they were less familiar with the market than were the domestic institutional investors.

---

[2] Company Act, 2006, Chapter V, Section 4.
[3] Taiwan Securities and Exchange Act, 2006, Article 26-3.
[4] For saving the space, the data regarding CEO duality are not shown. If readers need the data of CEO duality, contact with authors please.

Table 2. Correlation for variables of institutional investors.

Variable	RELWEIGHT		MANAGER	BLOCK	INDEP	PLEDGE	DUAL	LNTA	SYSTEMRISK	EPS
	Domestic	Foreign								
RELWEIGHT	1.000	1.000								
MANAGER	0.389 (0.000) ***	0.134 (0.000) ***	1.000							
BLOCK	0.182 (0.000) ***	0.292 (0.000) ***	−0.089 (0.000) ***	1.000						
INDEP	0.072 (0.000) ***	−0.261 (0.000) ***	−0.080 (0.000) ***	−0.128 (0.000) ***	1.000					
PLEDGE	0.034 (0.019) **	0.088 (0.000) ***	−0.090 (0.000) ***	0.031 (0.033) **	−0.130 (0.000) ***	1.000				
DUAL	−0.137 (0.000) ***	−0.145 (0.000) ***	−0.102 (0.000) ***	−0.002 (0.879)	0.010 (0.482)	−0.043 (0.003) ***	1.000			
LNTA	0.130 (0.000) ***	0.327 (0.000) ***	−0.097 (0.000) ***	−0.037 (0.010) **	0.018 (0.221)	0.098 (0.000) ***	−0.112 (0.000) ***	1.000		
SYSTEMRISK	0.015 (0.315)	−0.033 (0.022) **	−0.139 (0.000) ***	−0.156 (0.000) ***	0.120 (0.000) ***	−0.063 (0.000) ***	0.002 (0.905)	0.247 (0.000) ***	1.000	
EPS	0.139 (0.000) ***	0.148 (0.000) ***	0.025 (0.088) *	0.012 (0.407)	0.139 (0.000) ***	−0.089 (0.000) ***	−0.054 (0.000) ***	0.245 (0.000) ***	0.088 (0.000) ***	1.000

Note: RELWEIGHT is the preference of institutional investors' shareholding, including domestic and foreign. MANAGER is the managerial ownership ratio. BLOCK is the blockholder ownership ratio. INDEP is the independent director ratio. PLEDGE is the stock pledge ratio. DUAL is the CEO duality. LNTA is firm scale. SYSTEMRISK is the system risk. EPS is the earning per share. The number in parentheses is the p-value. *, **, and *** are denoted significant at 10%, 5% and 1% level, respectively.

237

5.2. Empirical Results Analysis

In this study, two models were used based on various managerial ownership ratio assumptions. The first regression model (Equation (1)) assumed a linear relationship between the shareholding preferences of institutional investors and the managerial ownership ratio. The second model (Equation (2)) was a piecewise regression model constructed by dividing the manager ownership at three points. The empirical results of Models 1 and 2 are presented in Tables 3 and 4, respectively.

Table 3. Shareholding reference of institutional investors for Model 1 (n = 4760).

Variable		Domestic	Foreign
β_0 :Constant	Domestic	1.151 (0.000) ***	—
	Foreign	—	−1.186 (0.000) ***
β_1 :MANAGER		0.006 (0.000) ***	0.003 (0.000) ***
β_2 :BLOCK		0.005 (0.000) ***	0.002 (0.000) ***
β_3 :INDEP		0.001 (0.171)	0.000 (0.831)
β_4 :PLEDGE		0.001 (0.048) **	−0.001 (0.002) ***
β_5 :DUAL		0.019 (0.209)	0.005 (0.666)
β_6 :LNTA		−0.091 (0.000) ***	0.040 (0.001)
β_7 :SYSTEMRISK		−0.025 (0.005) ***	−0.017 (0.015) **
β_8 :EPS		0.013 (0.000) ***	0.008 (0.000)
Adjusted R-squared		0.868	0.901
F-statistic		46.650 (0.000) ***	63.859 (0.000) ***
Hausman Test		162.502 (0.000) ***	181.155 (0.000) ***
Fixed/random effect		Fixed	Fixed

Note: RELWEIGHT is the preference of institutional investors' shareholding, including domestic and foreign. MANAGER is the managerial ownership ratio. BLOCK is the blockholder ownership ratio. INDEP is the independent director ratio. PLEDGE is the stock pledge ratio. DUAL is the CEO duality. LNTA is firm scale. SYSTEMRISK is the system risk. EPS is the earning per share. The number in parentheses is the *p*-value. *, ** and *** are denoted significant at 10%, 5% and 1% level, respectively. *n* is sample number of observations.

Table 4. Shareholding reference of institutional investors for Model 2 (n = 4760).

Variable		Domestic	Foreign
β_0 :Constant	Domestic	1.178 (0.000) ***	—
	Foreign	—	−1.102 (0.000) ***
β_1 :MANAGER		−0.008 (0.075) *	−0.006 (0.099) *
β_2 :(MANAGER − 10%) × a_1		0.021 (0.000) ***	0.009 (0.042) **
β_3 :(MANAGER − 20%) × a_2		−0.011 (0.006) ***	−0.001 (0.648)
β_4 :(MANAGER − 30%) × a_3		0.005 (0.133)	0.004 (0.133)
β_5 :BLOCK		0.005 (0.000) ***	0.002 (0.000) ***
β_6 :INDEP		0.001 (0.177)	0.000 (0.788)
β_7 :PLEDGE		0.001 (0.051) *	−0.001 (0.002) ***
β_8 :DUAL		0.020 (0.186)	0.005 (0.679)
β_9 :LNTA		−0.088 (0.000) ***	0.039 (0.001) ***
β_{10} :SYSTEMRISK		−0.024 (0.006) ***	−0.017 (0.016) **
β_{11} :EPS		0.012 (0.000) ***	0.007 (0.000) ***
Adjusted R-squared		0.869	0.901
F-statistic		46.585 (0.000) ***	63.731 (0.000) ***
Hausman Test		156.379 (0.000) ***	182.674 (0.000) ***
Fixed/random effect		Fixed	Fixed

Note: RELWEIGHT is the preference of institutional investors' shareholding, including domestic and foreign. MANAGER is the managerial ownership ratio. BLOCK is the blockholder ownership ratio. INDEP is the independent director ratio. PLEDGE is the stock pledge ratio. DUAL is the CEO duality. LNTA is firm scale. SYSTEMRISK is the system risk. EPS is the earning per share. The number in parentheses is the *p*-value. *, ** and *** are denoted significant at 10%, 5% and 1% level, respectively. *n* is sample number of observations.

Based on the results of Table 3, the blockholder shareholding ratio (BLOCK) and managerial ownership ratio (MANAGER) had significant and positive effects on both the domestic and foreign institutional investors' shareholdings. Thus, H1 and H3 are supported both for domestic and foreign institutional investors. This is consistent with the convergence of interest hypothesis (Morck et al. 1988).

However, the independent director ratio (INDEP) produced nonsignificant effects both on the domestic and foreign institutional investors (domestic : $\beta_3 = 0.001$, $p < 0.171$; foreign : $\beta_3 = 0.000$, $p < 0.831$). That is, the institutional investors did not consider independent directors capable of efficiently monitoring managers. That is due to the law requiring that listed firms hire independent directors does not increase the confidence of institutional investors in increasing their shareholdings, and the independent director ratio (INDEP) had nonsignificant effects on the foreign institutional investors' shareholdings. Therefore, H4 is not supported both for domestic and foreign institutional investors.

The stock pledge ratio (PLEDGE) has positive effect on domestic institutional investors' shareholdings ($\beta_4 = 0.001, p < 0.048$ **), but has negative effect on foreign institutional investors ($\beta_4 = -0.001,\ p < 0.002$ ***). The foreign institutional investors may consider that when directors collateralize shares and engage in over-leveraged transactions, the company may has higher risk. Therefore, H5 is only supported for foreign institutional investors.

The results for CEO duality are all nonsignificant (domestic: $\beta_5 = 0.019, p < 0.209$; foreign : $\beta_5 = 0.005, p < 0.666$) That is, whether or not the separation of CEO and chairperson of the board duties cannot improve or decrease institutional investors' shareholdings. Therefore, H6 is not supported both for domestic and foreign institutional investors.

From Table 3, the managerial ownership ratio has significant effects both on domestic and foreign institutional investors (domestic: $\beta_1 = 0.006,\ p < 0.000$ ***; foreign: $\beta_1 = 0.003,\ p < 0.000$ ***). The descriptive statistics table (Table 1) gave the mean of the managerial ownership ratio as 22%, thus, we divided the variable at three points, 10%, 20%, and 30%, to analyze the nonlinear relationship between the shareholdings of institutional investors and the managerial ownership ratio using the piecewise regression model. From Table 4, a nonlinear relationship was found between managerial share ownership and institutional investors' shareholdings; the latter decreased when the managerial ownership ratios were between 20% and 30%. If the managerial ownership ratio larger than 10%, it had positive effects on institutional investors' shareholdings (domestic: $\beta_2 = 0.021,\ p < 0.000$ ***; foreigm: $\beta_2 = 0.009,\ p < 0.042$ **). However, when the ratio increase to 20%, the effects will turn to negative (domestic: $\beta_3 = -0.011,\ p < 0.006$ ***; foreigm: $\beta_3 = -0.001,\ p < 0.648$), but the results for foreign institutional investors are nonsignificant. Consequently, H2 is only supported for domestic institutional investors.

5.3. Sensitive Analysis

5.3.1. Electronics and Nonelectronics Industry Analysis

Because half of the sampled firms are in the electronics industry, this study divided the samples into two categories, electronics and nonelectronics industries, to analyze the behavior of institutional investors.

The results of Model 1 for electronics and nonelectronics industries were shown in Tables 5 and 6. Comparing Tables 5 and 6, this study found that the independent director ratio (INDEP) only had a significant positive effect on the institutional investors for nonelectronics industry (domestic: $\beta_3 = 0.095,\ p < 0.080$ *; foreign: $\beta_3 = 0.173,\ p < 0.003$ ***). This indicates that they observed the law regarding listed firms and the hiring of independent directors. Further, most Taiwanese companies are family businesses, particularly in nonelectronics industries, where director and supervisor positions are held by family members and ownership interest is concentrated in only a few shareholders. Thus, they mind the function of independent directors for nonelectronics industry. However, for electronics industry, the independent director ratio (INDEP) had nonsignificant effects both on domestic and foreign institutional investors (domestic: $\beta_3 = 0.001,\ p < 0.268$; foreign: $\beta_3 = 0.000,\ p < 0.722$). Consequently, H4 is only supported for nonelectronics industry.

Table 5. Institutional investors' shareholding reference of electronics industry for Model 1 (n = 2256).

Variable		Domestic	Foreign
β_0 :Constant	Domestic	2.090 (0.000) ***	—
	Foreign	—	−2.253 (0.000) ***
β_1 :MANAGER		0.007 (0.000) ***	0.003 (0.000) ***
β_2 :BLOCK		0.007 (0.000) ***	0.002 (0.000) ***
β_3 :INDEP		0.001 (0.268)	0.000 (0.722)
β_4 :PLEDGE		0.002 (0.008) ***	−0.002 (0.000) ***
β_5 :DUAL		0.037 (0.119)	−0.039 (0.001) ***
β_6 :LNTA		−0.154 (0.000) ***	0.090 (0.000) ***
β_7 :SYSTEMRISK		−0.011 (0.408)	−0.004 (0.521)
β_8 :EPS		0.013 (0.000) ***	0.004 (0.003) ***
Adjusted R-squared		0.859	0.870
F-statistic		42.637 (0.000) ***	46.635 (0.000) ***
Hausman Test		135.240 (0.000) ***	88.666 (0.000) ***
Fixed/random effect		Fixed	Fixed

Note: RELWEIGHT is the preference of institutional investors' shareholding, including domestic and foreign. MANAGER is the managerial ownership ratio. BLOCK is the blockholder ownership ratio. INDEP is the independent director ratio. PLEDGE is the stock pledge ratio. DUAL is the CEO duality. LNTA is firm scale. SYSTEMRISK is the system risk. EPS is the earning per share. The number in parentheses is the *p*-value. *, ** and *** are denoted significant at 10%, 5% and 1% level, respectively. n is sample number of observations.

Table 6. Institutional investors' shareholding reference of nonelectronics industry for Model 1 (n = 2504).

Variable		Domestic	Foreign
β_0 :Constant	Domestic	−0.310 (0.316)	—
	Foreign	—	0.073 (0.827)
β_1 :MANAGER		0.005 (0.000) ***	0.004 (0.000) ***
β_2 :BLOCK		0.003 (0.000) ***	0.002 (0.004) ***
β_3 :INDEP		0.095 (0.080) **	0.173 (0.003) ***
β_4 :PLEDGE		0.000 (0.995)	0.000 (0.377)
β_5 :DUAL		0.007 (0.692)	0.051 (0.011) **
β_6 :LNTA		0.004 (0.843)	−0.026 (0.216)
β_7 :SYSTEMRISK		−0.050 (0.000) ***	−0.031 (0.018) **
β_8 :EPS		0.010 (0.000) ***	0.014 (0.000) ***
Adjusted R-squared		0.883	0.872
F-statistic		52.578 (0.000) ***	47.573 (0.000) ***
Hausman Test		52.926 (0.000) ***	80.673 (0.000) **
Fixed/random effect		Fixed	Fixed

Note: RELWEIGHT is the preference of institutional investors' shareholding, including domestic and foreign. MANAGER is the managerial ownership ratio. BLOCK is the blockholder ownership ratio. INDEP is the independent director ratio. PLEDGE is the stock pledge ratio. DUAL is the CEO duality. LNTA is firm scale. SYSTEMRISK is the system risk. EPS is the earning per share. The number in parentheses is the *p*-value. *, ** and *** are denoted significant at 10%, 5% and 1% level, respectively. *n* is sample number of observations.

These results imply that they focus on other factors, such as the managerial ownership ratio (MANAGER) and the blockholder ownership ratio (BLOCK). According to Tables 5 and 6, MANAGER and BLOCK have significant positive effects both on foreign and domestic institutional investors, Thus, H1 and H3 are all supported.

The CEO duality (DUAL) positively affected the shareholdings of foreign institutional investors of nonelectronics industry ($\beta_8 = 0.051$, $p < 0.011$ **), again largely because most nonelectronics industries in Taiwan are run as family businesses. The congruence between ownership and management ensures the alignment of director/supervisor interests with those of the company, which is consistent with the convergence of the interest hypothesis. However, the DUAL and PLEDGE had negative effects on foreign institutional investors of electronics industry ($\beta_8 = -0.039$, $p < 0.001$ ***). Therefore, H5 and H6 are only supported for foreign institutional investors of electronics industry.

The results of Model 2 for electronics and nonelectronics industries were shown in Tables 7 and 8. From Table 7, when the managerial ownership ratio increased, the shareholdings of both domestic and foreign institutional investors in the electronics industry increased (domestic: $\beta_2 = -0.453$, $p < 0.000$ ***, $\beta_3 = 0.331$, $p < 0.003$ ***, $\beta_4 = 0.132$, $p < 0.008$ ***; foreign: $\beta_2 = -0.002$, $p < 0.815$, $\beta_3 = 0.002$, $p < 0.570$, $\beta_4 = 0.005$, $p < 0.046$ **). Thus, there is a linear relationship exists between them. Thus, H2 were supported both for domestic and foreign institutional investors of electronics industry.

Table 7. Institutional investors' shareholding reference of electronics industry for Model 2 (n = 2256).

Variable		Domestic	Foreign
β_0 :Constant	Domestic	1982.901 (0.000) ***	—
	Foreign	—	−2.150 (0.000) ***
β_1 :MANAGER		−0.214 (0.246)	0.002 (0.806)
β_2:(MANAGER − 10%) × a1		−0.453 (0.000) ***	−0.002 (0.815)
β_3:(MANAGER − 20%) × a2		0.331 (0.003) ***	0.002 (0.570)
β_4:(MANAGER − 30%) × a3		0.132 (0.008) ***	0.005 (0.046) **
β_5 :BLOCK		−0.019 (0.630)	0.003 (0.000) ***
β_6 :INDEP		0.058 (0.000) ***	0.000 (0.582)
β_7 :PLEDGE		−0.043 (0.000) ***	−0.001 (0.000) ***
β_8 :DUAL		0.005 (0.262)	−0.041 (0.001) ***
β_9 :LNTA		−0.091 (0.627)	0.085 (0.000) ***
β_{10} :SYSTEMRISK		1.941 (0.000) ***	−0.004 (0.505)
β_{11} :EPS		−0.003 (0.010) **	0.004 (0.003) ***
Adjusted R-squared		0.033	0.871
F-statistic		1.230 (0.008) ***	46.484 (0.000) ***
Hausman Test		297.266 (0.000) ***	101.735 (0.000) ***
Fixed/random effect		Fixed	Fixed

Note: RELWEIGHT is the preference of institutional investors' shareholding, including domestic and foreign. MANAGER is the managerial ownership ratio. BLOCK is the blockholder ownership ratio. INDEP is the independent director ratio. PLEDGE is the stock pledge ratio. DUAL is the CEO duality. LNTA is firm scale. SYSTEMRISK is the system risk. EPS is the earning per share. The number in parentheses is the *p*-value. *, ** and *** are denoted significant at 10%, 5% and 1% level, respectively. *n* is sample number of observations.

Table 8. Institutional investors' shareholding reference of nonelectronics industry for Model 2 (n = 2504).

Variable		Domestic	Foreign
β_0 :Constant	Domestic	−0.189 (0.563)	—
	Foreign	—	0.166 (0.622)
β_1 :MANAGER		−0.009 (0.042) **	−0.006 (0.205)
β_2:(MANAGER − 10%) × a1		0.024 (0.001) ***	0.015 (0.039) **
β_3:(MANAGER − 20%) × a2		−0.010 (0.067) **	−0.006 (0.293)
β_4:(MANAGER − 30%) × a3		−0.002 (0.514)	0.003 (0.472)
β_5 :BLOCK		0.003 (0.000) ***	0.003 (0.001) ***
β_6 :INDEP		0.065 (0.273)	0.137 (0.026) **
β_7 :PLEDGE		0.000 (0.772)	0.000 (0.334)
β_8 :DUAL		−0.008 (0.693)	0.050 (0.013) **
β_9 :LNTA		0.000 (0.993)	−0.028 (0.189)
β_{10} :SYSTEMRISK		−0.046 (0.000) ***	−0.030 (0.021) **
β_{11} :EPS		0.008 (0.006) ***	0.014 (0.000) ***
Adjusted R-squared		0.880	0.872
F-statistic		54.470 (0.000) ***	47.200 (0.000) ***
Hausman Test		43.724 (0.000) ***	81.005 (0.000) ***
Fixed/random effect		Fixed	Fixed

Note: RELWEIGHT is the preference of institutional investors' shareholding, including domestic and foreign. MANAGER is the managerial ownership ratio. BLOCK is the blockholder ownership ratio. INDEP is the independent director ratio. PLEDGE is the stock pledge ratio. DUAL is the CEO duality. LNTA is firm scale. SYSTEMRISK is the system risk. EPS is the earning per share. The number in parentheses is the p-value. *, ** and *** are denoted significant at 10%, 5% and 1% level, respectively. n is sample number of observations.

According to Table 8, for nonelectronics industry, domestic institutional investors decreased shareholdings when the managerial ownership ratio were larger than 20% ($\beta_2 = 0.024$, $p < 0.001$ ***, $\beta_3 = -0.010$, $p < 0.067$ *, $\beta_4 = -0.002$, $p < 0.514$). For foreign institutional investors, shareholdings decreased when the managerial ownership ratios were between 20% and 30% ($\beta_2 = 0.015$, $p < 0.039$ **, $\beta_3 = -0.006$, $p < 0.293$, $\beta_4 = 0.003$, $p < 0.472$), although the results are nonsignificant. H2 is supported only for domestic institutional investors of nonelectronics industry.

5.3.2. Subsample Period during 2007–2008

The 2007–2008 financial crisis was a crucial period that resulted in the threat of total collapse of large financial institutions, the bailout of banks by national governments and stock market downturns worldwide. Consequently, the preferences of institutional investors may have been affected. Therefore, we focused on the period immediately following the crisis (2008–2010) to empirically analyze the relationship between corporate governance and the shareholdings of institutional investors. We analyzed two cases by splitting the sample into electronics and nonelectronics industries, based on the sample period during 2007–2008. The results are shown in Tables 9 and 10.

Table 9. Institutional investors' shareholding reference during financial tsunami for Model 1 (n = 1785).

Variable		Domestic	Foreign
β_0 :Constant	Domestic	−1.974 (0.022)**	–
	Foreign	—	−0.428 (0.064) *
β_1 :MANAGER		0.004 (0.132)	−0.001 (0.378)
β_2 :BLOCK		0.000 (0.967)	0.000 (0.698)
β_3 :INDEP		−0.005 (0.003) ***	0.000 (0.654)
β_4 :PLEDGE		0.000 (0.597)	−0.001 (0.131)
β_5 :DUAL		0.018 (0.631)	−0.032 (0.235)
β_6 :LNTA		0.116 (0.031) **	−0.013 (0.330)
β_7 :SYSTEMRISK		0.002 (0.857)	−0.019 (0.193)
β_8 :EPS		0.007 (0.140)	0.007 (0.003) ***
Adjusted R-squared		0.932	0.824
F-statistic		28.077 (0.000) ***	10.268 (0.000) ***
Hausman Test		87.049	133.939
Fixed/random effect		Fixed	Fixed

Note: RELWEIGHT is the preference of institutional investors' shareholding, including domestic and foreign. MANAGER is the managerial ownership ratio. BLOCK is the blockholder ownership ratio. INDEP is the independent director ratio. PLEDGE is the stock pledge ratio. DUAL is the CEO duality. LNTA is firm scale. SYSTEMRISK is the system risk. EPS is the earning per share. The number in parentheses is the *p*-value. *, ** and *** are denoted significant at 10%, 5% and 1% level, respectively. *n* is sample number of observations.

Table 10. Institutional investors' shareholding reference during financial tsunami for Model 2 (n = 1785).

Variable		Domestic	Foreign
β_0 :Constant	Domestic	−2.145 (0.017) **	—
	Foreign	—	−2.397 (0.000) ***
β_1 :MANAGER		0.015 (0.380)	0.005 (0.688)
β_2:(MANAGER − 10%) × a1		−0.012 (0.545)	−0.003 (0.829)
β_3:(MANAGER − 20%) × a2		0.002 (0.843)	0.001 (0.904)
β_4:(MANAGER − 30%) × a3		−0.003 (0.760)	0.001 (0.885)
β_5 :BLOCK		0.000 (0.965)	0.003 (0.072) *
β_6 :INDEP		−0.005 (0.003) ***	0.000 (0.706)
β_7 :PLEDGE		0.001 (0.542)	0.000 (0.802)
β_8 :DUAL		0.018 (0.647)	0.001 (0.971)
β_9 :LNTA		0.120 (0.027) **	0.113 (0.002) ***
β_{10} :SYSTEMRISK		0.003 (0.843)	0.006 (0.550)
β_{11} :EPS		0.006 (0.163)	0.000 (0.973)
Adjusted R-squared		0.932	0.960
F-statistic		27.822 (0.000) ***	48.702 (0.000) ***
Hausman Test		85.930 (0.000) ***	93.116 (0.000) ***
Fixed/random effect		Fixed	Fixed

Note: RELWEIGHT is the preference of institutional investors' shareholding, including domestic and foreign. MANAGER is the managerial ownership ratio. BLOCK is the blockholder ownership ratio. INDEP is the independent director ratio. PLEDGE is the stock pledge ratio. DUAL is the CEO duality. LNTA is firm scale. SYSTEMRISK is the system risk. EPS is the earning per share. The number in parentheses is the *p*-value. *, ** and *** are denoted significant at 10%, 5% and 1% level, respectively. n is sample number of observations.

From Table 9, domestic and foreign institutional investors valued the monitoring function of independent directors ($\beta_3 = -0.005$, $p < 0.003$ ***). However, the independent director ratio (INDEP) did not improve foreign institutional investors' investment confidence ($\beta_3 = 0.000$, $p < 0.654$). For other corporate governance variables, most estimated results are nonsignofcant, Consequently, H1, H3, H4, H5, and H6 are not supported.

According to Table 10, we discovered that the shareholdings of foreign institutional investors uniformly increased as the managerial ownership ratio increased, but are nonsignificant ($\beta_2 = -0.003$, $p < 0.829$; $\beta_3 = 0.001$, $p < 0.904$; $\beta_4 = 0.001$, $p < 0.885$). The managerial ownership ratio also positively affected the shareholdings of domestic institutional investors when a manager owned 20% of the equity; however, if firms owned less than 10% or more than 30%, the shareholdings of the foreign institutional investors declined ($\beta_2 = -0.012$, $p <$

0.545; $\beta_3 = 0.002$, $p < 0.843$; $\beta_4 = -0.003$, $p < 0.760$). But these estimated results are all not significant. Thus, H2 is not supported.

Most corporate governance variables had no significant effect on domestic or foreign institutional investors' shareholdings. These corporate governance variables did not improve institutional investors' shareholdings during the financial crisis period. By contrast, institutional investors paid attention to firms' profit or characteristics, such as the earnings per share (EPS) or firm scale (LNTA). This indicates that there is considerable room for improvement in Taiwan's corporate governance system. It is crucial that the government enhance corporate governance mechanisms to improve institutional investors' confidence during financial crises. Finally, the summarization with respect to six hypotheses is shown in Table 11.

Table 11. Summarization of hypotheses.

	Full Sample		Electronics		Nonelectronics		Financial Tsunami	
	Domestic	Foreign	Domestic	Foreign	Domestic	Foreign	Domestic	Foreign
H1	yes	yes	yes	yes	yes	yes	no	no
H2	yes	no	yes	yes	yes	no	no	no
H3	yes	yes	yes	yes	yes	yes	no	no
H4	no	no	no	no	yes	yes	no	no
H5	no	yes	no	yes	no	no	no	no
H6	no	no	no	yes	no	no	no	no

Note: Hypothesis 1 (H1): The larger ownership ratio, the higher institutional investors' shareholdings. Hypothesis 2 (H2): The relationship between managerial ownership ratio and institutional investors' shareholdings is nonlinear. Hypothesis 3 (H3): The higher blockholder ownership ratio, the greater the institutional investors' shareholdings. Hypothesis 4 (H4): The higher independent directors ratio, the higher institutional investors' shareholdings. Hypothesis 5 (H5): The higher the collateralized shares by directors, the lower institutional investor' shareholdings. Hypothesis 6 (H6): The higher CEO duality, the lower institutional investors' shareholdings. "No" represents the hypothesis is not supported. "Yes" represents the hypothesis is supported.

6. Conclusions

In Taiwan, corporate governance became essential after the 1997 Asian financial crisis. Furthermore, interest in the corporate governance practices of modern corporations has been renewed, particularly in relation to accountability, because of the high-profile collapses of numerous corporations during 2001–2002, most of which involved accounting fraud.

Since the institutional investors are important traders in Taiwan market, their preferences will affect investment strategies of other traders. This study investigated the correlation between preferences of institutional investors and corporate governance in Taiwan. This study applied the panel data regression model and piecewise regression model to determine whether hypotheses are supported.

Empirical results showed that the domestic and foreign institutional investors had dissimilar perspectives on corporate governance variables, such as collateralized shares by directors and CEO duality. The blockholder ownership ratio and managerial ownership ratio positively affected the institutional investors' shareholdings. Because most firms of nonelectronics in Taiwan are family businesses, foreign institutional investors pay particular attention to CEO duality. However, these corporate governance variables have not improved institutional investors' shareholdings during financial crisis periods; instead, institutional investors paid more attention to firm profits or characteristics than to corporate governance variables. Therefore, we conclude that the Taiwanese government should establish better corporate governance to improve institutional investors' confidence.

The sample data of this paper are obtained from Taiwan market, which is the emerging market. However, for Taiwan, many regulations of corporate governance have to improve. Further, there are many emerging markets in Asia, such as the Indian and Chinese markets. Thus, for further research, the methodology and issues can be employed to analyze and compare effects of corporate governance on institutional investors' preferences among other emerging markets.

Author Contributions: S.-L.L. was the author behind the main idea and objectives of the paper. Y.-H.L. collected and analyzed the data. S.-L.L. and Y.-H.L. drafted the manuscript. S.-L.L. completed further econometric estimations and revised the paper.

Funding: This research received no external funding.

Acknowledgments: We are grateful to the three anonymous referees for their helpful comments and suggestions.

Conflicts of Interest: The authors declare no conflict of interest.

References

Aggarwal, Reena, Leora Klapper, and Peter Wysocki. 2005. Portfolio Preferences of Foreign Institutional Investors. *Journal of Banking and Finance* 29: 2919–46. [CrossRef]

Appel, Ian, Todd Gormley, and Donald Keim. 2016. Passive investors, not passive owners. *Journal of Financial Economics* 121: 111–41. [CrossRef]

Beasley, Mark. 1996. An Empirical Analysis of the Relation between the Board of Director Composition and Financial Statement Fraud. *The Accounting Review* 71: 443–65.

Bebchuk, Lucian, Alma Cohen, and Scott Hirst. 2017. *The Agency Problems of Institutional Investors*. Discussion Paper. Cambridge: Harvard Law School.

Boyd, Brian. 1995. CEO duality and firm performance: A contingency model. *Strategic Management Journal* 16: 301–12. [CrossRef]

Cadbury, Adrian. 1992. *The Financial Aspects of Corporate Governance (Cadbury Report)*. London: The Committee on the Financial Aspect of Corporate Governance (The Cadbury Committee) and Gee and Co., Ltd.

Carleton, Willard, James Nelson, and Michael Weisbach. 1998. The influence of institutions on corporate governance through private negotiations: Evidence from TIAA-CREF. *Journal of Finance* 53: 1335–1362. [CrossRef]

Cao, Tingqui, Xiuli Yang, and Yuguang Sun. 2007. Ownership structure and corporate performance: Measurement method and endogeneity. *Economic Research Journal* 10: 126–37.

Chen, Ming-Yuan. 2006. Managerial ownership and firm performance: An analysis using switching simultaneous-equation models. *Applied Economics* 38: 161–81. [CrossRef]

Chiou, Jeng-Ren, Ta-Chung Hsiung, and Lanfeng Kao. 2002. A Study of the Relationship between Financial Distress and Collateralized Shares. *Taiwan Accounting Review* 3: 79–111.

Choe, Hyuk, Bong-Chan Kho, and René M. Stluz. 1999. Do Foreign Investors Destabilize Stock Market? The Korean Experience in 1997. *Journal of Financial Economics* 54: 227–64. [CrossRef]

Dahya, Jay, Laura Galguera Garcia, and Jos van Bommel. 2009. One Man Two Hats: What's All Commotion! *Financial Review* 44: 179–212. [CrossRef]

Daily, Catherine, and Dane Dalton. 1993. Boards of directors, leadership and structure: Control and performance implications. *Entrepreneurship Theory and Practice* 17: 65–81. [CrossRef]

Dahlquist, Magus, and Gorän Robertsson. 2001. Direct Foreign Ownership, Institutional Investors, and Firm Characteristics. *Journal of Financial Economics* 59: 413–440. [CrossRef]

Davies, J.R., David Hillier, and Patrick McColgan. 2005. Ownership structure, managerial behavior and corporate value. *Journal of Corporate Finance* 11: 645–60. [CrossRef]

De Miguel, Alberto, Julio Pindado, and Chabela de la Torre. 2004. Ownership structure and firm value: New evidence from Spain. *Strategic Management Journal* 25: 1199–207. [CrossRef]

Driffield, Nigel, Vidya Mahambare, and Sarmistha Pal. 2007. How does ownership structure affect capital structure and firm value? Recent evidence from East Asia. *Economics of Transition* 15: 535–73. [CrossRef]

Dahya, Jay, Alasdair Lonie, and David Power. 1996. The case for separating the roles of chairman and CEO: An anaylsis of stockmarket and accounting data. *Corporate Governance: An International Review* 4: 71–77. [CrossRef]

Dahya, Jay, and Nickolaos Travlos. 2000. Does the one man show pay? Theory and evidence on the dual CEO revisited. *European Financial Management* 16: 85–98. [CrossRef]

Faccio, Mara, and Meziane Lasfer. 1999. Managerial Ownership, Board Structure and Firm Value: The UK Evidence, Working Paper. Available online: https://papers.ssrn.com/sol3/papers.cfm?abstract_id=179008 (accessed on 31 December 2018).

Fama, Eugene, and Michael Jensen. 1983. Separation of Ownership and Control. *Journal of Law and Economics* 26: 301–25. [CrossRef]

Falkenstein, Eric. 1996. Preference for Stock Characteristics as Revealed by Mutual Fund Portfolio Holdings. *Journal of Finance* 51: 111–35. [CrossRef]

Florackis, Chrisostomos. 2005. Internal corporate governance mechanisms and corporate performance: Evidence for UK firms. *Applied Financial Economics Letters* 1: 211–16. [CrossRef]

Florackis, Chrisostomos, Alexandros Kostakis, and Aydin Ozkan. 2009. Managerial ownership and performance. *Journal of Business Research* 62: 1350–57. [CrossRef]

Gompers, Paul, and Andrew Metrick. 2001. Institutional Investors and Equity Prices. *Quarterly Journal of Economics* 116: 229–59. [CrossRef]

Griffith, John. 1999. CEO ownership and firm value. *Managerial and Decision Economics* 20: 1–8. [CrossRef]

Hermalin, Benjamin, and Michael Weisbach. 1991. The effects of board composition and direct incentives on firm performance. *Financial Management* 20: 101–12. [CrossRef]

Holderness, Clifford, Randall Kroszner, and Dennis Sheehan. 1999. Were the good old days that good? Changes in managerial stock ownership since the Great Depression. *Journal of Finance* 54: 435–470. [CrossRef]

Huson, Mark, Robert Parrino, and Laura Starks. 2001. Internal Monitoring Mechanisms and CEO Turnover: A Long-Term Perspective. *Journal of Finance* 56: 2265–97. [CrossRef]

Jensen, Michael, and Willian Meckling. 1976. Theory of the Firm: Managerial Behavior, Agency Cost and Ownership Structure. *Journal of Financial Economics* 3: 305–60. [CrossRef]

Jensen, Michael. 1993. The Modern Industrial Revolution, Exit, and the Failure of Internal Control Systems. *Journal of Finance* 48: 831–80. [CrossRef]

Kao, Lanfeng, Jeng-Ren Chiou, and Anlin Chen. 2004. The Agency Problem, Firm Performance and Monitoring Mechanisms: The Evidence from Collateralized Shares in Taiwan. *Corporate Governance: An International Review* 12: 389–402. [CrossRef]

Keasey, Kevin, Helen Short, and Robert Watson. 1994. Directors' ownership and the performance of small and medium sized firms in the UK. *Small Business Economics* 6: 225–36. [CrossRef]

La Porta, Rafael, Florencio Lopez-de-Silanes, Andrei Shleifer, and Robert Vishny. 1997. Legal determinants of external finance. *Journal of Finance* 52: 1131–50. [CrossRef]

La Porta, Rafel, Florencio Lopez-de-Silanes, Andrei Shleifer, and Robert Vishny. 1998. Law and finance. *Journal of Political Economy* 106: 1115–55. [CrossRef]

La Porta, Rafel, Florencio Lopez-de-Silanes, Andrei Shleifer, and Robert Vishny. 2000. Investor protection and corporate governance. *Journal of Financial Economics* 58: 3–27. [CrossRef]

Leuz, Christian, Dhananjay Nanda, and Peter Wysocki. 2003. Investor protection and earnings management: An international comparison. *Journal of Financial Economics* 69: 505–27. [CrossRef]

Li, Lingfeng. 2002. Macroeconomic Factors and the Correlation of Stock and Bond Returns. International Center for Finance Yale University Working paper, November, No. 02-46. Available online: http://www.scielo.org.co/scielo.php?script=sci_nlinks&ref=000129&pid=S0121-50512011000100012000033&lng=en (accessed on 31 December 2018).

McConnell, John, and Henri Servaes. 1990. Additional evidence on equity ownership and corporate value. *Journal of Financial Economics* 27: 595–612. [CrossRef]

McCahery, Joseph, Zacharias Sautner, and Laura T. Starks. 2016. Behind the scenes: The corporate governance preferences of institutional investors. *Journal of Finance* 71: 2905–32. [CrossRef]

Morck, Randall, Andrei Shleifer, and Robert Vishny. 1988. Management Ownership and Market Evaluation: An Empirical Analysis. *Journal of Financial Economics* 20: 293–315. [CrossRef]

Mudambi, Ram, and Carmeia Nicosia. 1998. Ownership structure and firm performance: Evidence from the UK financial service industry. *Applied Financial Economics* 8: 175–80. [CrossRef]

Mura, Roberto. 2007. Firm performance: Do non-executive directors have a mind of their own? Evidence from UK panel data. *Financial Management* 36: 81–112. [CrossRef]

Ng, Lilian, and Qinghai Wang. 2004. Institutional trading and the turn-of-the -year effect. *Journal of Financial Economics* 74: 343–66. [CrossRef]

Patton, Arch, and John Baker. 1987. Why won't directors rock the board? *Harvard Business Review* 65: 10–18.

Pi, Lynn, and Stephen Timme. 1993. Corporate control and bank efficiency. *Journal of Banking and Finance* 17: 515–30. [CrossRef]

Prowse, Stephen. 1993. The structure of corporate ownership in Japan. *The Journal of Finance* 47: 1121–40. [CrossRef]

Rosenstein, Stuart, and Jeffrey Wyatt. 1997. Inside Directors, Board Effectiveness, and Shareholder Wealth. *Journal of Financial Economics* 44: 229–50. [CrossRef]

Shan, Neeta, and Christopher Napier. 2014. *The Cadbury Report 1992: Shared Vision and Beyond*; Essay. Egham: Royal Holloway University of London. Available online: http://wwwdata.unibg.it/dati/corsi/900002/79548-Beyond%20Cadbury%20Report%20Napier%20paper.pdf (accessed on 31 December 2018).

Shleifer, Andrei, and Robert Vishny. 1997. A survey of corporate. *The Journal of Finance* 52: 737–38. [CrossRef]

Short, Helen, and Kevin Keasey. 1999. Managerial ownership and the performance of firms: Evidence from the UK. *Journal of Corporate Finance* 5: 79–101. [CrossRef]

Stoeberl, Phillip, and Bruce C. Sherony. 1985. Board Efficiency and Effectiveness. In *Handbook for Corporate Directors*. Edited by Edward Mattar and Michael Ball. New York: McGraw-Hill, pp. 12.1–12.10.

Minguez-Vera, Antonio, and Juan Francisco Martin-Ugedo. 2007. Does ownership structure affect value? A panel data analysis for the Spanish market. *International Review of Financial Analysis* 16: 81–98. [CrossRef]

Weisbach, Michael. 1988. Outside Directors and CEO Turnover. *Journal of Financial Economics* 20: 431–60. [CrossRef]

Yeh, Yin-Hua, and Tsun-Siou Lee. 2002. Corporate Governance and Corporate Equity Investments: Evidence from Taiwan. Paper presented at 9th Global Finance Conference, Beijing, China, May 27–29.

Zhang, Yu-Ren, Tay-Chang Wang, and Chung-Fern Wu. 2009. Evidence on the association between mechanisms of corporate governance and the portfolio held by foreign investors. *Journal of Management & Systems* 16: 505–32.

Journal of
Risk and Financial Management

MDPI

Article

The Impact of Exchange Rate Volatility on Exports in Vietnam: A Bounds Testing Approach

Vinh Nguyen Thi Thuy * and Duong Trinh Thi Thuy

Foreign Trade University, Hanoi 100000, Vietnam; trinhthithuyduong.ftu@gmail.com
* Correspondence: vinhntt@ftu.edu.vn; Tel.: +84-24-3775-1278 (ext. 112)

Received: 15 November 2018; Accepted: 27 December 2018; Published: 4 January 2019

Abstract: This paper investigates the impact of exchange rate volatility on exports in Vietnam using quarterly data from the first quarter of 2000 to the fourth quarter of 2014. The paper applies the autoregressive distributed lag (ARDL) bounds testing approach to the analysis of level relationships between effective exchange rate volatility and exports. Using the demand function of exports, the paper also considers the effect of depreciation and foreign income on exports of Vietnam. The results show that exchange rate volatility negatively affects the export volume in the long run, as expected. A depreciation of the domestic currency affects exports negatively in the short run, but positively in the long run, consistent with the J curve effect. Surprisingly, an increase in the real income of a foreign country actually decreases Vietnamese export volume. These findings suggest some policy implications in managing the exchange rate system and promoting exports of Vietnam.

Keywords: exchange rate; volatility; exports; ARDL; Vietnam

---

1. Introduction

In 2015, the exchange rate became a hot issue for Vietnam's economy with regard to concerns about China's devaluation of the Yuan, the increase of the federal fund rate of Fed, and the US dollar appreciation against many currencies in the world. Due to being pegged to the USD, the Vietnam Dong (VND) became more expensive against many foreign currencies, thus, the competitiveness of Vietnamese goods and the trade balance was affected negatively. The debatable policy question is whether a dong-pegged-to-the-dollar policy over the years remains appropriate. From a corporate perspective, does the stability of the VND against USD support enterprises to avoid risk in international business because the US dollar is the main payment currency, or enterprises may be adversely impacted by the uncertainty of bilateral exchange rates for currencies of different countries around the world? In the period of integrating into the world's economy, Vietnam could be seriously challenged by the increase in such risks, therefore, it is necessary to find a suitable exchange rate arrangement. Under that situation, on 31 December 2015, the State Bank of Vietnam issued Decision No. 2730/QD-NHNN to announce the way to determine the central rate of the VND against the USD, which would be used by financial institutions authorized to trade in foreign currencies. The rate is calculated based on three benchmarks: demand and supply of the Vietnam Dong, the movement of eight currencies of the countries having the largest weights for trading and investment with Vietnam, including the USD, the Euro, the Chinese Yuan, the Japanese Yen, the Singapore Dollar, the South Korean Won, the Thai Baht, and the Taiwan Dollar, and macroeconomic balance.

However, whether the exchange rate stability based on the eight major currencies really brings advantages to international trade or not is still a significant question because of the mixed results of theoretical, as well as empirical, studies on the impact of exchange rate volatility on international trade, although many studies also propose that mitigating exchange rate risk is very important to ensuring that the exports of a country achieve sustained stable growth. Moreover, in Vietnam, economists often study the impact of exchange rate movement on the trade balance, inflation, and economic growth, while studies concentrating on measuring and assessing the influence of exchange rate volatility are still limited, especially in regards to the macro approach. Therefore, it is worthwhile to investigate the effect of exchange rate volatility on exports in the Vietnam context.

For all of the above reasons, this paper investigates the impact of exchange rate volatility between VND and the basket of eight foreign currencies referred to in the central rate benchmark on exports of the Vietnamese economy using quarterly data from the first quarter of 2000 to the fourth quarter of 2014 and the Autoregressive Distributed Lag (ARDL) method of Pesaran et al. (2001). Pesaran's ARDL method shows having comparatively superior forecasting performance compared to the other techniques based on co-integration (Iqbal and Uddin 2013; Adom and Bekoe 2012). The result shows that export performance will be impacted by exchange rate volatility in the long run. A one percent increase in exchange rate volatility will reduce export volume significantly by about 0.11 percent. However, an appreciation of the domestic currency can adversely affect the competitiveness of Vietnamese exports in the international market in the short run, while the Vietnam Dong's devaluation will have positive impacts and improve exports in the long run. A surprising finding is that real foreign income has a negative impact on export volume of Vietnam in both the long run and the short run. The findings provide some implications for managers, policymakers, and entrepreneurs. The remainder of the paper is organized as follows: Section 2 reviews the theoretical background and econometric techniques for examining the effect of exchange rate volatility on exports. Next, Section 3 describes the model, methodology and relevant data used for quantitative assessment in the case of Vietnam. Then, the estimation results are discussed in Section 4. Finally, Section 5 concludes with a summary of findings and policy recommendations.

2. Theoretical Framework and Literature Review

Different theories exist in the literature regarding the impact of exchange rate volatility on exporter behavior. An increase in exchange rate volatility may be associated with either an increase or a decrease in the volume of exports, given plausible alternative assumptions.

Traditionally, it has been argued that exchange rate volatility will have a negative influence on exports. Clark (1973) analyses a very early example, in which a firm produces a homogenous commodity and exports its products entirely to one foreign market. In this basic model, the market is considered as perfectly competitive and imported inputs are not required. The firm receives payments for its exports in foreign currency and hedging possibilities are extremely limited. Owing to adjustment costs, the firm cannot change its output over the planning horizon. The unpredictable variation of the exchange rate, therefore, is solely blame for uncertainty about future export sales as well as future profits in domestic currency. For the sake of maximizing the expected value of utility, which depends on both the expected value and the variance of profits, the risk-averse firm would reduce its exposure to risk in response to higher volatility in the exchange rate. That is, the volume of production, and hence exports would be cut down in this circumstance. This simple model is also developed by a number of authors, for example, Baron (1976b); Hooper and Kohlhagen (1978), indicated the same conclusion that exchange rate volatility has a negative effect on exports.

However, all of those conclusions result from several restrictive assumptions. One obvious criticism of the traditional models is that the exporter's risk exposure is attributed solely to the exchange rate volatility, whereas it may depend on the availability of hedging techniques, diversification possibilities, the existence of imported inputs, and other factors. The rationale of this assumption is that forward exchange markets are just in infancy or even not appear in developing economies. In addition, transaction hedging may prove relatively expensive and challenging for some manufacturing firms with a long time between order and delivery. However, this is not the case with advanced countries, in which such markets are well-developed. For risk-adverse entrepreneurs who can hedge their contracts, a higher exchange rate volatility would not always deter exports, as noted by Ethier (1973) and Baron (1976a). Furthermore, the companies can minimize exchange rate risk in other ways; take multinational cooperation to be a good case in point. Being involved in a wide range of trade and financial transactions over numerous countries, it would see an abundance of diverse opportunities to offset the movement of a bilateral exchange rate, such as the variability of other exchange rates or interest rates. Relaxing the assumption of no imported intermediate inputs, Clark (1973) finds that the loss from the depreciation in a foreign currency to the exporter will be partly alleviated by lowering input cost. Likewise, if inventories are possible and firms can allocate their sales between abroad and home markets, a declining effect on export earnings will also be compensated. More generally, from a finance perspective, Makin (1978) argues that a diversified firm holding a portfolio of assets and liabilities determined in various currencies will be able to protect itself from exchange rate risks related to exports and imports. Finally, recent studies suggest that exchange rate volatility does not just embody a risk, but profit opportunities. For instance, as examined by Canzoneri et al. (1984), if a firm has ability to alter its factor inputs to benefit from changes in exchange rate without adjustment costs, a higher volatility may create greater probability to make profit. Gros (1987) derives a further version of model with the presence of adjustment costs, in which exporting can be seen as an option depending on capacity, taking advantage of favorable conditions (e.g., high prices) and to minimizing the influence otherwise. The value of the option rises as result of higher variability of the exchange rate, creating a positive effect on exports. Therefore, the effect of volatility remains ambiguous because the dominant direction depends on a case-by-case basis.

In the early models, the negative association between exchange rate volatility and expected export increases is supported in terms of risk aversion. The uncertainty of the exchange rate seems to not affect a risk-neutral firm's decision. Nonetheless, De Grauwe (1988) argues that the assumption of risk-averse agents is not adequate to ensure the direction of this link. What is relevant is the degree of risk aversion. An increase in risk, in general, has both a substitution and an income effect that work in opposite directions (Goldstein and Khan 1985). The substitution effect discourages risk-averse agents to export because it lowers the expected utility representing the attractiveness of the risky activity, while the income effects urges very risk-averse agents to increase their exports to avoid the possibility of a severe decline in the revenues. Taken together, these studies support the notion that even though firms are worse off with an increase in exchange rate risk, their response may be to export more rather than less.

All of the theoretical studies reviewed here support the notion that the net effect of exchange rate volatility on exports is ambiguous, as differing results can arise from plausible alternative assumptions and modelling strategies. Increased exchange rate volatility can have no significant effect on exports, or where significant, no systematic effect in one direction or the other.

Numerous empirical studies have been conducted in many countries and areas around the world to evaluate the impact of exchange rate volatility on exports. Again, the implications of the results of those studies confirm that, although exchange rate volatility has an impact on exports, the effect can be either positive or negative depending on the endowment of each country; whether empirical studies use aggregate data, sectoral data or bilateral data; and the econometric techniques applied.

The empirical literature using aggregate data tends to find weak evidence in favor of a negative impact of exchange rate uncertainty on the trade flows of a country to the rest of the world. Using the Engel-Granger method, Doroodian (1999) approximated volatility with both Autoregressive Integrated Moving Average (ARIMA) and Generalized Autoregressive Conditional Heteroskedasticity (GARCH) techniques to study the exports of India, Malaysia, and South Korea from the second quarter of 1973 to the third quarter of 1996. The results reveal significantly negative effects of exchange rate volatility on exports. Meanwhile, employing the Johansen approach of co-integration and using Autoregressive Conditional Heteroskedasticity (ARCH) method to calculate volatility, Arize and Malindretos (1998) found mixed results for two Pacific-Basin countries: volatility is shown to depress New Zealand exports, while its impact is positive in the case of Australia.

To sum up, the majority of empirical studies indicate that the relationship between a single country's exports and exchange rate volatility is statistically significantly negative in the long run, especially in developing countries, while others consider that there is the positive relationship in the short run or long run. The basis for empirical model development is mostly based on simple demand functions of exports. Relative prices, income, and volatility are often employed as determinants. There are two major problems facing the applied econometrics in these studies. Firstly, there has not yet been a standard exchange rate volatility proxy (Bahmani-Oskooee and Hegerty 2007). Some measure of variance has dominated this field, but the precise calculation of this measure differs from study to study. Later estimates have involved using the standard deviation of a rate of change or the level of a variable. Kenen and Rodrik (1986) draw attention to the moving standard deviation of the monthly change in the exchange rate, which has the advantage of being stationary. Utilizing newer time-series methods, Engle and Granger (1987) developed Autoregressive Conditional Heteroskedasticity (ARCH) as a measure of volatility in time-series errors, which is a widespread measure of exchange rate volatility in the literature. A broader perspective is adopted by (Pattichis 2003) who develops Generalized Autoregressive Conditional Heteroskedasticity (GARCH), which incorporates moving-average processes. These authors' estimates also have the desirable property of stationarity. Some measures are more popular than others, however, none stands out as the standard volatility proxy (Bahmani-Oskooee and Hegerty 2007). The second problem is the type of method used in estimating the empirical model. While the Ordinary Least Squares (OLS) was commonly used in the early papers, newer and more sophisticated techniques, including time-series and panel data methods, in recent studies have facilitated investigation of the sensitivity of exports to a measure of exchange rate volatility. The main goal of modern time-series analysis is to take into consideration integrating properties of the variables so that spurious results can be avoided. Some popular methods of time-series analysis in recent years are the Engle-Granger method, the Johansen method, and the bounds testing approach.

3. Exchange Rate Volatility Measurement

Exchange rate volatility denotes the amount of uncertainty or risk about the size of changes in the exchange rate. If the exchange rate can potentially be spread out over a larger range of values in a short time span, it is termed to have high volatility. If the exchange rate does not fluctuate dramatically, and tends to be steadier, it is termed to have low volatility. Additionally, real and nominal exchange rate volatilities are different for practical purposes. The properties of the method used to estimate volatility have also received lots of attention. Bahmani-Oskooee and Hegerty (2007) emphasizes the fact that a clearly dominant approximation for uncertainty has not yet emerged up to now.

In this paper, the exchange rate volatility is measured by the moving average of the standard deviation of exchange rates, which is typically used by a number of scholars such as Chowdhury (1993); Arize and Malindretos (1998); Kasman and Kasman (2005). This equation is as follows:

$$
\text{VOL}_t = \left[\frac{1}{m} \sum_{i=1}^{m} (\text{ER}_{t+i-1} - \text{ER}_{t+i-2})^2 \right]^{\frac{1}{m}} \tag{1}
$$

where m is the number of periods; and t is time and ER refers to the exchange rate index. In our study, m = 2.

Bagella et al. (2006) show advantages of effective exchange rate volatility comparing with bilateral exchange rate volatility and find that this variable performs much better than the bilateral exchange rate volatility measure. An important advantage is that the effective exchange rate reflects more sufficiently the stability of a country which might have low bilateral exchange rate volatility with a leading currency but absorb instability via variability of economic policies of its trade partners. Therefore, we use the nominal effective exchange rate between the VND and a foreign currency basket (NEER) to compute the exchange rate volatility. This selected basket consists of eight foreign currencies used by the SBV to refer to the central exchange rate from the beginning of 2016, including: USD (United States), EUR (EU), CNY (China), THB (Thailand), JPY (Japan), SGD (Singapore) KRW (Korea), and TWD (Taiwan). This option aims to assess the validity of the new exchange rate policy for export purposes. Following the splicing procedure proposed by Ellis (2001), this index is computed as:

$$\text{NEER}_t = \text{NEER}_{t-1} \frac{\prod_{j=1}^{8} \left(\text{NER}_t^j \right)^{\omega_{jt}}}{\prod_{j=1}^{8} \left(\text{NER}_{t-1}^j \right)^{\omega_{jt}}} \tag{2}$$

where NEER_t is the real effective exchange rate of Vietnam at time t; NER_t^j is the nominal bilateral exchange rate relative to currency of country j, measured as the number of units of the domestic currency per unit of currency of country j and expressed as an index; ω_{jt} is the weight assigned to the currency of country j at time t, reflecting the contribution of the country j to Vietnam's foreign trade, $\sum_{j=1}^{8} \omega_{jt} = 1$.

In Equation (2), the nominal effective exchange rate is calculated as the ratio of geometrically weighted bilateral nominal exchange rates in the current period and in the preceding period, using current weights, spliced onto the preceding level of nominal effective exchange rate. There are two main advantages associated with the use of this approach. Firstly, the weights are allowed to vary over time in order to account for the possibility that some countries may become more important trading partners. Otherwise, if actual trade shares move significantly and this is not taken into consideration, the effective exchange rate would give a misleading picture of the net effect of movements in particular bilateral exchange rates. Secondly, as changing weights are updated, it is important that the exchange rate index should be spliced together with the previous observation. Otherwise, in periods in which the weights change, it would not be clear whether a change in the NEER is reflecting changes in the weights or in the bilateral exchange rates, as we can see from a common calculation: $\text{NEER}_t = \prod_{j=1}^{8} \left(\text{NER}_t^j \right)^{w_{jt}}$. There are some prior studies using this approach, such as Moccero and Winograd (2006); Chinn (2006); Betliy (2002); Dullien (2005).

Data for bilateral exchange rates and trade weights are computed from International Financial Statistics (IFS) and Direction of Trade Statistics (DOTS) of IMF.

Figure 1 describes the volatility of NEER of the Vietnam Dong versus the eight currency basket for the period from the first quarter of 2000 to the fourth quarter of 2014. The degree of this volatility depends on the exchange rate policy and the fluctuation of foreign currencies in the world market. As can be seen from Figure 1, the NEER volatility fluctuated gradually from 2000 to 2007, dramatically increased during the following four years and decreased between 2012 and 2014.

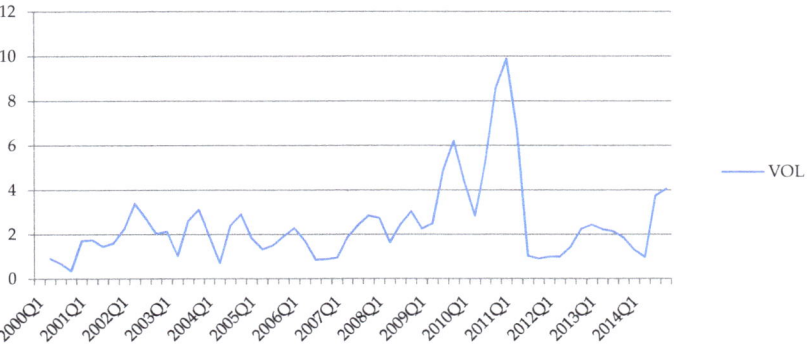

Figure 1. Vietnamese NEER volatility (2000 Q1–2014 Q4).

After introducing a new principle for setting the exchange rate in 1999, the volatility from 2000 to 2008 was relatively small as the official exchange rate was almost unchanged. During the period from 2008 to 2011, the State Bank of Vietnam had devalued three times the Vietnam Dong by approximately

10% and adjusted the trading band in commercial banks continuously (widened the band five times from ±0.5% to ±5% and then narrowed it back to 1%). These actions increased the exchange rate fluctuation. From 2012 to 2014, the official exchange rate remained stable except for a devaluation in June 2013 and the trading band was fixed at ±1%, therefore, the volatility was small.

4. Empirical Investigation

4.1. Econometric Model

According to the microeconomic theory, conventional demand functions are homogenous degree zero in terms of price and income (Deaton and Muellbauer 1980). To examine the impact of exchange rate volatility on exports, this study adds an exchange rate volatility variable to the traditional export demand function comprising consumers' income (or GDP) and relative price, which has been used in many previous studies such as Salas (1982); Gafar (1995); Matsubayashi and Hamori (2003); Ekanayake et al. (2010). The model is specified as follows:

$$X_t = \beta_0 + \beta_1 GDP\_F_t + \beta_2 REER_t + \beta_3 VOL_t + \varepsilon_t \tag{3}$$

where X represents real exports; GDP_F is real foreign income; REER is the real effective exchange rate; and VOL is the exchange rate volatility. With regard to the functional form, Khan and Ross (1977) suggest that a log-linear specification is better than a standard linear one on both empirical and theoretical grounds. That is, the former allows the dependent variable to react proportionally to an increase or decrease in the regressors and exhibits interaction between elasticities. Therefore, all variables in Equation (3) are expressed in logarithmic form. In Equation (3) we have the following expectations for the sign of the regression coefficients: According to the gravity theory of international trade, increases in real GDP of trading partners would be expected to result in greater real exports to those partners, therefore, $\beta_1 > 0$. Due to the relative price effect, the real exchange rate may lead to an increase in the volume of export, therefore, $\beta_2 > 0$. The relationship between the exchange rate volatility and export volume is ambiguous, thus, it is expected that $\beta_3 > 0$ or $\beta_3 < 0$.

When modelling the relationship between a set of time-series variables, it is important to take into account the stationarity of the data. When detecting a spurious regression problem among these series including a unit root, some methods are suggested to solve this problem. One of the simplest ways is taking the differences of the series and estimating a standard regression model. However, this method results in the loss of information that is meaningful for the level relationships. Provided that the first differences of the variables are used, it is impossible to determine a potential long run relationship in levels. Moving from this point, the co-integration approach associated with error-correction modelling was developed during the late 1980s. In this way, both the short run and long run relationship can be analyzed. The co-integration approach developed by Engle and Granger (1987) is suitable for the test based on the expectation of only one co-integrating vector being present. Further, the approach proposed by Johansen (1988) enables researchers to test the case that there is more than one co-integration vector by using the VAR model in which all the variables are accepted as endogenous. However, the important condition that must be met to perform these standard co-integration tests is that all series should not be stationary at levels and they should be integrated of the same order. In order to overcome this problem, Pesaran et al. (2001) have developed the bounds test approach. According to this method, the existence of a co-integration relationship can be investigated between the time-series regardless of whether they are I(0) or I(1) (under the circumstance that the dependent variable is I(1)). This point is the greatest merit of the bounds test over conventional co-integration testing. Moreover, this approach can distinguish dependent and independent variables and is more suitable than another method for dealing with small sample sizes (Ghorbani and Motallebi 2009). In addition, different variables can be assigned different lag lengths as they enter the model.

As reviewed by Bahmani-Oskooee and Hegerty (2007), while common variables in trade models are non-stationary series, most measures of exchange rate volatility are stationary. Therefore, the ARDL approach by Pesaran et al. (2001) is the most highly recommended to investigate the effect of exchange rate volatility on exports. There are some prior studies using this approach, such as De Vita and Abbott (2004); Sekantsi (2008); Yin and Hamori (2011); and Alam and Ahmad (2011). To implement the bounds test procedure, Equation (3) is modelled as a conditional ARDL error correction model as follows:

$$\text{LEX}_t = \alpha_0 + \beta_0 t + \sum_{i=1}^{l_1} \delta_{1i} \text{LEX}_{t-i} \sum_{i=1}^{l_2} \delta_{2i} \text{LGDP\_F}_{t-i} \sum_{i=1}^{l_3} \delta_{3i} \text{LREER}_{t-i} \sum_{i=1}^{l_4} \delta_{4i} \text{LVOL}_{t-i} + u_t \qquad (4)$$

$$\Delta \text{LEX}_t = \alpha_1 + \gamma_0 t + \theta_1 \text{LEX}_{t-1} + \theta_2 \text{LGDP}_{Ft-1} + \theta_3 \text{LREER}_{t-1} + \theta_4 \text{LVOL}_{t-1}$$
$$+ \sum_{i=1}^{l_1-1} \lambda_{1i} \Delta \text{LEX}_{t-i} + \sum_{i=1}^{l_2-1} \lambda_{2i} \Delta \text{LGDP\_F}_{t-i} + \sum_{i=1}^{l_3-1} \lambda_{3i} \Delta \text{LREER}_{t-i} + \sum_{i=1}^{l_4-1} \lambda_{4i} \Delta \text{LVOL}_{t-i} + u_t \qquad (5)$$

where LEX, LGDP_F, and LREER are the natural logarithms of real exports, real foreign income, and the real effective exchange rate (all data are seasonally adjusted); LVOL is the natural logarithm of the nominal exchange rate volatility of Vietnam; l_1, l_2, l_3, l_4 are lag-lengths; θ_1, θ_2, θ_3, θ_4 are long-run coefficients; and λ_{1i}, λ_{2i}, λ_{3i}, λ_{4i} are short-run coefficients (if the co-integration vector exists) and u_t is a random disturbance term.

According to Pesaran et al. (2001), the ARDL approach uses two main steps to estimate the level relationship. The first step is the co-integration test to determine whether a level relationship exists between the variables in Equation (4). The null hypothesis of no level relationship among variables is tested. This test is performed on the basis of comparing the computed F-statistic values with bounds on critical values which depend on the number of variables. Furthermore, some later studies propose the critical value table for special cases, such as the study by Narayan (2005) dealing with small sample size. For various situations, those authors give lower and upper bounds on the critical values. In each case, the lower bound is based on the assumption that all the variables are I(0), and the upper bound is based on the assumption that all the variables are I(1). If the estimated F-statistic falls below the lower bound we cannot reject the null hypothesis, so no co-integration is possible. If the F-statistic exceeds the upper bound, we conclude that we have co-integration. Finally, if the F-statistic falls between the bounds, the test is inconclusive. If the long-run relationship is established between the variables, the long-run and short-run coefficients can be obtained by using the ARDL approach. The appropriate lag orders of variables are chosen using the Schwarz Information Criterion (SIC).

4.2. Data and Data Sources

The study uses quarterly data from the first quarter of 2000 to the fourth quarter of 2014, including 60 observations. This period is used for research in order to minimize the problems associated with monetary policy changes. Data for real exports (EX) is collected from the General Statistics Office of Vietnam (GSO). Real foreign income (GDP_F) is measured by the export weighted GDP Volume Index of the twenty largest export partners during this period (United States, Japan, China, Australia, Singapore, Germany, Korea, Malaysia, United Kingdom, Philippines, Netherlands, Thailand, Canada, France, Indonesia, Switzerland, Belgium, Hong Kong, Italy, and Spain). GDP_F is calculated as follows:

$$\text{GDP\_F}_t = \prod_{j=1}^{20} (Y_{jt})^{\varphi_{jt}} \qquad (6)$$

where Y_{jt} is the real GDP of each partner, calculated by the GDP Volume Index, collected from the IFS dataset; φ_{jt} is the export weight assign to partner j at time t, computed by using data from the DOTS and $\sum_{j=1}^{20} \varphi_{jt} = 1$.

The real effective exchange rate index (REER) is defined in domestic currency terms (an increase in its value indicates a depreciation of Vietnamese currency) and is estimated by the geometric average, as in the following common equation:

$$\text{REER}_t = \prod_{j=1}^{n} \left(\text{NER}_t^j \frac{\text{CPI}_t^j}{\text{CPI}_t^{VN}} \right)^{w_{jt}} \tag{7}$$

where REER_t is the real effective exchange rate of Vietnam at time t; n is the number of trading-partner currencies in the trade basket; NER_t^j is the nominal bilateral exchange rate relative to currency of country j, measured as the number of units of the domestic currency per unit of currency of country j and expressed as an index; CPI_t^j and CPI_t^{VN} are consumer price indices at time t of foreign country j and Vietnam, respectively; and w_{jt} is the trade-weight assigned to currency of country j at time t, reflecting the contribution of the partner j to Vietnam's foreign trade, $\sum_{j=1}^{n} w_{jt} = 1$. Further, with the same rationale as Equation (2), Equation (7) is adjusted according to the splicing procedure proposed by Ellis (2001) to avoid biasing the result due to changing weights.

The currency basket includes the currencies of Vietnam's twenty largest trading partners during the period from 2000 to 2014, which are: USD (United States), JPY (Japan), CNY (China), KRW (Korea), SGD (Singapore), TWD (Taiwan), THB (Thailand), MYR (Malaysia), AUD (Australia), HKD (Hong Kong), IDR (Indonesia), INR (India), GBP (United Kingdom), KHR (Cambodia), PHP (Philippines), RUB (Russia), AED (United Arab Emirates), CHF (Switzerland), CAD (Canada), and EUR (19 Eurozone countries). The basket covered over 90% of Vietnam's total trade in every year since 2000. In addition, each selected partner accounted for at least 0.2 percent of total foreign trade during this period.

Data for trade values is collected from the DOTS, while bilateral exchange rate data and consumer price index data are collected from the IFS of IMF.

4.3. Results and Discussions

4.3.1. Unit Root Test

Prior to constructing our models, all variables are tested for stationary and the order of integration is determined. Augmented Dicker Fuller (ADF) tests are conducted including a drift term and both with and without a trend. The lag-lengths for ADF regressions are chosen using the Schwarz Information Criterion (SIC). Table 1 contains the results of the unit root tests.

Table 1. ADF unit root tests.

Variable	Level		First Difference	
	Constant	Constant and Trend	Constant	Constant and Trend
LEX	0.37	−1.46	−9.61 ***	−9.55 ***
LGDP_F	−0.64	−2.98	−4.92 ***	−4.89 ***
LREER	−0.39	−2.37	−4.46 ***	−4.61 ***
LVOL	−4.19 ***	−4.30 ***	−7.32 ***	−7.32 ***

Note: *** are respectively significant at 1%.

The results confirm that all the series are I(1), with the exception of the exchange rate volatility (LVOL), which is I(0). In other words, unit root tests show that the dependent variables are I(1) and the independent variables are a mixture of I(0) and I(1). Thus, the ARDL approach is more suitable than other approaches for examining relationships in levels of variables.

4.3.2. Bounds Testing for Level Relationships

Using Schwarz (Bayes) criterion to find optimal lags, the EVIEWS 9.5 software developed by IHS Markit (London, UK) suggests the model of ARDL (2,0,2,7).

A key assumption in the Bounds Testing methodology of Pesaran et al. (2001) is that the errors of Equation (6) must be serially independent. This requirement may also be influential in the choice of optimal lags for the variables in the model. We use the LM test to test the null hypothesis of no serial correlation. The result indicates that at the 1% significance level, we cannot reject the null hypothesis, therefore, the selected model is suitable to test the cointegration relationship between the variables.

Due to the small sample size, we use the critical value bounds given by Narayan (2005). The result of bounds testing is shown in Table 2.

Table 2. F-statistics to test the existence of long run relationships.

Model	Number of Regressors	Sample Size	Estimated F Test Value	Critical Values Bounds-Narayan (2005), Unrestricted Intercept and Unrestricted Trend					
				10%		5%		1%	
	k	n	F-Statistic	I(0)	I(1)	I(0)	I(1)	I(0)	I(1)
ARDL (2,0,2,7)	3	52	14.576	3.673	4.715	4.368	5.545	5.995	7.335

As can be seen from the table, the calculated F-statistic of 14.576 exceeds the upper bounds, this supports the existence of level relationships between real exports, real foreign income, real effective exchange rate and exchange rate volatility in the export equation. The selected ARDL model is rewritten as a single error correction model to identify long run and short run relationships.

4.3.3. Short run and Long run Relationship

By normalizing the exports, from the ARDL (2,0,2,7), the empirical results of the relationships in levels are presented in Equation (8):

$$LEX_t = 0.047t - 1.403LGDP\_F_t + 0.987LREER_t - 0.102LVOL_t + e_t$$
$$(0.004)*** \qquad (0.344)*** \qquad (0.139)*** \qquad (0.012)***$$

(8)

Note: *** are respectively significant of 1%, the standard errors are in parenthesis.

The estimation result suggests that all of variables could significantly explain the variation in exports at the 1% level of significant.

The estimated coefficient of VOL is about -0.11 percent, implying that the exchange rate volatility has a negative impact on real exports. A one percent increase in the volatility reduces Vietnamese exports by about 0.11%. This is in line with the theoretical models of the behavior of risk adverse exporters in Clark (1973); Kohlhagen (1978), etc.; Arize and Malindretos (1998) argue that higher exchange rate volatility will depress export volume through a rise in adjustment costs like irreversible investment due to higher uncertainty and risks.

At the macro level, this result is consistent with Qian and Varangis (1994) from considering the cases of developing countries. In these countries, the means of payment in international trade is in foreign currency and the degree of dollarization is fairly high (always above 15 percent in Vietnam), hence, the impact of exchange rate volatility is significant to economic activities. In addition, in developing countries like Vietnam, the derivative markets are underdeveloped, so that hedging may not only be limited but also costly. Another possible explanation for the long run negative impact of exchange rate volatility is that the higher the risk, the higher the value of options, leading to increased costs to ensure the future profit. This reduces the transaction volume in the market.

However, for the short run relationships shown in Table 3, all coefficients of the first difference of VOL are positive and statistically significant at the 1% level, indicating that if exchange rate volatility increases, export volume will increase in the short run. To sum up, the volatility of exchange rate has a positive and significant short-run effect on exports whilst, in the long run, volatility adversely affects export performance in Vietnam. This result is likely to be related to the simple model of De Grauwe (1988) arguing that the effect of an increase in risk can be decomposed into a substitution effect and an income effect. The substitution effect causes risk-averse firms to decrease export activities as the expected marginal utility of export revenues decrease, while the income effect leads risk-averse firms to boost export performance to avoid severe falls in revenues. Kroner and Lastrapes (1993) argue that enterprises may increase commercial activity as they expect the market to deteriorate in the future due to unforeseen fluctuations in the exchange rate. Thus, they quickly trade at the present time, trying to maximize profits to compensate for possible losses. Thus, in the short run, the income effect can offset the substitution effect, so exports will be encouraged. Alternatively, in the long run, enterprises may have more flexible responses to risks, such as transferring export goods to the domestic market and the cost of hedging becomes more expensive, so the substitution effect can dominate the income effect. This results in a decline in exports in the long run.

Table 3. The ECM for the selected ARDL model of output equation.

Regressors	ARDL (2,0,2,7)
ΔLEX(-1)	0.590 (0.116) ***
ΔLGDP_F	-2.653 (0.312) ***
ΔLREER	1.086 (0.301) ***
ΔLREER(-1)	-0.883 (0.333) **
ΔLVOL	-0.001 (0.001)
ΔLVOL(-1)	0.148 (0.019) ***
ΔLVOL(-2)	0.119 (0.017) ***
ΔLVOL(-3)	0.110 (0.015) ***
ΔLVOL(-4)	0.082 (0.014) ***
ΔLVOL(-5)	0.063 (0.012) ***
ΔLVOL(-6)	0.034 (0.012) ***
C	22.434 (2.225) ***
ECM$_{t-1}$	-1.709 (0.172) ***
Adj. R-Square	0.726
$\text{ECM}_t = \text{LEX}_t - (-1.403\text{LGDPF}_t + 0.987\text{LREER}_t - 0,107\text{LVOL}_t + 0,047t)$	

, * are respectively significant at 5% and 1% levels. The t-ratios are in brackets.

Surprisingly, at the 1% level of significance, the coefficient of the real foreign income variable is negative. The estimated result suggests that if real income of the main importing countries from Vietnam goes up by 1%, the export volume of Vietnam will go down by 1.4%. In addition, the GDP_F variable has a negative short-run coefficient, implying that real trading partners' income exerts a significant adverse effect on real exports of Vietnam in both the short run and the long run. This finding is different to the results of previous studies showing that the impact of foreign output on exports in Vietnam is positive. However, this discrepancy may be due to the fact that those studies have used the nominal values of GDP and exports while, in this paper, the data in real terms has been calculated. Moreover, Vietnamese exports remain low-grade in terms of technological content and added value. Most agricultural products and minerals are exported in their raw or preliminarily processed forms, therefore, an increase in the real foreign income may decline the expenditure on Vietnamese goods following the theory of Engel (1857) on necessary goods that the demand decreases as income increases.

The coefficient of the real effective exchange rate is significant at the 1% level in the long run equation, implying if real exchange rate increases by 1%, the export volume will increase by 0.99%. Therefore, an appreciation will hamper export performance in Vietnam. This is in line with the theory and many empirical studies suggesting that the REER value represents the competitiveness of Vietnamese goods in the international market. Nonetheless, the short-run coefficient of the REER variable is negative and highly significant. Thus, a depreciation of the domestic currency affects exports negatively in the short run, but positively in the long run, consistent with the J curve effect.

Table 3 provides the summary of the error correction representation of the estimated ARDL model. The empirical results indicate that the error correction term has the correct sign (negative) and is statistically significant. This is further evidence of co-integration relationships among the variables in the model. The estimated value of the error correction term implies that the speed of adjustment to the long run equilibrium in response to the disequilibrium caused by short-run shocks of the previous period is 170.5% in the export equation.

4.3.4. Diagnostic Testing

The diagnostic tests including the normality test, serial correlation test, and heteroscedasticity test generally provide satisfactory outcomes.

Finally, the stability of the long-run coefficients along with the short run dynamics are evaluated by applying the CUSUM and CUSUMSQ (Brown et al. 1975). The CUSUM test uses the cumulative sum of recursive residuals, whereas the CUSUMSQ test is based on the cumulative sum of the squared recursive residuals. As shown in Figure 2 both plots of CUSUM statistics and CUSUMSQ statistics stay within the critical bounds of the 5% significance level (represented by the pair of straight lines drawn at the 5% level of significance). These tests indicate no evidence of any significant structural instability. Therefore, the estimated results are stable over the studied time period.

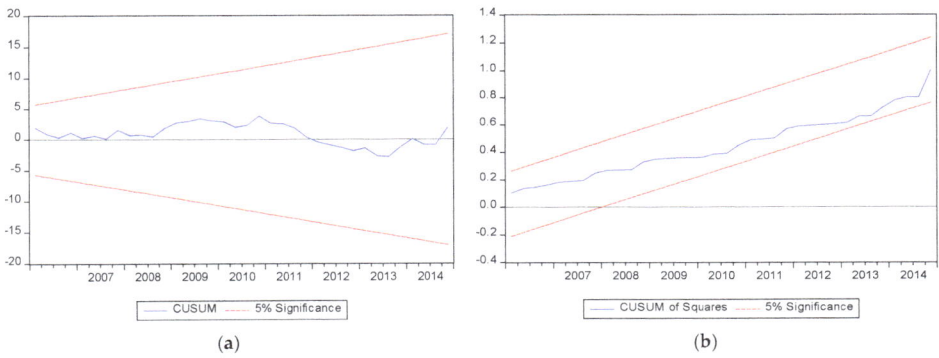

Figure 2. Plot of cumulative sum of recursive residuals recursive residuals (**a**) and cumulative of squares of recursive residuals (**b**). The straight lines represent critical bounds at the 5% significance level.

5. Conclusions

This paper aims to examine the impact of exchange rate volatility on Vietnamese exports performance during the period from the first quarter of 2000 to the fourth quarter of 2014. We use the Moving Average of Standard Deviation (MASD) model and nominal effective exchange rates computed by a weighted average of the nominal bilateral exchange rate of the Vietnam Dong against the basket of eight foreign currencies to measure exchange rate volatility. This paper also applies an approach called the Autoregressive Distributed Lag (ARDL) to investigate the existence of a level relationship among variables in the model and implements it using EVIEWS software offered by IHS Markit (London, UK). The advantage of this approach is that it is suitable for small sample size and regressors which are a mixture of I(0) and I(1).

It is found that there exists a co-integration relationship between real exports, real foreign income, real effective exchange rate, and nominal exchange rate volatility. In addition, the speed of adjustment to the long run equilibrium is fairly high.

The result shows that export performance will be impacted by exchange rate volatility in the long run. A one percent increase in exchange rate volatility will reduce export volume significantly by about 0.11 percent. One anticipated finding is that real foreign income has a negative impact on export volume of Vietnam in both the long run and the short run. As the income of trading partners increases, they tend to import fewer Vietnamese goods, which reflects that the position of Vietnamese goods in the international market remains low-grade. Finally, an appreciation of the domestic currency can adversely affect the competitiveness of Vietnamese exports in the international market in the short run, while the Vietnam Dong's devaluation will have positive impacts and improve exports in the long run. Since the inflation rate of Vietnam is unstable, it may impact the exporters' expectations of movement of real exchange rate. We will deal with this issue for our future empirical research.

These findings have some important policy implications. Firstly, for the State Bank of Vietnam, the conversion of the exchange rate regime from announcing a solid exchange rate between the VND and the US to announcing a central rate and cross rates with eight strong currencies is the right direction to promote export performance. The weighting for these currencies in the basket may be calculated based on stabilizing the nominal effective exchange rate with these eight currencies to reduce exchange rate uncertainty.

Secondly, besides considering exchange rate policy, it is essential for the government to adapt synchronous implementation solutions to overcome the bottlenecks in Vietnamese exports. Production cost, brand value, product quality, and technology content are key factors which threaten to decrease export competitiveness.

Finally, in the context of Vietnam, as the foreign currency derivatives market has not fully developed and there are potential risks in international business, enterprises needs a proper international trade strategy, including a long-term vision for risk analysis and forecasting, combined with the flexible use of risk hedging tools such as futures, options, swap contracts. In addition, exporters wishing to promote their international trade should not rely solely on the devaluation of the domestic currency, but on the long-term strategy in building their brand, defining their comparative advantages and increasing market access.

Author Contributions: V.N.T.T. designed the model and the computational framework and analyzed the data. D.T.T.T. carried out the implementation. V.N.T.T. and D.T.T.T. performed the calculations. D.T.T.T. wrote the initial manuscript with input from all authors. V.N.T.T. was in charge of the overall direction and planning, as well as revised the manuscript.

Funding: This research received no external funding.

Acknowledgments: We are grateful to three anonymous referees for their helpful comments and suggestions.

Conflicts of Interest: The authors declare no conflict of interest.

References

Adom, Philip Kofi, and William Bekoe. 2012. Conditional dynamic forecast of electrical energy consumption requirements in Ghana by 2020: A comparison of ARDL and PAM. *Energy* 44: 367–80. [CrossRef]

Alam, Shaista, and Qazi Masood Ahmad. 2011. Exchange rate volatility and Pakistan's bilateral imports from major sources: An application of ARDL approach. *International Journal of Economics and Finance* 3: 245–54. [CrossRef]

Arize, Augustine Chuck, and John Malindretos. 1998. The long-run and short-run effects of exchange-rate volatility on exports: The case of Australia and New Zealand. *Journal of Economics and Finance* 22: 43–56. [CrossRef]

Bagella, Michele, Leonardo Becchetti, and Iftekhar Hasan. 2006. Real effective exchange rate volatility and growth: A framework to measure advantages of flexibility vs. costs of volatility. *Journal of Banking* 30: 1149–69. [CrossRef]

Bahmani-Oskooee, Mohsen, and Scott. W. Hegerty. 2007. Exchange rate volatility and trade flows: A review article. *Journal of Economic Studies* 34: 211–55. [CrossRef]

Baron, David P. 1976a. Flexible exchange rates, forward markets, and the level of trade. *The American Economic Review* 66: 253–66.

Baron, David P. 1976b. Fluctuating exchange rates and the pricing of exports. *Economic Inquiry* 14: 425–38. [CrossRef]

Betliy, Oleksandra. 2002. Measurement of the Real Effective Exchange Rate and the Observed J-Curve: Case of Ukraine. Master's dissertation, The National University of Kyiv-Mohyla Academy, Kiev, Ukraine.

Brown, Robert L., James Durbin, and James M. Evans. 1975. Techniques for testing the constancy of regression relationships over time. *Journal of the Royal Statistical Society Series B* 37: 149–92. [CrossRef]

Canzoneri, Matthew B., Peter B. Clark, and Thomas C. Glaessner. 1984. The Effects of Exchange Rate Variability on Output and Employment. In *International Finance Discussion Papers 240.* Washington: Board of Governors of the Federal Reserve System.

Chinn, Menzie D. 2006. A primer on real effective exchange rates: Determinants, overvaluation, trade flows and competitive devaluation. *Open Economies Review* 17: 115–43. [CrossRef]

Chowdhury, Abdur R. 1993. Does exchange rate volatility depress trade flows? Evidence from error-correction models. *The Review of Economics Statistics* 75: 700–6. [CrossRef]

Clark, Peter B. 1973. Uncertainty, exchange risk, and the level of international trade. *Economic Inquiry* 11: 302–13. [CrossRef]

De Grauwe, Paul. 1988. Exchange rate variability and the slowdown in growth of international trade. *IMF Economic Review* 35: 63–84. [CrossRef]

De Vita, Glauco, and Andrew Abbott. 2004. The impact of exchange rate volatility on UK exports to EU countries. *Scottish Journal of Political Economy* 51: 62–81. [CrossRef]

Deaton, Angus, and John Muellbauer. 1980. *Economics and Consumer Behavior.* Cambridge: Cambridge University Press.

Doroodian, Khosrow. 1999. Does exchange rate volatility deter international trade in developing countries? *Journal of Asian Economics* 10: 465–74. [CrossRef]

Dullien, Sebastian. 2005. *China's Changing Competitive Position: Lessons from a Unit-Labor-Cost-Based REER.* International Trade. Munich: University Library of Munich.

Ekanayake, Ekanayake M., John Robert Ledgerwood, and Sabrina D'Souza. 2010. The real exchange rate volatility and US exports: An empirical investigation. *International Journal of Business and Finance Research* 4: 23–35.

Ellis, Luci. 2001. *Measuring the Real Exchange Rate: Pitfalls and Practicalities.* Sydney: Reserve Bank of Australia.

Engel, Ernst. 1857. Die produktions-und konsumptionsverhältnisse des königreichs sachsen. *Zeitschrift des Statistischen Bureaus des Königlich Sächsischen Ministeriums des Innern* 8: 1–54.

Engle, Robert Fry, and Clive William John Granger. 1987. Co-integration and error correction: Representation, estimation, and testing. *Econometrica* 55: 251–76. [CrossRef]

Ethier, Wilfred. 1973. International trade and the forward exchange market. *The American Economic Review* 63: 494–503.

Gafar, John. 1995. Some estimates of the price and income elasticities of import demand for three Caribbean countries. *Applied Economics* 27: 1045–48. [CrossRef]

Ghorbani, Mohammad, and Marzieh Motallebi. 2009. Application Pesaran and Shin Method for Estimating Irans Import Demand Function. *Journal of Applied Sciences* 9: 1175–79. [CrossRef]

Goldstein, Morris, and Moshin Khan. 1985. Income and Price Elasticities in Foreign Trade. In *Handbook of International Economics.* Edited by Ronald Jones and Peter Kenen. Amsterdam: North Holland, pp. 1041–105.

Gros, Daniel. 1987. *Exchange Rate Variability and Foreign Trade in the Presence of Adjustment Costs*; Montreal: Department of Economics.

Hooper, Peter, and Steven W. Kohlhagen. 1978. The effect of exchange rate uncertainty on the prices and volume of international trade. *Journal of international Economics* 8: 483–511. [CrossRef]

Iqbal, Javed, and Muhammad Najam Uddin. 2013. Forecasting accuracy of error correction models: International evidence for monetary aggregate M2. *Journal of International and Global Economic Studies* 6: 14–32.

Johansen, Søren. 1988. Statistical analysis of cointegration vectors. *Journal of Economic Dynamics and Control* 12: 231–54. [CrossRef]

Kasman, Adnan, and Saadet Kasman. 2005. Exchange rate uncertainty in Turkey and its impact on export volume. *METU Studies in Development* 32: 41–58.

Kenen, Peter Bain, and Dani Rodrik. 1986. Measuring and analyzing the effects of short-term volatility in real exchange rates. *The Review of Economics and Statistics* 68: 311–15. [CrossRef]

Khan, Mohsm S., and Knud Z. Ross. 1977. The functional form of the aggregate import demand equation. *Journal of International Economics* 7: 149–60. [CrossRef]

Kohlhagen, Steven W. 1978. *The Behavior of Foreign Exchange Markets: A Critical Survey of the Empirical Literature*. New York: New York University, Graduate School of Business Administration, Salomon Brothers Center for the Study of Financial Institution.

Kroner, Kenneth F., and William D. Lastrapes. 1993. The impact of exchange rate volatility on international trade: Reduced form estimates using the GARCH-in-mean model. *Journal of International Money and Finance* 12: 298–318. [CrossRef]

Makin, John Holmes. 1978. Portfolio theory and the problem of foreign exchange risk. *The Journal of Finance* 33: 517–34. [CrossRef]

Matsubayashi, Yochi, and Shigeyuki Hamori. 2003. Some international evidence on the stability of aggregate import demand function. *Applied Economics* 35: 1497–504. [CrossRef]

Moccero, Diego Nicholas, and Carlos Winograd. 2006. Real exchange rate volatility and exports: Argentine perspectives. Paper presented at Fourth Annual Conference of the Euro-Latin Study Network on Integration and Trade (ELSNIT), Paris, France, October 20–21.

Narayan, Paresh Kumar. 2005. The saving and investment nexus for China: Evidence from cointegration tests. *Applied Economics* 37: 1979–90. [CrossRef]

Pattichis, Charalambos. 2003. Conditional exchange rate volatility, unit roots, and international trade. *The International Trade Journal* 17: 1–17. [CrossRef]

Pesaran, Mohammad Hashem, Yongcheol Shin, and Richard J. Smith. 2001. Bounds Testing Approaches to the Analysis of Level Relationships. *Journal of Applied Econometrics* 16: 289–326. [CrossRef]

Qian, Ying, and Panos Varangis. 1994. Does exchange rate volatility hinder export growth? *Empirical Economics* 19: 371–96. [CrossRef]

Salas, Javier. 1982. Estimation of the structure and elasticities of Mexican imports in the period 1961–1979. *Journal of Development Economics* 10: 297–311. [CrossRef]

Sekantsi, Lira. 2008. The impact of exchange rate volatility on South African exports to the United States (US): A bounds test approach. *Review of Economic and Business Studies* 8: 119–39.

Yin, Fengbao, and Shigeyuki Hamori. 2011. Estimating the import demand function in the autoregressive distributed lag framework: The case of China. *Economics Bulletin* 31: 1576–91.

Journal of
*Risk and Financial
Management*

MDPI

Book Review

Book Review for "Credit Default Swap Markets in the Global Economy" by Go Tamakoshi and Shigeyuki Hamori. Routledge: Oxford, UK, 2018; ISBN: 9781138244726

Haifeng Xu

Department of Statistics, School of Economics, Xiamen University, Xiamen 360000, China; xhf1984@hotmail.co.jp or xhf1984@gmail.com

Received: 22 October 2018; Accepted: 24 October 2018; Published: 25 October 2018

Credit default swaps (CDS) came into existence in 1994 when they were invented by JP Morgan, then it became popular in the early 2000s, and by 2007, the outstanding credit default swaps balance reached $62 trillion. During the financial crisis of 2008, the balance of CDS was hit hard, and it dropped to $25.5 trillion in 2012. The role of credit default swaps in the financial crisis has attracted increased attention from regulators, market participants, and academics.

This book focuses on the CDS market and provides many important results using various advanced econometric methodologies. The book provides a comprehensive overview of global CDS markets and focuses on three main segments of CDS markets: Sovereign CDS markets, Sector-level CDS markets, and Firm-level CDS markets.

The main contents of the book are as follows. In the first part, around sovereign CDS markets, the book shows: (1) The causality between the spread of the sovereign CDS index and the banking sector CDS index; (2) The determinants of sovereign CDS spreads; and (3) The spillover effects across sovereign CDS rates. In the second part, it focuses on: (1) The causal relationships amongst financial sector CDS indices at the sector level; (2) Financial crises and their effects, by focusing on the CDS indexes of three financial industries; (3) The relationships between insurance sector CDS indices across countries; and (4) The dynamic relationship between bank sector CDS indices for several countries. In the final part, they examine: (1) The co-movement of bank CDS spreads of Eurozone banks; (2) The conditional dependence structure of the three main CDS indices; and (3) The dynamic interdependency of CDS indices in different cycles.

I strongly recommend this book to policymakers, investors, researchers, and graduate students, based on the following reasons. First, it summarizes a large number of literature and provides a helpful reference for researchers aiming to build a solid knowledge base about CDS markets and the financial crisis. Specifically, the introduction of every section describes the background and research progress, wherein academics will benefit from these parts.

Second, the book provides several empirical researches that apply advanced econometric methodologies. Empirical methodologies are explained in every section before application. Graduate students can use it as a textbook or supplementary reading material when studying time series analysis. The methodology in this book, which includes, but is not limited to the cross-correlation function (CCF) approach, auto regressive distributed lag (ARDL) bounds test approach, dynamic conditional correlation (DCC) GARCH model, copula-GARCH approach, dynamic equi-correlation (DECO) model, and the continuous wavelet transform.

Third, the results of this book are interesting and impressive. They are useful for market participants and policymakers who design and implement regulatory frameworks to ensure properly functioning financial markets. Furthermore, the book provides implications and discussions of the results. What is the economics behind the results? It is important to understand CDS and the financial crises at work behind our own actions.

Finally, the contents of this book cover well-studied sovereign CDS markets, as well as sector-level and firm-level CDS indices, suggesting it could make a major contribution.

Although CDS markets have experienced a significant rise and fall, CDS have many benefits if used appropriately. This book shows the benefits and provides guidance in dealing with existence problems.

Funding: This research received no external funding.

Conflicts of Interest: The author declares no conflict of interest.